# A HISTORY OF ARTISTS' FILM AND VIDEO IN BRITAIN

**1** *Seemingly So Evidently Not Apparently Then*, Frances Hegarty and Andrew Stones, site specific installation with live and recorded video at Sheffield Midland Station,1998.

# A History of Artists' Film and Video in Britain

David Curtis

 Publishing

First published in 2007 by the
BRITISH FILM INSTITUTE
21 Stephen Street, London W1T 1LN
The British Film Institute's purpose is to champion moving image culture in all its richness and diversity across the
UK, for the benefit of as wide an audience as possible, and to create and encourage debate.

The publisher and author gratefully acknowledge the support of
the Arts Council England and Central Saint Martins College of Art and Design
in the publication of this book.

Front cover illustration: Dryden Goodwin, *One Thousand Nine Hundred and Ninety-Six*, 1996.
Back cover illustrations: (top to bottom) Hans Richter and others, *Everyday*, 1929/67; David Larcher, *VideØvoid*,
1993–5; David Hall, *Television Interventions* (aka *Seven TV Pieces*), 1971; Ian Bourn, *The End of The World*, 1982;
(in background) Tony Hill, *Point Source*, 1973.
Cover design: Ketchup/SE14
Text set by D.R. Bungay Associates, Burghfield, Berkshire
Layout and design by Ketchup/SE14

Printed in the UK by Butler and Tanner Ltd, Frome, Somerset
British Library Cataloguing-in-Publication Data
A catalogue record for this book is available from the British Library
ISBN (pbk) 1–84457–096–7
ISBN (hbk) 1–84457–095–9

# Acknowledgments

This book was commissioned by and would not have seen the light without the encouragement of Rob White, sadly no longer an editor at the BFI. Rebecca Barden and Tom Cabot have ably picked up the project and steered it to its conclusion.

The following friends read the manuscript at various stages, and their comments and corrections have enormously improved it: A.L. Rees, Felicity Sparrow, William Raban, Guy Sherwin, Christophe Dupin, Malcolm Le Grice and Mike O'Pray. Biddy Peppin has lived with it as long as I have, and I'm grateful for her patience and her deft sub-editing. My colleagues at the Study Collection Steven Ball and Lara Thompson have been supportive throughout, and our intern Poppy Shibamoto helped organise many of the images. Gary Thomas at Arts Council England generously supported the making of colour plates, which we all believed was essential to this project. Too many individual artists to list here have replied to arcane questions and searched through cupboards for images, and I'm grateful to them for their support. All errors of fact and thought that remain are mine alone.

D.C., June 2006

# Contents

# Introduction

## ARTISTS

At the end of the 1920s, as commercial film production in Britain appeared on the edge of extinction, and as cinema as a silent art form seemed threatened by the literalness of sound recording, artists and writers joined the debate about film's future and potential. Particularly, they questioned cinema's dependence on visually opened-up but intellectually cut-down versions of stage melodramas. In 'An Open Letter to the Film Industry and to All Who are Interested in the Evolution of the Good Film' the Hungarian photographer, film-maker and teacher Laszlo Moholy-Nagy, living in London, wrote:

> Shall we look on while the film, this wonderful instrument, is being destroyed before our eyes
> by stupidity and dull witted amateurism? The unbiased observer cannot fail to see, to his great
> distress, that the film production of the world is growing more and more trivial every year. To
> the trained eye and mind, the present-day film can give no pleasure"[1].

Moholy argued that the industry's exclusion of 'the experimental film creator [and] the free independent producer' was bringing about its own downfall, and urged support for a 'pioneering group' of makers (himself no doubt included). More radically, Virginia Woolf speculated that cinema had yet to realise its potential as a purely visual language, in which 'thought could be conveyed by shape more effectively than by words'.[2]

This book is about how artists living and working in Britain[3] have continued this debate about the moving image's potential. It is a history of artists' engagement with the moving image in all its forms. The term 'artist' in this context is not confined to those painters and sculptors who occasionally make films (though they too made their contribution), but identifies people who have worked with the moving image with a particular freedom and intensity, often in defiance of commercial logic, and knowingly risking the incomprehension of their public. Importantly, film and video art as discussed here is not a phenomenon restricted to one form of exhibition space. Some artists have responded specifically to the darkened void of the cinema, others to the seat-less white cube of the gallery, yet others to domestic spaces and even television. For many the ideal space in which to show moving images has yet to be designed, and this history is in part that of an ongoing search for a more equitable maker–viewer relationship. At the same time, most artists are pragmatists as well as visionaries and have accepted the necessity of working with whatever space is closest to hand. In the 1920s, Fernand Léger (one of the artform's patron saints) could only show *Le Ballet mécanique* in cinemas because they were the only places equipped with the 35mm projector his film required, but who can say what his ideal showing space might have been? [4] The museum-world's frequent assumption that the only significant film and video artists are those who design their works for the gallery and sell them in limited editions has distorted many national collections and is indefensible in terms of what it leaves out. By this logic, museums should be stripped of all paintings not originally designed for their spaces. Out would go works made for chapels, cardinals' bedrooms, eighteenth-century dining rooms and nineteenth-century bourgeois sitting rooms, together with all prints and drawings, most photographs, etc. This book therefore takes an inclusive view of the subject, as museums should.

The subject matter in artists' films often reflects that of painting and poetry – portraits, still lives, the relationship of abstract forms, responses to landscape and particular environments, reflections upon the major events and stages in life, memory, identity, politics, human relationships. And, like other art forms, film reflects upon the nature of its own medium. And while some film artists work alone and conform to the stereotype of the solitary figure in the studio-garret, many work on projects with a close group of friends, and some act as the head of a team of professional collaborators – where, in this respect, their method becomes indistinguishable from that of mainstream cinema directors.

Often in this history, success for an individual has depended upon the existence of the critical mass of a group of sympathetic peers. For this reason, London as a cosmopolitan centre with a large media industry and strong international connections has proved an irresistible magnet, with which artists based in the regions have had at very least to negotiate a relationship. [5]

The terms 'artists' film' and 'artists' video' have only gained anything like wide acceptance in recent times. In the early days of cinema no film-makers described themselves as artists, though as the language of film developed during the inter-war period, terms such as 'the art of film' and 'film art' were widely employed in magazines such as *Close Up*. [6] Len Lye, Britain's first internationally important film artist, was described as 'an artist' in the 1929 Film Society programme note that introduced the screening of his first film *Tusalava*, but probably because he was still primarily associated with painting and sculpture. [7] And even towards the end of his film-making career, Lye referred to himself as 'an experimental film-maker' rather than film artist, perhaps to distinguish himself within the group of painters and kinetic artists with whom he associated. [8] Humphrey Jennings – another major figure in this history – painted, organised exhibitions, took photographs and wrote poetry in addition to his prolific film-making, and discussed the creative process most readily in terms of poetry, but he too never described himself as a film artist, and would probably have been content with Lindsay Anderson's description of him as 'the only real poet the British Cinema has yet produced'.[9] In the post-war period, the committee of the BFI's (British Film Institute) newly established Experimental Film Fund defined one of its aims as being 'to explore proposals to give the creative artist, such as the painter or composer, much closer control over the design and production stages of a film',[10] but the context remained firmly that of the development of the commercial feature film.

More self-evidently 'artist film-makers' were the several painters and sculptors and conceptual artists who in the early 1970s occasionally made films alongside their full-time practice in other media. Some made records of the evolution of works in other media (Liliane Lijn), others extended their painterly or sculptural ideas into a time-based form (William Pye), and some indeed made full-blooded time-based works in their own right (David Hall). Some of these film-making artists were the first recipients of funding from the Arts Council; others were among the few who had their work shown in commercial galleries during the same period.

The term 'artists' film' was possibly first officially used in the context of the setting up of an 'Artists' Films Sub-Committee' by the Arts Council of Great Britain in 1972, in response to what the Council then perceived to be a 'new activity'. But while happy to apply for 'funding for artists', the majority of applicants to the Arts Council would generally refer to themselves as 'film-makers', because film was their primary medium (following Lye, a decade earlier). When their video equivalents arrived in the mid-1970s they more helpfully answered to the title of 'video-artist', but this was primarily to distinguish themselves from their dominant film-making cousins.

Throughout the 1980s the terms film-maker, film-artist, experimental film-maker, and video-artist came to be used fairly indiscriminately, and embraced the growing number of artists who worked at the margins of the film or television industries, and who made what in industry terms would be described as experimental works. The term 'independent' was equally widely used from the early 1980s onwards, partly as a mark of solidarity with the contemporary political film avant garde, but later with the growing number of wholly commercial independents, it, too, lost most of its earlier associations. In the mid-1990s a generation of artists who worked exclusively in film or video, but who exhibited primarily in the gallery, chose deliberately to style themselves as 'artists' plain and simple, keen to stress that they were operators in the art-world of commercial dealers and public collections. Now in the 21st century, *all* these terms – plain 'artists', 'film-artists', 'video-artists' and 'film-makers' – have currency.

## ECONOMICS

One factor that has shaped the history of artists and film more than any other has been the absence, till very recently, of any form of commercial market for the works produced. The moving image has been an art form uniquely devoid of its own sustaining economy.

The artists' films we have from the inter-war period, before public subsidy to artists was available, consist of sponsored films or of one-off experiments made covertly at the film industry's margins, and works by a very few well-connected amateurs. The former involved the serious compromise of working at the government's or a commercial manufacturer's behest, yet these include almost all the works that made the reputations of Jennings and Lye; the latter remained few in number because artists found no way of recovering their costs. It was not until the mid-1980s with the advent of Channel Four that public broad-casting became an intermittent source of income for a very few artists, and not till the mid-1990s that any were able to make a living by selling to individual collectors and public collections. To survive, the majority have always had to find work in some other film-related field; in education (which began to take film seriously in the mid-1970s), or technical sup-port of the commercial industry (camera-person, editor, etc.), or the sponsored film in its new guises: the corporate film; TV advertising; the music video. Public subsidy – available from the BFI from the 1950s and from the Arts Council and its Regional Arts Associations from the 1970s – never provided artists with an income, though it may have given the lucky few a psychological boost at significant moments in their careers, and did provide some of the infrastructure of workshops and viewing spaces that made film and video-making an attain-able dream for many more.

A commercial industry containing many more independent cinemas and producers, and the earlier development of a multi-channel broadcasting environment *might* have encour-aged the development of a niche market for artists' film. But, in practice, artists have fared little better in countries where the film and television industries were more open and less monop-olistically structured than in Britain.[11] Thus the historic problem for artists, and all independent voices in the moving-image area, has been the fundamental disparity between the high material costs of film-making and the low likely return from distribution and sales. To an individual maker, the price of film equipment and film laboratory charges – both based on the economics of the feature film and television – remained prohibitively high throughout most of the 20th century. This imbalance only began to change with the development of a widespread amateur market based on 16mm and 8mm/Super 8 film equipment in the 1960s and 1970s, then video cameras and recorders in the late 1970s and 1980s, and the arrival of professional-standard video-editing systems designed for home computers in the late 1990s. It was the advent of DVD players and reliable video projection equipment also in the 1990s that re-awoke the interest of the commercial art market, dormant after a brief flurry in the early 1970s, making artists' films and videos a viable saleable commodity, and so providing a chosen few artists with a return on their outlay.

Low-budget methods therefore feature strongly in the history of artists' film and video. These include using borrowed or 'amateur' equipment; making collage-films from waste footage found in industry dustbins, or abstract imagery hand-painted or scratched directly into the filmstrip, or silent films (avoiding the complicated apparatus of recording and syn-chronising film-sound). The desire to minimise costs also helped motivate the setting up of production collectives and workshops – such as Unit Five Seven, the London Film-makers' Co-op (LFMC), the Berwick Street Film Collective, London Video Arts, and Sankofa.

For some artists, the classic cinema-theatre developed by the commercial film industry not only failed as a source of income, but fell short as a social space. The dream shared by many has been to show work in a domestic-scale setting – where repeated viewings might lead to greater familiarity – as through re-reading a piece of literature or re-viewing a painting[12]. The film clubs run *by* and *for* film enthusiasts that came into being in the 1920s established another context, and introduced a tradition of alternative viewing-spaces that continues till today. A domestic scale was also the appeal of Super 8 film – adopted by several artists in the 1980s, notably Derek Jarman, whose enthusiasm did much to promote its use, often showing work in his own loft. Some tried to sell copies of their works on this home-movie format, though the practice never extended beyond a core of enthusiasts. But the dream of an alternative home-based market began to become more credible in the 1990s with the advent of personal libraries of VHS tapes and DVDs.

If unlikely to make an income from the exhibition of their work, artists could at least try to influence its distribution. The idealism of film society enthusiasts replicated itself – particularly in the post-war years – in small specialist commercial film distributors, some of whom added artists' films to their lists. But more typically, artists developed strategies for self-promotion and collective distribution, notions which first seriously took root in the mid-1960s, following precedents established in the USA.

A history of the changing patterns of activity and of the changing definitions of 'artists' film/video' in Britain could be constructed entirely from the pages of the many limited-circulation magazines and books self-published by artists and others over the decades. Magazines such as *Close Up* and *Film Art*, from the 1920s–30s, *Sequence* (which spawned Free Cinema) in the late 1940s and early 1950s, *Cinim* in the 1960s, *Afterimage* in the 1970s, and *Independent Media, Undercut,* and *Filmwaves* in the 1980s and 1990s, have marked the emergence of new movements and theories, provided space for manifestos and warnings against errors of thought and practice, and recorded the ongoing business of self-definition. Artists have never been slow to talk-up the distinctiveness of their own work, and to theorise the ideas that had shaped it. And in the absence of interest from the daily press, many have by default become reviewers of their own and colleagues' works.

If the odds against progress have sometimes seemed overwhelming, the history of artists' film has been characterised by an inextinguishable optimism; a sustaining belief that a production and distribution economy, and appropriate viewing spaces *might* one day be established. The first part of this book provides an account of the many ways in which artists have responded to these challenges and circumvented the inevitable difficulties, inventing institutions, or adapting and influencing those they encountered, in order to get their work *made* and *viewed*. The second part describes some of their individual achievements.

## NOTES

1.  'An Open Letter from Moholy Nagy,' *Sight & Sound* vol. 3 no. 10, 1934.
2.  'The Cinema' first published in *Arts*, June 1926; reprinted in Michael O'Pray (ed.), *The British Avant-Garde Film* (Luton: Arts Council/University of Luton Press, 1996).
3.  Its scope includes both artists born in Britain and those from elsewhere who have worked in Britain.

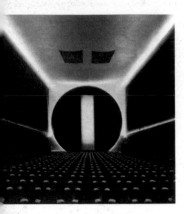

**2** Frederick Keisler's Film
Guild Cinema, New York;
see Footnote 4.

4. Léger was however a friend of Frederick Keisler who designed the remarkable experimental film-screening space the Film Guild Cinema (1928) on 8th Street New York, in Keisler's words an 'entire building … as a plastic medium dedicated to the Art of Light'. Unpublished papers quoted in *AFI Tribute to Anthology Film Archives' Avantgarde Film Preservation Program* (New York, MOMA 1977).

5. At least two thirds of the British-based moving-image artists listed in the LUX online distribution catalogue live in London. The proportion of artists represented by commercial dealers is probably even higher.

6. Following the lead of prior French avant-gardists – see Richard Abel, *French Cinema: The First Wave, 1915–1929* (Princeton, NJ: Princeton University Press, 1984).

7. Programme of 1 December 1929.

8. 'Is Film Art?', *Film Culture*, vol. 29, 1963; reprinted in Wystan Curnow and Roger Horrocks (eds), *Figures of Motion: Len Lye/Selected Writings* (Auckland, NZ: Auckland University Press, 1984).

9. *Sight & Sound,* April–June 1954.

10. 'Experimental Film Fund 1951–9' [uncredited], *1951–1976 Catalogue of BFI Productions* (London: BFI, 1977).

11. Not least, the USA.

12. Perhaps most eloquently articulated in lectures by the American pioneer Maya Deren, where she proposed the idea of 'chamber cinema', as in chamber music; see Maya Deren, *Essential Deren, Collected Writings on Film* (Kingston, NY: McPherson & Co., 2005).

# Part 1

# 1.1 Artists

The Film Society : Little Magazines : Internationalism and Festivals : Schooling Artists :
The London Filmmakers Co-op : Into the Gallery : Video as Video : The 1990s

## THE FILM SOCIETY

*History*

Film-making by artists in Britain began in the second half of the 1920s and, as with many such creative bursts, coincided with a period of intense speculation about the future of the art form. In the last years of silent cinema, the commercial studios of France, Germany and Denmark had produced feature films that were highly individual, strongly visual and bore the mark of their individual authors – simultaneously expanding the language of commercial narrative film, and laying the foundations of today's 'art cinema'. But new technological developments, such as full-colour film stocks and reliable sound film technologies, seemed to change the nature of film radically, upsetting past certainties. And commercial film-makers throughout Europe were becoming anxious about the growing domination of production from the USA.

In London, the Film Society[1] (1925–39) provided a space for viewing new films and encouraged debate about cinema. Its once-a-month screenings were run by a group of intellectuals from many different disciplines – film, literature, the visual arts – initially brought together by the desire to see foreign films, and the need to circumvent Britain's cumbersome censorship and film licensing laws. Adrian Brunel and Ivor Montagu, both working at the fringes of the film industry, were two of the Society's founders, and while artists such as the sculptor Frank Dobson, the painter/writer Roger Fry, the designer E. McKnight Kauffer, and the illustrator Edmund Dulac constituted a small minority among its members, they were none the less essential to its mix. The breadth of members' professional interests was matched by the eclecticism of the Society's programming. Typical of what was to follow, its first programme of 25 October 1925 included the wholly abstract animations *Opus 2-3-4* (1923–5) by the German painter and later documentary maker

**(Opposite)** *Point Source*, Tony Hill, 1973.

**3** The logo designed by E. McKnight Kauffer, spliced onto all film-prints shown by The Film Society.

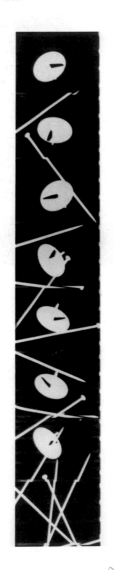

Walther Ruttmann, the comedies *How Bronco Billy Left Bear Country* (Essanay USA c. 1915), *Champion Charlie* (Chaplin / Essanay 1916), Brunel's 'burlesque' *Topical Budget* (1925), and Paul Leni's expressionist feature film *Waxworks* (Germany 1924). Programmes regularly featured episodes from Mary Field and Percy Smith's popular natural history series *Secrets of Nature*, reflecting Montagu's training as a zoologist and interest in scientific film, and might include demonstrations of new colour processes and sound-film systems, designed to be of interest to film industry members such as David Lean, Michael Powell and Alfred Hitchcock, and experimentalists alike.[2] Oskar Fischinger's *Experiments in Hand Drawn Sound* (aka *Ornament Sound* 1932) were shown together with Laszlo Moholy-Nagy's similar translation of images into sounds *A B C in Sound* (1933). Silent feature films were usually accompanied by a full orchestra, but even the problem of sound could be approached experimentally. Jack Ellitt, a modernist composer who was also Len Lye's preferred sound editor, provided 'non-synchronous' musical accompaniments to silent films for the Society throughout the 1934–5 season.

The Society made it possible for artists to see the work of their film-making contemporaries abroad. It staged the first English screenings of Rene Clair's *Entr'acte* (France 1924), Fernand Léger's *Le Ballet mécanique* (France 1924), and works by Sergei Eisenstein, Man Ray, Marcel Duchamp, Germaine Dulac, Charles Scheeler and Paul Strand, Dziga Vertov, and many others, where possible introduced by their makers. In addition to Brunel and Montagu, British artists and experimenters who exhibited at the Society included Len Lye, John Grierson, Oswell Blakeston, Francis Bruguiere, Kenneth Macpherson, Desmond Dickinson, Alberto Cavalcanti, Humphrey Jennings, the partnership of Anthony Gross and Hector Hoppin, and many others. The formal style of the Society's programme notes, which refer to directors and technicians alike by their titles ('Mr Richter' etc.), evokes screenings received in respectful silence, but Montagu reports this was not always the case. *Entr'acte* appropriately provoked a near riot:

> cries and catcalls rang out, pundits within the audience came within an ace of punching each other. Frank Dobson was sitting near Clive Bell, whose excitement was fever pitch in defence of what he regarded as an unjustly denigrated opus of genius, Dobson murmured pensively afterwards: 'Makes one [wonder] what they say of one's own work, doesn't it'.[3]

While it encouraged interest in film-making, the Society held back from direct involvement in film production. However in 1929 it invited the German painter/film-maker Hans Richter to direct an experimental film-making workshop to accompany a lecture series given by Eisenstein. The workshop was held in an attic above Foyles bookshop in Charing Cross Road, and attended by (among many others) Eisenstein, Lye, and a young Basil Wright.[4] But the Society's focus remained firmly on exhibition and, almost by default, on distribution, as other societies and even commercial cinemas sought to show works that the Society had imported. The significance of the Society to Britain's emerging film avant-garde was its function as a venue for showing work, and the promise it extended of a critical response from a group of interested peers. In this the Society acted as a role model for many similar groups throughout Europe and America.

Politically inspired film-makers of the period had even greater reason to form groups in order to get their films seen while avoiding censorship. Kenneth Macpherson and Henry Dobb, the film critic of the left newspaper *The Sunday Worker*, had proposed a scheme to enable workers' groups to see important films at a price they could afford. After a legal struggle with

**6** The Film Society 'workshop' group; with Richter (left) Eisenstein (with policeman's helmet), Jimmy Rogers at the camera, Basil Wright (glasses and cigarette), Len Lye (extreme right, seated) and others.

*The start of margin*

**7** *Peace and Plenty*,
Ivor Montagu with
Norman McLaren, 1939.

local authorities which seemed determined that the privileges of a film society should be restricted to the wealthier middle-classes, this was effectively realised by Ralph Bond and others with the setting up of the Federation of Workers' Film Societies in 1929. A national distribution organisation Kino followed in 1934. The Federation brought together the interests of making and exhibiting groups such as the Socialist Film Council, the London Workers Film Group, and the Workers' Film and Photo League (itself an association of amateur groups). Montagu left the Film Society to set up the Progressive Film Institute (its name a dig at the recently founded and strenuously apolitical British Film Institute), which was to engage directly in political film-making, and to distributed films such as Eisenstein's *Potemkin* to leftist groups. The Depression of the early 1930s, the rise of Fascism in Europe and the Spanish Civil War were reflected in the theme of films such as *Bread* (1934) made by the Workers' Theatre Movement, Montagu's *Defence of Madrid* (1937), made with animator Norman McLaren as cameraman, and his *Peace and Plenty* (1939).[5]

## LITTLE MAGAZINES

Film's potential was debated in a growing body of critical writing in the 1920s and 1930s. Films screened at the Film Society and its more political counterparts were reviewed by the commercial film press with a mix of interest and suspicion. The Film Society's founding coincided with, and contributed to, the beginnings of serious film journalism, and many Society regulars were also journalists in positions of influence. Iris Barry, another founder member, became a prominent film journalist in the 1920s, and established the role of film critic at the *Daily Mail*. Montagu was the first film critic of *The Observer* and *The New Statesman*. And reviews appeared in unexpected contexts such as the *Architectural Review*, where Oswell Blakeston discussed 'Len Lye's Visuals', and previewed his own film made with Francis Bruguiere, *Light Rhythms* (1930).[6]

More important to the development of an active film-making culture were the debates generated in specialist film magazines. Of these, *Close Up* (1927–33) and *Film Art* (1933–37) were the most significant, though Robert Herring's literary magazine *Life and Letters Today* (1928–50) also made an important contribution. *Close Up* was edited by Kenneth Macpherson from *Kenwin*, a modernist pavilion at Riant Chateau in Territet, Switzerland, built by his partner Bryher (Annie Winifred Ellerman, heiress to a shipping fortune). This artistic pair together with the poet HD (Hilda Doolittle) formed Pool Films to produced three short films credited

to Macpherson, and the feature-length work *Borderline* (1930), so
*Close Up* viewed developments from the engaged perspective of
practising film-makers.[7] Its contents included a mix that would be
familiar again in the little film magazines of the 1960s and 1970s;
manifestos, theory, passionate and often highly subjective responses
to new films, campaigns (for example against censorship) and trade
gossip. In addition to its publishers, its regular writers included
Blakeston, Herring, the author Dorothy Richardson (close friend
of H. G. Wells) and the psychoanalysts Barbara Low and Hans
Sachs, with occasional contributions by Gertrude Stein and many
others. Eisenstein contributed nine articles over the years – including his first published writings in English. *Close Up*'s informal and
often conversational style of journalism is typified by a long essay
by HD on Dreyer's *The Passion and Death of a Saint* [*Joan of Arc*],
who wrote:

> I know in my mind that this is a great tour de force, perhaps the
> greatest. But I am left weary, a little defiant. Again why and why and
> why and just, just why? Why am I defiant before one of the most
> exquisite and consistent works of screen art and perfected craft that
> it has been our immeasurable privilege to witness? [Later answering …] This great Dane Carl
> Dreyer takes too damn much for granted. Do I *have* to be cut into slices by this inevitable
> pan-movement of the camera, these suave lines to left, up, to the right, back, all rhythmical
> with the remorseless rhythm of a scimitar?. [etc.]

**8** *Close Up* – the cover image
is from Macpherson's lost film
*Monkey's Moon*, 1929.

*Close Up*'s less well known (because more hand-to-mouth) but even more adventurous rival
*Film Art* was edited and published by another film-maker, B. Vivian Braun, who also briefly ran
the Forum Cinema, 'London's advance-garde cinema'.[8] Like *Close Up*, *Film Art* included
reviews and polemic by film-makers including Robert Fairthorne,[9] Blakeston, Braun himself,
Irene Nicolson and Andrew Buchanan, and guest articles by Man Ray, Laszlo Moholy-Nagy
and others. An article on 'Abstract Film' by S. John Woods was criticised in a letter by Man Ray
who thought Woods had failed to understand Surrealism, and had mis-described Ray's films
as 'experiments': 'I affirm that I have never tried to invent anything, and I have never made …
an experiment. The discoveries and the accidents of science have provided ample means for
a lifetime of experiment'.[10] Braun and Basil Wright together wrote a 'Manifesto Dialogue on
Sound' for the third issue in 1934, calling for its more imaginative use.

**9** Flier for *Film Art*, 1934, and
for two films now missing

## INTERNATIONALISM AND FESTIVALS
In Britain in the 1920s and 1930s, as in Europe and the USA, the international circulation of
more experimental and political cinema was strongly opposed by the established commercial
industry, and it became clear that one of the functions of film clubs and societies might be to

**10 (right)** The Themerson's
magazine *fa*, Poland, 1937.

**11 (far right)** B. Vivian Braun's
short-lived *New Cinema*.

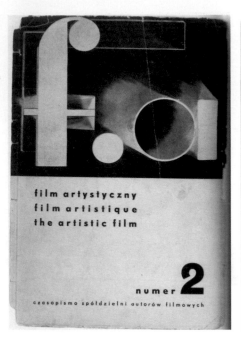

develop international networks to facilitate the distribution of films. The importance of this role is reflected in a Film Society programme note that accompanied its screening of Joris Ivens and Mannus Franken's *Rain* (1929), which makes much of the fact that its makers 'are the principal officers of the Film Liga of Holland [1927–33] … with branches in each of the Dutch university towns. Through the principal activity of the Liga consists, as does that of this Society its chief model, in the study of otherwise rarely seen films, the officers have themselves produced several films'.[11] Similarly, the notes for *Manhatta* (1926) by Sheeler and Strand and *The Loves of Zero* (1928) by Robert Florey give pre-eminence to the Film Art Guild of New York, ahead of the film-makers' names.[12] Through these networks, the Polish artists Stefan and Francisca Themerson, founders of Warsaw's Co-op of Film Authors, visited London in 1936 and organised a programme of films by Lye, Grierson, Cavalcanti and Wright shown in Warsaw in 1937, and arranged for the publishing of articles by some of the artists (Lye, Grierson and Moholy-Nagy) in the first issue of their magazine *'fa' (the artistic film,* 1937). Amos Vogel, who as a post-war refugee in New York would found the most influential film society of the period, Cinema 16 (1947–63), saw and was inspired by a programme of English films at a film society screening in Vienna in 1938. 'The whole notion of documentary became important to me because of [*Night Mail* (1936)] … I realised that this was a really poetic film. … *Song of Ceylon* (1934) was also tremendously important to me'.[13]

To strengthen these international links, delegates at the Congrès de La Sarraz in Switzerland in 1929, including Montagu, Richter, Eisenstein, Franken, Alberto Cavalcanti from France, and the futurist artist Enrico Prampolini from Italy, attempted to set up an international association of film societies and cine clubs. Seven nations signed up to the 'International League for the Independent Cinema'; the clubs' common distrust of the influence of the commercial

**12** La Sarraz group portrait including Walther Ruttman (striped shirt), Bela Balaz (next right), Eisenstein, Richter and Montagu (behind Ruttmann, to the left).

industry reflected in their resolution that 'to maintain the character of the Leagues as non-profit-making organisations, … no commercial or semi-commercial association could affiliate as a voting member'. Support for production was also on the agenda. A 'Cooperative de Film Independent' was to be located in Paris as a production centre, with 25,000 French francs to be raised as starting capital.[14] This, like the International League itself, was a dream that came to nothing.

More successfully, the La Sarraz meeting seeded the idea of regular gatherings of the international film avant-garde community, to screen work and exchange ideas, which was achieved over the following decades through a succession of experimental film festivals, forums and competitions. Experimental work featured at the Brussels International Film Festival in 1935, where Grierson could boast, 'Great Britain carried off the first award and almost all the others in the documentary class'.[15] *Song of Ceylon* won the documentary prize, and Lye's *Colour Box*, which 'defied all categories', was awarded a special medal. But this was not yet a specialist experimental festival. These began after the war in 1949, when the Royal Belgian Film Archive held the first of its international experimental competitions, usually staged at the seaside town of Knokke-le-Zoute.[16] Although the 1949 festival included new work from the USA by Maya Deren, Kenneth Anger, Sydney Peterson, Mary Ellen Bute, John and James Whitney and others, the European contribution to the event was predominantly retrospective – a

**13** Design by Pierre Alechinsky (of the Cobra group of artists) for the 1949 Knokke Festival.

review of the pre-war achievement – made poignant by the absence of so many of the artists represented: Richter, Man Ray, Mclaren, Moholy-Nagy, Lye and others, who had left Europe for the USA.

The Knokke festivals ran irregularly till 1974, and represented a rare opportunity for successive generations of new artists from North America and Europe to meet and see each others' work. The 1958 festival moved to Brussels to coincided with a World's Fair, and made a feature of multi-screen films, including the three-screen *Magirama* by Abel Gance, pioneer of the form in 1926 with *Napoléon vu par Abel Gance,* and – a link across decades – Kenneth Anger's *The Inauguration of the Pleasure Dome* (1954) re-versioned in multi-screen for the festival. Stan Brakhage attended the 1958 festival and encouraged other young American artists to enter.

Art Film

> Though I know American filmmakers are generally disillusioned about film contests, myself sharing the disillusionment in retrospect, I really feel that this contest will prove all it's cracked up to be, and film will perhaps really be considered as an art form for the first time in its history. My correspondence with [Jacques] Ledoux [the festival director] only serves to strengthen this belief. You might pass this along.[17]

Americans who showed work included Hy Hirsh, Madeline Turtalot, Jordan and Jane Belson – whose work screened alongside that of the Europeans Georges Franju, Agnes Varda, Peter Kubelka, Roman Polanski, Robert Breer (then living in Paris), and others. At the 1963/64 Festival, Jack Smith, Ron Rice and Bruce Conner from the USA exhibited alongside Anthony Balch and Walerian Borowczyk from Europe; in 1967/8 Paul Sharits, Michael Snow and George Kuchar from the USA showed with Steve Dwoskin, Alfredo Leonardi, Willhelm and Birgit Hein, Yoko Ono, Jeffrey Shaw and John Latham from Europe.

These encounters were also important to writers and critics. Karel Reisz showed his first film *We are the Lambeth Boys* (1958) at the 1958 festival, and reviewed the event for *Sight & Sound*, puzzling over the wisdom of bringing innovative feature films and experimental shorts into one programme. 'The filmmaker who wants his work to connect with commercial pro-duction – either as a precedent or as protest – is after a different thing from the abstractionist and introvert who seeks an elite-cinema for the minority.' Confessing his preference for the former, he found the work of Brakhage and Deren 'symbol-happy', but warmed to the 'intri-cate symmetry and invention' of Len Lye's scratched animation *Free Radicals* (1957), which he compared to the work of J. S. Bach. The debate about what it was appropriate to *in*clude and *ex*clude in experimental festivals would rumble on over the years. Also reviewing the 1958 festival, the un-named correspondent of the *Continental Film Review* regretted the absence of a stronger native movement in Europe:

> Over the past five years, we have, in a number of articles, dwelt on the lack of an avant-garde, an experimental school in Europe – a fact that the commercial cinema would regret in a future decade. There have been, of course, a number of avant-garde filmmakers who began their esoteric careers in the twenties and thirties and are today continuing their work (because

of the war) in other countries – particularly in America. This poses a number of interesting questions. How long, for instance, can one continue to be an experimentalist – invariably in the short film form? How long is it before experiment gels into a style that must give birth to works complete and repetitive? In other words, the experimental film is very much the sphere of the young filmmaker – for the most part amateur or the private work of a professional technician. The big surprise of the Brussels Competition has been the discovery of so many comparatively unknown filmmakers working in this field.[18]

[He] goes on to call for more cinemas to show this work, and for encouragement to be given to 'genuine experimental film-makers – as distinct from merely amateur film-makers'.

Also at Brussels in 1958 were several London-based film distributors, including Charles and Kitty Cooper of Contemporary Film (founded 1951), Bill Polanka of Connoisseur Films, and John Gillett from the BFI. From then onwards, these distributors began to license films by US and European artists for distribution in 16mm in Britain, and work by Deren, Varda, Breer, Brakhage and others began to be seen in Britain's network of university and amateur film societies, now numbering over 600.[19] By the time of the founding of the London Film-makers Co-op in 1966, there were already more than 50 works from the international inter- and post-war avant-garde in circulation in Britain.[20]

The nineteen-year-old American critic P. Adams Sitney (already publishing his magazine *Filmwise*) attended the 1963 festival, and later admitted that 'many of the filmmakers whose work I have most been most deeply concerned with I first encountered at that 1963 competition'.[21] Michael Kustow, newly appointed director of London's Institute of Contemporary Arts (ICA), was at the 1967/68 festival, and describes the experience of being a festival audience-member, and the reception of Don Levy's experimental feature *Herostratus* (1967), soon to open the ICA's new cinema.

[The screening] began at midnight and finished well after 2a.m. It held the audience of a thousand people absolutely rapt. More remarkable still, those thousand people had been watching films solid for the previous five days, ten hours a day. [...] The audience ... consisted of the most difficult spectators in the world: filmmakers judging each other's work. For days we had watched Underground American movies shot in superimposed images on 16mm stock (naked boys wrapped in the Stars and Stripes); French *hommages a Genet* (electronic music and lowering homosexuals); a Japanese film of unbelievable sadism [*The Embryo* (1966) by Koji Wakamatsu], which I counted the most despicable work I've ever seen (and of which the director wrote 'I want very much to let the world know that such fantastic films are being produced in Japan one after another'); films made by computers (a cybernetic mountain labouring for a year to produce an eight-minute animated molehill). Our eyes were aching, red-rimmed. We were suffering from severe anxiety symptoms, the sort ... that come when you've sat through ten cinematic stinkers in a row, flee to the bar and grab a drink, and are suddenly hit (laughter, cheering from the auditorium) by the terrible fear that maybe the *eleventh* film was *the* film, the jewel beneath the garbage pile.[22]

**14** Steve Dwoskin at a
festival in Mannheim in
November 1975 (anticipating
Spain's rebirth).

**15** Poster design by
Dwoskin for the second NFT
Avant-garde Festival, 1973.

Stephen Dwoskin (from London) won the Solvay Prize at the 1967/68 Knokke event and, perhaps encouraged by this success, a larger English contingent including Anthony McCall, Mike Dunford, Richard Woolley and Anna Ambrose (all prize winners), David Hall and Tony Sinden, William Raban and Marilyn Halford participated in the 1974/75 festival. Peter Gidal reviewed it for *Studio International*, using the occasion to note juror Sitney's failure to under-

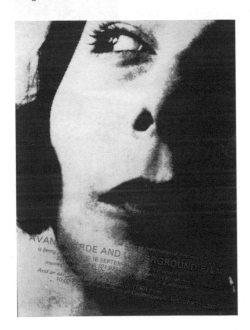

stand structural film properly, and to lament the Belgian pre-selectors' preference for 'quasi-surrealist meanderings', which had led to the exclusion of his own and John Du Cane's work from the official competition. Le Grice, he reported, boycotted the event 'out of principled opposition to the competitive aspect of the festival'.[23]

In Europe, other experimental festivals began to fill the gap years between the Knokke events: the 2mme Festival du film de demain in Basel in 1954 (where, surprisingly, the American James Broughton represented Britain[24]), Oberhausen with its focus on the whole range of short films from 1958, the Rencontres Internationales Jeune Cinema at Hyeres/Toulon from 1968 to 1983, and a series of International Avant-garde Festivals held at the BFI's National Film Theatre in London in 1970, 1973 and 1979, organised by various English experimental film groups.[25] In contrast to Knokke and Toulon, and in the spirit of the times, these London festivals were definitively non-competitive and consciously a gathering of the tribes. In the 1970s, art-exhibition organisers began to take interest in the moving image. *Prospect 71 Projection*

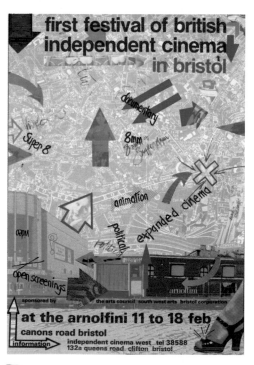

in Dusseldorf was exclusively devoted to lens-based media and both video and film made a strong showing at Documenta 6 (1977), with Hall showing alongside Paik, Emshwiller, Douglas Davis, Joan Jonas, Kubota Shigeko and others from the USA and Japan, and Le Grice, Raban and McCall showing with Paul Sharits, Tony Conrad and artists from the Lodz Workshop of Film Form.[26]

By the 1980s the field of avant-garde festivals was fragmenting, and both national and international events in Britain as elsewhere began to specialise in particular areas – the short film, animation, experimental film, video, expanded cinema and installation, and, later in the 1990s, interactivity and digital work.

A series of national events in Britain in the 1970s announced that the many forms of the moving image were now firmly established, not just in London but in many of England's regional cities. The First National Festival of Independent Film was held in Bristol in 1975, and brought together the avant-garde of artists with a political film-making wing, under the stewardship of the newly formed lobbying group, the Independent Filmmakers Association (IFA) founded the previous year. Reviewing the event in his regular column 'Visions' in *Studio International*, Le Grice questioned 'the main underlying assumption of the festival', and observed 'there can be very little point of contact between Mike Dunford and Derek Jarman' (the former a politically-minded formalist; the latter an unrepentant Romantic/gay activist). But he concluded that:

> there were sufficient points of contact between some of those working within political groupings and experimental makers to convince me that the process [of bringing them together] should continue. The experimental film-makers should continue to be exposed to the problem of 'accessibility', counteracting the tendency to become simply incorporated into the 'art-world' where the formally sophisticated audience is most readily found. At the same time, the political film-makers should be made aware of the poverty of sensibility and reactionary conventionality of much of their film-form. That the process of interaction can be productive was shown most by *Night Cleaners* (1975) by the Berwick Street Collective[27].

This debate on form and content was taken up by an *International Forum on Avant-garde Film* at the Edinburgh Film Festival in 1976, with Le Grice, Marc Karlin of the Berwick Street Collective, Annette Michelson, Hollis Frampton and many others as speakers,[28] amplified by Peter Wollen's influential article 'The Two Avant-gardes' of 1975.

**16**  The avant-garde moves outside London to meet the independent sector; the Bristol festival of 1975.

**17**  International visitors to the1973 festival:  Kurt Kren, Tom Chomont, Jonas Mekas (and Cynthia Beat). Polaroid portraits by Roger Hammond.

*[Handwritten note: First ... composition in London]*

Television has been attacking us
all of our lives,
now we can attack it back

Artists' video    Community video    Performances

Closed circuit installations    Video graphics    Tape library

Live events you can
take part in    Giant TV screen    At the gallery
in the Park

**The Video Show**
first festival of independent video at the Serpentine Gallery

1–26 May  Weekdays 12–8  Sundays 11–8  Kensington Gardens  London W2  Admission free

Arts Council of Great Britain

**18** Video arrives: *The Video Show*, Serpentine Gallery, 1975

In the summer of 1975 'The Video Show – first festival of independent video', held at the Arts Council's Serpentine Gallery in London, was the first substantial British survey of this still-new medium. Under a poster-headline proclaiming 'Television has been attacking us all of our lives, now we can fight it back' (the words of Korean/US video-pioneer Nam June Paik), it, too, pursued an inclusive selection policy, bringing together tapes by many community and political groups, work by international artists such as Dan Graham, William Wegman and the Vasulkas, and installations and performances by rising British stars such as David Hall, Susan Hiller and Tamara Krikorian. The month-long programme included a repertory of tapes shown on monitors. Some American tapes came with the smart logo of the Castelli-Sonnabend Gallery, New York, on the front – introducing the novelty of a well-heeled commercial gallery with a substantial stake in moving-image media. Interest by British galleries had been limited; many British artists disapproved of limited-edition works in principle; certainly any hope that a market might develop in Britain proved premature. But the Serpentine show was widely reported in the art and even daily press.

Expanded cinema – multi-screen work and films with a live performance element – had been a feature of the 1973 London festival. In the *Village Voice,* Mekas recognised the importance to the British scene of this new form:

> Some of the best work done by the London film-makers is in the area of 'expanded cinema'.
> … they are not repeating history: the London group picked up (or overlapped) what was done
> in New York and San Francisco and went further …The London school is deep into structural
> researches into process art, and formal explorations of space.[29]

The year 1976 saw a whole festival devoted to gallery-based installations at the *Expanded Cinema Festival* at the ICA in London, selected by a committee led by Ron Haselden and Tony Sinden with a catalogue edited by Deke Dusinberre and Gray Watson. Caroline Tisdall bravely summarised the artists' aims for readers of *The Guardian*:

> Most of these filmmakers are involved in some kind of examination of the medium itself. They
> explore the nature of film, the cine-camera or projector, rather than telling stories … Many
> use quite modest means, 8mm film being as frequent as 16mm. Some experiment with multi-
> screen projection, as Warhol did. Others extend the concept of cinema so the projector or
> beams of light that bring the image to the screen become part of the area of interest; almost a
> sculpture of light and space. The time and duration aspect fascinates others and is analysed or
> demonstrated in anything from four minutes to seven hours. [30]

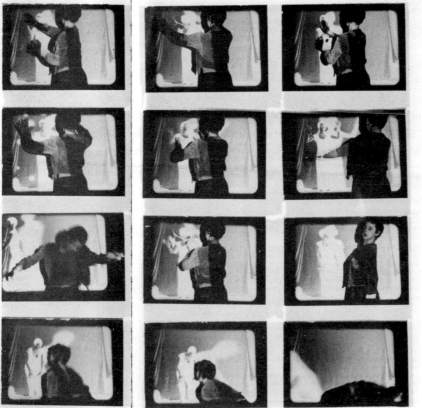

**19 (above)** David Hall and Tony Sinden's *101 TV Sets*, at the Serpentine's *The Video Show.*

**20 (left)** Marilyn Halford performing *Hands, Knees and Boomsa Daisy*, 1973, as illustrated in the catalogue to the *ICA Expanded Cinema Festival*, 1976..

David Hall and Tony Sinden's installation *101 TV Sets* (1975) had been a spectacular feature of *The Video Show* at the Serpentine, and video installations were featured for the first time at the Tate in a small display – confusingly also called *The Video Show* – organised by the education department in 1976. Video artists gained their own festival in the modestly scaled but important *Artists Video,* held annually at Biddick Farm Arts Centre in Washington New Town, between 1976 and 1980, in which installations were a central feature. Similarly inspired by *The Video Show*'s success and by its inclusive policy, a loose coalition of video users – artists, community and political groups – organised an annual National Video Festival at Bracknell's South Hill Park media centre, from 1981 to 1988, mixing themed programmes of tapes with installations. Throughout the 1980s, this would be the occasion for the launching of new work by established artists, students, groups and distributors, supported by the linked bi-monthly magazine *Independent Media*.

The amateur film gauge Super 8 gained its own annual Super 8 Festival in Leicester in 1984. As early as 1965, the writer Ray Durgnat had urged use of the medium while discussing the work of 'the 8mm poet' Jeff Keen:

**21 (top)** The design used each year for Artists' Video, at Biddick Farm, Washington.

**22 (above)** Video's annual gathering at Bracknell.

Why take notes when you can make pictures? An 8mm camera is the ballpoint of the visual world. Soon (and the sooner the better) people will use camera-pens as casually as they jot memos today. Filmmakers will make 'rough drafts' of their films as rapidly as painters dash off preliminary sketches. And the narrow gauge can make finished works of art.[31]

But while Keen, Bruce Lacey, Robert Stuart Short, Victor Musgrave and others soldiered on through the 1970s, it took Jarman's endorsement (and the 'buzz' surrounding the showing of Super 8 work by his protégés John Maybury and Cerith Wyn-Evans at the ICA in 1981) to stir up wider interest, and the momentum for a festival.

The new but short-lived technology of video-walls formed the core of the first Video Positive biennial festival held in Liverpool in 1989, and large-scale installations and interactive works became its speciality in subsequent years. The LUX Centre's Pandaemonium biennials held in London in 1996, 1998 and 2001 attempted to bring film and video back together, reflecting the convergence brought about by the arrival of digital technology. Behind all these festivals lay the impulse to meet fellow artists and to see their work. And for the majority of artists still outside the economies of commercial galleries and cinema releases, such events also presented a welcome spur to the making of new films and tapes.

## SCHOOLING ARTISTS

Artists' film and video first became the specialist subject of an art/film-school course with the setting up of Fine Art Film at Saint Martins School of Art in London in 1972. Prior to that, artists had to make do with non-specialist film courses, often linked with photography, such as those at Harrow School of Art and the Polytechnic of Central London. The only institution uniquely devoted to practical film-making in the early 1960s was the London School of Film Technique (LSFT) founded in 1956[32] (London International Film School from 1974), but as a privately run independent school it offered no grants or scholarships, and its approach to film-making was conservative, based on workshops led by freelance and retired industry technicians.[33] Grants and scholarships were one of the attractions of the Royal College of Art's (RCA) post-graduate two- and three-year MA practical courses and a PhD, established in 1961. Here, too, the course was ostensibly focused on future industry practitioners, but the presence of Peter Gidal on the staff from 1972, and Steve Dwoskin and writer/film-maker Noel Burch from 1973 – all under the leadership of Stuart Hood – attracted artists and other progressive film-makers. The RCA had one of the earliest colour TV studios in the country – the result of a donation by ATV – the only place outside the BBC where experiments were

**23** Anne Rees-Mogg greets Peter Gidal (plus film) at Chelsea School of Art, c. 1975, recorded by Le Grice.

possible with broadcast television technology. And from 1974 to 1986, its interdisciplinary Environmental Media Department attracted many artists who then gravitated to film, or more often to video. There:

> at any one time, a studio may contain projected slide and film images, video monitors showing pre-recorded and/or 'on camera' material, constructions and painted surfaces, light and sound projection and performance activities. That all these systems should be on hand is considered crucial to the Department's creative work.[34]

At undergraduate level, film-making began to infiltrate fine-art courses throughout the 1960s, though often it was not till much later, if at all, that these courses openly re-named themselves as 'Film', or 'Time-Based Media' (Maidstone College of Art's designation from the mid-1970s), or its equivalent. Clive Latimer and John Bowstead established a Light Sound Workshop at Hornsey College of Art in the mid-1960s, which offered access to Super 8 film among other media, but came to grief during the student uprising of May 1968 when Latimer was sacked for siding with the students.[35] Hornsey's loss was the North East London Polytechnic's gain (NELP, now University of East London), for Latimer with Guy Sherwin established film-making in the Communication Design course there in 1971, and NELP became – with Saint Martins School of Art – one of the most consistent nurturers of artists' film-making in Britain. NELP's first cohort included John Smith, Lis Rhodes, Tim Bruce and Ian Kerr, joined in the next year by fine-art students Steve Farrer, Cordelia Swann and Penny Webb, all significant figures in the development of film in the 1970s. John Latham and Malcolm Le Grice had independently introduced film into the painting course at Saint Martins in 1965–66, and Le Grice. who was also teaching at Goldsmiths College, developed film and video there at about the same time. Sheffield Polytechnic's Fine Art course included film from 1967, Chelsea School from 1968, David Hall's Audio Visual Workshop at Maidstone began in 1972, film in Fine Art at Reading University after 1973 with Ron Haselden and William Raban, and so on. Film benefited from the climate of freedom and experiment that characterised many fine-art departments in the late 1960s and early 1970s. Students were encouraged to shift disciplines, to explore sound and environmental constructions, print media, music. Some formed rock bands, (Blur, Pulp from Saint Martins), others entered the advertising industry, some became film/video artists. Film/video was one medium among many.

It is arguable that the influence of the Film Society continued even into the early 1960s, when Thorold Dickinson was appointed as the Slade School Film Unit's first director, later Professor. A production assistant and film-editor in the early 1930s, Dickinson had

**24** The first show by NELP staff and students at the London Filmmakers Co-op, 1975.

been responsible for the 'presentation and technical preparation' (subtitling, etc.) of the Society's film prints between 1930 and 1932. After directing feature films including *Gaslight* (1940) and *Queen of Spades* (1948), and a period of working for the United Nations Department of Information in New York, he was invited in 1960 to set up the first British university department devoted to film studies, at University College London, with initial funding raised from the industry by the BFI. His academic model was the Film Studies department at Pisa University, but his Film Unit was significantly based within an art-school, the Slade, and had the active support of the Slade Professor, the painter William Coldstream, himself a film-maker in the 1930s and yet another former Film Society member. Dickinson was not an admirer of artists' films, nor of experiment for its own sake, but his screening-based seminars were illuminated by his practical knowledge of film-making, and by his experience of dissecting films on the Film Society editing table. He could also draw on his personal friendship with many of the great figures of inter- and post-war cinema. He placed the practice of studying sections of a film on an editing-table, then projecting the film complete in the cinema, at the centre of the Slade Film Unit approach to film studies.[36] The course contained no practical element, but it nonetheless attracted and produced as many film-makers as academics, and the first cohort of students included the scholar-makers Lutz Becker and Lisa Pontecorvo, the writers Ray Durgnat and Charles Barr, and makers Peter Whitehead and Don Levy – all important figures in the shaping of film culture from the late 1960s onwards.[37] A later generation of students included the critic-curators Simon Field and Deke Dusinberre, the scholar Annette Kuhn, artist Ken McMullen and Channel 4's commissioning editor for Independent Film, Rod Stoneman.

**25** Thorold Dickinson, c. 1950.

## THE LONDON FILMMAKERS CO-OP

By the mid-1960s the young painter Malcolm Le Grice and the young sculptor Barry Flanagan had joined John Latham on the staff at Saint Martins School of Art, and independently they began making films alongside their work in other media. With their very different approaches to the medium – one hands-on, the other more detached – Le Grice, Latham and Flanagan's teaching at Saint Martins helped shape some of the most important films by artists of the late 1960s and early 1970s – the so-called structural film-making associated with the London Filmmakers Co-op (Le Grice) and the conceptual and minimal film and video work associated with the emerging small commercial galleries and artist-run spaces of the early 1970s, (Latham/Flanagan). The ideas and energy of these divergent groups emanating from Saint Martins were one of the catalysts to the explosion of activity that occurred around the turn of the decade.

Le Grice's approach to film was coloured equally by his training as a painter at the Slade which stressed truth to materials, and the experimental approach to art and media that characterised the early 1960s; the latter shared with Latham and Flanagan. This background made it unsurprising that Le Grice would provide the vision for a practical film-making workshop at the London Filmmakers Co-op (LFMC).

Founded in 1966, the LFMC had initially been little more than another film society, distinguished only by its unusual commitment to experimental film. It grew from the programme

**26** The London Filmmakers
Co-op 'founders'
photographed by *Town*
magazine, 1966. (l. to r.)
Steve Dwoskin, Andy Meyer
(visiting New York filmmaker),
Simon Hartog, Bob Cobbing
and Harvey Matusow.

of activities organised by Bob Cobbing, sound-poet and film enthusiast, who for a living
managed Better Books paperback bookshop at the corner of New Compton Street and Charing
Cross Road, in central London. Cobbing had established this cramped shop and its basement as a venue for readings, installations and screenings, and film-makers from all parts of
the UK and abroad were among the many artists who gravitated to its door.[38] Jeff Keen,
Kenneth Anger and Robert Pike were among those who showed films there in the early 1960s,
to audiences seated among the book-stacks and tables. John Latham, Yoko Ono and Kurt
Kren showed work as part of the *Destruction in Art Symposium* of September 1966, organised
by Cobbing and Gustav Metzger. In the same year, Oswell Blakeston, the experimental film-
maker/writer of the 1930s, now an author/painter surviving by reviewing art for *What's On in
London,* encountered an installation by Keen and writer/performer Jeff Nuttall.

**27** Installation by Jeff
Nuttall, Better Books
basement, 1966.

The cellar gallery at 94 Charing Cross Road is a perfect home for an exhibition in which one may encounter a ghost of soiled linen in a corner. But what, you may ask, is it all about? Some years ago some dustmen started a museum in London; and then the surprise was to see the amazing objects which people abandon, such as stuffed heads of cross-eyed tigers. But Jeff Nuttall and Jeff Keen rely on the magic of what obviously should have gone into the dustbin: crumbled bits of cellophane, burnt coloured cartons, sinister lengths of piping. They thrust them together into some outrageous ensemble which (and here lies their art) somehow comments on our sex habits, our routines, our victimisations.[39]

The first Filmmakers' Co-op had been established in New York by Jonas Mekas in 1962 as a specialist distributor of experimental film, and by the mid-1960s Mekas was looking for a base for a European satellite. The presence in London of New York film-makers Steve Dwoskin and Andy Meyer encouraged Cobbing to take on film distribution, closely following the American model, and with the hope of an eventual donation by Mekas of a collection of American work. With film-maker Simon Hartog, and critic Ray Durgnat joining the group, the London Filmmakers Co-op was formed.[40] Responding to the Co-op's birthday twenty-five years later, Durgnat listed the elements that had contributed to that moment:

The 1966 Co-op was a response to American (not Soviet) models, and related upsurges (beatniks, bebop, Humph's, folk and skiffle, an Albert Hall poetry reading, psychedelia, flower power, the Arts Lab, the *Oz* trial). I wrote a third of the LFMC's first catalogue with one hand, while writing for *Oz, IT* and *Movie,* and teaching 'bourgeois' art history with the other. The general *zeitgeist* was non- (but not anti-) academic, a late bloom of Bohemia-and-backwoods counter-culture, reinvigorated by popular affluence; apolitical anarcho-libertarian. Come-all-ye.[41]

Le Grice's workshop was initially associated with the Drury Lane Arts Laboratory, an artist-run space for experimental film, theatre, poetry and performance founded by Jim Haynes in 1967, where I, another Slade-trained painter, was cinema-programmer. As its name suggests, the Arts Laboratory placed emphasis on making as well as presenting, and it was this combination that attracted Le Grice, who was looking for a base for production and exhibition for himself and his Saint Martins' and Goldsmiths' students, among them Fred Drummond and Roger Ackling, and later William Raban, Gill Eatherley and Annabel Nicolson. He began with hand-built equipment, a converted projector as a film-printer, wooden processing tanks and drying racks constructed from wooden discs and dowel rods. By 1969, his workshop group and the LFMC had joined forces and were housed at the second, Robert Street Arts Laboratory – the Institute for Research in Art and Technology (IRAT 1969–71). There, powered by Le Grice and Drummond, the film workshop had its own space, and acquired its first professional film developing and printing machines, which both dramati-

**28** Drury Lane Arts Lab's rarely used logo.

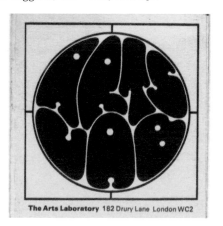

**The Arts Laboratory** 182 Drury Lane London WC2

**29** Poster by Biddy Peppin, 1968.

cally reduced film-making costs, and gave artists control over aspects of the film-making process previously denied to them.[42] Until video and computer-based editing became widespread tools in the late 1990s, the only other way in which an artist might make a substantial body of work without funding was to use the amateur gauge of Super 8, as David Dye and Derek Jarman notably did for part or all of their careers. The Co-op workshop gave artists for the first time a sense that they could make work using the newly established 'professional' gauge (for TV) of 16mm equipment, independently of sponsorship or funding. The explosion of film-making that followed was dramatic. In the year 1973, at the workshop's next home in Prince of Wales Crescent, Le Grice made nine films, Roger Hammond five, Annabel Nicolson ten, Stuart Pound six, and John Du Cane an astonishing sixteen; almost all of them self-funded. Self-processed film also offered the possibility of near-immediate feedback, the opportunity to see what you had just shot and respond to it – the norm in video, but till this moment inconceivable in film. Mike Leggett recalled being inspired by tests he made on the printer at Co-op workshop and making the film *Shepherd's Bush* (1971) the same night, then showing it the next day in the cinema.[43] This immediacy was still enough of a novelty in the mid-1970s for artist and workshop-worker Steve Farrer to mount a virtuoso performance in which he filmed an audience as it arrived at a screening at the Co-op's Fitzroy Road building and, a few minutes later, fed the developed film as it emerged from the processing machine, through a hatch in the wall and straight into a projector, so audience saw itself arriving.[44] But to most film-makers, immediate feedback was just one further aspect of a new, intimate involvement with the materials of film-making.

At the Robert Street Arts Lab, IRAT, I was again programming the cinema, and the repertory of artists' films I could include in its daily screenings also expanded at this time, as a

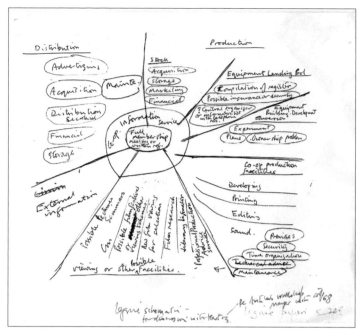

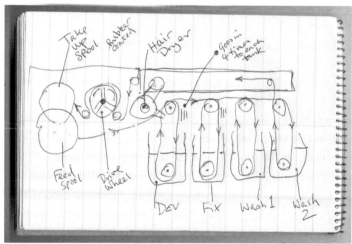

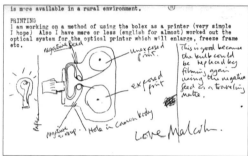

**30 (top left)** The key relationship of film production, distribution and 'viewing' (exhibition) at the Co-op, as mapped by Le Grice and Hartog c.1969–70.

**31 (top right)** Le Grice, c. 1969.

**32 (above)** Schematic drawings by Malcolm Le Grice of Co-op's home-made printer (in a letter to Birgit Hein), and processor, c. 1970.

result of the long-awaited donation of a collection of American works to the London Co-op by Mekas. P. Adams Sitney had presented an *International Exposition of New American Cinema* at the ICA in Dover Street in 1964, and he returned in 1968 with the much larger series *The New American Cinema*, which screened at the National film Theatre (NFT) and toured to twelve regional university campuses. This collection included work by thirty artists, among them Brakhage, Anger, Breer, Landow, Sharits and Snow. And it was these prints that returned to London in 1970, to become the core of the London Filmmakers Co-op collection, and thus part of IRAT's repertory. For many British artists, these prints represented the first opportunity to see contemporary and historic work by their American peers.

Funded by subscriptions alone during its early years, the London Filmmakers Co-op – with its workshop, its screening space and collection of prints – established itself as the centre of an intense film-making movement. Based in one short-life building after another, its collection of equipment and its black-box exhibition space were one attraction, but an equal draw to many was the sense of common purpose and shared commitment to film experiment. The Co-op became a mutual support-group and ideas factory. Le Grice claimed 'what makes the London Filmmakers Co-op significantly different from other similar units in Europe is its continual emphasis on film-MAKING. A purely "distribution" facility is no basis for the day-to-day communication between makers, which allows the building of a cooperative *for* film-makers *by* film MAKERS'.[45] Raban, who became a key workshop organiser in its Prince of Wales Crescent incarnation, traced the 'ideals of the creative laboratory' back to Dziga Vertov and his *Kino Eye* in the Soviet Union of the 1920s: 'Vertov's idea that experimentation should be at the forefront of all film production was the essential message. This … was picked up [by us] in the 1960s and early 1970s, just as it had been by the Dziga Vertov Group in Paris of 1968 by Godard and Gorin.'[46] Peter Gidal and others saw their work at the Co-op in the 1970s as gaining stature from being part of a collective enterprise, avoiding the individualist path.

The emphasis on experiment had impact on the space designed by Co-op members for showing films. The Drury Lane Arts Lab cinema famously had no seats but a deep foam carpet-covered floor (it was housed in a low-ceilinged basement); IRAT's cinema had a very large projection box and connecting 'window' to cater for the needs of multiple projection, but otherwise was conventional, with fixed rows of cinema seats. In the Co-op's own subsequent buildings, these gave way to loose seats in a flat-floored black box, to better cater for

**33 (top left)** Poster by Biddy Peppin, 1968.

**34 (top right)** Gidal's first solo show, 1969.

**35 (above)** Robert Street Arts Lab / IRAT schedule, 1970.

performances and simultaneous projection on more than one wall.[47] And this unconventional configuration was re-created even in the Co-op's final architect-designed lottery-funded building the LUX in 1997. From the beginning of the 1970s to the end of the 1990s the Co-op cinema usually ran two screenings a week, mixing new work with a repertory of avant-garde classics, each generation of programmers giving their own inflection to – in Le Grice's phrase – 'the history we need'. Annabel Nicolson, who succeeded Gidal, emphasised the links with music and performance art; later programmers such as Lis Rhodes (1975–76) Deke Dusinberre (1977–78), and Cordelia Swann (1983–85), brought in more historical programmes, international work and single-artist retrospectives. James Mackay (1979–80) and a number of Slade School post-graduate students introduced the annual *Summer Show* where everything that had entered the distribution catalogue in the preceding year was given a screening, (often shown in alphabetical order, echoing the egalitarian inclusivity and startling juxtapositions of its Royal Academy namesake).

The Co-op's new orientation towards production didn't suit everybody. Some were discouraged from joining by the Co-op's perceived cliqueishness, and its apparent focus on one school of film-making. Artist John Hilliard who briefly used its facilities described it as being like a private members' club with no known rules of admission.[48] Founder-member Steve Dwoskin expressed frustration at the dominance of the workshop membership within the organisation, to the detriment – as he saw it – of distribution. He withdrew his films in the early 1970s, and placed them with The Other Cinema, which promised selection and active promotion. Several new culturally committed distributors were active in the early 1970s, all touting for business. Some like The Other Cinema were not-for-profit organisations; others such as CineGate, Politkino, Derek Hill's Short Film Service and its associated New Cinema Club, 24 Frames, and Vaughan-Rogosin Films were ostensibly commercial, though few made

**36** At 'the Diary' (the Filmmakers Co-op at Prince of Wales Crescent), 1971. (Clockwise from top left) Mike Dunford and Annabel Nicolson, Dunford and Roger Hammond, Le Grice. Polaroid portraits by Hammond.

**37** The Other Cinema staff, as portrayed in their catalogue of 1975.

**38** The London Filmmakers Co-op's first catalogue, designed by Dwoskin.

a profit. The American 'stars' of the period, Mekas, Shirley Clarke, Andy Warhol and Kenneth Anger, all placed their films with commercial companies in Britain, to the disappointment of the Co-op group.

For many, distribution remained the Co-op's most important function. Even film-makers outside the core group of workshop users were attracted by the Co-op's radical commitment to accept into distribution *every* film submitted to it, and to promote all films in its catalogue equally. This was the most important idea borrowed from Mekas's New York model, and represented an extraordinary act of empowerment. By simply publishing a list of films in distribution, the Co-op stated 'these films exist', challenging the blanket of invisibility that had bedevilled artists' film since its beginning. Catalogue descriptions of works were supplied by the artist and printed as submitted, good or bad, clear or obscure. Individual promotion was left to the artist, who was expected to refer any expression of interest back to the Co-op. In all this, London practice was paralleled by a growing network of Co-ops in mainland Europe, in Paris, Munich, Hamburg, Amsterdam and Rome.

But the London Co-op took its egalitarian principles further than most of its siblings, and decided that all salaried posts (which it had from the mid-1970s onwards) should be held for a maximum of one year for cinema, two for workshop and distribution, to ensure that the advantage of paid employment should be shared. This decision had long-term consequences. Positively, it meant that over the years the Co-op provided dozens of artists with skills, equipping them to be film teachers, technicians, projectionists, and distribution workers in other organisations, almost incidentally providing the Co-op with a valuable network of contacts. The original relationship with Saint Martins and Goldsmiths through Le Grice was soon paralleled by links with film-making at the Royal College of Art and Chelsea, through Co-op worker Peter Gidal and key Co-op 'executive' member Anne Rees-Mogg. Later waves of ex-workers provided links with film and art departments in North East London Polytechnic, Exeter, Newcastle, Maidstone, Brighton and Sheffield. Equally positively, the rapid turnover of workers at the Co-op and its inevitable bias towards the young (the Co-op's low pay and spartan working conditions were not designed to attract the old) meant that each new generation of film-makers was likely to find a sympathetic response at the Co-op, and possibly jobs. Film festivals organisers, in search of the

**39** Installing the Co-op's longest-surviving home at 42 Gloucester Avenue, c. 1979, and the same space, completed, as drawn by Agnes Hay, a young filmmaker just arrived from Hungary. **40** Journalist and filmmaker John Du Cane (photos by Hammond).

latest crop of British artists' films, could expect to see a good proportion of them in the Co-op's collection. Negatively, the fixed-term employment rule meant that those with experience – who knew how to work the film processing and printing machines; who knew the contents of the Co-op catalogue and had an understanding of programmers' and educationalists' needs; and who knew the selectors for important exhibitions and festivals – were ejected, just when their accumulated knowledge might have paid dividends. In this sense Dworkin had been right.

This absence of a collective memory and state of almost permanent flux also gave the organisation problems when it came to seeking funding for its activities; public funders moved more slowly and expected continuity in communication. The Co-op didn't achieve revenue funding from the BFI till the mid-1970s, and never felt that its worth was adequately financially recognised. More significantly, it meant that the Co-op grew out of touch with the needs and expectations of its older members, and could be cavalier even in its treatment of its rising stars. Chris Welsby – riding a wave of interest in film installations and landscape film in the late 1970s – loyally offered to show his new six-screen *Shore Line Two* (1979) at the Co-op. Afterwards, he complained bitterly of the Co-op's 'inefficient organisation, lack of interest [and] apathy', and withdrew his films.[49] Many senior figures mutely accepted that they would have to continue to be their own agents, and to broker their own relationships with exhibitors. But the Co-op held to its principles and its egalitarian approach finally ended only when it merged with its sister organisation London Video Arts (LVA)[50] to create the LUX in 1997. Then, in the face of an impossibly expanded community of artists and pressure from its funders, it accepted the conventions of permanent employees and the selection of work taken into distribution.

**41**  Peter Gidal in Prince of Wales Crescent, Polaroid
portrait by Hammond.

**42**  Annabel Nicolson and Paul Burwell's *Readings*, 1977.

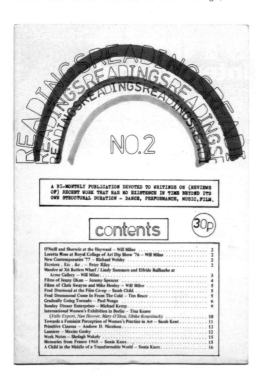

The Co-op's model of operation acted as a catalyst to other groups in one further way. From the early 1970s, artists associated with the Co-op had begun to articulate the concept of 'an integrated practice', by which they meant maintaining a close relationship between the acts of making and exhibiting work, so that each would provide feedback to the other in a virtuous circle. This built on Le Grice's early intuition that 'day-to-day communication between makers' was central to the Co-op's – and artists' – development. Le Grice and Mike Leggett were core members of the lobbying group the IFA, where this philosophy provided common ground with other early political film collectives and workshops such as Cinema Action (1968– ) and Amber Films (1968 onwards). And 'integrated practice' was the mantra of the growing number of second-generation workshop-based political film groups, such as the Bristol Filmmakers' Co-op and Sheffield Independent Film, and became enshrined in workshop revenue funding agreements with Channel 4 and in the 'Workshop Declaration' agreed with the film union the ACTT in 1982, a code of practice which 'legitimised' certain forms of low-budget film-making.[51] But by the end of the 1980s the phrase through overuse had come to mean little more than 'we make and show films'.

When Gidal took over the running of the Co-op's cinema in September 1971, he re-orientated its weekly programme to give stronger emphasis to new British work, and remarkably persuaded the London listings magazine *Time Out* to take copy from him each week, to promote the shows. As a journalist, his see-sawing mix of sharp insight and slang was infectious, and he rarely disguised his true opinion. His ambivalence is transparent as he announces a screening of Jonas Mekas's film diaries at the Co-op:

> Although I find bits of the film loose, highly romantic and all-embracingly naive, I also feel that if you are going to make personal cinema diaries, if you are going to believe in this cinema aesthetic, then Mekas's films represent the epitome of that style. In scenes where millionaires have weddings on huge estates with some asshole cleric performing the ceremony, underground cinema surely ends. But as part of the diary situation this is unprejudiced seeing. On the other hand, all embracing harmoniousness, tolerance of this sort can obviously become dangerous. Mekas's work should be seen. It betrays itself beautifully.[52]

During this period, issuing written texts that promoted artists' film-making and new approaches to film became almost as important to those involved in the Co-op as making film. Du Cane was another regular contributor to *Time Out*, and provided the first serious appreciations of Larcher, Le Grice, Gidal and others in page-long articles. The magazine *Art & Artists* produced a special 'Film Issue' in 1972, with articles by David Dye, Simon Field, Gidal, Le Grice and Nicolson. Le Grice himself gained a monthly column 'Film', then 'Vision', in the leading art journal *Studio International* from 1973, reviewing local and international events and monitoring the achievements and shortcomings of the art establishment, as it responded – or failed to respond – to artists' film. *Studio International* produced its own 'Film Issue' in 1975, and a 'Video Art issue' in 1976. The first crop of books appeared, assessing the international scene and attempting to recover and describe the art form's history. My *Experimental Cinema* (1971) was written in 1969–70, overlapping my involvement in the Robert Street Arts Lab; Dwoskin followed with *Film Is* (1975) and Le Grice with *Abstract Film and Beyond* (1977).[53] More unexpectedly, journalists not part of the Co-op's inner circle were also showing interest. Throughout the late 1960s and early 1970s, Gordon Gow wrote about artists' films in his column dedicated to the non-standard gauges of 8mm and 16mm in *Films and Filming*, and in the later 1970s Verina Glaessner, Claire Johnston, Jan Dawson and Tony Rayns were among those who contributed features on 'independent' film and 'the underground' to *Time Out*, *City Limits* and *Sight & Sound*. Academics associated with *Screen*, the BFI-funded journal of the Society for Education in Film and Television, such as Stephen Heath and Peter Wollen, also noted these developments, writing articles themselves[54] and occasionally making space for contributions by the more engaged historians Deke Dusinberre and A.L. Rees and practitioners Gidal, Le Grice and Stuart Marshall. All this attention generated a level of awareness of the Co-op group rarely equalled in its later years.

Echoing the links between film-making groups and self-published magazines of the 1930s, Co-op film-makers produced their own magazines. Durgnat, Hartog and Crick produced *Cinim* (1966–68), the Co-op's first official magazine, which survived a circulation of a few hundred for three issues. Du Cane ambitiously launched *Light One* (1973), while juggling his reviewing for *Time Out* and his most productive period of film-making, not surprisingly

**43** Artists' film is acknowledged by the art press; *Art and Artists*, 1972 (image from Le Grice's *Horror Film*); *Studio International*, 1975 (image from Chris Welsby's *Seven Days*).

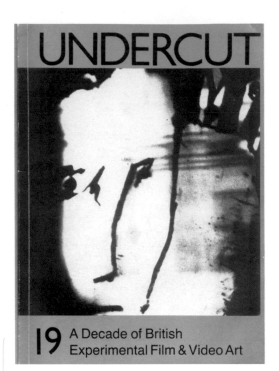

A Decade of British
Experimental Film & Video Art

**44** *Undercut*, the final issue
1990, (image from Lis
Rhodes' *A Cold Draft*).

stopping at one issue, a monograph on Michael Snow. Nicolson, busy film-making and programming the Co-op cinema, published a review magazine *Readings* (1977 – three issues) with musician Paul Burwell, which reflected their shared interest in film and performance; and Raban – keen to encourage international links – published *Filmmakers Europe* (1977–81, 22 issues), a poster/broadsheet providing lists of screening venues across Europe and America, film courses, forthcoming festivals, reviews, comparative charts of lab costs, and news.[55] A second Co-op magazine *Undercut* (1981–90, 19 issues) was produced by a collective within the collective, again achieving a tiny circulation, but providing an important launch-pad for new artists and writers. The struggles during *Undercut*'s gestation in 1979–80 reprised the Co-op's earlier agonising over its egalitarian principles.

> Articles discussing areas of work, and not specific films, would help to break down rather than enforce, the existing selectivity (the small minority of films which enter public discourse through being mentioned in art magazines or 'perspectived' by the Arts Council). [The latter a reference to the contemporary Arts Council exhibition *A Perspective on English Avant Garde Film*] … The Co-op's policy of non-promotion should be interpreted as a refusal to select individual films/makers, not a refusal to publicise or contextualise the work cooperatively.[56]

The unsigned writer, almost certainly Mike Leggett, then quotes a prediction by Le Grice: 'There is an inherent weakness in non-promotion which eliminates persuasion and taste-forming which are [then] open to competitors'.[57] (Other curatorial perspectives were rarely welcomed by the Co-op group.) But over the next decade, the *Undercut* collective bravely made its editorial choices – often an attenuated and painful process – and visibly demonstrated its alertness to 'the new' in the avant-garde: feminist film, landscape film, work by black artists, Scratch video, the romantics associated with Jarman, gay and lesbian cinema and more.

From the mid-1970s to the mid-1990s, the Co-op continued to be a magnet to young artists, and provided a dependable showcase for their work. Many new groups and factions as they emerged happily colonised the organisation, and were able to sufficiently re-shape it to their own image to feel at home there, expressing their difference through seasons of film screenings, festivals, and the occasional angry public meeting. But it was no longer the only home available. Video artists had their own production and exhibition needs and by the mid-1970s had organised their own structures, as would digital artists in the 1990s (for example, the London work-space Backspace, and the magazine *Mute*). The demand for women-only workshop sessions and screenings proved divisive, and the Co-op suffered a major trauma in 1979 when many women withdrew to set up the women-only distribution company Circles

– Women's Work in Distribution, coinciding with their withdrawal from the Arts Council's exhibition *Film as Film*. Circles re-invoked the tighter focus and cohesion of the early Co-op. It stayed small; its artists (notably its founders Lis Rhodes, Tina Keane, Annabel Nicolson, Jo Davis and co-ordinator Felicity Sparrow) sometimes worked together on projects, and it bravely refused public funding – the artists initially each contributing £20 towards its start-up costs. It moved to the Four Corners workshop in East London in 1982, where as its distribution activity expanded, it was able to hold women-only screenings in tandem with Four Corners' own programme of events involving the local working-class community. Inevitably, money became a problem, and eventually Circles merged with Cinema of Women (COW) to form Cinenova in 1991 (COW itself being the residue of the Cine Sisters (1979–91), which in turn had inherited equipment from London Women's Film Group (1972–78), an organisation associated with Mary Kelly, Claire Johnston and others).

The pluralism that characterised artists films' in the 1980s was reflected in the growth of smaller specialist groupings, and a new accommodation with the private sector. It saw the establishment of the black artists' groups Black Audio Film Collective and Sankofa, both founded in 1983, and both initially associated with the Co-op, and the involvement of commercial production companies such as Mayavision, Koninck, Tall Stories, K.D. Digital and Illuminations, which offered a production base to artists undertaking works of scale and ambition, such as Jayne Parker, Patrick Keiller, Richard Billingham and Andrew Kotting.

In the late 1990s, with some coercion from the funders, the Co-op and LEA (London Electronic Arts) finally accepted that their common objectives were more important than their differences, and they came together to create the Lottery funded *grand project* that was the digital-friendly but ill-fated LUX Centre, in an episode described later.

**45** *Circles* first catalogue, 1980.

## INTO THE GALLERY

The common perception that the video installation is an invention of the 1990s – born miraculously free of any evolutionary history – is understandable, if wholly wrong. Certainly, dealers in the 1990s succeeded in marketing the film video installation as a limited-edition commodity where their 1970s predecessors had failed, but the modern form of the installation in all its diversity was the product of long period of experiment shared by the post-Caro generation conceptualists with their commercial gallery shows, and by members of the Co-op and future LVA groups, exhibiting mostly in artist-run and public sector spaces. What the many artists from the Co-op, LVA and conceptualist groups shared was an interest in challenging the conventional screen/spectator relationship – by opening it out – allowing the spectator to approach the image, to walk in and around the space of projection, and to experience the

*Gallery space s.*

*Video brought hour.*

**46** (above) Sequence of
drawings for the animation,
*Emergences of Continuous
Form*, Jeffrey Shaw, 1966;
(below) *Emergences of
Continuous Form* in projection
(with balloons), at Better
Books, 1966.

**47** (below right) Drawing of
loop projection installations,
1969–71 by Tony Morgan.

work in different ways. By the middle of the 1970s, most of the conceptual artists had abandoned film and video, but the evolution of installations and performance-related work was carried forward into the 1980s and 1990s, latterly predominantly but not exclusively by video artists.[58]

In the inter-war period, portable film projection equipment was rare, and the exhibition of artists' films was necessarily confined to the conventional cinema space. The availability in the 1960s of portable 8mm and 16mm projectors liberated artists, and film began to colonise other sites and spaces. As early as 1967, the artist Scotty had shown films in the gallery at the Drury Lane Arts Lab, making a visible feature of a rare portable 35mm projector, and his performance of keeping it fed with reels of found images. A year earlier, Jeffrey Shaw projected film into an environment of smoke, balloons and hanging screens in a performance at Better Books,[59] and throughout the late 1960s and early 1970s, he and the Event Structure Research Group (which included John Latham and others) would project into translucent plastic 'inflatables' in galleries, public parks and other environments. Tony Morgan showed loops of film (which allowed for continuous exhibition for as long as the loop lasted) at *Strategy – Get Arts* in Edinburgh in 1969, and again at *The Floor Show* at the Lisson Gallery in 1972, hinting at the possibility of permanent film installations.

Film was also included in a series of survey exhibitions in the early 1970s that showcased contemporary developments in art in all media – and which deliberately broke with convention in their choice of venues and forms of display. One hundred artists took part in the London version of *Art Spectrum* (1971) at the Alexandra Palace in London, selected for the Arts Council by an eclectic group including performance artist and film-maker Stuart Brisley, gallerists Annely Juda and John Dunbar (Indica Gallery), and film-maker and 'outsider'-art collector Victor Musgrave.[60] In a space associated with trade fairs rather than art shows,

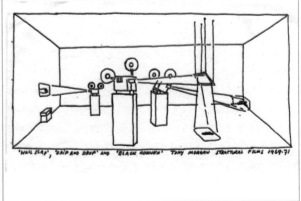

a repertory of films was shown in a side-aisle, and included works by Leggett and Breakwell, Bruce Lacey, Conrad Atkinson and Mark Boyle, and the first (and only) group-showing of a collection of self-documentation films by sculptors recently funded by the Arts Council. *Prospect 71 – Projection* in Dusseldorf (1971) was a similarly catch-all event, this time international in scope, and organised by Konrad Fischer, Jürgen Harten and Hans Strelow, at least in part inspired by Dusseldorf-based Gerry Schum's radical approach to exhibition. There, the British contribution included twelve film-makers and two photographers.[61] Video was more prominent in the media-mix in *A Survey of the Avant-Garde in Britain* (1972) organised by Rosetta Brooks and Siggi Kraus at Gallery House in London, which included the spectacular installation *60 TV Sets* by David Hall and Tony Sinden, videos by Denis Masi, and films by Raban, Gidal, Latham, Anthony McCall and others, and *An Evening of Artists' Film and Video* at the Walker Art Gallery in Liverpool (June 1973) which included many of the same cast, with the addition of video works by William Wegman (USA) and Bruce McLean.

**A Survey of the Avant-Garde in Britain**

October 2nd - 15th 1972

VOL. 3

**GALLERY HOUSE LONDON**

**48** Catalogue to *A Survey of the Avant-Garde in Britain*, 1972.

Uniquely in these shows, Co-op film-makers and their conceptual film and video counterparts appeared side by side; the former hostile to the commodification of the art-object, the latter at least accepting, if not always whole-heartedly embracing it; ideas rather than objects being the common denominator.[62] The links between conceptualism and early structural film were explored further in *Structures & Codes* at the Royal College of Art (1975) which included films by John Blake, Gidal and David Lamelas, alongside work in other media by Latham, John Stezaker and Stephen Willats, and in *Structure and Function in Time* (also 1975) at Sunderland Arts Centre, again organised by Rosetta Brooks, featuring many of the same artists. However, by this date, many conceptualists (among them Hilliard, Flanagan and Masi) had abandoned film or like Blake and Morgan, moved abroad.

**49** *Ambient-Vision*, Jane Rigby, 1979 – schematic drawing for installation in the Acme Gallery.

Though historically important as announcements of the arrival of a 'new art', these big mixed-media shows rarely provided a sympathetic physical environment for the showing of film, and the most significant developments in the installation in the 1970s took place in the more familiar contexts of the Co-op's black box and the controllable environment of the gallerist's white cube. The expanded-cinema work of the group of artists who showed with Le Grice as Filmaktion first seen at Galley House in 1973 (Raban, Eatherley, Nicolson and David Crosswaite) essentially involved *performance* with the moving image, but also included static sections in which composite images were built from overlapping or adjacent projections of film-loops. Long loops suspended from hooks in the exhibition space, rotating slowly as the projectors chewed their way through them, became a familiar sight in galleries at this time. Some artists worked to transform the images on the loop, as it turned (Nicolson,

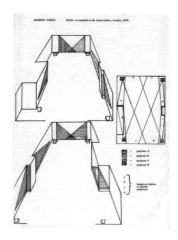

**50** Synchronised multi-screen projection, *Thames Barrier*, William Raban, 1977.

Rhodes); some used loops to animate all four walls of the gallery, or joined up the projected images to create panoramas (Jane Rigby, Chris Welsby); some combined loops with slide projections (Eatherley, Tim Head), or photographic still images (Haselden, Sinden, Darcy Lange). Some created visual paradoxes and jokes (Morgan, Dye), others pure light-sculptures (Brian Eno, Anthony McCall).

Continuous film installations – in contrast to video – were always limited in duration by the length of the loop (rarely more than three or four minutes), and its vulnerability as it hung in space. The cost of replacing loops meant that installations generally were shown for a day or two, and rarely more than a week. In multi-screen installations there was the additional problem that film projectors would soon run out of synch, and most artists designed their works to accommodate this drift. However, technology developed for the trade-fair market provided solutions towards the end of the 1970s with interlocked projectors, used for example by Raban in his film *Thames Barrier* (1977),[63] and film 'loop-absorbers' ('loopers' to Americans) first introduced to the art-world with the exhibition *Film as Film* in 1979, that allowed for the continuous projection of loops of up to thirty minutes long.

By the end of the 1970s, video had taken over as the preferred medium for installations, though Welsby, Steve Farrer, Jane Rigby and others would continue to make substantial installations in 16mm, and John Maybury and his generation would re-discover multi-screen film in the more flexible form of Super 8 in the mid-1980s. In the 1990s, just when 16mm installations were about to be declared dead, 16mm and loop-absorbers were chosen by a new wave of installation artists including Tacita Dean and Steve McQueen.

## VIDEO AS VIDEO

Video art, and artists' first engagement with broadcast television, began to make their appearance at the very end of the 1960s. As so often, changes in technology – the arrival of the first domestic portable video recorders and experimental colour cameras in the professional sphere – provided one driver, but artists were also responding to the growing dominance of broadcast television in daily life. Activity was initially limited, simply because opportunities for access to video equipment and the apparatus of broadcast television were so rare. None the less, in the short span of the five years 1966–71, Lutz Becker was working experimentally with engineers at BBC television in London, David Hall was shooting his *TV Interruptions* in Edinburgh for Scottish Television, John 'Hoppy' Hopkins at IRAT was showing off one of the

*Intro of Video/TV*

first Sony Portapaks to arrive in Britain (loaned to him by John Lennon), and the artist/entre-preneur Gerry Schum was in England shooting works (on film) for TV with Richard Long, and later Gilbert and George for his Fernsehgalerie (TV Gallery) in Germany.

Hopkins, a successful freelance photographer in the early 1960s, was associated with many of the 1960s Underground's more colourful enterprises. He was one of the founder-editors of the alternative newspaper *The International Times*; he ran the classic underground nightclub the UFO Club, where Mark Boyle created some of the most innovative light-shows of the period with house-band Soft Machine; and he was associated with The Free University in Notting Hill. At the Robert Street Arts Lab, IRAT, he formed the group TVX and promoted video as a medium for reflecting and mediating social change.[64] In a letter to the Arts Council seeking funding in 1969, he wrote:

> we have been looking at society in terms of the disaffiliated and other groups within it, and
> have developed the concept of Social Matrix in which to describe our findings. The Social
> Matrix is a map of society seen from the individual's point of view, and we feel it will be of
> tremendous use to any group or government wanting to communicate with the disparate and
> decentralised activity that is now part of young society.[65]

The hint of Mass Observation-like detachment in this statement was atypical. Most of Hoppy's work, like that of the other social and political groups who discovered video, responded to its potential for an immediate engagement with and possible empowerment of its audience. And, famously, Hoppy went on to demonstrate video as a tool in guerrilla action, with his team's invasion of David Frost's television studio during a live interview with Yippie activist Abbie Hoffman in November 1970, and his record of a drugs raid on the Robert Street Arts Lab (IRAT) in June the same year, shown the same day on BBC2's *Late Night Line-up*.[66]

Many artists among the first generation of those who engaged with video responded more to the formal challenge of its very visible technical limitations. Early video was restricted to a black and white image; cameras were heavy to hold and slow to respond to changes in light; images 'bled' if you moved the camera fast; and, most restricting of all, editing was almost impossible apart from live-mixing of images; these became material qualities to be worked with. But video also came into its own as a medium to record process and performance, and to relay a live image from one space to another. Many works of this period were made in a single take; video found use as a 'mirror', and consequently author-introspection was rife.

As the portable non-broadcast technology became more soph-isticated in the early 1970s, a growing community of artists began to work with it, particularly when art-schools recognised the relative

**51** Colour and video projection; novelties in the age of black and white monitors. John Hopkins and Fantasy Factory, 1976.

cheapness of production using the new medium. Videotape could be re-used; there was no need for expensive film processing; QED. Video artist Stuart Marshall later acknowledged the importance of facilities in colleges such as Maidstone, Brighton, Coventry and the Royal College of Art to the sustaining of video art in its early days.

> At this time many colleges were setting up media departments and investing in video technology. Many early video art productions took place in these art departments which provided the only resource centres of any sophistication. … The commercial gallery system in Great Britain has never shown interest in the exhibition or distribution of artists' video and has therefore never provided institutional support for video practice.[67]

Initially, when it came to exhibition, video works could only be shown on TV sets or monitors, making video a natural child of the gallery, rather than of the cinema-space.[68] And, contrary to Marshall's protestations, commercial galleries *did* show an early albeit short-lived interest in the medium. In the early 1970s, the Lisson, Nigel Greenwood, Jack Wendler, Robert Self, Angela Flowers and other galleries regularly or occasionally exhibited video works (and sometimes films), and notionally offered them for sale, despite the soon-evident lack of any real market.[69] But the work these galleries exhibited was made by conceptual artists (mostly ex-sculptors) for whom film and video was generally one medium among many used, and who were content to participate in the commercial gallery system, however notional the return. Marshall (from a media studies background) approached video from a very different perspective. Paradoxically, even as this private-sector initiative was failing, video became even more firmly rooted in gallery spaces in the early 1980s with the advent of playback decks that could be set to re-wind and re-play automatically, potentially giving the work a continuous presence. The context was now the growing number of public-sector galleries dedicated to showing contemporary art such as the Serpentine Gallery in London, the Ikon in Birmingham and the Arnolfini in Bristol, and smaller artist-run spaces. This technology remained the standard till projection systems became widely available in the 1990s, allowing video to replicate cinema's world of black boxes and round the clock performance.

**52** Video as light sculpture, *Place #11*, Brian Eno, 1986.

Video came of age, and caught the wider public's attention, with the widely reviewed *The Video Show* at the Serpentine Gallery in 1975, and the Tate education department's version in 1976. *Studio International* responded by publishing a *Video Art* issue in May 1976 co-edited by Hall to coincide with the Tate show, containing a declaration by Hall of British video art's independence 'British Video Art: Toward an Autonomous Practice', and articles on his work and that of Roger Barnard, Brian Hoey, Tamara Krikorian, Mike Leggett, Marshall, Stephen Partridge, the partnership of Hopkins and Sue Hall, and others. This blitz was completed by a *Video Art* special edition of the BBC's *Arena* programme, for which Hall made *This is a Television Receiver,* and which included extracts of works by Peter Donebauer, and American artists Peter Campus and Ed Emshwiller.

Hall's campaigning included the demand for a separate organisation to distribute video and represent video artists' interests, and in 1976 he secured Arts Council funding for some equipment and a catalogue for a new organisation, and was able to announce its creation in the pages of *Studio International*.

> With the ever-pressing need in this country for a centrally located organisation to promote, show and distribute independent work in video art, I am pleased to announce that … just such an idea has been realised in the shape of London Video Arts. … It has been initiated by a group of video artists and will operate as a strictly independent non-profit-making organisation. Finances are virtually non-existent at this stage, but approaches are being made to appropriate funding bodies for support. Eventually, LVA hopes to provide a venue for the showing of tapes, installation and performances.[70]

*[handwritten margin note: THE OTHER CINEMA MAIDSTONE (UCA)]*

Hall, Krikorian and Partridge had worked together at Maidstone College of Art where Hall had established a media workshop in 1972, and together they provided LVA's vision and energy in its early years, with artist David Critchley who became its first paid organiser in 1981, and Marshall and Hoey as other early activists. Soon LVA had an office in Wardour Street, Soho,[71] in a building also occupied by The Other Cinema, the Women's Film & TV Network, the IFA and other independents; a little island of alternative practice in the traditional heart of the capital's media industry. LVA's first distribution catalogue published in 1978 stated that 'anyone working experimentally and anyone documenting artworks in the medium is eligible for inclusion in the LVA library', but this Co-op-like egalitarian invitation had disappeared by the time of its second catalogue in 1984, and did not resurface. LVA was never embarrassed by the idea of selective promotion, nor would it insist on short-term contracts for its workers. It had learned, perhaps, from the Co-op's experience. A small pool of production equipment was established in 1981, and was greatly enlarged thanks to regular funding from Channel 4 from 1983, and from the Greater London Council from 1984. This investment prompted the move of LVA's office and new edit suites to 22 Frith Street, Soho, by happy coincidence next door to the building from which John Logie Baird had sent the world's first experimental television transmissions in 1926. (Hall would memorably recreate Baird's first fragile images in his tape *Stooky Bill TV* (1990).) Re-housed more than once, these production facilities remained a busy centre of production for artists till the late 1990s, when they, and the whole notion of artists' collective equipment-based video workshops, were finally made obsolete by the ubiquity of domestic, computer-based editing systems.

LVA's launch party was held at the Air Gallery in Shaftsbury Avenue, and for its first few years, it held occasional screenings

**53** *Studio International* celebrates Video Art. David Hall's *This is a TV Receiver*, 1976, the cover image.

**54** LVA' first distribution catalogue, designed by David Critchley

**55** Card for Marty St James and Anne Wilson's environmental installation, *Hotel*, 1989

there, and in other artist-run spaces in London such as 2B Butler's Wharf from 1976,[72] the Acme Gallery from 1979, the Ayton Basement in Newcastle from 1980, and occasionally even at the Filmmakers Co-op. And while its aspiration to control its own exhibition space for installations was initially frustrated, the core group energetically programmed installation work and group shows for other venues, such as *Video Towards Defining an Aesthetic* organised by Krikorian for the Scottish Arts Council Gallery (1977), *Video Art 78* organised by Hall and Partridge for the Herbert Art Gallery, Coventry (1978), and Hoey's annual *Artists' Video* festival at Biddick Farm from 1976. In 1979 the Air Gallery moved to larger premises in Rosebery Avenue, and LVA secured the use of its basement for regular monthly screenings, with access to the rest of the building for a major installation shows, in effect realising Hall's dream. The annual *Video Installation Shows* of 1981–84 were organised by LVA's new distribution worker Jeremy (Jez) Welsh with the Air Gallery's director Robert McPherson and exhibition organiser Iwona Blazwick, and included the first showing of important pieces such as Tina Keane's *Demolition Escape*, Mick Hartney's *Between the Lines*, Krikorian's *Time Revealing Truth* and Mineo Aayamaguchi's *Landscape,* all of 1983. On a later occasion, Marty St James and Anne Wilson converted the entire building into their live-in video-based fantasy environment *Hotel* (1989).

In the mid-1980s, Welsh organised two innovative shows jointly with the ICA, *Channel 5* (1985) and *Channel 6* (1986), which, as their titles were intended to suggest, reflected the current optimism about the potential role of Channel 4 as a space for artists, and a wider debate about how video art could be brought more fully into the public arena. *Channel 5* was timed to coincide with Channel 4's transmission of *The Eleventh Hour: Video, I, 2 and 3* – a showcase of video work mostly by British artists selected by Rod Stoneman and introduced by the critic Sean Cubitt. To complement this series,

Welsh commissioned installations for the Air Gallery, and a programme of screenings and seminars at the ICA. *Channel 6*, which appeared simultaneously at the ICA, the Air Gallery and the London Filmmakers Co-op, celebrated LVA's tenth birthday, with more installations under the banner *Scanners*, and 'works for the street' in the forms of a nine monitor *Video Window Box* display. In the period of Scratch video and television commissions in the later 1980s, and with the closure of the Air Gallery, LVA's distribution and exhibition activity seemed to lose momentum, till it refocused its activities round sale of works to television, and experimented with tape sales aimed at a domestic market, the latter perhaps inspired by the success of artist George Barber's self-published VHS release of *The Greatest Hits of Scratch Video Vol. 1* in 1985. Significantly, a mid-1980s show organised by Tina Keane and Michael O'Pray for the Tate Education department, *The New Pluralism* (1985), mixed film and video and marked a shift in curatorial interest away from media specificity, anticipating the 1990s phenomenon of media convergence.

Not on LVA's agenda, at least not officially, was collaboration with NeTWork 21, an artist-run pirate TV channel which operated intermittently in South London in 1986–87, using airwaves perilously close to those of ITV. Originating some material on Video 8 – including an interview with Marguerite Duras – its eclectic schedule included tapes lent by Jarman and Maybury, clandestinely-shot footage of a Diamanda Galas concert at The Albany, German rock bands, and assorted Scratch videos. It was a brief taste of the alternative programming theoretically possible in a multi-channel age, which the commercial realities of the 1990s signally failed to deliver.

Like Le Grice, Hall knew that a regular mouthpiece was important to the development of the art form, and he too secured a column 'Video' in *Studio International* which appeared throughout 1976, and which became a record of triumphs and disappointments at home and abroad, and a source of advice and rebuke to funding bodies. After this ceased, the momentum was maintained by Mick Hartney, video artist and important video teacher at Brighton Polytechnic, who established a 'Video and Performance' column in *Art Monthly* throughout 1982–83, sometimes shared with Krikorian, and carried on by O'Pray till 1988. Marshall and other video artists contributed occasionally to the Co-op's *Undercut* magazine, and many of LVA's later distribution catalogues contained long contextual articles, but surprisingly no group of artists felt the urge to start a separate, video-specific magazine for artist-led debate and theorising. Perhaps video was already sufficiently tied into the art-world with its convention of exhibition catalogues and established art magazines to make such an initiative unnecessary. The wider video constituency that included political and social video-making groups alongside artists – the constituency that annually gathered at the *National Video Festival* at Bracknell – did provide a reader-

**56 (opposite top right)** LVA's steering committee meet in Maastricht during the Video Manifestie, 1977; (l. to r.) Tamara Krikorian, [unnamed Dutch observer], David Hall, Stephen Partridge, David Critchley, Roger Barnard.

**57** The first issue of video's house-journal *Independent Video* (later *Independent Media*).

ship for a news and reviews monthly *Independent Video* from 1980 (*Independent Media* from 1986), which valuably grew a new generation of critics such as Steven Bode, Nik Houghton, Julia Knight and Sean Cubitt, and the maker-writers Jez Welsh, Cate Elwes and Michael Maziere. From 1989 onwards, Bode would write regularly for *Videographic*, a glossy trade journal targeted at advertisers and users of Soho's digital post-production 'facilities-houses', marking the moment when video art and the graphics of high-commerce were at their closest.[73] Later still, digital and web-artists would gain a magazine in their own image in *Mute*.

## THE 1990s

As television had challenged the supremacy of the artist-organised screenings and shows in the 1980s – bringing artists' work to vast new audiences, if fitfully, and in ways over which the artists had limited control – so did the re-emergence of commercial galleries as players in the field in the 1990s. Capitalising on the display technologies pioneered by artists and public sector galleries in the 1980s, they re-introduced the notion of film and video works as saleable limited-edition commodities – backed by individual promotion and the strenuous lobbying of critics and crucial international networking that powers the international market. This time they succeeded commercially where their 1970s predecessors had failed, achieving the one-in-ten rate of hitting the jackpot with a particular artist or work that constitutes viability in the art-world, as it does for Hollywood studios and feature films. Among the first to be interested were the Lisson Gallery (a lone survivor from those which had shown film and video

**58** Video art meets the world of advertising and special effects; the post-production house-journal *Videographic*. Cover mage by John Maybury

**59** Environmental installations in the 1990s; *Gamma*, Jane and Louise Wilson, 1999.

in the 1970s), the Anthony Reynolds Gallery, Matt's Gallery, and Maureen Paley/Interim Arts (run by Paley who in an earlier incarnation had been associated with both the Co-op and LEA[74]). But the majority were wholly new to the scene.[75] Significantly, almost all the artists they represented were from the rising yBa (young British artists) stars and their international equivalents; the artists who had pioneered the form during the previous decades were passed over, a few because they refused commodification, the majority because their work was simply unknown to the new generation of entrepreneurs and curators. The newly opened LUX Centre – the combined residue of the Co-op and LEA – bravely announced its intention to enter the field by creating its own white cube space and issuing price lists of exhibited works, and cleverly employing the rising yBa curatorial star Gregor Muir as gallery director, but this experiment fell with the rest of the organisation in 2002, before it could be truly tested.

## NOTES

1. Sometimes mistakenly referred to as 'The London Film Society', as in the 1972 Arno Press NY reprint of its programme notes. Scotland had its equivalents, the Edinburgh Film Guild from 1930, and the Glasgow Film Society from 1931.

2. 'Hitchcock, an alumnus of the Film Society, experimented with sound in *Blackmail* (1929), and later hoped to collaborate with Lye in a shock ending for *Secret Agent* (1936): when the train crashed to destruction, the film was to appear to burn up in the projector, an effect created by Lye's animation. It came to nothing, but he always continued to nurture his idea of smuggling avant-gardism into the industry.' Peter Wollen, 'Together', *Sight & Sound*, 1996.

3. Ivor Montagu, 'Old Man's Mumble, Reflections on a Semi-Centenary', *Sight & Sound*, Autumn 1975.

4. Eisenstein's lectures introduced his ideas for the first time to English-speaking audiences. The resulting workshop film *Everyday* was finally edited by Richter in 1967, when he also added sound.

5. For an account of this period, see Bert Hogenkamp, *Deadly Parallels: Film and the Left in Britain 1929–1939* (London: Lawrence and Wishart, 1986).

6. *Architectural Review*, vol. 72, July 1932.

7. Macpherson's involvement with the magazine – and with Bryher – ended in 1933; in New York he co-produced Hans Richter's film *Dreams That Money Can Buy* (1944) and wrote occasionally for Parker Tyler's magazine *View*, then retired in 1947 to life as a writer in Italy, where he died in 1971.

8. He launched two other journals dedicated to 'advance-garde' cinema, *Film* (1933) and *New Cinema* (1936) which both folded after one issue.

9. See his 'The Principles of the Film', 1933, reprinted in Michael O'Pray (ed.) *The British Avant-Garde Film* (Luton: University of Luton Press, 1996).

10. *Film Art*, vol. III no. 8, 1936.

11. Film Society programme note, 12 April 1931.

12. *Manhatta* 13. November 1927; *Loves of Zero* 13 January 1929.

13. Scott MacDonald, 'An Interview with Amos Vogel', *Cinema 16: Documents Towards a History of the Film Society* (Philadelphia, PA: Temple University Press, 2002).

14. Mannus Franken's account written in 1929, quoted in 'La Sarraz and Holland' – a paper by Jan de Vaal of the Netherlands Filmmuseum, Amsterdam, for the 1979 La Sarraz Reunion, organised by FIAF. The

seven signatories were France, England, Italy, Spain, Switzerland, the USA and the Netherlands.

15. John Grierson, 'The Documentary Film', *The Manchester Guardian Commercial*, 31 January 1936.

16. In 1946, the Art in Cinema Society in San Francisco mounted an international season of screenings at the San Francisco Museum of Art, perhaps unconsciously celebrating the successful migration of many avant-garde film-makers from Europe to the USA. *Art in Cinema* remains unique in USA history in that works from overseas outnumbered those of the host nation.

17. Scott MacDonald, 'Letter to Amos Vogel from Stan Brakhage 12/2/57', *Cinema 16: Documents Towards a History of the Film Society* (Philadelphia, PA: Temple University Press, 2002).

18. 'Experimental Films at Brussels (1)', *Continental Film Review*, May 1958.

19. This number is cited by Peter Cargin in 'Alternative Cinema', *Film*, no. 58, Spring 1970.

20. For an account of the growth of 16mm independent film distribution in the inter-war period, see Don Macpherson (ed.), *Traditions of Independence* (London: BFI, 1980), and for the post-war, see Margaret Dickinson (ed.) *Rogue Reels – Oppositional Film in Britain 1945–90* (London: BFI, 1999), though both focus primarily on political film. See my 'List Man : Movies' in *IT*, vol. 15, June 1967 for a contemporary list of artists' films in distribution.

21. 'A Conversation on Knokke and the Independent Filmmaker', P. A. Sitney, Annette Michelson, *Art Forum*, May 1975. Sitney had already published several issues of his journal *Filmwise*. He went on to write the best account of the rise of the American avant-garde, *Visionary Film* (New York: Oxford University Press, 1974).

22. *The Magazine of the ICA*, April 1968. My own experience at the 1967/68 festival was more positive. I saw for the first time the work of Gregory Markopoulos, Paul Sharits, Mike Snow, and Willhelm and Birgit Hein. Two years later I curated a homage to Knokke at the Robert Street Arts Laboratory, re-creating in seven programmes its transatlantic mix and the contrasting definitions of 'experiment' in its successive festivals. See 'Report from Knokke' in *IT*, 19 January–1 February 1968; also my 'diary' of the period: *English Avant-Garde Film – An Early Chronology* first published in *Studio International*, November–December 1975, reprinted in Michael O'Pray (ed.), *British Avant-garde Film* (Luton: University of Luton Press, 1996).

23. '5th Experimental Film Competition at Knokke', *Studio International*, February 1975.

24. With his *The Pleasure Garden* (1952), shot in London.

25. International Underground Film Festival 1970; Festival of International Avant-garde Film 1973, Film London 1979. Simon Field and I nominally organised the first two of these, David Parsons, Penny Webb and others the third. After the first, Gidal wrote of its importance, 'you did an absolutely incredible job of getting all the people and films together; the results were very positive even on a pure basis of exposure to film (for me and other film-makers)'. Postcard to the author, September 1970.

26. This German alertness to avant-garde art was also reflected in the magazine *Interfunktion* (1968–75); Le Grice contributing to issue 4, March 1970. A 'Film Documenta' had been planned for 1968, but was 'cancelled because of Sitney's Tour' – letter from John Collins to Ulrich Herzog, 4 June 1968. Artist Birgit Hein programmed film for the 1977 event.

27. Malcolm Le Grice, 'Vision', *Studio International*, February 1975.

28. The full list is a remarkable round-up of key players of the period: (1) Adriano Apra, Victor Burgin, Regina Cornwell (2) Ben Brewster, Serge Daney, Hollis Frampton, Annette Michelson, (3) Chantal

Akerman, Malcolm Le Grice, Constance Penley, Paul Sharits, (4) Birgit Hein, Marc Karlin, Joyce Wieland, Peter Wollen, (5) Raymond Bellour, Peter Gidal, Yvonne Rainer, Michael Snow, with Ian Christie and Claire Johnston chairing sessions.

29. 'Movie Journal', *Village Voice*, 27 September 1973.

30. Caroline Tisdall, 'Expanded Cinema', *The Guardian*, 9 January 1976

31. Raymond Durgnat, 'Flyweight Flicks', *Films and Filming*, February 1965. The Leicester Festival survived till 1988.

32. It had been proposed as a course at the privately run Heatherly School of Art.

33. The history of the relationship between the three institutions offering industry-recognised film-making courses – the LSFT, the RCA and the National Film and Television School (founded in 1971) – is torturous, and deserves a study of its own. Some of the more radical May '68 generation of LSFT students were involved in Le Grice's first film workshop at the Drury Lane Arts Lab, attracted by its promise of censorship-free film-processing.

34. Peter Kardia (course director), in *Cross Currents*, a review of mixed media work associated with the department, organised by Cate Elwes and Chrissie Iles, 1984. Paradoxically, this show may have inadvertently hastened the department's demise. The RCA's new Rector Jocelyn Stevens reportedly observed, 'They were having a ten-year retrospective when I came here. Frankly it was rubbish, sculptors playing with mirrors, fine art students working without discipline. I cannot justify spending taxpayers' money on such rubbish'. Simon Robertshaw, 'Selling the Goods', *Channel* 6 catalogue, LVA/ICA 1986.

35. Other part-time lectures at Hornsey included Mark Boyle and Stuart Brisley; Brisley and Marc C. Chaimowicz also taught at Maidstone.

36. See his pamphlet *Should Britain Have a Film School?* 1963 [BFI Library].

37. The Slade Film department survived till the early 1980s. Malcolm Le Grice and I studied painting at the Slade in the early 1960s, and attended many of the Dickinson screenings.

38. Cobbing was already running a film society Cinema 65, with Crick, Collins and others, which mutated into the Filmmakers Co-op.

39. 'Around the Galleries with Oswell Blakeston', *What's On In London*, 17 June 1966.

40. Other key founder members were Harvey Matusow, John Collins and Philip Crick. For a history of the early days of the London Filmmakers Co-op see Webber/Kurcewitz www.lfmc.org ; for the early days of the (New York) Filmmakers Co-op see David James (ed.), *To Free The Cinema* (Princeton, NJ: Princeton University Press, 1992).

41. 'Cooped in a Co-op?', *Art Monthly*, November 1991.

42. The cost of these machines was covered by a gift of £3,000 from the Living Theatre's benefactor Victor Herbert. Aware (thanks to Sitney) of Herbert's interest in the American Underground film, I visited him in Paris to suggest this investment; Le Grice followed up with a letter, and Carolee Schneemann who was staying with Herbert at the time convinced him to say 'yes'.

43. Sound interview with Deke Dusinberre, July 1975. He suggests it was the first film printed at the Co-op's re-located workshops at The Dairy, Prince of Wales Crescent.

44. Reported by Anna Thew in 'Relating', unpublished text by Annabel Nicolson.

45. Le Grice papers – undated draft response to 'The London Filmmakers Co-op' by Irving Washington, *Time Out*, 21 January 1971.

46. 'Filmaktion: some founding principles of the LFMC' talk given by Raban in Barcelona in 2002.

47. At Prince of Wales Crescent, mattresses provided the seating, and the screen was a painted white artist's canvas on a stretcher.

48. Michael Snow conference, Arnolfini Gallery 2001.

49. Chris Welsby, 'Report of Co-op Cinema Show: 16 November 1979 6–10 pm', *Filmmakers Europe*, no. 18, 1979.

50. LVA briefly became London Video Access, then London Electronic Arts (LEA) from 1994.

51. Most artists' film-making fell outside this Faustian pact, though it was important to a few, including Leggett; and was honoured in name in artists' television funding schemes in the 1980s.

52. *Time Out*, 11 February 1972 Gidal's *Time Out* prose sometimes got him into trouble; this, a few months later, earned a place in *Private Eye*'s 'Pseud's Corner', 16 June 1972, submitted by the writer Paul Hammond: 'Hollis Frampton's *Zorn's Lemma*. An absolutely hypnotic film. A total reconditioning, restructuring of our linear rationalistic conceptions. It's on a par with *Wavelength* and *Blowjob* in the sense of revelation of film as film. It initiates processes in the viewer not only of re/de-culturisation, but also forces one to deal with structures in their newly conceived serial alterations as well as in their basic forms. Finally one is left with a new alphabet in dialectic relation to "normal". An incredibly beautiful, strong film.'

53. *Experimental Cinema* (London: Studio Vista, 1971; New York: Universe Books, 1973); it was part of series which included *Experimental Painting* by Stephen Bann (1970), *Experimental Architecture* by Peter Cook (1970) and *Experimental Music* by Michael Nyman (1974). *Film Is* (London: Peter Owen, 1975); *Abstract Film and Beyond* (London: Studio Vista, Cassel & Collier Macmillan, 1977).

54. Such as Stephen Heath's afterword to Peter Gidal, 'The anti-narrative', vol. 20 no. 2, 1979; Peter Wollen, '"Ontology" and "materialism" in film', vol. 17 no. 1, 1976; Al Rees, 'Conditions of Illusionism', vol. 18 no. 3, 1977.

55. There were many more: *Cinemantics*, 3 issues 1970, *Afterimage* 1970–85, *Cinema* 1968–71, *Framework* 1974–1992, *Independent Media* 1982–91, *Vertigo* 1993–, *Filmwaves* 1997– etc.

56. 'LFMC Working Party: Proposal for a Co-op Magazine', 1979. LFMC papers at BAFV Study Collection. See Nina Danino and Michael Maziere (eds), *The Undercut Reader Critical Readings on Artists' Film and Video* (London: Wallflower Press, 2003).

57. Malcolm Le Grice, 'Some Thoughts on recent Underground Film', *Afterimage*, vol. 4, 1972.

58. For a chronology of milestones in this field in the late 1970s and through the 1980s, see 'Video Installations in the UK', Jez Welsh, *Video Positive 1991*, catalogue 1991.

59. *Emergences of Continuous Forms*.

60. Other versions of *Art Spectrum* took place simultaneously in Scotland, the North, Wales, Ulster, Central England and the non-London South, to celebrate the newly-formed Regional Arts Associations. Only London's showcased 'new art'.

61. Film and video: Barry Flanagan, Hamish Fulton, Gilbert and George, David Hall, John Hilliard, David Lamelas, John Latham, Bruce McLean, David Tremlett, Tony Morgan and Malcolm Le Grice; photographs: Roger Cutforth, Victor Burgin (plus Lamelas, Tremlett *et al.*).

62. A juxtaposition of attitudes recreated by the exhibition *On General Release*, Norwich Gallery 2002.

63. Raban used three interlocked projectors bought for *Filmmakers on Tour* by the Arts Council.

64. Became Centre for Advanced Television Studies (CATS) on moving with the Co-op to Prince of Wales Crescent in 1971.

65. Letter to Andrew Page at the Arts Council 12 December 1969. In files at BAFVSC. Hoppy later received some equipment from the Arts Council, and encouragement from the Minister of Technology, Tony Benn.

66. For an illuminating account of early video in Britain and the best assessment of Hoppy's contribution to the field, see Mick Hartney 'InT/Ventions: some instances of confrontation with British broadcasting', in Julia Knight (ed.), *Diverse Practices* (Luton: Arts Council/University of Luton Press, 1996).

67. 'Video Per Se (The British Experience)', Stuart Marshall, *LVA Catalogue*, 1984.

68. Large-scale video projection had been demonstrated at the Festival of Britain, and small-scale at IRAT, but both were prohibitively expensive and cumbersome.

69. Other commercial galleries showing film and video in the 1970s included Situation, PMJ Self, the Robert Fraser Gallery, and Gimpel Fils.

70. Hall in *Studio International*, January 1977: LVA became LEA (see earlier note) and became part of the Lux Centre in 1997.

71. Briefly, it had an office at 12–3 Little Newport Street.

72. Founded by Alison Winckle, David Critchley, John Kippin, Steve Partridge and others.

73. Later he became director of the touring and commissioning agency the Film and Video Umbrella, and introduced the work of many new artists through the Umbrella's catalogues and leaflets.

74. She contributed to *Undercut* and jointly selected the touring programme *Genlock* (1988) with Welsh.

75. Among those consistently showing film and video were Anthony D'Offay, White Cube, Frith Street Gallery, Laurent Delaye, Sadie Coles HQ, and Victoria Miro.

# 1.2 Institutions

Sponsored Films : Museums and Collections : Post-War Recovery : Experimental Film Fund :
The Arts Council : The BFI : Funders and Broadcasters

## SPONSORED FILMS

The slow flow of artists' film-making in the 1920s, associated with the Film Society and the little film magazines, became a flood in 1930s in the new context of public information films and advertising, and largely as the result of the persuasive powers of a man with a vision, John Grierson. Grierson had studied philosophy and literature in Glasgow, but became interested in mass communication while conducting a study of immigration problems in Chicago in the mid-1920s. There he met the journalist Walter Lippmann who helped shape his belief that society could never be improved unless it was educated to understand its own nature. Full of ideas and theories about film's potential to fulfil this mission, Grierson returned to Britain in 1927 and secured a post at the government's Empire Marketing Board (EMB 1924–33), a body set up to promote and protect British trade with its Empire. Within this uninspiring but well-resourced agency, he created a film production unit with a remarkably free agenda 'to inform society'. It took Grierson two years of persuasion – and the making of a film to demonstrate the power of the medium – to convince the EMB to invest in film-making:

> I was telling governments that they should do this and that, but when the British Government said: all right so show us a picture, well … I made a film about the sea and about fishermen, the morning, the day and the night of the sea, and the fishermen against the sky. It was called *Drifters* [1929] and it made a startling impression at the time. It was something altogether new to be looking at ordinary things as if they were extraordinary …[1].

The desire to see ordinary things as if they were extraordinary made Grierson value artists, or 'specialists in looking and seeing' as the painter William Coldstream defined them.[2] As he built his team of film-makers, Grierson looked for people who shared his belief that 'the ordinary affairs of people's lives are more dramatic and more vital than all the false excitements [the

**(Opposite)** *Around is Around* (detail), Norman McLaren, 1951.

**60** John Grierson in his twenties (BFI Stills Collection).

cinema] can muster'.[3] First to be involved were Basil Wright, a twenty-three-year-old Cambridge graduate, fired up by seeing *Drifters* at the Film Society, soon followed by a further Cambridge cohort that included Edgar Anstey, Arthur Elton, Stuart Legg and Humphrey Jennings. Jennings was a poet/painter, and others who joined later – Len Lye, Coldstream and Paul Rotha – were all art-school trained, but to Grierson, *all* his team were 'artists', and he brought in freelance collaborators from many other fields, among them the composer Benjamin Britten, the poet W. H. Auden and writer Laurie Lee.

After *Drifters,* Grierson's only direct involvement with making rather than producing film was with *Granton Trawler* (1934), and he focused on performing as impresario to the talents he had attracted. If many of the 300 or more films made during the next decade by the EMB and its successor the GPO (General Post Office) Film Unit were simply functional, the film-makers were at least able to bring subjects to the Board, and Grierson had freedom to seek commissions from outside the organisation if the EMB itself was not interested in them. If he spotted a talent, Grierson would find a way to use it. He encountered Norman McLaren as a student at Glasgow School of Art and invited him to the unit – and persuaded the GPO to fund a figurative hand-painted film by him. Len Lye brought him samples of his hand-painted abstract film footage, and Grierson gave him a contract, paid him a fee and let him get on with his experiments, again persuading the GPO to use the results to sell the Parcel Post. He imported the venerable Robert Flaherty, the American director of *Nanook of the North* (1922) and *Moana* (1926), both to work on films in Britain and to act as mentor to younger talents

**61** Len Lye (with spray-pipe) working on a film c. 1936 (Len Lye Foundation).

**62** Flaherty shooting *Man of Aran*, 1933–4 (BFI Stills Collection).

such as Wright. He defended his artists when a film changed radically during its making. The Tea Board expected Wright's *Song of Ceylon* (1934) to be delivered as four short travelogues, rather than one extended poem, and 'Grierson spent three and a half hours convincing them to allow the film to be finished. *Song of Ceylon* was an unusual film for its time, and the Tea Board did not know what to make of it'[4].

Some of Grierson's imported artists were more comfortable in the film world than others. Coldstream, attracted by a sense that film could perform a social function that painting couldn't in the Depression, saw 'great possibilities with the GPO for making films myself', but suffered withdrawal symptoms from painting. He wrote to a friend:

> Grierson has offered to employ me permanently … If I work hard, I will become a junior director within one year … [But] When I go to see Roger Fry, I am particularly torn. His rooms – hung with Seurats, Renoirs, Bonnards and smelling of the smoke of French cigarettes – are so alluring to me … coming from the hideous mess of the ledger branch of the [Post Office] Savings Bank [where he was working on a film], and the grim little offices of film business managers in Wardour Street. It is easy on rational grounds to dismiss … the individualistic culture of a man like Fry, as being unrealistic and unsuitable at such a time as this, but it is difficult to wean our feelings from tradition.[5]

**63** Norman McLaren drawing film images, 1940s (National Film Board of Canada)

He returned to painting after three years with the GPO, but later admitted 'I doubt whether I should have had what conviction I have now in painting, if I hadn't been in it'.[6]

The unit was a success, but the EMB was abruptly closed by the government in 1933 when tariff-reform made its original purpose irrelevant. The EMB Secretary Stephen Tallents was offered an equivalent appointment at the GPO and, as a condition of the move, took the film unit with him, and its mix of internal commissions and work undertaken for other agencies continued. The Brazilian-born French-based film-maker Alberto Cavalcanti joined the Unit in 1934, succeeding Grierson as its head in 1937, and remaining in post till the war. Cavalcanti – older than his colleagues and bearing the aura of a senior member of the European avant-garde – had been attracted by the opportunity to work in an experimental way with the unit's newly installed sound recording system.[7] The fruits – often more surreal than realist – were seen in films such as *Song of Ceylon*, the bizarre *Pet and Pott* (1934), *Coalface* (1935), *Night Mail* (1936) and Lye's *N or NW?* (1938).

In a memoir, Cavalcanti wrote:

> In the GPO we worked in conditions which were similar to those of craftsmen in the Middle Ages, and as a result *who* contributed *what* to the films made by the unit is often unclear. The work was collective, and each person's films were discussed by everyone else. If the film of a companion requires some assistance, it was offered'.[8]

Dai Vaughan (a notable film editor of the 1960s) suggests that this collective approach was sometimes reflected in the treatment of subjects, and that a film like *Night Mail* (1936) 'gives form to a myth *oppositional* to that of the Great Artist, in a way that the verbal literature of film has so conspicuously failed to do'.[9]

The films made by artists in this context of public information were often given full circuit releases, and were seen on the big screen by millions. Cavalcanti boasted to his former French colleagues that 'in Britain, more than a thousand cinemas have shown *Night Mail*; and while it received a long ovation of applause, the commercial film that accompanied it ended in complete silence'.[10] Len Lye was delighted by the general release given to his *A Colour Box* (1935) after its Film Society premiere, and collected reviews in his scrapbook from a dozen regional city newspapers as it appeared in cinemas across the country. Even when the major film distributors were unhelpful, there was the film society network. Rotha recalled:

> As filmmakers [we] learned from Bob Flaherty that no film, however good, ever sold itself. He
> had gone out in the States and mobilised special audiences to go to their local movie theatre to
> see his film *Moana*. We in Britain used the film society movement, spreading every year, as a
> showcase for our films, and wherever possible made an appearance and spoke about the film.
> No commercial distributor was interested in publicising documentaries: we were, and did'.[11]

Grierson left the GPO in 1937 to found the Film Centre, essentially a clearing house for documentary projects.[12] With his encouragement, many of the original members of his team were setting up their own companies (touchingly also called Units). Anstey had left to found the Shell Film Unit in 1934, where Lye and Jennings made their *The Birth of the Robot* (1935–36); Rotha and Legg founded the Strand Film Unit in 1935, and Basil Wright the Realist Film Unit in 1937, with Jennings, Cavalcanti and Harry Watt remaining at the GPO. With the outbreak of war, the GPO Unit once again changed ownership and title, and became the Crown Film Unit in 1940, answerable now to the new Ministry of Information (MOI), but as with the EMB, the MOI also commissioned films from the other 'independent' Units.

Grierson spent the war setting up the National Film Board of Canada, drawing on his EMB and GPO experience. The MOI was initially uncertain what to do with the team it had inherited:

> According to Harry Watt, there was a longish spell when nothing at all happened because no
> instruction came through: then Cavalcanti took it upon himself to send us out. This is where
> Cavalcanti was great. He said 'History is being made. We can't sit here'. All the members of
> the unit, which included Watt and Jennings, went out and shot everything that looked interest-
> ing, and a film was quickly put together' [*The First Days* (1939)].[13]

Still without a contract, Cavalcanti took the raw film to Wardour Street where Pathé agreed to distribute it – and to retrospectively pay for its making.

Jennings became the dominant figure of the war years. He had first joined the GPO with Coldstream in 1934, then left to work with Lye at Shell, and to organise the International

**64** Alberto Cavalcanti
(BFI Stills Collection).

Surrealist Exhibition in 1936. He returned to the GPO with his enthusiasm for documenting daily life renewed by his involvement in Mass Observation – 'an anthropology of our own people' – co-founded with Legg, Charles Madge and poet David Gascoyne. This pursuit had its purest expression in his film work in his essay on workers' pastimes, *Spare Time* (1939) – but his creative energies reached their peak in his war work.

> I should theoretically be very tired at the end of a picture. But I don't think I am: I don't think it's work so much as war … or maybe it's middle-age but I don't feel middle-aged, on the contrary – younger than ever. There's nothing so exhila-rating as seeing even a few ideas one has long had really coming into being on the screen.[14]

**65** Humphrey Jennings with pianist Dame Myra Hess. (BFI Stills Collection)

At the war's end the new Labour government abolished the Ministry of Information 'all too cheerfully and without a thought as to what we might be losing',[15] and the Crown Unit moved to the Central Office of Information, to which Grierson returned to become Controller of Films in 1948. Crown was now a studio-based unit, and its wings had been clipped. 'Bas [Wright], I think, had tried to get it set up on the same basis as the Canadian Film Board – you know, that they decided what films to make, and then made them. But the Civil Service moved in and said, "No you can't do that. You will have to do what's ordered by Government departments"'.[16] In this new context, Jennings's future looked less than certain. He had risen to prominence during Grierson's absence, and with Cavalcanti's encouragement. Now based at Wessex Films, he clashed with Grierson over ideas for his Festival of Britain film *Family Portrait*, complaining to a friend:

> [Grierson] could not – would not – pass the present piece of writing – he would not even call it a draft treatment – without a clear statement of aims. … This was also to be for *my* benefit – to help me get wise to myself. And then out poured a mass of personal insults laced with insensibilities and backhanded compliments such as I have never been treated to even by Grierson. … 'This piece of writing of mine – full, no doubt of clever literary illusions – but no shape – no form – no beginning, middle or end – such philosophy as it had was "fascist" – its scholarship thoroughly second-hand – its politics amateur – the confused product of a neuras-thenic who had been living in the luxury of the feature world and who had now trailed his impracticality, desire to overspend, and self-pity across twenty-odd pages which would run to ten reels of films and £60,000 of production costs!'.[17]

He nevertheless completed the film. The Crown Film Unit itself was finally dissolved in 1952 by the new Conservative government (that which also hastened to flatten the Festival of Britain Exhibition site).

Many of the sibling Units survived into the post-war era. The GPO reclaimed its team and turned its focus towards the new medium of television. Anstey formed British Transport Films in 1948 which in the 1960s would fund John Schlesinger's *Terminus* (1961) and host Ian Breakwell as an artist in residence in the early 1970s,[18] linking with other generations of film-making artists. He also served as as a member of the Arts Council Arts Films committee well into the 1970s. Shell continued without him, and made many popular films on nature and landscape – including John Betjeman's filmed guides to the English regions. But the age of the sponsored film as a reliable source of work for artists was over.[19]

## MUSEUMS AND COLLECTIONS

An unforeseen beneficiary of the Film Society's policy of striking new English-intertitled prints of all the films it showed was the archive and distribution arm of the new British Film Institute (BFI), which had been founded in 1933 'to encourage the use and development of the cinema'. In 1935 the BFI established its National Film Library as a national agency to collect and preserve film, one of the first of its kind.[20] During 1941–2, many of the Film Society's extraordinary collection of film prints, including works by Leger, Vertov, Moholy-Nagy and others, were donated to the National Film Archive (as it became), which in turn made them available through the BFI to film societies and educational institutions in 16mm prints from the 1960s onwards, representing a visible link with a previous era of experiment. In the inter-war period, the BFI interpreted its educational purpose rather narrowly and did little to promote experiment in film, though its educational house-journal *Sight & Sound* (founded before the Institute itself, in 1932) did occasionally publish articles about the artistic fringe – such as a manifesto by Moholy-Nagy in 1934 and the text of a lecture by Cavalcanti on Len Lye in 1947.[21] Its ability to act was heavily compromised by its initial dependence on the industry's good will (it only gained direct treasury funding in 1949), and began to exercise its independence with the appointment of Denis Forman as Director in the same year.[22] The creation of the NFT in 1952 (following the success of the Festival of Britain's Telecinema in 1951), and the BFI's simultaneous decision to involve itself in production through a new Experimental Film Fund, were the product of Foreman's willingness to seize the moment and take risks. *Sight & Sound* was similarly given a new lease of life with the arrival in 1950 of some of the young writers and future film-makers associated with the Cambridge University film magazine, *Sequence*.[23]

Other archives of the period were more proactive in their approach to collecting works by artists. The Royal Belgian Film Archive, founded in 1938, used its Experimental Festivals as a means of augmenting its collection, making the donation of prints a condition of the acceptance of its prizes. Well-informed of what artists were doing, and with its good connections with the experimental community, it also bought prints to complement these donations. In Paris, the archive of the Cinémathèque Française created by the twenty-one-year-old enthusiast

Henri Langlois in 1936 reflected its founder's eclectic tastes, which included avant-garde work of the 1920s, 1930s and 1950s. Controversially in some quarters, Langlois' archive expended almost as much energy on showing work as conserving it, and the classic films of Duchamp, Clair, Man Ray and Bunuel were constantly in its cinema's repertory.

In the same year that Britain's National Film Archive was founded, 1935, the Museum of Modern Art in New York (MOMA) established its film collection, with Film Society founder member Iris Barry as its first curator and programmer of its daily screenings, which began in 1939. The Museum's first director Alfred H. Barr Jr. had from the beginning intended that industrial design, film and photography be included in the collection, but it was with Barry's appointment, and through her collecting policy, that MOMA visibly demonstrated film's status as one of the modern visual arts. Justifying this policy, Barry wrote:

> People who are well acquainted with modern painting or literature or the theatre are amazingly ignorant of modern film. The work and even the names of such masters as Gance, Stiller, Clair … Eisenstein … are, one can hazard, practically unknown to the Museum's Board of Trustees … It may be said without exaggeration that the only great art peculiar to the twentieth century is practically unknown to the American public most capable of appreciating it'.[24]

The museum's daily screenings included artists' films and classic Hollywood feature films side by side, without apology, following the Film Society's example. In London, Barry's poems had been discovered by Ezra Pound, and he had introduced her to T. S. Eliot, Arthur Waley, Wyndham Lewis and the Vorticist circle of painters and sculptors. With this background and her experience as a journalist, she could write about painting and film with equal authority, a rare quality in a film archivist.[25] She retired in 1951, but MOMA continued to acquire artists' films for its collections.

**66** Iris Barry, c. 1940, from the MOMA New York memorial leaflet, 1980.

In post-war Europe, the decision of most major national art collections about whether and how to collect film and video was often similarly dependent upon the initiative of an interested senior curator. Pontus Hulten, who himself had made experimental films in the 1950s, committed Stockholm's Moderna Museet to exhibiting film within its exhibition programme from its founding in 1956,[26] and when he became the Pompidou Centre's first director in 1976, ensured that it, too, actively pursued and collected work by contemporary film and video artists, alongside the classics of the 1920s and 1930s avant-garde. The National Library of Australia established its Film Study Collection in the 1950s and enthusiastically collected artists' film during the 1970s and the Stedelijk Museum in Amsterdam began collecting films by artists in late 1960s, and videos from the 1980s. In Britain, the Tate bought tapes by Gilbert and George from *The Evening Before the Morning After* show at the Nigel Greenwood Gallery in 1973, but then very little else until the early 1990s, when commercial galleries once again began selling film and video. In the same year as this purchase, Malcolm Le Grice used his column in *Studio International* to urge a more proactive approach. Congratulating its education department on a recent season of 'structural film' organised by Mick Hartney, he suggested that the Tate should follow MOMA's example and 'build up a collection of film work, giving it the same status as painting and sculpture', and he outlined a vision of an exhibition policy for film.

> There are three important areas for which the Tate could be the ideal context: (1) an historical repertory of avant-garde film, regularly presented as an aspect of the Tate's permanent art exhibition; (2) a regular series of showings by individual film-makers, introduced by them, beginning with a complete review of home-grown production; (3) occasional special presentations of installation and cinema in the round, work prepared for the gallery situation'.[27]

His advice was ignored; film remained the responsibility of the education department, with only rare excursions into the territory by the exhibitions and collections staff over the next two decades. One apparent obstacle was the Tate Trustees' decision only to collect works published in limited editions. To many artists, the idea of a limited edition of a film was an anathema; film's infinite reproducibility was one of its attractions, offering an escape from the trap of the unique, therefore materially valuable art-object, also making film a conceptually purer, and (arguably) more democratic medium. (Though most artists would soon admit this democracy of access was more virtual than actual; many works never got beyond one or two copies.) The Arts Council, which saw purchasing works for its Collection as a primary means of supporting living artists, similarly failed to include film and video till the mid-1990s. It had the excuse that from the 1970s it was already supporting film-making artists with grants of production and exhibition funds. None the less, the absence of film and video works from the 1970s and 1980s in the Arts Council Collection of contemporary British art – which in size exceeds that of the Tate – was, and is, anomalous.

## POST-WAR RECOVERY

A chance to look forward, perhaps even to kick-start a new wave of experimental activity came in 1951 when the post-war Labour government staged the Festival of Britain on London's South Bank as a celebration of national achievement and renewal, that also marked the 100th anniversary of The Great Exhibition. A committee which included John Grierson was appointed to select films to be shown across the country and in the Festival's own futuristic Telecinema.[28] Designed by the modernist architect Wells Coates, the Telecinema incorporated Britain's first 'full-screen television' projection system, and was to be run by the BFI. The Committee's task was to endorse and commission films that reflected this forward-looking spirit, yet 'experiment' was not high on its list of priorities. Of the artists who might contribute, they had few of the pre-war generation of film-makers to call upon, though documentaries were contributed by Wright and Jennings. The Telecinema was also equipped to show the latest cinema novelty – 3-D film, and Norman McLaren – now working in Canada – was persuaded to contribute

two stereoscopic abstract films, *Around is Around* and *Now is the Time* (both 1951), using dots and loops created on an oscilloscope – surely inspired by the pioneering experiments in a similar technique by Mary Ellen Bute, with whom he briefly worked in New York in 1939.

Another project associated with the Festival was the *Painter and Poet* series (1951), for which eight artists including Henry Moore, Mervyn Peake, Ronald Searle, Michael Ayrton, and John Rothenstein were invited to choose a poem and provide a series of illustrations for it, which the producer/animator John Halas undertook to put under the camera and turn into a film. Though the results were conventional rostrum-work, and hardly the meeting of minds across disciplines that *might* have advanced film language, the series is interesting as an early manifestation of the desire to involve visual artists in the film-making process 'for the good of film'. This engagement became one of the objectives of the BFI's Experimental Film Fund, the only significant public sponsor of short films during the 1950s and 1960s. In subsequent decades, television executives and public-funding committees were moved by similar motives to involve visual artists in digital video-graphics and live-action post-production, as in the BBC's *Painting With Light* video paintbox series (1987) to which David Hockney and Howard Hodgkin contributed, and the Arts Council's *High Tech* scheme for digital art with Channel 4 (1995–96).

A new funding body for the arts – the Arts Council of Great Britain (ACGB) [29]   had been established in 1946, with responsibility for supporting artists and exhibiting their work. Like the Festival of Britain, the Arts Council was a manifestation of the post-war Labour government's desire to bring culture to the people in an accessible and affordable form, and evolved seamlessly out of the Council for Entertainment, Music and the Arts (CEMA 1940–46) which had successfully organised exhibitions and entertainment for troops and public during the war. The government's earlier recognition of the British Film Institute led to film being excluded from the Arts Council's remit, a decision that set in concrete in ministerial minds a distinction between 'film' and 'art' that has yet to be repaired.

**67** Artwork for the series *Painter and Poet*, 1951; Henry Moore and Mervyn Peake. (BFI Stills Collection)

**68** 3-D abstraction at the Festival of Britain, *Around is Around*, Norman McLaren 1951.

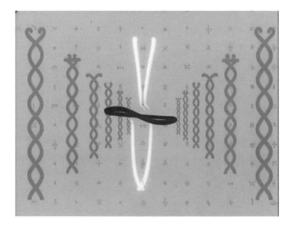

Though the extent of its interest in film waxed and waned over the decades, the Arts Council was initially quick to show it recognised the importance of the art form. One of its first peacetime exhibitions was *The Art of the Film* (1945),[30] a photographic survey in two parts – *The History of American Movies* borrowed from the Museum of Modern Art in New York, and a larger section on European film 1920-45 selected by Roger Manvell – that together toured Britain. More significantly in the light of later developments, the Arts Council also began to support the making of documentaries on the arts, with the BFI acting as its distributor. Many of its early commissions were intended as a permanent record of its exhibition-making at the Tate and later at its own newly-built Hayward Gallery, and included Basil Wright's *Stained Glass at Fairford* (1956) and Guy Brenton's *The Vision of William Blake* (1958). At very least, the art world had recognised that film could also help broaden the audience for the arts, though not till 1968 did the Council appoint a committee to advise on this area of work, and not until 1972 did it formally support the making of artists' films[31]. The television arts documentary was an innovation of the 1950s, with classic TV monographs being perfected by John Read in films such as his *Henry Moore* (1951), and a new form of popular arts journalism pioneered by Kenneth Clark's ATV series *Is Art Necessary?* (1958–59) and *Tempo* (1961–64), and by the BBC's *Monitor* programmes (1958–65) edited by Hugh Weldon. Weldon's commissions included occasional experimental forms, such as Ken Russell's fly-on-the-wall-meets-pop-video *Pop Goes the Easel* (1962), a highly personal response to British Pop Art.

## EXPERIMENTAL FILM FUND

The BFI's Experimental Film Fund evolved out of the Telecinema Production Committee, adopting its new name and purpose in 1952. Among its aims, defined by committee members in 1953, was 'to explore proposals to give the creative artist, such as the painter or the composer, much closer control over the design and production stages of a film'.[32] Beyond this, the fund had no clear policy, and dealt with any demands as they came in, and *when* it had funds available. Between 1952 and 1965 it received only two injections of money from the government's Eady tax on cinema box-office receipts given with the reluctant agreement of the trade,[33] plus a one-off £10,000 grant from the Gulbenkian Foundation in 1961; otherwise it was dependent upon the modest income from sale and rental of previously funded works. At this time its trickle of funding included very few works by artists, perhaps because its public profile was so low, or because its connections through its advisory committee were primarily with the industry. Of the most prolific film artists then working, Margaret Tait, John Latham and Bruce Lacey, Tait alone applied for funding, and was turned down. The year 1966 (coincidentally the year of the founding of the London Filmmakers Co-op), marked an important change with the announcement of a regular income for the committee from the Labour government's radical and expansive Arts Minister Jennie Lee, a new name, the BFI Production Board, and the appointment of a full-time Head of Production, Bruce Beresford. Beresford was not unsympathetic to artists and experiment, but the most significant investments of his era perpetuated the Fund's established policy of supporting 'first films' and 'calling-card' shorts by future television,

**69** Lorenza Mazzetti during the filming of *Together*, 1955 (BFI Stills Collection).

commercials and feature-film directors, such as Tony and Ridley Scott, Stephen Frears, Kevin Brownlow, Michael Darlow, Jonathan Gili, but included the Board's one feature investment (one that nearly sunk the Fund), *Herostratus* by Don Levy.

The cultural phenomenon now firmly associated with the Experimental Film Fund in the 1950s is Free Cinema, the critically-inspired beginnings of England's 1960s 'New Wave' of fea-ture film-making, and its younger counterpart, the Manchester-based documentary group Unit Five Seven. Free Cinema was never a unified production group, but a journalistic and cura-torial attempt to create a movement out of a number of disparate works that showed evidence of a new approach to film-making – a marketing initiative in modern parlance. Its origins lay in the writings by Lindsay Anderson, Penelope Huston and Gavin Lambert for the Oxford University Film Society journal *Sequence*.[34] From the late 1940s, *Sequence* had argued against the middle-of-the-road journalism of *Sight and Sound,* with its connoisseurship, notions of 'quality' and attachment to wartime realism, arguing instead for a re-engagement with the poetic/modernist tradition exemplified by Lye and Jennings. By 1950 Lambert had won over the opposition and become editor of *Sight & Sound,* making it a mouthpiece for the new critical approach. *Free Cinema* was the title originally given by Anderson (as editor) to a review by Alan Cooke in *Sequence* in 1951 of works by Deren, Anger, Francis Lee, Curtis Harrington, Joseph Strick and McLaren, shown at the New London Film Society the previous November. Cooke discussed San Francisco's *Art in Cinema* series, but states 'I prefer to group the films under Free Cinema [because …] they have one achievement in common, an express-ive and personal use of the medium'.[35] Anderson re-used the term Free Cinema in a manifesto announcing the first of what became a series of six programmes of films for the NFT under the same banner, selected by himself and film-maker Karel Reisz, and shown between 1956 and 1969. The first programme was accompanied by a joint statement, signed by those con-tributing films; Anderson, Reisz, Lorenza Mazzetti and Tony Richardson:

These films were not made together; nor with the idea of showing them together. But when they came together, we felt they had an attitude in common. Implicit in this attitude is a belief in freedom, in the importance of people and in the significance of the everyday.

*As film-makers we believe that*

*No film can be too personal.*

*The image speaks. Sound amplifies and comments.*

*Size is irrelevant. Perfection is not an aim.*

*An attitude means a style. A style means an attitude.*[36]

The series also featured 'Free Cinema' from overseas, including work made by Lionel Rogosin, Norman Mclaren, Georges Franju, Jan Lenica, Walerian Borowczyk, Roman Polanski, François Truffaut and Claude Chabrol, so was in effect a mini festival of contemporary new waves. Most but not all of the domestic contributions were documentaries, some sponsored by the commercial film Units set up by former GPO employees; other connecting threads being the contribution to many of camerawork by Walter Lassally, and help, editing or production advice by Anderson.

Even at the time, some questioned how 'free' these films were, and what right they had to represent themselves as radically different? The third NFT programme was pointedly followed a few weeks later by a season of documentaries from one of the new commercial TV companies Associated Rediffusion, that titled itself *Captive Cinema*, mocking Free Cinema's pretensions. Rediffusion's 25-minute portraits of working-class men – *Sewermen, Tramps, Street Cleaners,*

**70**  Michael Grigsby shooting *Enginemen* 1958 (BFI Stills Collection).

et al. – made for *Look in on London* (1956/57) were praised by Huston in *Sight and Sound* as examples of television having made the valuable discovery that 'people are interesting', but she was loyal to her former *Sequence* colleagues, and concluded that:

> from the point of view of art … there can be a danger in too great an immediacy, in the loss of perspective, distance, shape and balance of the whole. The very qualities that give these television programmes their force and impact are at odds with the requirements of art, which needs time, deliberation, the ability not merely to catch people at their most revealing moments but also to express an attitude towards them.[37]

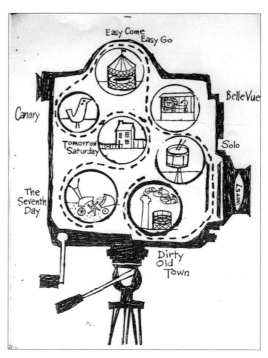

**71** The first filmmakers' journal of the post-war era, the *Unit Five Seven Newsletter*, 1959.

Ray Durgnat, revisiting this juxtaposition a decade later, came down firmly on the side of television, seeing these same NFT programmes as demonstrating 'just how timid, how remote, even for its time, Free Cinema was'.[38]

By contrast with Free Cinema, Unit Five Seven was a truly collective production group, which coalesced around common beliefs and a pool of equipment – initially a Bolex camera, lens and tripod – and a five shilling-a-week subscription by members to 'accumulate some cash reserves in order to prevent sudden personal financial strain when filmstock etc. for future productions is required'.[39] Started by Michael Grigsby and seven other Granada Television Network employees and trainees, together with two enthusiasts from the Manchester College of Art and Technology, it was later joined by the Hungarian émigré Robert Vas who, like Grigsby, remained wholly committed to the field of documentary. The link with Free Cinema was inevitably through Lindsay Anderson who heard of the Unit's activities, made contact, and helped get support from BFI funds for its first production *Enginemen* (1959), and secured its inclusion in the sixth programme in the Free Cinema series. Grigsby spelled out his aspirations for the Unit in an *Open Letter* in the first issue of the group's newsletter.

> I want to see the cinema play an important part in the life of the community; [I want cinema to be] a place at which one can find work of an entertaining, stimulating, and sincere nature; a place from which one emerges feeling vital and alive, and NOT like a limp rag! The cinema influences, in this country, eighteen million people per week; it can do good; it can do harm. At the moment British films are doing a great deal of harm, for virtually every subject they tackle is seen through the same pair of rose-tinted spectacles. And this will give rise to a false sense of values and an irresponsible outlook on life'.[40]

He sees 'healthy signs emerging' with *Room at the Top* and *Look Back in Anger* because their 'impetus … stems from documentary', and he suggests that experiment in the low-budget documentary form could lead to experimentation with feature films, though this was not the direction he himself eventually pursued.

Unit Five Seven only held together till 1963–64, and its output was small; possibly five completed films out of an announced slate of eight, the best known apart from *Enginemen* being Grigsby's *Tomorrow's Saturday* (1962), Robert Vas's *The Vanishing Street* (1962, nominally attributed to the group) and Brian Cosgrove's *Canary* (1962) an award-winning animation. Cosgrove later founded the successful Manchester-based TV cartoon production studio Cosgrove Hall, with fellow Unit Five Seven member Frank Hall. But the Unit had unwittingly pioneered a model of mutual support and collective endeavour to which others would turn repeatedly in the 1960s and 1970s.

A near-contemporary variant on the collective model was Mithras Films, which first came together to make *Gala Day* (1963), a record of the Durham miners' annual celebration, funded by the Experimental Film Fund. Mithras's members included John Irvin, David Naden and Dai Vaughan who met as members of the first cohort of the London School of Film Technique in 1956 (where an influential fellow student was Arnold Wesker), and freelance photographer Maurice Hatton, another Manchester College of Art alumnus. Mithras criticised Free Cinema's lack of a social agenda, and in Hatton's words, aspired 'to make films which were more socially relevant, without negating the artistic ... more *potent* than we thought Free Cinema was'.[41] In its early days, its members were all paid the same wage and collectively agreed on projects they would undertake.

## THE ARTS COUNCIL

The 1970s and 1980s were the decades when public funding had most impact on the development of artists' films, with the Arts Council and the BFI responding in different ways to the flood of film and video talent emerging from arts schools and higher education. The Arts Council initially acted as a commissioner and subsidiser of artists' work, then increasingly a supporter of its exhibition. The BFI, together with Channel 4, was the most significant supporter of production workshops and distribution resources, and a significant but less frequent funder of artists' film-making.

The Arts Council's involvement with arts documentary-making in the 1950s and 1960s has already been described. At the time of Hugh Evans's appointment as the first film officer in the Art department in 1968, the concept of 'documentary' was being expanded to include works in which artists themselves notionally documented the creation of a sculpture or painting. David Hall's *Vertical* (1969) and Derek Boshier's *Link* (1970) were the first of these, and immediately challenged the need for a pre-existing work; they were unapologetically works in their own right, and documented nothing but an idea. The initiative was continued by Evans's successor Rodney Wilson in 1970, and a group of works by Bill Lundberg, Derek Boshier, Ivor Abrahams, Anthony Donaldson, Nicholas Munro and William Pye, which more closely adhered to the brief, were shown as a group in the exhibition *Arts Spectrum* (1971).

In 1968, while at the Arts Lab in Drury Lane, Le Grice and I had urged both the BFI and Arts Council to recognise that film-making could be an artist's full-time activity, and that this

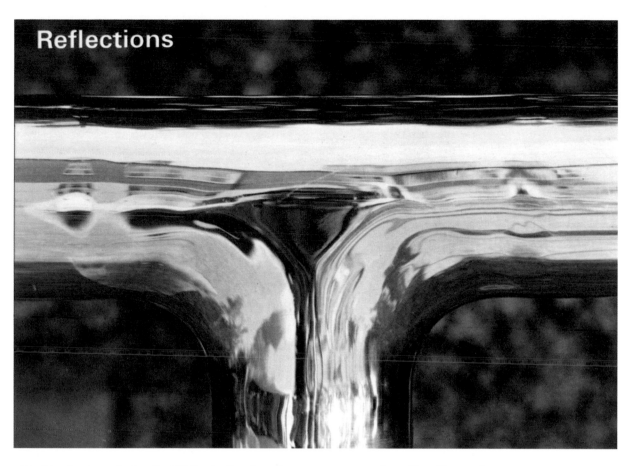

**Reflections**

**72** Promotional card for one of the first Arts Council's 'films by artists', William Pye's *Reflections*, 1972.

was at least as important as the BFI Production Board's current preoccupation with calling-card commercial short films (entrées to the film industry) and the Arts Council's films about, or by, painters and sculptors. Le Grice was eventually invited onto the Production Board, but not till 1972. I was co-opted onto the Arts Council's New Activities Committee in 1969, which was set up to advise the Council on how it should respond to the current outpouring of experimental work in all media. I resigned early on, obviously having failed to impress my colleagues of film's needs, for after two years of deliberation the primary beneficiaries of the funding that became available were fringe theatre, and (of more use to film) Peter Sedgley and Bridget Riley's SPACE Ltd [42] (founded 1968), and its later sibling the Acme Studios and Housing Association (1972). These organisations secured ex-industrial buildings for artists' studios and living spaces and in the 1970s helped to house the London Filmmakers Co-op and artist-run galleries and spaces including the Air and Acme Galleries, 2B Butler's Wharf, Matt's Gallery, Interim Arts, and many other film-friendly organisations.

By 1972 Wilson had persuaded his Arts Council colleagues that the sheer number of active film-making artists merited attention, and an Artists' Film Subcommittee was set up (a subcommittee of the documentaries committee), to consider film-making and exhibition proposals from artists. [43] Until its dissolution in 1999, this committee would be a modest but consistent supporter of artists' work in England, and the only specialist committee dedicated to this area of work.[44]

Once or twice a year, the Arts Council would accept proposals from artists for specific film or video projects, and these were considered by a committee of unpaid peers – artists, critics, academics and curators – following the Arts Council's non-democratic, but time-honoured practice. Demand always exceeded the money on the table, and the relative needs of new makers versus old, film versus video, large budget versus small, exhibition or publishing[45] versus production, would be argued time and again. Periodically the committee agonised about the folly of expecting artists to be able to fix their ideas on paper before lifting the camera. Offering bursaries in response to an existing body of work provided one answer to this problem, and as video entered the frame, the Arts Council jointly funded annual production bursaries at a number of equipment-rich art-schools and polytechnics: the Royal College of Art in 1974, Maidstone 1978, then Newcastle and Brighton, with Reading and Exeter also open to film.

With so little money available, there were inevitable arguments about where the borderline fell between artists' works (clearly an Arts Council responsibility) and innovative or experimental film and video works (arguably still the responsibility of the BFI). These boundary disputes might be thought of little interest in any other context, but from time to time they managed to engage even government departments, as the Arts Council and the BFI (and later the Film Council) fought over responsibility for this tiny area.[46] At the coalface, harmonious working relationships generally prevailed. There was, for example, an unwritten agreement that made the funding of film and video workshops – which benefited the whole spectrum of independent makers – a responsibility shared by the BFI and the Arts Council-funded Regional Arts Associations, often in partnership with local authorities such as the Labour-controlled Greater London Council (GLC), and, after 1982, Channel 4 Television. Support of distribution organisations was also accepted to be largely a BFI concern.

Being based in the Art department where much of the activity was exhibition organising, a natural question was how to encourage the screening of work. An early initiative was the *Filmmakers on Tour* scheme (1976–89), which encouraged artists to present their work to audiences in person, by automatically subsidising speakers' fees and travel expenses. The scheme was also intended to help film clubs and small galleries to show what they might see as high-risk work, and its use helped consolidate the growing network of screening spaces in artist-run galleries and film workshops. It was also used by art colleges to supplement visiting-artist programmes, where, according to a satirical account by the film-maker and *Biff* cartoonist Chris Garratt, 'audiences of reluctant students were padlocked into the lecture theatre on pain of failing their

**73** The first *Film-makers on Tour*, prospectus, 1976.

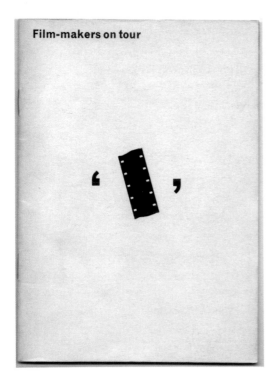

Film-makers on tour

continuous assessments. … [and] for those who had failed to make their escape under the cover of darkness ... the dreaded Post Filmic Discussion'.[47] Artists' reports to the Arts Council more often told of migrating (with at least part of the audience) to the pub.

*The New Art* (1972) – a survey of conceptual and minimal art organised by Anne Seymour for the Hayward Gallery – was one of the Arts Council's first exhibitions to include the moving image alongside painting and sculpture, and bravely (given the limitations of the current technology) included installations as well as films performed 'on the hour'. Film and video were included in many of the Arts Council's regular sampling of contemporary art practice through-out the 1970s – its *Hayward Annual* exhibitions. Also at the Hayward Gallery, *Identifications* (1973), a survey of Gerry Schum's artists' TV commissions, was the first Arts Council exhibition to be dedicated exclusively to the moving image, followed by *The Video Show* (1975) at the Serpentine Gallery, and the international survey show *Perspectives on British Avant-garde Film* (1977) at the Hayward Gallery.[48]

*Film as Film* (1979), also at the Hayward Gallery, was its most ambitious exhibition proj-ect until the 1990s, and was remarkable for a number of reasons. Based on the exhibition *Film Als Film, 1910-Bis Haute* organised by Birgit Hein and Wolf Hertzogenrath for the Cologne Kunstverein, it presented a linear history of 'formal experiment in film' through a collection of still images – artists' original drawings, film-structure diagrams and frame-blow-ups – and complete projected films. It broke new ground in the presentation of the moving image in the gallery in its use of the relatively untried technology of film-loop projectors – fourteen of them. It was also famously opposed by leading British feminist film-makers, who withdrew from participation in its selection committee in response to its 'male' construction of history. Lis Rhodes wrote:

**74** The moving image occupies the Hayward Gallery: *Identifications*, 1973; *Perspectives on British Avant-garde Film*, 1977; and (overleaf) *Film as Film*, 1979.

> The history presented here is the illustration of a philosophical ideal, the meshing of moments to prove a theoretical connection. It is as though a line could be drawn between the past and present, and pieces of a person's life pegged on it; no excep-tions, no change – theory looks nice – the similarity of item to item reassuring – shirt to shirt – shoulder to shoulder – an inflexible chain, each part in place. The pattern is defined. Cut the line and chronology falls in a crumpled heap. I prefer a crumpled heap, history at my feet, not stretched above my head'.[49]

Though it stuck to its chronological structure, the exhibition's thesis was more 'crumpled' than its German model, 'formal film' being stretched to included many non-formalists such as Cocteau, Bunuel, Cornell, Burroughs, Dulac and Deren and Menken – all missing from the Cologne original. But Rhodes was right to the extent that its selection of contemporary figures focused on the Co-op/Le Grice/Gidal school, and their international equivalents (though

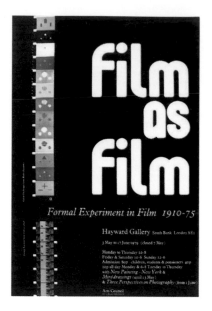

Gidal himself, with characteristic contrariness, resigned from the selection panel in solidarity with the women). Most of the Arts Council's group shows of contemporary work that followed in the 1980s were more catholic in their scope (and were in turn criticised for that).

Richard Cork and I had selected films for the British Council's major exhibition of contemporary British Art, *Arte Inglese Oggi* (1976, Milan), and after joining the Arts Council, I proposed a joint Arts Council/British Council international touring exhibition, *A Perspective on English Avant-garde Film* (1978), which I curated with Deke Dusinberre. There had been some hard feeling among the post-1960s generation of European artists about the exclusion of their work from the repertory and collection of Mekas's Anthology Film Archives, and about the continuing circulation of purely American accounts of the contemporary avant-garde film, such as *New Forms in Film* (1974) curated by Annette Michelson for the Lausanne Museum of Art.[50] Anthology's version of history would appear in exhibition-form at many European museums over the next decade, and its selection of films shaped many of their permanent collections. As a result, there developed a strong sense that it was time to fight back, and to assert abroad the strength of British work.[51]

The success of *A Perspective...,* which included works by twenty-four artists and toured thirty countries, led to further Arts Council/British Council collaborations. *The Elusive Sign – British Avant-garde Film & Video 1977–87* curated by Catherine Kinley of the Tate, the critic Mike O'Pray and artist Tamara Krikorian was followed by four jointly-funded and internationally-toured *ICA Biennials* (1990, 92, 95, 97) with the actor Tilda Swinton, and critics Peter Wollen, John Wyver and B. Ruby Rich as successive selectors. *The Elusive Sign* proved as controversial with the Co-op and LEA community as had *Film as Film*, but for different reasons. *The Eluded Decade R.I.P.* complained LEA's Michael Maziere, and *Who's Eluding Who?* asked Co-op member Anna Thew;[52] their complaints – beyond predictable lists of the 'excluded' – included the age of some of the featured artists and, more seriously, the absence of a unifying aesthetic or political stance in the exhibition. The avant-garde was indeed ageing, and entering the pluralist 1980s; a reality already acknowledged by the curators of a Tate education department season *The New Pluralism* (1985), Mike O'Pray and Tina Keane.

The Arts Council also organised small-scale film and video exhibitions to tour in Britain. The earliest were adaptations of shows staged by other organisations, and included *Cubist Cinema* (1983) originally designed for the Tate education department, and *Recent British Video* (1983) for the British American Arts Association. The committee supported touring proposals from artists' organisations such the women's distribution collective Circles' *Her Image Fades As Her Voice Rises* (1983) curated by Lis Rhodes and Felicity Sparrow (a late reply to *Film as Film* that supplied more of the missing history), and *Black Women and Invisibility* (1986) curated by June Givanni.[53] Subsidy of UK touring proposals became the second consistent strand of Arts Council provision for the art form, and has continued in different forms till today. By the mid-1980s, the Council's own touring projects were being handled by the semi-autonomous Film and Video Umbrella with Mike O'Pray as its curator (its title opportunistically borrowed

**75** (left) Subsidised film tours: *Black Women and Invisibility*, Circles, 1986; (below) *Subverting Television*, Film and Video Umbrella, 1985:

from the Dance department's similar but older dependency, the Dance Umbrella). The Umbrella's exhibition format was simple: two or three 60–90-minute programmes of films or tapes, plus a poster/broadsheet that could be used as a programme note. O'Pray selected and wrote many of these, but often involved other curators, and co-opted existing programmes to give them wider circulation. Its second year, 1985, saw the tour of *Subverting Television: Deconstruct/Scratch/Alter Image* selected by Mark Wilcox, Alex Graham, Andy Lipman and others, *Of Angels and Apocalypse: Derek Jarman* which coincided with a special issue of *Afterimage,* and *Recent British Super 8 Film* – highlights from Leicester's Super 8 Festival, curated by Jo Comino and Laraine Porter. *Surrealist Traces* in the same year helped cement a funding partnership with the BFI, and gave the opportunity to make the Umbrella an independent client, which it became fully in 1987. Moira Sweeney and Jez Welsh were other curators brought on board by O'Pray in the early years to widen the scope of its programming. With Steven Bode's appointment in 1989 the Umbrella took a new direction and became one of the most assured programmers of new media in Europe. It renewed itself again in the late 1990s – now fully under Bode's direction – as a major commissioner of video installations, funded largely by Lottery money. Across the years, the Umbrella has remained remarkably consistent in its focus on working with large and small regional venues to build up their programme of moving-image exhibitions.

A funding experiment of the 1980s was investment in a chain of video access libraries – collections of arts documentaries and artists films transferred to tape

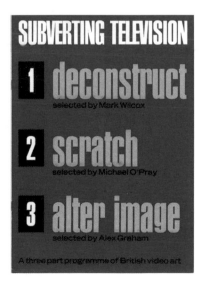

– that could be viewed on demand for a fee. The ICA in London had floated the idea as early as 1978, and opened its Videotheque in 1981, which was soon joined by libraries at the Midland Group in Nottingham, the Arnolfini in Bristol, the Basement Group/Projects UK, Newcastle, jointly with the Newcastle Polytechnic, Sheffield Central Library and others. The Arts Council provided each venue with a core collection of arts documentaries, and money for equipment and the first round of tape-purchases from artists. Rod Stoneman, at that time the cinema programmer at the Arnolfini, welded the venues into a circuit and secured further funding for touring collections that visited each site for a six-month period.[54] The concept was popular with the public but proved labour-intensive, (digital technology, which might have streamlined the system, was still in the future), and none of the host organisations managed to sustain the running costs. Most had closed by the end of the 1980s, with the ICA struggling on with ever-reducing opening hours into the early 1990s.

Throughout this period, the Committee's core budget that supported artists' applications for production funds continued to grow, if modestly. As the number of artists emerging from college grew exponentially, it became harder to pretend that Arts Council funding could support even just the most talented newcomers, or meet the expectations of the increasing number of established artists. At the same time, the number of publicly funded galleries and artists organisations interested in film and video had grown in number, as had the number of film-wise independent curators. Responding to these changing circumstances, from the early 1990s the Committee offered commissioning funds to organisations and curators prepared to promote and exhibit new work, in effect delegating the decisions about *who* to fund to others who might add value to the award. This in effect encouraged the creation of a 'market', though one almost entirely sustained by arts and education funding. Arguably, the nurturing of this 'market' contributed to the re-emergence of commercial activity in the field in the early 1990s, consolidating the concept of the installation as a saleable commodity (for good or ill), and securing the interest of the major national collections. It more certainly gave visibility to the benefiting artists, and experience of commissioning in the area of the moving image to a new generation of curators. Some artists saw this as the Arts Council's abdication from responsibility. In an article summarising the 1980s, Jez Welsh complained:

> The latest Arts Council policy puts the cart firmly before the horse by suggesting that curators
> should decide what kind art artists should make. ... The real problem is that video artists have
> effectively been locked out of the funding structure – it is no longer possible to get funding
> simply because you need to make work.[55]

In reality, the vast majority of works made by artists had always been self-funded, but Welsh's observation perhaps marked a final burial of the expectation that the State should provide. Few of the 1990s generation of artists would have any such illusions. With broadcast-quality domestic cameras and professional editing programmes on their personal computers, they already enjoyed complete technological autonomy. Exhibition and distribution remained the challenge.

The 1990s saw the introduction of a National Lottery in Britain as a means of raising money for 'good causes'. In 1994 the Arts Council became the distributor of the fifth-slice of the Lottery revenue that had been allocated to the Arts. This was earmarked exclusively for capital projects (bricks and mortar), and the unexpectedly large annual sum came with numerous restrictions and half-revealed objectives imposed by the Treasury. In the process of grappling with new 'non-judgmental' criteria, prior value systems were upturned, and bizarre inequalities emerged between the new and old streams of funding. While in one part of the Arts Council a committee of artists struggled to distribute £100,000 equitably between ten film or video projects from sixty proposed by their peers, elsewhere in the same building non-specialist Lottery officers could rubber-stamp the spending of £150,000 on a single video installation, with no competing bids. It took until the end of the decade for common priorities and criteria to be established. The Lottery upheaval hastened the regionalisation of the Arts Council and the delegation of all funding for individual artists to the regional offices (which many said was long overdue). It prompted the creation of the Film Council, which robbed the BFI of many of its funding responsibilities, and placed a large question-mark over the funding of more radical film-for-cinema experiments. It also precipitated the demise of the Arts Council's own film department, which was considered too 'hands-on' in the new environment.

The Lottery proved an equally mixed blessing to artists' film and video organisations. The Film and Video Umbrella wisely kept in check any appetite for bricks and mortar, and concentrated on modest requests for equipment, and regular funding for commissioning, as did the occasional commissioner of films, the Artangel Trust. The London Filmmakers Co-op and London Electronic Arts had both been seeking re-housing throughout the late 1980s, and were high on the BFI's list of priorities for capital support even before the Lottery came into existence. With BFI and Arts Council encouragement, and in a partnership with a commercial property developer, they submitted plans to the Lottery for purpose-built shared premises, and gained funding in 1995. Their new home, the LUX Centre, opened in Hoxton Square in 1997 and contained a cinema space, a gallery, workshops and offices. Despite a doubling in revenue funding, it soon became apparent that costs were greatly exceeding income. The workshops failed to attract enough paying clients and the ambitiously programmed six-days-a-week cinema operation and gallery lost more than anticipated and, crucially, the developer who continued to own the site began to seek a commercial return on his investment in what had become overnight a fashionable area of London.[56] The two organisations merged to cut costs, adopting their building's name as their new single identity, but still lost money.[57] Finally, the new building was forced to close in 2002. A year later, a new, slimline LUX rose from the ashes as a distribution-only organisation, which is how it successfully continues today with Arts Council funding.

**76** Lottery funding – the Lux building in Hoxton Square, 1997

The FACT Centre, which opened in Liverpool in 2002, was another Lottery capital development. The Foundation for Art and Creative Technology grew out of Liverpool's successful biennial Video Positive Festival, and its between-years programme of commissioning and touring, organised by its director Eddie Berg and guest curators. FACT also had pioneered a subsidised exhibition equipment loan service MITES (Moving Image Training and Exhibition Service), the brainchild of the artist Clive Gillman, which loaned and installed equipment, and trained curators in its use, serving venues as large as Tate Modern and as small as Prema Arts Centre in Ulay, Gloucester. FACT's programme and MITES' resources formed an important catalyst to the greater visibility of video in Britain in the 1990s. Sustained by increased Arts Council revenue funding, and in a happy marriage with Liverpool's only independent art-house cinema, the Centre has its own exhibition spaces, and laboratories for project development. Now a substantial organisation, FACT's challenge will be to remain as outward-looking and as fleet-of-foot as its former self, and as in touch with tomorrow's rising stars as its competitors – not just the Umbrella and LUX, but the newly buoyant video-interested commercial galleries.

## THE BFI

The BFI Production Board that Malcolm Le Grice was invited to join in 1972 had already sporadically supported film-making artists. Bruce Beresford, the Board's Head of Production in the late 1960s, had been a member of the Sydney-based underground film group UBU, and his film-making in England had been associated with the *OZ* generation of journalists and satirists Richard Neville, Barry Humphries and Germaine Greer. He was receptive to the anarchic spirit of Jeff Keen, and to the psychedelic imagery of Mark Boyle's lightshows, and both were given grants in the late 1960s. He had invited the painter and occasional film-maker Derek Boshier onto the Board, and films by Tony Sinden and David Hall had been funded. As Le Grice attended his first meeting in September 1972, the Board was waiting to hear the outcome of the Attenborough Committee's review of the Arts Council's involvement in film production. The BFI had been alarmed by the extent to which the Arts Council was stretching the definition of 'arts documentary', and in response to its complaints, the government had appointed a committee chaired by Richard Attenborough to review the problem.[58] The Attenborough Report (1973) decided in the Arts Council's favour, confirming that it should 'embrace and encourage filmmaking as a fine art activity', but the Board continued to give grants to artists, and in the next two years supported Steve Dwoskin, Stuart Pound, Peter Gidal, Gill Eatherley, David Crosswaite, Chris Welsby and others, reflecting the impact of Le Grice's arguments for the Co-op generation.

Of greater long-term consequence, Le Grice immediately argued for support for the new phenomenon of culturally-committed film and video groups – an 'area of film-making in England which is not receiving public assistance'. He had the Co-op in mind, but he also championed the growing number of other potential applicants. In response to this agitation, Le Grice was asked to prepare a report on groups for the Board, and visited over twenty organisations around the country to assess their needs. His report was rejected 'by a [Board] heavily loaded against this awareness',[59] but as a gesture, an ad hoc group-support fund was created, and in 1974 small equipment grants were made to CATS & Graft-on, the Berwick Street Film Collective, London Women's Film Group, Liberation films, Cinema Action, the West London Theatre Workshop, and others.[60] The same arguments were being made at this time to the Regional Arts Associations – the new semi-autonomous bodies in the English regions which received funding from both the Arts Council and the BFI. Amber Films received Northern Arts funding from 1971, and Chapter Video Workshop in Cardiff from the Welsh Arts Council from 1974. The more experimentally-orientated Film Work Group and Four Corners were among several groups that applied for office and workshop funding to Greater London Arts in 1974, where Keith Griffiths, himself a new-generation film-maker, was film officer.[61] As different sources of funding opened up in the late 1970s and early 1980s, best-guessing their gate-keepers' preferences and tailoring applications to fit became a familiar pastime.

When in 1975 the Production Board returned to its discussion of group funding, Peter Sainsbury, an assistant in the department, and about to become its most influential head, complained about the 'lack of product' from the workshops that had benefited from the Board's first tentative funding experiment, though he enthused about the 'remarkable developments … in the field of non-broadcast video' pursued by some. This time, the Board approved group funding in principle, and its support became a core element of BFI policy, though as Sainsbury's lack of enthusiasm became clear, responsibility for workshops (as opposed to group-submitted production applications) was moved to the Regional (Funding and Development) Department, where it was developed through partnerships with the Regional Arts Associations. For Sainsbury, much workshop production was mired by its lack of interest in aesthetics, and in Le Grice's words (from his review of the First National Festival of Independent Film) the 'reactionary conventionality of its film-form'. The antagonism between workshops and the Board became mutual. Speaking for the workshops, Alan Fountain, film officer at East Midlands Arts, and later Channel 4's first commissioning editor for Independent Film and Video, remarked:

> we suspect that the fantasy of the Production Board is to create a cinema in Britain of Fassbinder, Bertolucci or Truffaut. We have never had such a cinema in Britain, and we don't want such a cinema; we don't want this tacky glamour of the metropolitan EEC bourgeoisie. We have a completely different cultural conception.[62]

Group subsidy – providing workshop facilities to an identified cultural or geographic community, or support for a broadly outlined collective body of work – established a pattern to which the Greater London Council and Channel 4 could turn as they implemented their commitments to support 'cultural groups' (GLC from 1976) and the 'independent sector' (Channel 4 after 1982). The GLC's determination to reflect the cultural diversity of London in its arts funding (an aspect of funding that neither the Arts Council nor BFI had engaged with seriously at this time) was reflected in its support from the early 1980s of the Oval Video Project, Ceddo (set up by Menelik Shabazz and Imruh Bakari), Black Audio Film Collective, Sankofa and Retake Film and Video, which nurtured a rising generation of young black, Asian and gay film and video artists, including Connie Giannaris, Julian Cole, John Akomfrah and

**77** Sally Potter shooting
*The Gold Diggers* (1983) –
Babette Mangolte at extreme
right (BFI Stills Collection).

Isaac Julien. Group subsidy became a distinctive British phenomenon, developed to an extent unequalled elsewhere in Europe. It became particularly associated with Channel 4, largely because of the size of the channel's commitment, which had reached £1 million annually by 1984. However, measured in terms of success in encouraging artists, the most significant investment in workshops and groups preceded the channel's entry into the field.[63]

Like Griffiths, but unlike his predecessors at the Board, Sainsbury had been schooled in the new independent sector – he had been one of the founders of the independent distributors The Other Cinema, and was an editor of *Afterimage* with Simon Field and Ian Christie – so he came armed with knowledge and clear agenda. In an editorial in *Afterimage 4* (1974) inspired by recent viewings of Jean Luc Godard's *Vent d'Est* and Hollis Frampton's *Zorn's Lemma* he called for a 'new cinema' that would unite 'the underground of London and New York' with the 'avant-garde cinema' of France. This call was echoed and elaborated by the critic and film-maker Peter Wollen in his celebrated article 'The Two Avant Gardes' in the film issue of *Studio International* (1975), which similarly concluded that 'it is crucial that the two avant-gardes should be confronted and juxtaposed'.[64] The parameters of this debate provided Sainsbury with his constituency. In a later unsigned editorial in *Afterimage 7* (1978) he saw the two strands as 'joint protagonists – in an 'epistemological cinema' – a 'cinema of enquiry', but now suggested that:

> the simple opposition of two avant-gardes is no longer an adequate model … Increasingly film practice has acknowledged the complex questions raised by the introduction of speech and writing, and the reappraisal of narrative strategies. Here film-makers of different 'generations' associated with the London Co-op join the established current of independent production, broadly political in its concerns, which sees the necessity of re-thinking the place of language and narrative within a politics of representation'.[65]

Three years into post, he saw convergence already happening, and welcomed artists from the Co-op group into the fold.

Paradoxically, as Sainsbury wrote this, the Board's support for the Co-op group was already waning, and by 1981 had all but dried up.[66] Only Le Grice, Raban (with Marilyn Halford) and Sally Potter would sufficiently engage with the 'the complex questions raised by the introduction of speech and writing', and the mission was more predictably realised though the Board's support of feature-length works by Laura Mulvey and Peter Wollen (1977), Berwick Street Collective (1978), Peter Greenaway (1978 and after), a trilogy of films by Terence Davis (1976–83); Chris Petit (1979) and after a break Derek Jarman (1985). The most characteristic results of the Sainsbury years were a series of theory-driven low-budget feature films investigating social, political and historical themes, including works by Ed Bennett, Richard Woolley, Anthea Kennedy and Nick Burton, Anna Ambrose and Sue Clayton and Jonathan Curling; a new wave celebrated in the extraordinary catalogue *The New Social Function of Cinema*.[67] This gave details of just eleven films, devoting most of its pages to an intensive guide to the new structures and politics of the independent film.[68] Sainsbury wrote:

> While the BFI has always distanced its production funding from the obviously commercial … it has – over the past four years – quite conspicuously pursued a policy resulting in even less marketable films. It has done so for good reason. The generation of film-makers applying to the Board for production funds in this recent period have been frequently concerned with nothing less than a reinvention of the communication process itself.[69]

His brave words were prophetic; the films *were* less marketable, and a decade later, not one of these 'Post-Straubian costume dramas' (as they came to be known by the disrespectful) was listed in the last two BFI Production catalogues (1995 & 1998).

Support of short films including work by artists would revive with the *New Directors Scheme* (1987–99), under Ben Gibson's directorship. This period also saw the BFI making its first significant investment in works on video, with notable examples by George Snow, George Barber, Rick Lander, Cerith Wyn Evans and David Larcher. It also saw memorable feature-length films by Jarman, Isaac Julien, Margaret Tait, Chris Newby, Patrick Keiller and Andrew Kötting, mostly made in partnership with television. With the advent of the National Lottery in 1994, the Production department had hopes of a more financially secure future but, like its Arts Council equivalent, it became a victim of administrative changes, and its funding powers were transferred to the Film Council in 2000.

**78** *The New Social Function of Cinema*, 1981

## FUNDERS AND BROADCASTERS

With the arrival of Channel 4 in 1982, both the BFI and the Arts Council entered a period of partnership with – and some have argued a dependency upon – television. Even before the channel went on air, the Arts Council had secured an agreement that it could depend upon up to c. £150,000 annually towards its programme of documentary-making, and the BFI had gained a subvention of £420,000[70] (rising to £500,000 by the mid-1980s) towards the work of the Production Board. Jeremy Isaacs, the Channel's first Chief Executive, had chaired the Board, and was familiar with the aspirations of the independent sector. These agreements gave the channel the right to transmit the results without further cost. Though neither was designed to benefit artists' film, they opened the door to a series of ongoing funding relationships in later years. Prior to this, television had been an occasional patron of artists' experiments, largely as a result of the initiative of individual BBC producers such as Mark Kidel and Anna Ridley.

Given its charter commitment to 'encourage innovation and experiment', Channel 4 was surprisingly slow to risk giving airtime to work by artists. Unusually in the British context, the channel was designed as a publisher-broadcaster with no studios or production staff of its own, and was instead largely dependent upon ideas submitted by independent producers. One of the first artists' series on-air was *Alter Image* (1983), a showcase for visual and performance art assembled by Jane Thorburn and Mark Lucas, commissioned by the Youth Programmes editor, Mike Bolland, who later commissioned Anna Ridley's series *19:4:90*. The channel's first Arts editor Michael Kustow – former director of the ICA – was probably its most adventurous patron of artists, if an infrequent one. His commissions included John Wyver's series *Ghosts in the Machine* (1986) which introduced the work of American artists Bill Viola, Gary Hill and others to British audiences long before they were discovered by the gallery-world, and Peter Greenaway's innovative graphic video-paintbox collaboration with the painter Tom Phillips *A TV Dante* (1987). Paul Madden commissioned Anna Ridley's series of original works for television *Dadarama* (1984) with contributions from John Latham and others, and her multi-episode versions of Ian Breakwell's *Continuous Diary* and *Christmas Diary,* which started their transmissions in the same year.

Alan Fountain, the channel's Independent Film and Video editor, was responsible for the channel's substantial workshop investment. While the majority of his commissions went to social and political film-makers, one early commission (made through the partnership with the Arts Council) resulted in four interview-based profiles of artist film-makers shown in 1983, each followed by the transmission of several of the artist's works.[71] Fountain's workshop funding had included equipment given to LVA, and the series *Video 1.2.3* (1985), assembled by Terry Flaxton and critic Sean Cubitt, featured the work of many LVA artists. Rod Stoneman, appointed Fountain's assistant in 1985,[72] was more open to work by artists. From 1988 to 1994 the Arts Council and Channel 4 jointly ran an open submission scheme that funded four or five works each year, *The 11th Hour Awards* (either 'the last moment' or a recognition of the 11p.m. graveyard slot in the evening schedule into which most of Fountain and Stoneman's commissions, and occasional but invaluable purchases, were shoehorned).[73] Open submissions were nothing new to the channel, but the novelty of the scheme was that the selection of projects was made by a group of artists and critics, with Stoneman as the channel's sole representative, in a position to be outvoted; the channel of course retained the ultimate veto which was not to transmit. Fifty-four works resulted from this partnership, all but one of which were transmitted. This relationship provided the model for the channel's 'new talent' scheme with the BFI, the *BFI New Directors,* which incidentally funded work by some artists, despite its emphasis on narrative and even, in its final incarnation, imposition of a given theme. The diverse collection of material that resulted from these schemes was showcased in the more alluringly titled transmission slots *Midnight Underground, The Dazzling Image* and (less happily) *The Shooting Gallery.* Commissions to artists remained rare outside these schemes, but Stoneman notably directly funded Gad Hollander's *The Diary of a Sane Man* (1985), David Larcher's *EETC* (1986) and *Granny's Is* (1989) and Le Grice's *Sketches for a Sensual Philosophy* (1988). Other partnerships with the Arts Council included a scheme for experimental animation *Animate!* (1990 onwards), *Black Tracks* (1995) which commissioned music-related subjects from new black artists and film-makers, building on the Council's earlier Black Arts Video scheme (1991–94), and the *High Tec Awards* (1995–96) which involved brokered access to professional digital post-production technology.

In these partnerships, there were surprisingly few 'no-go' subjects for the broadcasters. Erect penises worried them, but less so than total silence, or (the ultimate taboo) the absence of any image. But to its credit, Channel 4 even permitted *that* as it transmitted Derek Jarman's last work *Blue* (1993) – seventy minutes of an empty blue screen, but with a rich sound-tract, which also remarkably involved a simultaneous broadcast in stereo by BBC Radio 3. For their part, artists tended to bring to these schemes whatever projects they were working on at the time, grateful for the exposure to a wider audience, but rarely showing real interest in the television

**79** *Angel,* Mark Wallinger, 1996

context. An exception was the unfailing attraction for artists great and small of the idea of making false adverts to be placed among the real ones, or advert-like unexplained interruptions to the flow of TV's evening schedule. Artists were often surprised to discover this was not a new idea (Hall had been at it since 1969), and none provided an original enough variation to persuade the selectors.[74]

Advert-length works were, however, the subject of the Arts Council's first funding relationship with BBC television, *One Minute Television* (1990–93), which commissioned eight works each year to be dropped into BBC2's late-night arts programme *The Late Show.* This series was followed by several partnerships with the BBC based on the idea of pairing creators from different disciplines, which included *Dance for the Camera* (1991–2003) and *Sound on Film* (1995–97), to which artists such as John Smith, Jayne Parker and Mike Stubbs contributed. One of the last of these was *Expanding Pictures* (1997 only), which ostensibly paired film artists and performance artists, but which memorably provided the first broadcast exposure for three artists of the yBa generation, Gillian Wearing, Sam Taylor-Wood and Mark Wallinger. The fragility of the concept of a 'limited edition' – the art-world convention that restricts the copying of photographs, prints and tapes to a fixed number to protect their monetary value – was nicely demonstrated when a number of the works resulting from this scheme were offered for sale in West End galleries in editions of three or five copies, in the same week as their BBC transmission. Half a million viewers saw them on the box, and no doubt many legally recorded them off-air for their own personal collections, slightly expanding the authorised edition.

The funders' entanglement with broadcasting was another source of irritation to some artists. In his end of 1980s rant already cited, Jez Welsh saw the Arts Council and BFI providing Channel 4 with 'cheap television – so cheap it can afford not to show it'.[75] From a different corner, John Wyver suggested that artists (and funders) were missing the point that television was an art form in its own right, and were pathetically holding onto 'a definition of video [art] by subculture'.[76] An interesting middle ground where television responded to the power of the individual voice, the artist's signature, was identified by artist Jon Dovey of Gorilla Tapes in another late 1980s issue of *Independent Media*.

> There are particular qualities of video as a medium that make it possible to have a production process that is both involving and inclusive of the participants … The BBC Community Programmes Unit has, at long last, got round to giving some of their clients video equipment to go away and make their own programmes with, virtually unaided by the BBC'.[77]

Some of the *Teenage Diaries* and *Video Nation* shorts produced by the BBC Community Programmes Unit had the urgency, emotional directness and even the formal rigour of some of the earliest works of video art, though it is unlikely that any of their makers would have claimed to be artists. Both Peter Wollen (in 1992) and Wyver (in 1995) included examples in their selections for the *ICA Biennial of Independent Film and Video*.

## NOTES

1. John Grierson, 'I Remember I Remember' (1970), quoted in Ian Aitken (ed.), *The Documentary Movement, An Anthology* (Edinburgh: Edinburgh University Press, 1998). *Drifters* (1929) was first shown at the Film Society, with Eisenstein's *Potemkin* which was receiving its first show in Britain after a protracted battle with the Censor.
2. Coldstream: letter to 'Rake' [Dr John Rake, an amateur painter and life-long friend], 8 March 1933, Tate Archive: 'I suppose we can call an artist a sort of eye-merchant. Specialist in looking and seeing – and so painting, drawing and photography [and film] are all his business.'
3. Forsyth Hardy, *Grierson on Documentary* (London: William Collins, 1946).
4. Basil Wright interview with Ian Aitken, 1987, in *The Documentary Movement, An Anthology*, op. cit.

5. Coldstream letter to 'Rake', [undated 1934] Tate Archive. This must be a retrospective thought, for Fry died in 1932.

6. Coldstream letter to 'Rake', 6 April 1937, Tate Archive.

7. 'Grierson turned to me and said – "Stay with us, enjoy yourself and explain your ideas about sound to the team. We have done nothing of this nature yet"'. Alberto Cavalcanti, *The British Contribution* (1952), reprinted in Aitken, *The Documentary Movement, An Anthology*, op. cit.

8. Alberto Cavalcanti, *The British Contribution*, op. cit.

9. Dai Vaughan, *Portrait of an Invisible Man – the Working Life of Stewart McAllister Film Editor* (London: BFI, 1983).

10. Alberto Cavalcanti, 'The Neo-Realist Movement in England', in *Le Rôle Intellectuel du Cinema* (Paris: 1937), translated in Richard Abel, *French Theory & Criticism. 1907–39* (Princeton, NJ: Princeton University Press, 1984).

11. 'Afterthought' (1972), *The Documentary Movement, An Anthology*, op cit.

12. Grierson and Arthur Elton both remained associated with the Centre till their deaths in the early 1970s.

13. Elizabeth Sussex, 'Cavalcanti in England' *Sight & Sound,* Autumn 1975, much reprinted including Macdonald and Cousins (eds), *Imagining Reality, The Faber Book of Documentary* (London: Faber & Faber, 1996).

14. Letter to Cicely Jennings, 28 July 1942, *Humphrey Jennings Filmmaker Painter Poet* (London: BFI, 1982).

15. Grierson, quoted by Rotha, 'Afterthought' (1972), *The Documentary Movement, An Anthology*, op. cit.

16. John Taylor (Crown Unit Producer 1946–48) in Dai Vaughan, *Portrait of an Invisible Man – the Working Life of Stewart McAllister Film Editor*, op. cit.

17. (Letter to Ian Dalrymple), Kevin Jackson, *The Humphrey Jennings Film Reader* (Manchester: Carcanet, 1993).

18. *The Journey* (1975) was the result.

19. Anstey's greatest post-war achievement may have been his discovery and patronage of Geoffrey Jones (1931–2005), a brilliant if profoundly conservative director, cameraman, editor, and star of BTF and Shell Films in the 1960s: *Shell Spirit* 1961; *Snow* 1962, *Rail* 1965, etc.

20. The first was the Svenska Filmsamfundet Arkiv in Sweden, founded in 1933; the next Goebbels's Reichsfilmarchiv in 1934–5. See Penelope Huston's *Keepers of the Flame* (London: BFI, 1994) and Raymond Borde, *Les Cinematheques* (Lausanne: Editions l'Age d'Homme, 1983).

21. *Sight & Sound*, vol. 3 no. 10; vol. 6 no. 4.

22. This followed the publication of the Radcliffe Report (1948) and the BFI Act (1949); before that, it depended on a small grant from the Cinematograph Fund administered by the Privy Council, and originating from a tax on the Sunday opening of cinemas.

23. For an account of the early days of the BFI its post-war film-funding role see Christophe Dupin's 'Early Days of Short Film Production at the BFI: Origins and Evolution of the BFI Experimental Film Fund (1952–66)' in *The Journal of Media Practice*, 2004.

24. *The Public as Artist* (New York: MOMA, 1932).

25. Her *Cubism and Abstract Art* (New York: MOMA, 1936) includes a discussion of abstract film, and her description of the Museum's film collection in *Art in Our Time* (New York: MOMA, 1939) gives one of the first accounts in English of the French painter Léopold Survage's planned abstract film *Le Rythme coloré* (1914). Born Frieda Crump, she had two children by Lewis, who wouldn't marry her (she dispatched them to an orphanage). See Paul O'Keeffe, *Some Sort of Genius: A Life of Wyndham Lewis* (London: Jonathan Cape, 2000).

26. The museum fully opened with *A propos Eggeling: Avant-garde Film Festival* in 1958.

27. 'Vision' *Studio International*, vol. 186 no. 959, October 1973.

28. 'Telekinema' on the building itself; 'Telecinema' in most contemporary documents.

29. Funding recommendations were made locally by the UK nations; responsibility was fully delegated to them in 1994, ACGB becoming the Arts Council of England (ACE).

30. Notionally organised by CEMA, the exhibition toured under the new name from September 1945.

31. The first Arts Films committee appointed consisted of Alan Bowness, Richard Cork, Douglas Lownes, George Melly, Sam Rhodie and Colin Young.

32. 'Experimental Film Fund 1951–59' in John Ellis (ed.), *Catalogue of BFI Productions 1951–76* (London: BFI, 1977).

33. £7,000 in 1953 and £5,500 in 1956.

34. *Sequence* (1947–52), later published by the London Film Club, and edited at different times by Anderson, Huston and Lambert.

35. 'Free Cinema', *Sequence*, Winter 1951. Gregory Markopoulos contributed an article to the same issue. The screening was organised by Olwen Vaughan, former Secretary of the BFI (1936–45), and was introduced by Grierson.

36. *Free Cinema 1*, NFT, 5–8 February 1956.

37. 'Captive or Free', *Sight & Sound*, Winter 1957.

38. 'Brain Drains: Drifters, Avant-Gardes & Kitchen Sinks,' *Cinema*, no. 3, June, 1969.

39. *Unit Five Seven Newsletter*, Autumn 1959 [BFI Library].

40. *Newsletter*, ibid.

41. Hatton, in Jane Wood, *Gala Day and The Challenge: A Study of Two Films*. Footnote 6. BA Dissertation, Humanities, Ealing College 1982 [BFI Library].

42. Founded 1968; SPACE = Space Provision, Artistic, Cultural, Educational.

43. This became the Artists Film and Video Subcommittee in 1976, following David Hall's lobbying, and gained equal gender representation *c*. 1980 thanks to committee member Lis Rhodes's persuasions, and no doubt influenced by the bad press surrounding recent all-male artist exhibitions selected by all-male juries at the Hayward and Serpentine Galleries.

44. I joined the Committee in 1973, and resigned to become a staff member in 1977, and was complicit in most of its decisions after that date.

45. Over the years, committee supported the magazines *Undercut, Afterimage, Independent Media, Filmwaves, Pix* and *Vertigo,* some with the BFI as a partner.

46. The Attenborough Committee began considering this subject for the government's Office of Arts and Libraries in 1971 and 1973 legitimised the Arts Council's support of artists' film. There were several attempts by the BFI in later years to overturn the decision. For a detailed history of this relationship see Peter Mudie's PhD thesis, *The Project – Structural/Materialist Film at the London Filmmakers Co-op (1968–80)* (Perth: University of Western Australia, 2001); Christophe Dupin's PhD thesis, *The British Film Institute as a Sponsor and Producer of Non-commercial Film: A Contextualised Analysis of the Origins, Administration, Policy and Achievements of the BFI Experimental Film Fund (1952–1965) and Production Board (1966–1979)* (London: Birkbeck College, University of London, 2005), and Michael Maziere's paper, *Institutional Support for artists' Film & Video in England* at www.studycollection.org.uk.

47. 'L'Avant Garde et apres', Chris Garratt, *Vivid,* magazine of the Cornwall Video Resource, 1994. Garratt was enrolled on the scheme, and also made use of it as a polytechnic film teacher. Initially there were just eight artists on the scheme. 'Video' was recognised in the scheme's title from 1980, and the number of enrolled artists peaked at 90 in 1985.

48. INNO 70 (1970), a month-long event organised by APG (Artists' Placement Group) at the Hayward Gallery, may have been the very first – featuring screenings by Brisley, Dwoskin, Gidal, Hall/Sinden, Latham, Leggett, Lange and Raban, alongside displays by APG business partners British Steel, ICI *et. al.*

49. I is Rhodes, 'Whose History? Women and the Formal Film', *Film as Film* (London: Arts Council of Great Britain, 1979), reprinted in Michael O'Pray, *The British Avant-Garde Film* (Luton: University of Luton Press, 1966).

50. But held in Montreux.

51. Other Arts Council supported correctives to the 'Anthology view' included the tour of *Films by American Artists* (1981) curated by Regina Cornwell, and *American Video* (1983) curated by Mark Nash, which reflected different aspects of a gallery-based film and video practice not part of the Mekas, Michelson and Sitney narrative.

52. Both in *Independent Media,* issue 74, February 1988, which also contained a more favourable assessment by Nik Houghton.

53. These initially formed part of a *Modular Scheme* proposed to the Arts Council (1980) by Guy Sherwin from the Filmmakers Co-op (adopted 1982), in which the Council supported distributors' touring proposals. There had been anxiety that the Arts Council's own touring would undermine the position of the Co-op, LEA and Circles, though most Arts Council exhibitions involved renting or buying work from these distributors.

54. *Network One* (1984) curated by Mike Stubbs was one such touring programme.

55. Jez Welsh, 'Resigned NOT Resigning', *Independent Media*, no. 103, September 1990.

56. Fatally, the financial experts at the Lottery failed to spot the vulnerability of the LUX development to rising property values.

57. This formally marked the end of the London Filmmakers Co-op, and London Video Arts after nearly forty years, and thirty years respectively.

58. Stanley Reed, the BFI's Director, hoped that the money the Arts Council was spending on film might be transferred to Production Board, to augment its modest budget.

59. This section draws from Le Grice's papers in the BAFV Study Collection. Le Grice continues, 'In a minority of one, I must frequently have sounded like a frustrated Old Testament Prophet' (draft of a letter of resignation to be sent to Keith Lucas, BFI Director, 1975).

60. CATS & Graft-on consisted of Hoppy and Sue Hall; the Berwick Street Film Collective members included Marc Karlin, James Scott, Humphrey Trevelyan; London Women's Film Group (1972–78) included Esther Ronay, Mary Kelly and Claire Johnston.

61. The Film Work Group was formed by film and painting students graduating from the RCA in 1974, Anna Ambrose, Ed Bennett, Stewart McKinnon, Phil Mulloy, Clive Myer, and Nigel Perkins; Four Corners was formed by graduates from the London International Film School in the same year – Wilf Thust, Joanna Davis, Mary-Pat Leece, and Ron Peck. Paul Hallam, Richard Taylor and Lis Rhodes joined later. They also received funding for the film *On Allotments* in 1974.

62. Julian Petley, *Landmarks* (exhibition catalogue) (London: British Council, 1989). One of the disappointed applicants to the Board during this period was gallerist Siggi Krauss – who proposed a video workshop attached to his gallery.

63. Other workshops supported by Channel 4 included Amber and Trade Films in Newcastle, Northeast Films, Sheffield Independent Films, Cinema Action and Frontroom in London, and later Scrin (Wales), and workshops in Belfast, Bristol, Birmingham, Derry, Edinburgh, and Leeds.

64. *Studio International*, vol. 190 no. 978, November–December 1975; Wollen saw the First Festival of Independent British Cinema of the same year as a hopeful sign; his article formed a key text at the *International Forum on Avant-garde Film* at the Edinburgh Film Festival in 1976.

65. Editorial, *Afterimage*, no. 7, 1978.

66. Between 1972 and 1976, the Board supported Co-op members, Gill Eatherley, Stuart Pound, David Pearce, William Raban, Peter Gidal, Mike Dunford, Chris Welsby, and experimental work by Peter Greenaway (shorts), Tony Sinden, Peter Donebauer and Stephen Dwoskin. Between 1976 and 1986, the only Co-op members funded were Gidal, Raban and Halford, Le Grice and Lis Rhodes.

67. Bennett *The Life Story of Baal* (1978); Phil Mulloy, *In the Forest* (1978); Wooley, *Brothers and Sisters* (1980); Kennedy and Burton, *At the Fountainhead* (1980); Ambrose, *Phoelix* (1979); Clayton and Curling, *Song of The Shirt* (1979).

68. 'Art Cinema and the Question of Independence'; 'Decolonising the Unconscious'; 'Independent Cinema and Cultural Democracy'; 'Distribution and Exhibition – The Practices of the Women's Movement'; 'The Cinema Workshops – New Models of Cinema'; 'Questions of Democracy and Control in Film Culture', and more. *The New Social Function of Cinema* (London: BFI, 1981).

69. Peter Sainsbury, 'Production Policy', *The New Social Function of Cinema*, op. cit.

70. 1982/83 BFI Annual Report.

71. *Jeff Keen Films, Margaret Tait Filmmaker, Normal Vision: Malcolm Le Grice, Seeing for Ourselves: Women Working in Film (Circles),* directed by Margaret Williams for Arbor International.

72. He had been a Channel 4 independent film and video consultant from 1983 to 1985.

73. From 1992 called *Experimenta;* the channel contributed three-quarters of the budget and gained rights to two transmissions. The artists retained copyright. There were no obligatory themes or required lengths, just a maximum budget.

74. Proof that interruptions *could* still happen in the ratings-conscious 1990s included David Mach's *The Clydeside Classic* for Channel 4 (1990), four apparent inserts into the evening schedule, David Hall's spots for MTV (1993), and more surprisingly, the Tyne Tees TV supported *Search* (1993) by Wendy Kirkup and Pat Naldi.

75. Jez Welsh, 'Resigned NOT Resigning', *Independent Media*, no. 103, September 1990. In reality almost all the works produced by these schemes *were* screened by the broadcasters; the sometimes long delay between completion and screening was frustrating to artists.

76. Most memorably in 'The Necessity of Doing Away with Video Art', *LVA Catalogue,* 1991, reprinted in Julia Knight (ed.), *Diverse Practices* (Luton: University of Luton Press and The Arts Council, 1996).

77. Jon Dovey, 'Talking Television,' *Independent Media*, no. 95, December 1989 [except, he might have added, in the editing].

Part 2

## 2.1 Film and Fine Art

The Camera **:** Landscape **:** Portrait **:** Still Life **:** Collage **:** Pop Art **:** Absurd **:** Psychedelic **:**
Sculptors' Films **:** Abstraction **:** Figurative Animation

### THE CAMERA

The story of mainstream cinema is that of the triumph over all other possibilities of a highly
encoded narrative language – the child of narrative painting and theatre – delivered with a standardised 24/25 frames-a-second pulse. In addition to questioning the dominance of story-telling
in cinema, artists have less frequently, but more radically, unpicked and re-thought the basic
mechanisms of film-recording and exhibition, often looking to early cinema and pre-cinema
moving-image technology as they did so. Re-considering the machinery of film and video
was a phenomenon of the 1970s onwards, reflecting increasing familiarity with, and ease of
access to, technology, and expanding notions of display. Early cinema had also reflected the
other traditional subjects of painting – landscape, portrait and still-life and these too offered
models that artists might develop.

The diversity of optical toys in the 19th century suggested the many different directions
cinema's development *might* have taken. From flip-books to zoetropes, these toys were made
for the domestic market, and could be enjoyed anywhere. Similarly, early film cameras also
served as projectors and could be set up in any space, domestic or public. This informality of
the moving image vanished with narrative cinema's success and the demand for theatre-like
performance spaces, and was only partially regained in the age of videotape, and finally
more fully recovered (at least in the developed world) in the digital late-90s, with video-
phones, the internet, and palm-held DVD players.

Early films could be shot at different speeds (permitting the extremes of slow-motion and
time-lapse photography) and could be projected at any speed, making the act of projection
into a performance. It is probable that a film pioneer such as Charles Goodwin Norton, who
already had an established and sophisticated magic-lantern show when he added film to his
repertoire, would have 'played' his film projector, as he would play his triple-lens lantern.
Varying the way in which he cranked his projector's handle, he could analyse photographed
movement, and implicitly the whole film phenomenon, by playing the film forwards and

**(Opposite)** *The Eye and the
Ear* (detail), Stefan and
Franciszka Themerson, 1945.

**80** *Rough Sea*, James
Bamforth Company, 1900.

backwards, speeding it up or slowing it down, and even momentarily 'freezing' the image. Norton's short 'actualities' made at the
turn of the century, such as *Horse Drawn Traffic in the Euston Road*
(1899), were topographic, and might reveal little more than the
choreography of street activity, but *Rough Sea* (1900) in the catalogue of his Yorkshire contemporary James Bamforth, a single shot
of the visual turmoil of waves breaking on a pier, verges on abstraction, and would have presented an invitation to exploit all the
possible permutations of projection. But by the 1920s projection had
become standardised, and the public could see these marvels of
manipulated time *only* in the context of a new genre of film, the
scientific short, popularised by Mary Field and Percy Smith's series
*Secrets of Nature*.

In the 1970s, artists with access to variable speed cameras and
domestic projectors would re-introduce the elements of analysis and
performance into their work, at both the filming and projection stages. Yoko Ono's Fluxus
film *no5* (1968) used a scientific camera to shoot a 333 frames-per-second close-up of John
Lennon's face curling into a smile through fifty minutes; Ian Breakwell and Mike Leggett used
another scientific tool, an analysis projector that could run at two frames-per-second, to show
their *Unword* (1970), a condensed-time record of a number of performances by Breakwell;
and the whole area of 'expanded cinema' developed by Le Grice and others challenged the
orthodoxy of audiences seated in rows, the single screen, and images appearing at 24 frames
per second.

Some 1970s artists went further, and re-thought the standard apparatus of mainstream
cinema; its cameras, projectors and lenses. Returning to pre-cinema basics, Tony Hill (b.1946)
toured a one-man-show during the 1970s and 1980s that included *Point Source* (1973), a
work of pure shadow-play, using a strong light-source and an array of baskets, sieves and

**81** Between movement and
stasis: *Unword*, Ian Breakwell
and Mike Leggett, 1970.

 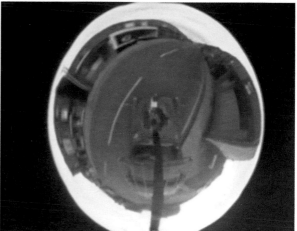

grids that enveloped his surrounding audience in a vertiginous display of spinning patterns. Also frequently included was his *Floor Film* (1975), which required audiences to stand on the screen, where they were enveloped by images projected through mirrors from above. These works could be staged wherever he found an audience, giving him the freedom of a nineteenth-century showman. Even in his more conventionally exhibited works, a consistent theme in Hill's work has been the destruction of familiar frames of reference. His *Expanded Movie 1* (1973) presented Lumière-like scenes of incidental street-life, squeezed and stretched to extremes through anamorphosis; *To See* (1982) showed the world through the 360-degree eye of a hemispherical reflector. He built special camera-mounts and cranes – such as the *Up and Over Crane* and *Falling Over Slowly Machine*, to achieve uncanny movements that upturn the spectator's relationship with gravity and the horizon. He described the surprising effect of the latter:

**83** Tony Hill: *Point Source* (above left), 1973, and *To See* (above), 1982

> a man with long hair holding a bottle of milk falls over sideways; seen strictly orientated to the man, he remains standing, the ground pivots about his feet, the milk slides up and out of the glass and shoots off sideways, and his hair is pulled sideways towards the ground as if by a magnet … This simple change of view exposes the action as the relative motion of two objects.[1]

These visually striking techniques endeared Hill's work to the world of advertising and music videos, as in an earlier age they might have caught the eye of the designers of novelty cinemas in World's Fairs and Expos, and led to his participation in many commercial projects. His non-commercial work is distinguished by the gradual way in which he explores the parameters of a particular effect by providing a game-like structure for the viewer to engage with. In *Downside* Up (1985), for example, he slowly increases the reach of the 'up and over' movement, then employs different sizes of cranes in contrasting environments, carefully choreographing his camera's movement through an array of structures and architectural spaces.

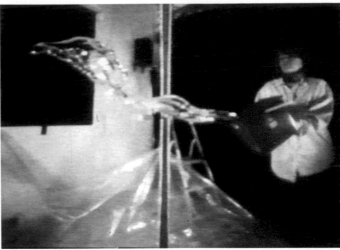

**83** *Water*, Tim Macmillan, 1983 (above right) and one of his hoop-shaped cameras.

The artist Tim Macmillan has challenged the assumption that the film-camera invariably records the passing of time. While still a student at the Slade, Macmillan (b.1959) built cameras as sculptures that were conceptually completed by the instantaneous exposure of a length of film. He realised that if a lens and a shutter were positioned in front of each separate film-frame and this entire sequence of individual frames was exposed simultaneously, then projecting the resulting film–strip would give the appearance of travelling through *space* – equivalent to the length of the strip – while *time* remained frozen. His early works such as *Water*, *Cat* and *Jump* (all 1983, each thirty seconds long) have all the qualities of 'primitive' cinema; the images of the figure, cat, splash-of-water suspended in mid-air round which the camera travels, are unstable, partially fogged and varied in exposure – imperfections he would later iron out, but which add to the films' charm. His invention of the 'time-slice' was later widely exploited by science and advertising, and replicated by computer technology in mainstream films such as *The Matrix*. Shown as a gallery installation, his own most startling and thought-provoking work was *Dead Horse* (1998), shot in a slaughter-house, which captured the instantaneous muscular-spasm of a huge animal as the bolt that kills it enters its head. The camera's movement round the beast reveals its executioner (initially out of shot), and its extraordinary frozen pose – every muscle in tension; all four feet simultaneously off the ground – and allows the viewer an uncomfortably long confrontation with the normally elusive moment of death.

Both Hill and Macmillan accepted cinema's core phenomenon of still images cohering into movement when projected in rapid succession; Steve Farrer (b.1952) challenged even this, spending ten years perfecting his *Machine* (1988) which explored the boundaries of the persistence of vision. His apparatus was both camera and projector, echoing the technology of early cinema, but its mechanism was shutter-less and moved the film continuously sideways (so no individual 'frames' were taken), while the body of the camera spun on its axis. When the speed of camera-rotation and film-movement synchronised, a clear image regis-

84 A strip of film (with enlargement) shot on Steve Farrer's *The Machine* 1988; the machine itself (below left), and seen suspended within its circular screen at the Diorama (below right).

tered, each rotation of the camera capturing a complete 360-degree panorama, joined seamlessly to the next. Projected, the image swept round its enclosing circular screen like a light-house beam, appearing to illuminate the part of the scene on which it fell. Refreshed by each subsequent sweep, movement within the image just registered. The phenomenon was so unusual that it inevitably re-invoked the first experience of seeing projected movement. The *Machine* was used to film scenes of incidental life; friends on the beach and artist-colleagues at work. With *Goodnight Ladies, Goodnight* (1999), Farrer employed a conventional

**85** Looped multiple superimposed actions in Steve Farrer's *Goodnight Ladies, Goodnight*, 1999.

35mm camera, but defied the customary linear sequence of events by arranging for time to seemingly continue, yet overlap and repeat endlessly, and without visible interruption. His subject was a detailed self-portrait in which the artist is seen simultaneously as multiple selves engaging in domestic tasks, eating, ironing, watching TV, climbing a ladder to a distant bed where other figures await; each 'self' occupying its own section of the screen-space, each appearing and disappearing at different points in the cycle. Farrer achieved this by creating a long loop of film that passed repeatedly through the camera, recording a different performed action with each cycle; and carefully plotting his movements in an otherwise blacked-out space. The dispersal of the narrative across the screen-space and the spatial flatness of the image are closer to the pictorial conventions of early Renaissance painting than to those of contemporary cinema. On this occasion, Farrer had felt challenged to explore the possibilities of the loop by a dismissive earlier remark by the critic Stuart Morgan.

Like the avant-garde itself, experimental cinema has come to seem a thing of the past, its techniques pilfered by the mainstream, its precepts no longer viable. When the filmmaker Steve Farrer's exhibition opened recently at *Milch* in London, the first thing that caught visitors was a moving loop of film [part of his installation *Crossing the Line* (1996)]. For many observers, the metaphor could not have been more apt: indeed, it could be argued that as the year 2000 approaches, avant-garde filmmakers are more and more obviously caught in a loop, and that for this very reason the entire *Milch* event was based on a defunct aesthetic as well as an unrealistic estimate of where cinema is now.[2]

The approach of the millennium, and perhaps more provocatively the arrival of cinema's centenary in 1996, seemed to stimulate a surge of interest in 'defunct' moving-image technologies and their aesthetics. The *International Symposium of Shadows*, a celebration of eccentric technologies, was held in London's dockland West India Key Warehouses in 1996, organised by the 'shadow engineers' Loophole Cinema (artists Greg Pope, Paul Rogers and Keely Macarow). The event attracted artists and performers from all over Europe, and demonstrated how widespread was the interest in creating an alternative history of moving images and shadow-play. Some of the assembled machines – such as Simon Lewandowski's *Stumbling Machine* (UK 1996),[3] the heat-powered micro-worlds built into 35mm slides by Julien Maire (France) or Thomas Bartels witty *Projecting Sculptures* (Belgium) – recalled the 1960s sculptor Jean Tinguely's humanisation of machinery through its engagement in absurd, motorised performance. Others seemed more utilitarian – Joost Rekveld's *Installation 13* (Holland 1995), David Rokeby's *Interactive systems* (Canada) and the inter-

active projections of the group Flicker (UK), designed solely to produce engaging or spectacular visual phenomena. In all of them, the spirit of pre-cinema and early cinema was
manifest.

    Another maverick apparatus-making artist of the 1990s was Steven Pippin (lauded by
Morgan, even as he lost patience with Farrer), who achieved some celebrity and certainly a
gallery career by turning railway-carriage toilets and Laundromat washing machines into
effective cameras, capable not just of taking images (using their orifices as lenses) but also

**86** Shadow performance by
Loophole Cinema, 1993.

**87** Documentation of
Steven Pippin's *Laundromat*
photography, 1997.

chemically developing and fixing them. The
whole process was recorded on film, that documentation becoming the saleable work of art
in the time-honoured tradition of much conceptual art.[4] His later television-sculptures, in
which the guts of a TV were enclosed in a transparent vacuum-filled bubble (rendering them
silent), provided a convincing sculptural object,
but seemed curiously contrived in comparison
with his earlier adaptations.[5] Other artists keen
to take cinema back to its origins included
Jennifer Nightingale, who has made pinhole-
camera films, and those who have re-worked
Edweard Muybridge's analyses of human and
animal locomotion, among them Anne Rees-
Mogg, Fred Drummond and George Snow.

## LANDSCAPE

Of the traditional subjects carried over from painting into early film, landscape was the most popular for several reasons. Audiences could be expected to respond to an immediately familiar subject, such as a view of the street outside the hall where the film was to be shown, or a 'living' version of an image well-known from still photography, such as the Niagara Falls, or simply a spectacular visual phenomenon such as vertiginous perspectives seen from a train crossing a high steel-frame bridge. (Moving vehicles were a gift to the early topographic film-makers.)

**88** Alexander Promio in Liverpool, *Panorama pris du chemin de fer electrique*, 1897

The films made in cinema's first years by the Lumière brothers were just seventeen metres long, roughly one minute of projection, but occasionally a subject offered such a challenge that a longer study resulted. The Lumière brothers' cameraman Alexandre Promio (1868–1926) – who spent several months in England and Ireland in 1897, was clearly astonished by the commercial prosperity of Liverpool docks, then at their height, and this prompted two individual reels, *La rade* and *Entree dans Clarence Dock,* and a remarkable four-reel sequence travelling through the port's tangle of warehouses, steamers and three-masted ships, *Panorama pris du chemin de fer electrique I–IV,* shot from an elevated light railway used to transport workers along the waterfront. Silent, and without explanatory titles or framing narrative, early studies such as these were presented to the viewer simply as landscapes, and were open to different interpretations by the viewer to an extent inconceivable in the age of travelogues and the determining voice-over. As early as 1900, narrative and the explanatory inter-title began to impose themselves, and not until after the Second World War would such intense focus be placed again on the challenge of making landscape the sole subject of a film. That said, the narrative sound-film had its compensations. In the documentary context of the 1930s, where human interaction with the landscape became the subject, film-makers found constructive ways of setting voice against landscape images – poetically as in Basil Wright's *Song of Ceylon,* or heroically, as in Flaherty's narrative *Man of Aran* (both 1934), discussed later.

The Scottish artist Margaret Tait (1918–99) was probably the first film-maker to construct a film around her response to a particular landscape. Trained as a doctor, Tait had spent the war in India, where the culture, the relationship of people to land, and the light made a deep impression on her. Intending to make a film on the subject, she enrolled at the Centro Sperimentale film school in Rome to learn film craft, and there she observed Rossellini, De Sica and others at work. On completing the course she returned to her native island of Orkney, and began to make her distinctive, low-key but incisive portraits of people and places. Her *Orquil Burn* (1955) documents a local stream ('burn' in Scots), following its course from the sea to its source in a marshy landscape, in hand-held but essentially static shots. This sequence of images moves progressively further into the particular landscape, and the viewer quickly learns that the present image contains clues as to the location of the next, and so on. Coincidentally, there are similarities between the structure of this early film of Tait's and

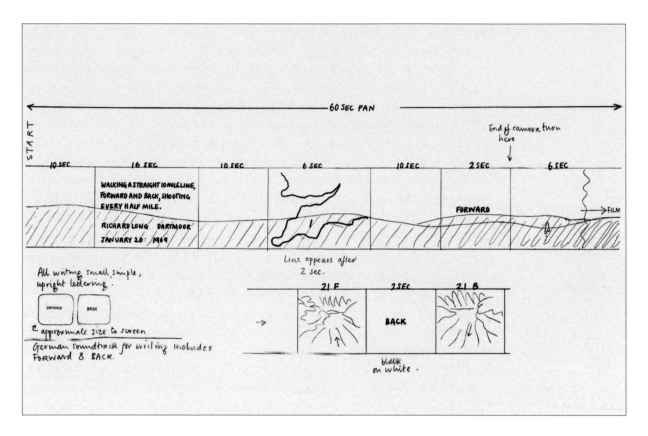

Richard Long's *Walking a Straight 10 Mile Line Forward and Back Shooting Every Half Mile (Dartmoor, England, January 1969)* (1969), one of his films made with Gerry Schum. In their search for ways to engage and sustain the viewer's interest with limited subject matter, both Tait and Long adopted a formal solution, stations on the line of a walk, that anticipates the 'structural' landscape films of Raban and particularly Welsby. Tait accompanied each shot with a voice-over observation, Long simply located his walk with a title giving location, time and direction (forward or back); neither was ever as formal again. In Tait's later landscapes such as *The Big Sheep* (1966) and *Landmakar* (1981), people and their interaction with the land, rather than simply the topography, became the primary subject of the work; in Long's one later film project *Stones and Flies* (1988 directed by Philip Haas) his walks and art-making in the southern Sahara were documented in a more conventional form. The challenge of capturing landscape in the raw on film was next picked up by a small group of artists associated with the Filmmakers Co-op in the early 1970s.

In March 1975, the American-born critic and London Filmmakers Co-op organiser Deke Dusinberre curated a season *Avant-garde British Landscape Films* for the Tate Gallery education department, presenting the work of this generation of 'young filmmakers who are making important movies in the area of avant-garde cinema'.[6] The striking feature of this work was the way it combined a passionate attachment to imagery of mountains, clouds, seascapes, parks and rural pastures, familiar from the work of British Romantic painters such as Cozens, Joseph

**89** Richard Long, schematic drawing for *Walking a Straight 10 Mile Line Forward and Back Shooting Every Half Mile (Dartmoor, England, January 1969)*, 1969.

Wright of Derby, Constable *et al.*, with a modernist determination to make visible all the processes involved in the film-making. As Dusinberre wrote in his printed notes for the season 'they assert the illusionism of cinema through the sensuality of landscape imagery, and simultaneously assert the material nature of the representational process which sustains that illusionism'.

Dusinberre's programmes were dominated by the work of Chris Welsby and William Raban. Raban (b.1948) studied painting at Saint Martins School of Art, and was making images directly from nature as he began his film-making, seeking ways of capturing time within the image. Raban described his painting as 'moving towards making physical documentation of specific changes occurring within landscape situations. The images … were the self-formed paint marks on canvas, being the product of a direct organic process'.[7] These 'prints' included impressions made on canvas wrapped to a tree-trunk and left for several months to allow weathering and mould stains to develop, and the instantaneous record made by spilling thinned oil paint onto the sea, and capturing the trace of the breaking wave on paper. Film attracted him because it allowed light and the passage of time to be recorded more directly. Raban's basic strategy for recording the interaction of landscape and weather (his way of getting *movement* into the static landscape image) was to use the single-frame mechanism on his tripod-mounted camera, and to record one frame of film every few minutes, to accelerate the rate of change.

His first film *View* (aka *View Film* 1970) recorded a river-scene through the changes of a winter day, compressed into five minutes; for *Colours of This Time* (1972) he took a new exposure every twenty seconds, but held the shutter open continuously between each frame, to 'record the imperceptible shifts in colour temperature in summer daylight, from first light until sunset'.[8] More ambitiously, *River Yar* (1971–72) made with Chris Welsby, was designed for two-screen projection, and recorded the same Isle of Wight view of a small tidal estuary over three weeks in Spring and Autumn. Spring begins with a normal-speed fourteen minute sunrise, while next to it, Autumn rushes ahead, compressing each passing day into a minute. After a section in which the days – left and right – pass in synchronisation, Autumn breaks into

**90** Exploring colour temperature – William Raban, *Colours of This Time*, 1972

real time to show the sun setting through fourteen minutes into darkness. In fact the film emulsion struggles to record the waxing and waning light, recording only darkness for long sections. Talking to John Du Cane at the time, Raban stressed the importance of experiment in his approach.

> When we arrived at this mill, it was getting dark and we were due to start filming at sunrise next morning. We bolted the camera to this windowsill without seeing the landscape. We decided to point the camera south because we wanted all the shadows to be apparent, and there was a decision to include some sky in the frame, but otherwise we made no aesthetic/romantic decisions in terms of composition … I'd hate people to see my films as romantic in that way: I'm dealing with specific quantities – the films aren't just pretty colours, or optical effects, but precise investigations'.[9]

With *Broadwalk* (1972) Raban began to look for subjects beyond those found in the natural world. The basic pulse of three frames a minute that continuously records the Broad Walk in Regent's Park for twenty-four hours, is complicated by superimpositions, recapitulations and overlapping sound recordings – signalling his growing interest in the workings of cinema as a potential subject, and the more abstract representation of relationship of film-time to 'real' time, and time experienced in projection and viewing. None of his films after this time could be described as purely about landscape, though landscape remains a strong interest through-out his work. (His contribution to Filmaktion and his documentary-based work are discussed later.). The quasi-scientific mode of investigation was carried forward by his *River Yar* partner Chris Welsby (b.1948), who has continued to work with landscape till the present.

Welsby studied painting at Chelsea School of Art and acknowledges the influence of the 'systems' painters Malcolm Hughes, Peter Lowe and Jean Spenser, then on the staff. Systems and mathematical sequence-structures were also part of contemporary avant-garde film practice, derived from Fluxus film-games and made internationally popular by the structural film movement. Michael Snow's three-and-a-bit-hour, highly systematic study of wilderness landscape *La Région Centrale* (Canada 1971) was a work widely discussed and held in some awe, though not actually screened in Britain till the 1973 Festival. From Europe, Heinz Emigholz's *Schenec-Tady I & II* (1972–3) shown at the same Festival offered another model of system-based shooting. In his own films, Welsby's enthusiasm for systems was always tempered by his desire to oppose 'what is structured, measured, systematic and predictable, [with] what in nature is quite the opposite'.[10] Systems were a way of capturing the fluctuating patterns of movement and light resulting from the Earth's rotation and the tidal pull of the Moon – and the equivalents in daily life caused by human traffic. Sometimes the system itself was dependent upon random external factors; the passing of pedestrians in *Parkfilm* (1973),[11] the strength and direction of the wind in *Wind Vane* (1972), *Tree (fragment)* and *Anemometer Film* (both 1974), the movements of a moored boat in *Estuary* (1980), or the pattern of cloud-cover in *Seven Days* (1974). He described this interaction of order and chaos as it shaped *Seven Days* as:

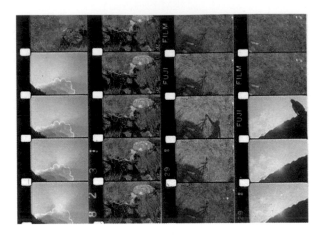

**91** Performing landscape:
Chris Welsby, *Seven Days*,
1974

a balance between a mechanistic structure – the sun rises and sets, the time-based interval – and the vagaries of the Welsh landscape – when it was sunny and when it wasn't – which you couldn't predict. The film attempts a symbiotic relationship between camera/structure, filmmaker and the landscape. As the structure begins to disintegrate or become obscured by the storm, the balance is destroyed, and the result is ultimately death-like'.[12]

Making the film, Welsby, aided by his then partner the photographer/filmmaker Jenny Okun, camped on the side of Mount Carningly in Wales, and gathered seven days' worth of weather, systematically sweeping the landscape from one horizon to the other, from east to west. They exposed one frame of film every ten seconds from sunrise to sunset, the camera tracking the sun's position in the sky, or (when the sun was shining) its own shadow on the ground; sound being sampled every two hours. Like Long's walks, the film-making was in effect a performance, even an endurance test, with the completed work its record. At an opposite extreme, the structure of *Streamline* (1976) was given by a single overhead tracking shot that surveyed ten yards of a streambed from a few feet above the rushing water. Here, the straight line of the track serves as 'a metaphor for technology':

> Just the idea of a straight line traversed at a regular speed could not be *less* dramatic. … Whatever 'dramatic' content there is in the film comes from the stream, where it gets louder and softer, where there is a still patch, and where the sensation of a straight line gets destroyed because the motion of the water is too strong'.[13]

Several of Welsby's films had been made for twin- or triple-screen projection, to be performed, as his single-screen work was, in the cinema. With *Shore Line* (first version 1977), he took the radical step of making a work designed for showing *continuously* in a gallery, and this soon became his preferred context for this work. Of this change Welsby commented:

> I have always felt that the work is more readily understood in the fine art context. The concerns of cinema (as opposed to film) though undeniably of interest and relevance to my way of working have always been a peripheral consideration. … Although still primarily cinematographic [these installations] … allow the viewer the freedom to choose the duration of his or her participation in the work.[14]

*Shore Line*, shown first at the Acme Gallery, and in 1981 at the Tate, involved six projectors mounted on their sides, each showing the same fifteen-foot film loop of a beach scene, the image joining up to form a seemingly continuous line of breaking waves. Photographs became part of his installations from this time, and for the gallery version of *Estuary* he

included panels showing different forms of record or 'trace' of the weather patterns that had contributed to the moored boat's movement; the artist's log-sheets, satellite photographs, meteorological charts and barometric trace-sheets.

**92** *Shore Line*, Chris Welsby, 1977, as installed at the ACME Gallery.

The other landscape artists active at this time included Renny Croft, Jane Clark and Mike Duckworth, all included in Dusinberre's Tate screenings, and a little later, Martin Hearn, Alan Renton, Martin Sercombe, and John Woodman. Duckworth and Hearn's film-making pursued the idea of performance and body-actions as a way of structuring perception of space and scene, developing from Long and John Hilliard, and at a distance Robert Morris (*Mirror*, USA 1969) and Richard Serra (*Hand Catching Lead*, USA 1968), as Welsby had. Duckworth's *Body Arcs* (1973) documents four self-filmed movements, the landscape swirling in the background while the camera spins, while Hearn's *Central Figure* (1976) and *Figure Spiral* (1978) involve the interplay of a moving camera and a remote, motionless figure as a pivotal point in the landscape. Croft's early works such as *Stream Walk* and *Hill Walk* (both 1973) used multi-screen techniques to explore contrasts in the scene such as enclosed and open spaces. Later he increasingly explored photographic issues such as 'framing' and the relationship between the still and moving image; issues that would have been familiar to contemporary landscape photographers such as Long and Hamish Fulton, though not pursued by them on film. *Attermire* (1976) documents the way in which the topography of the land appears to change as one walks through it, one landscape feature (the Sugar Loaf Hill, near Settle, Yorkshire, in this film) first seeming distinct, then merging into another (Attermire Scar), as a line of viewpoints is traversed. His *Three Short Landscape Films* (1979) almost didactically contrasts stillness and motion, black and white and colour, silence and sound, close-up and distant view, scanning the scene in permutated combinations. Renton's landscape films employed some of the systematic procedures devised by Welsby, but with a particular emphasis on the role of natural and artificial light. *Shadow Trace* (1977) follows the movements of a tree's shadow across the ground; *South Stack* (1976) documents a lighthouse as night falls; *Flash Frames* (1979) animates the dusk landscape by momentarily illuminating distant features such as trees with flash-light. Martin Sercombe's *Track* (1980) and *East Coast* (1982) similarly use systematic frame-by-frame moving camera techniques to document the characteristics of particular landscapes. Woodman was principally a photographer (working with Roger Poley); their multi-image still works used leaves, sticks and bits of paper to reveal patterns of movement in the landscape, anticipating the transient interventions into the natural scene of Andy Goldsworthy. In Woodman's films, such as *Pebbles* (1979), the multiple image with its opportunity to make comparisons and see relationships, occurs either by splitting the projected image into four separately filmed sections, or by contrasting time-lapse studies across two screens.

Dusinberre's 1975 show coincided with the period of most intense interest in the problems of landscape among the Co-op group, and by the time that *Undercut* produced its 'Landscape' issue in 1983, with its linked series of installations at B2 Metropolitan Wharf[15] and Air Gallery (organised by Mike O'Pray), this form of activity was already in decline. After this, landscape provided a metaphorical image (as in the work of Chris Newby, Cordelia Swann, even John Smith), or a diaristic record (as in Derek Jarman's Super 8 films) or a pretext for some other form of perceptual or material exploration (as in later Raban, Le Grice,

**93** Heroic landscape: Tony Sinden, *Dichotomy*, 2000.

Joanna Millett and Michael Maziere), but the topography itself was often almost incidental. Where it survived, the urge to record particular landscapes had become infused with issues of individual identity and consciousness typical of the late 1980s. Sharon Morris and Nick Collins (b.1953) were both drawn to ancient and remote landscapes that bear the trace of human habitation. *Cylch Yr Ynys* (*Circle of the Island* 1989) by Morris is her response to a windswept Welsh island; *Cornish Winter Reeds and Skies* (1980) and *Sanday* (1988) by Collins both attempt to 'engender a sense of time' – both historic time and time-passing in the present – 'through the particular quality momentary events have in an almost featureless landscape'.[16] Many of Collins's more recent works have also reflected on domestic spaces and history-bearing fragments of the contemporary cityscape.

**94** *Redshift*, Emily Richardson, 2001.

Landscape in the work of video artists of the 1970s and 1980s – Tamara Krikorian, Elsa Stansfield, Mick Hartney and others – rarely forms the central subject. The restricted image-size and low resolution of video made it hard to provide the scale and detail of image needed to evoke depth and to particularise the view. But an early exception was Brian Hoey's *Tir Na Nog* (1982), made – like the work of Collins and Morris – in response to the Celtic wilderness. Fifteen years later, modern video cameras and digital projection systems allowed Tony Sinden (b.1946) in a late development in his career to produce a series of spectacular landscape installations, beginning with a multi-screen work made in response to a period of residency in Durham Cathedral in 1995, *Approaching the Dissolve*. The series of individual works that constitute *Deluge* (1998), made for Artsway in Hampshire, juxtaposed an image of concentrated urban life – a shopping centre escalator – with the turmoil and force of a Yorkshire waterfall. *Dichotomy* (2000) similarly intercut the spectacular scenery of the Yosemite National Park in the USA, with images of napalm explosions in Vietnam and the artist at the wheel of his Ford Mustang – a meditation on the contradictory meanings of the American landscape to a European visitor. Other artists to juxtapose natural forces and the human world have included Nick Stewart in *Surface Tension* (1994) and *Reflective Surface* (1997) and Chris Meigh-Andrews in *The Stream* (1985–87)[17] and *Eaux d'artifice* (1990), a video-wall fountain, and *Streamline* (1991), and Emily Richardson, with her Welsby-like time lapses of seascapes, forests and even the night sky *Redshift* (2001) and *Nocturne* (2002).

The late twentieth-century urban and suburban landscape found a consistent champion in Patrick Keiller, who set out to explore in film 'the poetics of everyday surroundings – the way that some subjectivities, in particular literary or artistic subjectivities, transform experience of urban and other landscapes',[18] combining voice-over, an almost invariably static camera and long-held, usually un-peopled shots. In Keiller's work, words determine the reading of the image; in Tacita Dean's films such as *Sound Mirrors* and *Bubble House* (both 1999), she explores narratives

**95 (above)** *Descent*,
Catherine Yass, 2002.

**96 (above right)** *Centrale*,
Mark Lewis, 1999.

implicit in bizarre architectural structures. The cold beauty of the often unplanned spaces between buildings prompted Karen Mirza and Brad Butler's *Non-Places* (1999), and Catherine Yass's *Descent* (2002), a vertiginious study of the void between the Canary Wharf towers, shot upside-down by a camera descending the outside of a skyscraper in fog, shown as part of her Turner Prize exhibition. Yass exploits the camera's ability to animate deep perspectives, a phenomenon familiar to Promio in the 1890s when shooting his Liverpool panoramas, and a century later to Darren Almond shooting *Schwebebahn (Day 2)* (1995), his study of Wuppertal's extraordinary overhead monorail; Ken McMullen filming his installation *Chicago Loop* (1998) and Matthew Noel Tod his *Jetzt im Kino* (2003) where Berlin's U-bahn provides his connecting image (the ghost of Godard's *Alphaville* (1965) haunts them all). Others who have intensely scrutinised details in the urban scene have included Michael Landy, in his study of an improvised pavement display outside a store-front *Appropriation* (1990 for three monitors) and William English in films such as *Dining Room* (also 1990).

Landscape and urban space have increasingly come to dominate the installations of Mark Lewis (b.1957 Canada), after an earlier series of works derived from classic cinema: *Upsidedown Touch of Evil* (1997), *Peeping Tom by Mark Lewis* (2000) etc. In *Centrale* (1999), *North Circular* (2000) and *Smithfield 2000* (2000), the camera, either rigidly fixed or performing a single, highly formal movement, exposes a roll of film without any cuts, during which the ambiguities and visual complexities of a space are slowly unravelled, with an intended nod to the Lumière brothers' one-shot films. Typically, in *Centrale* a Soho street-scene viewed through a café window appears to be the meeting place of two people, but its puzzling representation of space (cars vanish as they cross the mid-point of the screen) and our growing awareness of the presence of a mirror undermine our trust in its 'primitive' realism.

## PORTRAIT

Portraits were less common than landscape in early cinema; the format of cinema was after all 'landscape'. After the initial celebratory images of the Lumière family at breakfast made in the first two or three years of cinema, intimate groupings of film-makers' family, friends and colleagues become rare.[19] The genre was presumably considered inappropriate to the large public arena of the cinema, unlike the domestic and contemplative spaces for which most portraits are painted. Predictably the few portraits that are listed in film catalogues after 1900 were of celebrities performing their public roles – Edward VII greeting his Russian cousin at Cowes, etc. Yet it is hard to imagine that the early camera operators did not at some time use their new apparatus to record their baby's first steps, their aged parents smiling slightly anxiously into the camera, a child decked out in fancy-dress outfit, as would the millions of owners of new cameras in the post-Box-Brownie decades. But if they did, it seems these records were not considered worth preserving by their offspring (possibly because the technology needed to view them was only available in public spaces). There are some stilted and self-conscious home movies made by the wealthy on the new 'amateur' gauge of 16mm from the late 1920s, but film portraits shot by artists only begin to appear in the 1950s, with the greater availability of 8mm and 16mm cameras.

**97** *Portrait of Ga*, Margaret Tait, 1952.

Margaret Tait was also among the first true film-portraitists. One of her earliest, *Portrait of Ga* (1952), has the simplicity of a home-movie – she filmed her mother looking shyly into the camera, smoking, and skipping down a winter-sunlit road, accompanying the image with an unsynchronised recording of her strongly accented Orcadian voice responding to the artist's questions. The sound of particular voices was important to Tait. Her longest and most ambitious portrait *Landmakar* (1981) observed her Orcadian neighbour Mary Graham Sinclair as she single-handedly ran her windswept croft. Tait followed the daily tasks of farming through the seasons – ploughing, stacking the corn, looking for the eggs of geese that have strayed – filling out the portrait of this 'poet of the land' (Tait's phrase). As in her mother's portrait, the film-maker's off-screen prompts engage the subject: 'MT: 'I see you as creating the beauty of the land'; MGS: 'Some beauty!'.[20] In *Hugh MacDiarmid – A Portrait* (1964), the words of three poems suggested parts of the film's structure. In un-emphatic voice-over, MacDiarmid recites in Lallans, the dialect of the Scottish Lowlands which he famously championed. Tait described the process:

the lines [from Somersault]

> *'I lo'e the stishie*
> *O' Earth in space*
> *Breengin' by*
> *At a haliket pace'*

suggested to me the poet as a circus performer enjoying balancing on the hire wire, or a thin line

> *'A wecht o' hills*
> *Gangs wallopin' owre,*
> *Syne a whummlin' sea*
> *Wi' a gallus glower'*

and I asked Christopher [MacDiarmid] if he thought he could walk along as if he was balancing the earth, making the earth turn round with his own foot'.[21]

Few in number, her portraits of family and friends are among her most memorable works.

Of the same generation but from a different world, Anne Rees-Mogg (1922–84) based most of her films on aspects of autobiography and the self-portrait. She described herself as the black sheep of her privileged, West Country family, and her films can be seen as being in part an attempt to explain herself to her adoptive offspring, her students at Chelsea School of Art and colleagues at the London Filmmakers Co-op, while at the same time flying the flag for a different form of 'personal cinema', thought by some to be old-fashioned and out of date. Cinema also was a consistent subject. *Grandfather's Footsteps* (1983), a portrait of her great-grandfather the Reverend Henry Giles Savory, was as much about his passion for photography as about him, and *Sentimental Journey* (1977), about the destruction of a family house,[22] begins with a long speculation about the proper subject of films and approaches to film-

**98** The Rev. Henry Giles Savory in Cheddar Gorge c. 1850?, Anne Rees-Mogg, *Grandfather's Footsteps*, 1983.

**99** *A Portrait of David Hockney*, David Pearce, 1970.

making. The earlier *Real Time* (1974) followed a journey back to that home, then in use as County administrative offices, while a sort of seminar on film-making takes place in the car. Her former student Anna Thew gave a flavour of its soundtrack in a memorial note:

> The language is simple … as one of four 100-ft rolls of film records the motorway drive West and homewards, 'I love that clock' is intercut with the drone of traffic sound. Bright red poppies tremble on the verge as the reel is changed. Anne drives the length of film time in her Ford Cortina. 'Film is a succession of still photographs.' Film is a thing. Film is a 100-ft roll of daylight reversal, with flare-outs and clapper boards consciously included. The mistakes 'Oh shit!', or 'Have you got a watch?' are set on an equal foot with a reading of T. S. Eliot'.[23]

Thew's own films contain many incidental portraits in their richly collaged mix – notably that of her mother in *Hilda Was a Good Looker* (1986), but Rees-Mogg's strongest influence was perhaps on David Pearce (another of her Chelsea students) and David Finch, who knew her through the Filmmakers Co-op. Pearce's *Portrait of David Hockney* (1970) shared her informal, conversational style, the subject's body language more important than his speech. Finch's *Man of Stones* (1989) constructed a portrait of a stern father as much through visual metaphor as through the family archive of images, while *Stone Steps* (1992) engaged family members in re-assembling the workings of a former terraced home – now a shell. Here the artist was overtly the intermediary – his siblings addressed him through the camera:

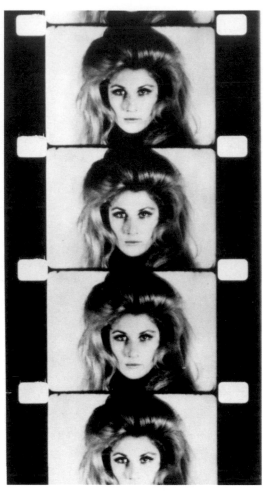

**100 (above)** *Man of
Stones*, David Finch 1989.

**101 (above right)**
Jane Holzer in *The Thirteen
Most Beautiful Women*,
Andy Warhol, USA, 1964–5.

respond[ing] to my questions with caution, revealing something of their characters and our
relationships. Trying to describe a 'family', the film maps people, places and time, searching
for an image as an aid to navigation, like the Plough and the Pole star, which my father always
said I should know about.[24]

In the mid-1960s in New York, Andy Warhol had dramatically thrown a spotlight on the potential of film as a portrait medium, while – almost incidentally – showing how the 'missing'
portraits of the early years of the 20th century might have appeared. His multi-part series, the
*Screen Tests* and *13 Most Beautiful Women*, made in the two years 1964–65, employed a
technique that would have been immediately familiar to the Lumières. Shot with an immobile
camera, and assembled from unedited 100-foot rolls of film (the standard length), they were
shown title-less and silent. Only his framing and lighting were entirely 1960s; head and shoul-
ders in tight close-up, starkly lit and printed in rich velvety black and white (as in the
contemporary photographs of Bill Brandt or David Bailey), as was his radical decision to proj-

ect the films at the silent speed of 16fps, slowing their pace and extending their length. Of Warhol's American peers, Gregory Markopoulos was the first to respond to this challenge. His *Galaxie* of portraits of thirty-three New York stars (1966) followed the silent, one-roll-per-sitter rule (though punctuated by the sound of a bell), and gained visual complexity from his characteristic in-camera editing and superimpositions (he would re-run the film through the camera for a second time or more, adding further layers of imagery with each pass).

**102** *Heads*, Peter Gidal, 1969 (l. to r.: Charlie Watts, Marsha Hunt, Francis Bacon).

**103** *Description 1970*, Tony Morgan, 1970.

Markopoulos migrated to Europe in the mid-1960s, where he continued to make portraits, including several shot in England.[25] Closer to Warhol's model, and among the first works to show his influence in England was Peter Gidal's *Heads* (1969), made while Gidal was still a student at the Royal College of Art. In the early 1960s, Gidal (b.1946) had frequented The Factory in New York, and *Heads* catalogues the artistic beau-monde of London into which he had moved, as Warhol might have done, but with an austerity that would become his own trademark. Silent and black and white like Warhol, but under-lit and tightly framed to the point of severe cropping, the film became – in his phrase – an essay in 'clinical subjectivity', a first step in his long journey into the denial of 'representation'.[26] Influenced in turn by Gidal, Roger Hammond's *Some Friends* (1973), shot in David Larcher's studio next to the Filmmakers Co-op in Prince of Wales Crescent, recorded some of his and Larcher's close circle of film-making colleagues, again shot silent and in long takes, but with the twist of being based on Polaroid portraits held in-shot by the film-maker as he filmed, and sometimes shown in negative.[27] His friend and contemporary Fred Drummond used the same technique in his *Kurt Kren Portrait* (1976).

Many of the films of Tony Morgan (b.1938) involve portraiture in some form. In *Camera* (1971), he, a mirror and his camera perform a double self-portrait, lasting the length of a roll of film. *Description 1970* was made as he and a group of Dusseldorf-based friends prepared the exhibition *Strategy: Get Arts* for showing in Edinburgh. In it, various kinds of 'description' are observed. Women describe their male partners; sometimes apparently from memory, and sometimes accompanied by the image of a different man; film describes the video image, and 'objectivity' is questioned.[28]

The *Short Film Series* begun by Guy Sherwin (b.1948) in 1975, and con-

tinuing to 1979 with occasional additions thereafter, contains several portraits, most memorably *Portrait with Parents* (1975), a self-portrait shot in front of a mirror, so that the artist, his
hand-cranked camera and his co-subjects can be seen in the same frame. The *Series* is discussed
later, but it is worth noting that, as in much of his work, Sherwin here deliberately adopted the
method of the film pioneers – not just making works the length of a single film-roll, shooting
in black and white and silent, but also developing the film himself for maximum control of the
image. (He might have boasted, as the Lumières did, that 'not only did I [shoot] those films,
but the first strips … were developed by me in enamelled iron slop buckets containing the
developer, then the washing water and the fixative. The positives were similarly printed, and
I used as source of light a white wall with the sun shining on it'.)[29]

All of Gilbert and George's art-making (Gilbert Proesche b.1943;
George Passmore b.1942) is a form of self-portraiture, since the
artists invariably feature in their own work, and all of it – paintings, performance and film/video alike – was and is deeply
influenced by Warhol. *A Portrait of the Artists as Young Men* (1972)
observes them smoking cigarettes, as *Gordons Makes Us Drunk*
of the same year observes their drinking, mirroring Warhol's portrait
of *Henry Geldzhaler* smoking a cigar (1964), and *Drink* (aka *Drunk*
1965) in which film-maker Emile de Antonio downs a litre of
scotch. In front of the camera, Gilbert and George reveal only the
mask-like personas they have maintained since 1969, when they
first presented themselves as 'living sculpture'. These early videos

were instigated by (and shot by) the German artist Gerry Schum, and the artists' occasional involvement in film-making seems to have been dependent upon the initiative of others (rather as Warhol depended upon the technical and entrepreneurial skills of Jonas Mekas and Gerard Malanga). After the four early films/tapes, they only once returned to film when invited by Philip Haas to collaborate on a feature-length work, also an extended self-portrait, *The World of Gilbert & George* (1981).

**106** *Chat Rap*, John Scarlett-Davis, 1983.

Another keen portraitist, Derek Jarman (1942–94) drew from a different side of Warhol's films in his own Super 8 home-movies. What appealed to him was the films' intimate record of the studio-life and circle of friends and lovers of an openly gay artist. Jarman's own portraits such as *Miss Gaby* and *Andrew [Logan] Kisses the Glitterati* (both 1971), *Duggie Fields* and *Ula's Fete* (both 1974), similarly draw performances out of visitors to his Factory-like Bankside studio (or to Logan's next door), though their shooting style is intimate and informal, full of colour, and accompanied by romantic popular music.[30] As might be expected, portraits are also scattered throughout the work of the circle of young artists encouraged by Jarman, including Cerith Wyn-Evans (the subject of several paintings by Lucian Freud), and John Maybury, whose subjects included another Freud regular, the performance artist and gay icon Leigh Bowery. (The work of Wyn-Evans and Maybury is discussed later.) John Scarlett-Davis (b.1950), editor and assistant director on a number of Jarman's films, including Jarman's first music video, made his own highly stylised set of portraits of friends from the art-world fringe *Chat Rap* (1983), exploiting video's live feedback, heightened colour, music and fast editing. His own brand of Warhol-like fascination with glamour and personality set the visual style for British youth television for the next two decades. Closer to the tradition of Anger and Cocteau than Warhol, Steven Chivers (b.1958) explored a decadent sensuality through the combination of elaborate costume, theatrical décor and opera music in his portrait *Prima Dilettante* (1984) of his muse, the slide-tape artist Holly Warburton, with whom he frequently collaborated. Marty St James and Anne Wilson made a speciality of multi-screen and 'expanded' video portraits in the late 1980s. Their three portraits *Julie Walters, Sally Burgess and Duncan Goodhew* (all 1990) were the first video works to be commissioned by the National Portrait Gallery. Both women, actress and opera singer, appear in close-up on vertical screens within ornate picture frames, and hold the viewer for twenty minutes with their vocal assaults, becoming literally talking-pictures. *Goodhew* (the Olympic gold medallist swimmer) is shown in his watery element fragmented across eleven screens, paralleling the artists' contemporary fourteen-screen *Video Portrait of Shobana Jeyasingh*, the classical Indian dancer, made for the Camden Arts Centre. From the 1990s St James working solo has made a number of more muted and sometimes disturbing self-portraits (video and still), expressively modifying and distorting his own image using digital technology. The Irish-born artist Vivienne Dick made memorable Super 8 portraits of members of New York's artistic punk subculture in the 1970s such as Lydia Lunch in *She Had Her Gun All Ready* (1978), and returned to the theme in *New York Conversations* (1991) and *London Suite* (1989), in which impromptu dialogue filled out the portrait of a circle of friends.

Warhol's film-primitive approach to portraiture influenced a new generation in the 1990s following the *Andy Warhol: A Retrospective* show at the Hayward Gallery in 1989, with its accompanying screenings of his films at the NFT. His cool detachment suffuses the work of many of the yBa (young British artists) generation, and particularly the films of Gillian Wearing (b.1963), Sam Taylor-Wood (b.1967) and Richard Billingham (b.1970). *English Rose* (1996), made jointly by Wearing with two other rising yBa stars Tracey Emin (b.1963) and Georgina Starr (b.1968), is a witty variant on Warhol's frequent ploy of asking his subjects to impersonate famous personalities. Already rising celebrities themselves, Wearing, Starr and Emin impersonate each other in caricature, subverting fixed portrait-identity while offering an ironic view of success in the art-world. In her solo work, Wearing has taken this role-playing in portraiture to more profound levels, in works such as *2 Into 1* (1996) and *10–16* (1997). In the former, twin sons face the camera and cruelly dissect their mother's character, and she more gently theirs; the artist making the mother provide the synchronised voice for the children's words, and

**107** *2 Into 1*,
Gillian Wearing, 1996

they hers; the effect being humorous, disturbing and doubly revealing of their relationship. Even more disturbingly, in the latter film, children voice their fears and fantasies through the bodies and mouths of mature adults. Wearing made her own contribution to the intoxicated-portrait genre with the multiple-subject three-screen *Drunk* (1999), made as an installation for the Serpentine Gallery. For it, she befriended a group of down-and-outs and transplanted them, plus cans and bottles, into the disorientating white void of a photographer's cyclorama, where they perform awkwardly, emotionally naked, to each other, and to the camera. Her intention was more analytical than that of her predecessors:

> I was interested in capturing the elements of psychological behaviour of the uninhibited.[…]
> Originally I wanted to create a busy group scene, with a mass of characters and different activity
> going on at the same time, like a scene from Bruegel; for it to have the same abandonment and
> lack of inhibition, together with a high level of detail. But then I moved on from that. What I
> wanted was to bring it down to an essence – a pattern of different emotions that people go through
> when drunk – the build-up, the violence, the caring aspect, the falling down and sleeping'.[31]

In *Snapshot* (2005) seven formally contrived (vertically hung) 'portraits' of different women stand in for decades in a single unidentified woman's life, and in their styling reflect seven decades of the society that she was part of; with the woman's rambling spoken reminiscences the only clue to their connection.

More directly indebted to Warhol was Sam Taylor-Wood's portrait *David* (2004), an hour-long video commissioned by the National Portrait Gallery, in which the English football team captain David Beckham is show asleep, naked to the waist. The prone and available body offers Beckham's adoring fans exactly the opportunity for voyeuristic pleasure that Warhol had given himself in *Sleep* (1963), his first film, a six-hour portrait of his lover of the time, the poet John Giorno. Many of the portrait-subjects in Taylor-Wood's films and installation were chosen for a particular facial quality, or some popular association, or both, such as the well-worn face of Marianne Faithful that continuously occupies one of the five screens of her installation *Third Party* (1999).

> She [Faithful] gives the work an immediate feeling of context, which would be difficult to
> express in another way. It would be hard to find a character who looks like they went to all
> those great parties in the 60s, who was a bit of a hippie, took loads of drugs and is now at a
> party in the 90s. But using someone like Marianne Faithful, it's already there'.[32]

Elsewhere, Taylor-Wood focused on the surface expression of emotions as in *Method in Madness* (1995) where an actor recreates an emotional breakdown in response to some unrevealed crisis; a more extreme version of Georgina Starr's tape *Crying* (1993). Richard Billingham's video portraits are less calculated, and more a return to the amateur's intuitive response to the camera and the desire to make a record of close family and friends. Famous for his huge, confrontational but uncritical photographs of his working-class family's chaotic

**108** *Fishtank*,
Richard Billingham, 1988.

and restricted lives, Billingham began in the mid-1990s to made videos in the same environment, not initially intending to show them, but 'using the camcorder to find out how people really speak',[33] thinking the tapes might help him write dialogue for screenplay about his student life. *Liz Smoking* (1998), *Ray in Bed* and *Tony Chopping* (both 1999) are typical of his straightforward titles. *Fishtank* (1988), made for the Illuminations and BBC 2 series *TX,* gathered together a series of such episodes (in some of which a tank of tropical fish appears), which were cut together by Dai Vaughan. Like early sound-period Warhol films, Billingham's portraits are startling in their evidence of the prevalence of non-sequiturs and incoherence in everyday behaviour and patterns of speech. Other portraits by members of the yBa generation include Lucy Gunning's three-monitor *Malcolm, Lloyd, Angela, Jane* (1997), Jaki Irvine's *Margaret Again* (1994) and the remarkable feature-length *Zidane: a 21st Century Portrait* (2006) by Douglas Gordon and Philippe Parveno.

## STILL LIFE

Still life – a genre almost as popular in still photography as in painting – is rare in film, the concept making little sense unless the scene can be animated in some way. Arthur Melbourne Cooper's *Dreams of Toyland* (1908) imagined a still life of children's toys performing a dream-recreation of a busy high-street, the sunlight sweeping across the scene as his stop-frame camera recorded it, adding another inadvertent layer of interest. Le Grice's first film *China Tea* (1965) was a still life of cups and saucers shot with a highly mobile camera, a strategy he repeated a decade later in *Academic Still Life (Cezanne)* (1976), this time more consciously replicating the multiple viewpoints that the Cubists had deduced from the French master. Returning to the theme in the late 1980s, Le Grice took advantage of digital editing technology to permutate different patterns of camera movement in *Digital Still Life* (1988).

Mike Dunford's *Still Life With Pear* (1974) carefully deconstructed the process of its own making (discussed later), while Lucy Gunning unknowingly contributed a gentler structural form in her early Super 8 *Two Tomatoes and a Saucepan Lid* (1991), in which the tomatoes roll about vigorously, asserting life over still-ness. There are several still lives in Sherwin's *Short Film Series,* animated by the movement of the sun recorded in time lapse, or shifts in focus, or of

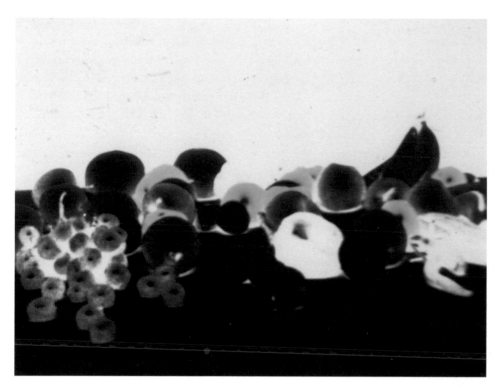

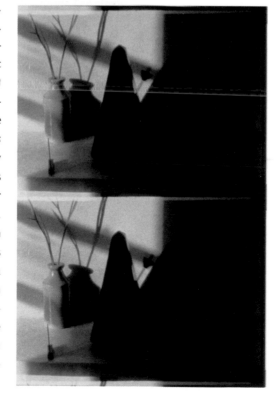

**110 (below)** *Metronome, Candle and Clock*, from *The Short Film Series*, Guy Sherwin, 1976.

aperture (that alter both light and depth of field): *Metronome, Candle and Clock, Vermeer Still Life, Window Frame, Tap* et al. (1975 onwards). Jenny Okun's *Still Life* (1976) reflects on the muta-bility of colour in photography and the elusiveness of photographic truth. Engaging the older medium of painting, she applied paint to the objects in a still life, challenging 'the impossibility of trans-forming an image from colour negative to colour positive on the same filmstock'.[34] Tamara Krikorian's early video still life *Vanitas* (1977) was, as its title suggests, essentially an allegory of the fragility of all images, and is described later. Similarly, Sarah Pucill's still lives such as *You Be Mother (1990)* and *Milk and Glass* (1993) are, in her own words, 'a form of self-portrait' (and again are discussed later). An enigmatic contribution to the genre was made by Graham Young's series *Accidents in the Home* (1984–87) in which still lives are animated by bizarre, unexplained intrusions, for example, a wind-up propeller-plane flying through the scene in slow-motion in *# 17 Gas Fires* (1984). More recently, Sam Taylor-Wood con-tributed *Still Life* (2001) to the genre, a time-lapse study of the rotting of an elaborate composition of fruit, its collapse and growth of mould providing an appropriate reflection upon the corrupt-ibility and temporality of all images.

## COLLAGE

Collage, the Cubist and Dada technique giving new meanings to found fragments, played its part in the development of narrative film in the 1920s and 1930s, as had the insights of psycho-analytic theory. Russian film montage theories, which suggested that in editing the sum of two images could equal more than its parts, to create a 'third' meaning, arrived too late to have much impact on silent cinema in Britain, and arguably only bore fruit in the 1960s in the works of the new international avant-garde of Kenneth Anger, Peter Kubelka, Gregory Markopoulos. But the simpler idea that context can be radically changed by editing, and that

**111** *Crossing the Great Sagrada*, Brunel and Montagu, 1924.

wholly new meanings can be constructed from assembled scraps of found film, has been explored at different times by many film-editors. If the patron saint of montage was Eisenstein, the patron saints of *collage* included in the 1920s Man Ray and Fernand Leger (France), and Esfir Schub and Dziga Vertov (Russia). Like montage, collage flowered again in the 1960s notably in the work of Bruce Conner (USA), Gianfranco Barucello and Alberto Griffi (Italy), and in the 1990s of Martin Arnold (Austria) and Yervant Gianiccian and Angela Ricci-Lucchi (Italy). Man Ray's assemblages of cinematic scraps were well known to Film Society members as was Léger's *Le Ballet mécanique,* and Vertov's *Enthusiasm, Symphony of the Don Basin* (1931) was shown by the Film Society in the year of its making, though Schub's classic feature-length work assembled from news-reels *The Fall of the Romanoff Dynasty* (1927) wouldn't become known in Britain till the 1970s. Of these, *Le Ballet mécanique,* with its abrupt cuts and relentless repetitions, and Vertov's *Man with a Movie Camera* (1929), with its active camera-eye and sections of programmatic editing,[35] became key reference works for the structuralists of the 1970s. Bruce Conner's *A Movie* (1958), a collage of shots of the precarious and the disastrous that builds from the humorous to the apocalyptic (made when he was working for the film archivist/collector Raymond Rohauer) was among the films he exhibited at the Robert Fraser Gallery in London in the late 1960s, in a show primarily dedicated to his collaged reliefs and sculptures. *A Movie* may have inspired Scotty's first collage films (dicussed later), but its influence would be mostly felt on successive generations of MTV music-video makers across the globe.

Adrian Brunel (1892–1958), as the Film Society member with responsibility for inter-titling foreign-language films, was fully aware how sequence could alter meaning, and exploited this knowledge in a series of ten 'burlesques' (skits) made during the 1920s, many of them jointly with fellow-founder Ivor Montagu (1904–84). *Crossing the Great Sagrada* (1924), a parody of *Crossing the Great*

*Sahara* of the same year and of the whole contemporary genre of travelogue/expedition films,
was largely assembled from found-footage
linked by elaborate intertitles: a stock-shot of
Venice's Bridge of Sighs standing in for
'Blackfriars Bridge', an African shoreline cap-
tioned as 'Wapping', and so on.[36] *Cut it Out*
(1925) made fun of the film censor's obsession
with domestic propriety; *So This is Jolly Good*
(1925) mocked the pretensions of an already
failing commercial industry. One of the last,
*Brunel and Montagu* (1928), is a one-minute
one-line-joke response to the imminent arrival
of talking pictures; convinced of financial ruin,
the pair commit suicide by jumping off their

**112** *A Study in Movement*,
C. Denis Pegge, 1948

Wardour Street office roof, but take a bow a moment later, through the magic of cinema.
The happy reprieve was misplaced, for in the event their inter-titling and editing company
(known informally as Brunel and Montage) was out of business within a year, killed, so Brunel
felt, by the coming of sound.

C. Denis Pegge's *A Study in Movement* (1948) is a both a historical curiosity and a small
mystery. An assemblage of shots 'from cine-magazines' of poodles being paraded in a formal
garden, clouds, ships, steam engines and workers making things with machines, it was edited
to stress similarities in patterns of movement, and incidentally gives a picture of a dog-
obsessed, class-divided Britain. No-one else was working like this at the time. Pegge would
seem to have been a writer/occasional film-maker (one of several in this history), and here he
may have worked with an industry editor (his earlier published novel-length scenario for a film
'poem' *Bombay Riots*[37] has an introduction by the feature director Anthony Asquith, so he certainly had friends in the industry). But did this film ever get exhibited publicly? Little is
recorded.

Collage's potential for surreal revelation through disturbing juxtapositions, latent in Pegge's
film, is fully realised in the works of Robert Stuart Short (b.1938), who started his first film *Bois-
Charbons,* a study of Paris street signs and graffiti, in 1956 and completed it (with the benefit
of the fresh contributions from recent civil unrest) in 1968. Short is a pre-eminent scholar of
surrealism[38], and most of his films such as *Barbareveuse* and *The Voluptuous Martyrdoms of
the Magnificent Masturbators* (both 1971) have taken the form of collages of shots, still images
and whole sequences from Hollywood, mostly re-filmed from the screen. He wrote:

> This solitary nocturnal activity grew out of and continues to go alongside the making of
> collages, assemblages events and performances. Both by choice and necessity [this] is a
> cinema of poverty which celebrates the intimate peculiarities of the 8mm gauge with total
> conviction. It shares the surrealists' suspicion of formalism, over-determined means, cheap

sentiment naturalism and overt political commitment. In love with the virtualities of the film, it presents a stream of night thoughts about movies that might have been. Its monsters and its martyrs, definitively expelled from their original framework in the narrative cinema, assume new identities and borrow new meanings'.[39]

His *arte povera* method had its contemporary counterpart in the work of Barucelllo and Griffi, and further back, in the collage films of the American artist Joseph Cornell.

Working in the early 1960s, Don Levy (b.1932–d.198?) had his own supply of documentary material to draw from when making his *Five Short Film Poems* (prosaically re-titled by the BFI *Don Levy Programme* 1967). As well as the out-takes and discarded footage from two films he had made for the Nuffield Foundation *Time Is* (1964) and *Crafts of Fez* (1967), and *Opus: Impressions of British Art & Culture* (1967) for the British Council, he was able to use test shots from his ambitious feature film *Herostratus,* still in progress. The *Poems* were probably made as a form of light relief during the latter's protracted birth-struggles (see below), but the wit and sharpness of their image-by-image counterpoint with words or sounds makes Levy's subsequent withdrawal from film-making after the trauma of *Herostratus* the more regrettable.[40]

Artists associated with structural cinema and Scratch video similarly plundered found footage for its ready-made meanings that could be used as building-blocks in collage, or for their inherent rhythms, or both. Le Grice's contributions starting with his collection of scrap footage *Castle One* (1966) are discussed later; other examples include Chris Garratt's *Commercial Break* (1980), a rhythmic re-cutting of a primitive *Daz* commercial, and Steve Hawley and Tony Steyger's *Drawing Conclusions – the Science Mix* (1982) which similarly chopped up and mixed two washing machine commercials, one contemporary, one from the 1950s. Scratch video, a phenomenon of the first half of the 1980s, involved the 'sampling' and repeating found images and sounds recorded from broadcast television, often using domestic editing equipment, thereby making a new work. *Gorilla Tapes* was the collective name of Scratch video artists Jon Dovey, Gavin Hodge, Jean McClements and Tim Morrison, who met at the video workshop at Luton and made an immediate impact with their sharp, no-budget political tapes, collaged from old film footage and the TV news imagery of the mid-Thatcher years. In *Commander in Chief* (1984) they cut up President Reagan's Normandy Beach speech and, by deleting key words, turned his supposed defence of liberty into a nakedly imperialist manifesto, thus 'reveal[ing] the true message behind the man-

**113** *Commander in Chief,*
Gorilla Tapes, 1984.

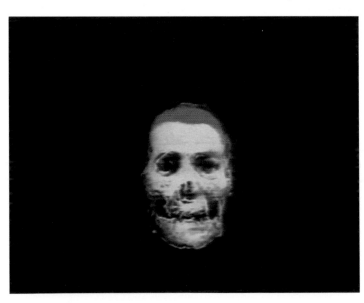

ufactured mediation of News and politics',
according to a group statement. The success of
their Thatcher/Reagan collage satire *Death Valley
Days* (1984), which made productive use of
Reagan's years as a Hollywood actor, gained
them commissions from Channel Four's *The
Media Show,* after which their energy ran out
(and academia beckoned) – though Hodge
made an excellent homage-documentary on
their spiritual master in *Zygosis – John Heartfield*
(1988). Other exponents included the Duvet
Brothers – Rik Lander and Peter Boyd McLean
(*Blue Monday* and *Laughing Girls*, both 1984) –
and George Barber. Barber was always the most
polished of these artists, and *Tilt* (1983) showed

his ability to make seductive, easy-viewing pieces from feature film fragments overlaid with
his own imagery, while maintaining a subversive undercurrent in his rapid-fire cut-ups such
as *Yes Frank No Smoke* (1984). Sandra Goldbacker and Kim Flitcroft were other contributors to the successful VHS publishing venture led by Barber, *The Greatest Hits of Scratch
Video Vols 1 & 2* (1985/6).

The two collage films made by Paul Bush (b.1956), in a career that has included animation and live action, constitute a more radical return to Schub's practice of carving a new
narrative out of pre-existing images. *Lost Images* (1990) was made in response to an invitation to make a one-minute film for screening on late night television. He proposed a précis
of a day's viewing in the form of sixty one-second fragments extracted from the transmitted programmes, to be assembled on the day of transmission, and selected on the basis of their

visual strength alone. *Rumour of True Things*
(1996), also made for television, presented a
journey through the modern world entirely constructed from non-fiction footage. 'The images
were not made by me, but by other filmmakers,
specialists from other areas such as doctors,
radiologists and the military. They are things
the public never see. My idea was to put these
records together in an attempt to make a portrait
of Western society'.[41] They revealed an unre-
liable world, bereft of human contact, where
objects and even colours seemed to take on
non-naturalistic meanings.

In the 1990s, the film archive (or, by this
time, the video store) also proved a fertile feed-

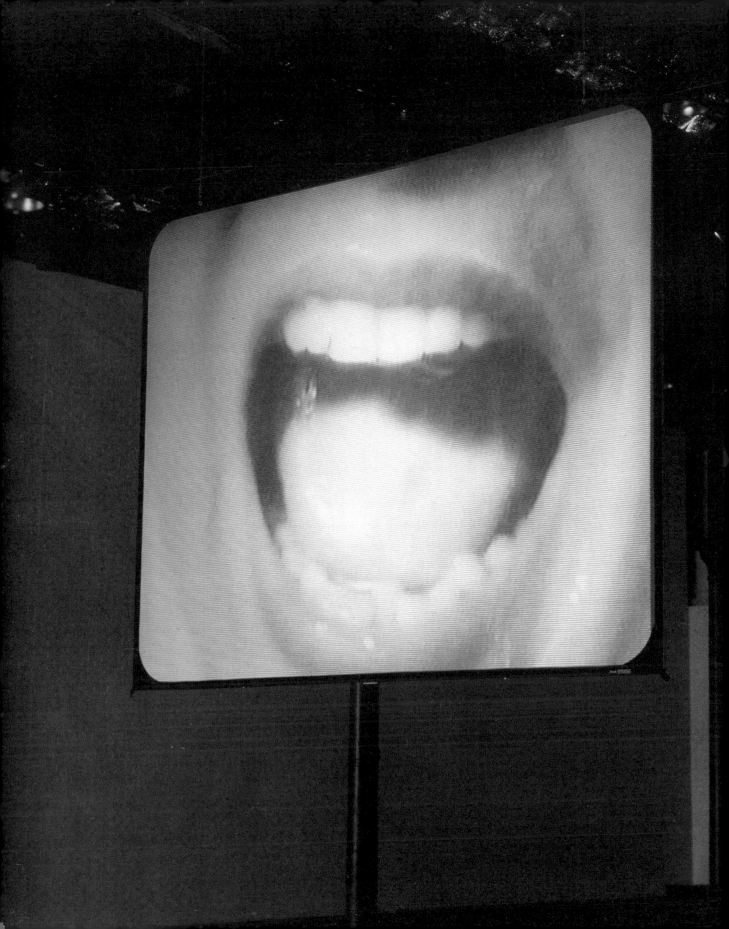

ing ground for the yBa generation, especially Douglas Gordon (b.1966) and Mark Dean (b.1958). Gordon looked afresh at existing footage, re-timing it in his slowed-down version of Hitchcock's film, his *24 Hour Psycho* (1993), duplicating its imagery across two screens as in *Through the Looking Glass* (1999) (Travis Bickle, with gun at the mirror: 'You talkin' to me?') or playing the same sequences on two more screens with a delay or at different speeds, as in *Déjà-Vu* (2000) which nicely confuses any narrative logic in the film noir *D.O.A.* (1950). Rarely, but strikingly, he rescues some sense of humanity in potentially voyeuristic imagery taken from medical archives by engaging the viewer's empathy, as in his *10ms1* (1994), a man struggling to stand up, or *Hysterical* (1995), a bizarrely masked woman fainting in the arms of two male attendants. Pleasure gained from the guilt implicit in cinematic voyeurism is closer to his heart, and exemplified in the throw-away (and paradoxically *not*-archive footage) *A Divided Self I & II* (a new take on fist-fucking). His image-making, like Hitchcock's, reflects an incomplete escape from a sternly religious childhood, with good and evil still slogging it out in the background. This is never more clear than in his brilliant *Between Darkness and Light (after William Blake)* (1997), in which two feature films *The Song of Bernadette* (Henry King 1943) and *The Exorcist* (William Friedkin, 1973) – saint and devil – do battle projected onto the same translucent screen, back to back, with their images and soundtracks merging. The result is an ever-changing (thanks to unequal-length loops), chaotic but productive interweaving of different representations of possession and spirituality, in which the chance combinations of dialogue and the choreography of camera and action are sometimes astonishingly apt. By contrast, Mark Dean's appropriations from Hollywood are more like votive offerings; tiny scraps of footage – a gesture by Judy Garland, a *look* by Brando – isolated and looped to drain them of any hint of narrative (other than the broad narrative of celebrity), so we can adore and worship. Dean's art is in his twin-screen (or multi-screen) pairing of images, which set in place little new ideas, neatly summarised in his titles: *Nothing To Worry About (Easy Rider/Frenzy-6)* (1996), *Scorpio Rising 2 (The Gospel According to St Matthew/Hells Angels on Wheels)* (1998), *Carrio/On (Carrie/Carry On)* (2001).

## POP ART

Pop Art liberated British painting in the 1950s and early 1960s from the social realist concerns of the 'Kitchen Sink' school, by drawing upon 'a visual octave outside the range of fine art' in painter Richard Smith's phrase; an 'octave' which included many borrowings from cinema and television imagery. While the movement arrived too early to result in many films by artists – the apparatus of film-making was still too rarely available – it profoundly changed attitudes towards art-making, and in due course would help propel the explosion of filmmaking of the 1970s. Of this change, the critic John Russell wrote:

> for many though not all of its participants, Pop was a resistance movement: a classless com-
> mando which was directed against the Establishment in general, and the art-Establishment in
> particular. It was against the old-style museum-man, the old-style critic, the old-style dealer
> and the old-style art-collector. ([Rayner] Banham later described its success as 'the revenge of

**116 (opposite)** *24 Hour Psycho*, Douglas Gordon, 1993

the elementary schoolboys'.) Much of the English art-world at that time was distinctly and unforgivably paternalistic. Pop was meant as a cultural break, signifying the firing-squad, without mercy or reprieve, for the kind of people who believed in the Loeb classics, holidays in Tuscany, drawings by Augustus John, signed pieces of French furniture, leading articles in *The Daily Telegraph* and very good clothes that lasted for ever.[42]

The first artist of the Pop generation to work with film was Richard Smith, whose *Trailer* (1960), apparently consisted of appreciative close-ups of consumer expendables such as cigarette packets, soda siphons, watches, cakes and car-tyres, 'shot more in the style of Busby Berkeley than Eisenstein'. Though the film is now lost, its imagery is reflected in two paintings bearing the same title.

Eduardo Paolozzi (1924–2005) provided British Pop with its richest image-source. His magpie collection of illustrations and diagrams torn from nineteenth-century books, instruction manuals, American magazines, advertising and packaging, filled his *Scrapbooks* of 1947–52 and 1960–62, and fed his series of cut-and-paste collages and prints, collectively called *Bunk*. He shared his scrapbook material with friends and colleagues in the form of a proto-cinematic performance at the first meeting of the Independent Group at the ICA in Dover Street in 1952, using an epidiascope projector that allowed movement and rapid substitutions under the lens. The photographer Nigel Henderson describes Paolozzi 'struggling for words' during the show 'because he considered the works' powers of association to be self-evident.[43] Paolozzi's first animated film *History of Nothing* (1963) draws from the same visual

**117** *History of Nothing*,
Eduardo Paolozzi, 1963

archive, and allows him to construct loose chains of image-associ-
ation and mini-narrative events, but it lacks the pop colours of the
originals (it was shot in black and white presumably to save money),
and suffers from slightly monotonous pacing. *Kakafon Kakoon*
(1965) has colour and a score by Elizabeth Lutyens, but was made
from the later post-Pop lithographs, and was shot by a commercial company, which introduced gimmicky focus changes and
erratic camera movements.[44] Film never did Paolozzi justice.

A more cinematic transposition between painting/print-making
and film was made in *Richard Hamilton* (1969), ostensibly a documentary about the most cerebral of British Pop artists, made for
the Arts Council by James Scott, in fact a collaboration of equals,
made without commentary, which brilliantly inter-cuts clips from
Hollywood movies, American magazine ads and newsreels with
related images from Hamilton's paintings. Scott's similar collaboration with Ron Kitaj of 1967 was suppressed at the latter's
insistence, and his *The Great Ice-Cream Robbery* (1971) which
records Claes Oldenburg's response to London at the time of his Tate
retrospective (and an encounter between the police and the epony-
mous ice-cream salesman) is more conventional, despite its two
screen format and use of Oldenburg's Super 8 home-movie
footage[45]. Ken Russell's *Pop Goes the Easel* (1962) made for the
BBC's *Monitor* arts series, which saluted the RCA Pop-generation

**118** *Sailing Through*,
Nicholas Munro, 1971.

graduates Peter Phillips, Derek Boshier, Peter Blake and Pauline Boty, with its absence of
commentary similarly transcends the documentary form, and was remarkable for its time.
Boshier (b1937) himself made *Link* (1971), a slightly literal-minded (and sexist) chain of visual
associations between disparate pop-culture signs and images, and Nicolas Munro recorded
the surreal sight of the ten plastic-coloured boat-sculptures that constitute his *Regatta Piece*,
adrift in a sea of ripe barley in *Sailing Through* (1971), both forming part of the Arts Council's
experiment in giving artists money to document their own work.

Arguably the most successful film-making Pop artist is Jeff Keen (b.1923), maker of over forty
films in as many years, though he is rarely mentioned by art historians in discussions of the
movement. Keen draws on the imagery of popular culture more consistently than even Paolozzi,
but his work has a subversive and aggressive edge not generally shared by Pop, which derives from
his co-allegiance to Surrealism and even Dada. His first important film *The Autumn Feast* (1961),
made with the Italian poet Piero Heliczer, is a *flâneur* film, the poet and the cameraman stalking
the street, and seizing the image, to the accompaniment of Heliczer's poetic off-screen ram-
blings. Heliczer moved on to join Andy Warhol and Jack Smith's wide circle in New York, and
provides an interesting physical link between Keen and these similarly productive recyclers of
Hollywood kitsch. Keen subscribes to Pop's enthusiasm for comic-book imagery, but is as much
attracted by the iconic status of comic-book heroes and villains, as by the graphics that frame them.

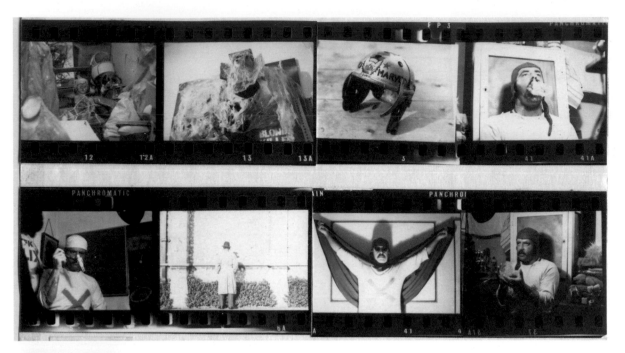

Baudelaire wrote a thing on … children's attitudes to toys. The fact that they were richly coloured and that children couldn't resist picking them up and playing. And I think that's the great thing about comics. They … have that kind of, not exactly primitive quality, but they are outside the world of bourgeoisie art … I like the fact that they were printed so badly, the colours overlapping; it gave them a certain rawness. They were [also] hermetic! … They obey a law unto themselves – you get Doll Man and Plastic Man and you know they are going to act in a certain physical way. Plastic Man would burst from frame to frame and go through the story – a kind of driving force. Those early characters were creatures of instinct acting directly, as distinct from characters in novels who are always questioning their feelings.[46]

In an interview with A.L. Rees, Keen identifies the driven, one-dimensional characters that populate his films with the heroes and heroines of the ancient myths and dramas.[47] In the multi-episode *Mad Love* (1978) these mythic creatures act out classic scenes of *l'amour fou* drawn from cinema, literature and art: *Picasso's Birthday, Return of the Wasp Woman, Bandits of Love*. The films' bizarre costumes, lurid colour, comic-like sets, graphics and jokes seduce the viewer with their Pop Art charm; while the rapid editing, layers of superimposition, and aggressive soundtrack deliver a Dada slap in the face. Keen describes *White Dust* (1972) as:

a home movie/serial edited and superimposed in the camera, filmed with no script and no post-cutting. [He is the ultimate 'no-budget' film-maker.] The film opens with a series of establishing shots: the sea – the actors – certain streets. From these images narrative threads emerge and dissolve again – through linking tableaux and film-star poses – to celebrate the lost world of adventure serials and B-Movies.[48]

Extending his homage to cheap Hollywood, he makes photocopied 'books of the films' and cardboard cut-out sculptures of film characters that in another world might grace the fleapit foyer.

Anthony Scott ('Scotty', b.1941), a conceptual artist whose star shone brightly but briefly in the late 1960s, more literally appropriated the imagery of film and television. Details of his contribution to the Destruction in Art Symposium (DIAS 1966) are unrecorded, but perhaps anticipated the 'Metamorphosis of Art Catalogues into Art Object' (through the act of shredding) he staged at the Lisson Gallery in May 1968. His film-making reversed this process – and involved gathering found footage from amateur film sales and film-industry waste-bins, and splicing it together. His first Super 8 film *Our Honeymoon Winter Sports Atomic Bomb Explosion* (1967) took four years to make and exhausted his interest in constructive montage. In 1968 he announced the multi-form *The Longest Most Meaningless Movie in the World* – a wholly random assemblage of footage – allowing endless opportunities for the chance encounters that so pleased the Surrealist filmgoers.

**119** Jeff Keen: (opposite top) *Marvo Movie*, 1978, (opposite below) *The Cartoon Theatre of Dr Gaz*, 1979 and (above) the book-of-the-film, *Mad Love*, 1978.

The 35mm version [he made others in 16mm, 8mm and promised even a 9.5mm one] … includes sections of still photographs. A beautiful 16-frame sequence of a stencilled 'NCR NEW YORK' contributed by George Brecht. Peter Howe has contributed most of the stills footage, but he doesn't do very much work on 35mm these days. 'The dagger enters the heart of the man who doesn't pay his taxes, and the hunchback sings from the bell-tower, while the nightclub announcer swings into the pool on a microphone lead'. World premiere of the first 16 reels (approx. five hours) of the *Movie* happened at the Arts Lab London Thursday August 8th 1968 at 8.30p.m. It all began with a wheel of fire, one flame after another, until a composite combustion was arrived at, at the end of part one. After *cine-verite, projection-verite*; projecting images onto street scenes, up warehouse walls, onto clouds, chase people about with projector mounted on a bogey like a studio TV camera.[49]

(The latter a reference to the fact that after its premiere screening in the Arts Lab's seatless basement cinema, the portable projector was moved into the ground floor gallery, where it ran continuously – sometimes projecting out through the front window – during all opening hours for the next eight days.) Scotty and his films appeared everywhere in the late 1960s, but he vanished after the 1970 Festival, leaving his *Swiz* magazines (another pop-culture collage project) as his only visible legacy.

## ABSURD

Running in parallel with Pop – and sometimes feeding it – was an older strand of playful-
ness in film-making that celebrated shaggy dogs, the fey and the absurd, and could trace its
artistic roots back to the music hall and beyond. Massingham (*And So To Work*) and Montagu
(*Bluebottles*) contributed pre-war examples to the genre, but among the first post-war exponents were the visiting American artist James Broughton and the indigenous Bruce Lacey.

   Broughton (1913–99) arrived in Britain to attend a screening of his films at the 1951
Edinburgh Film Festival, and finding himself among sympathetic film-enthusiasts, Wright,
Anderson and Denis Forman in London, stayed and made *The Pleasure Garden* (1952–3),
an extended parable of love/life-spirit repressed then finally released, featuring his lover of the
time Kermit Sheets as the apparently heterosexual pan-figure. The ruined gardens of Crystal
Palace provided the location, and the film's astonishing cast of British character actors caught
in their youth included Hattie Jacques (sublime as a balletic fairy godmother), John Le Mesurier
(chief grouse), Jill Bennett *et al.*, and in a bit part, the film-maker's mentor and producer
Lindsay Anderson. When finances ran out, the project was rescued by Basil Wright's mother,
Forman secured an empty government cutting-room, and 'Michael Balcon of Ealing Films
loaned us handcuffs, a hearse and a base fiddle, while enough members of the British Board
of Film Censors portrayed the official spoilsports.'[50] The film opened to favourable reviews (engi-

**120** *The Pleasure Garden*,
James Broughton, 1952–3.
(BFI Stills Collection)

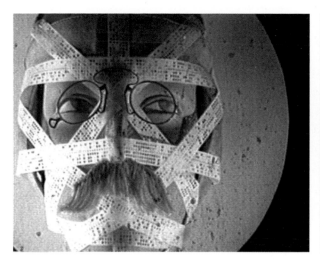

neered by Anderson's flatmate Gavin Lambert of *Sight and Sound*) and went on to receive a special prize at Cannes in 1954, presented to Broughton's delight by Jean Cocteau.

**121** *Everybody's Nobody*, Bruce Lacey and John Sewell, 1960

Bruce Lacey (b.1927) began his involvement with film while at Hornsey School of Art, in a series of films written and directed by the influential BBC graphic designer John Sewell, Lacey acting, developing storylines and designing sets and costumes. In *Head in Shadow* (1951) he played a blind innocent adrift in Islington, and in *Agib and Agab* (1954) contributed to a bizarre Arabian Nights fantasy. Still with Sewell, *Everybody's Nobody* (1960) introduces and systematically explored the Lacey automaton persona – now fully integrated with graphic sets and shot, lit and edited with great style. Lacey also contributed props and costumes to other productions including the music series *Cool for Cats* (Associated Rediffusion TV, 1956–61) and Dick Lester's early short *The Running, Jumping and Standing Still Film* (1962), a mixture of a more theatrical whimsy with the anarchy of the radio comics *The Goons*. From the mid-1960s his partner and collaborator was Jill Bruce and he shot his own films, making a *How To ...* series *Kiss 1* (1967), *2* (1968) and *How to Have a Bath* (1971), describing them as 'documents of human behaviour (for the benefit of Martians)',[51] the latter knowingly recapitulating the theme of Massingham's wartime instructional film *The Five Inch Bather*. Often Lacey presented his films as part of a live theatrical performance, and many featured his robot persona. He chose to work without establishment support, and to remain and operate in what most people would then have described as the amateur sphere of 8mm production. Using friends as cast and crew and organising his own screenings, he passed round a hat for contributions in what would become a time-honoured fundraising model for many film-making artists thereafter. An exception was *The Lacey Rituals* (1973), an introduction to family life featuring Bruce, Jill and their children, which was funded by the Arts Council. He also contributed to stage shows such as *An Evening of British Rubbish* with the Alberts, Ivor Cutler and Joyce Grant at the Comedy Theatre in 1974.

In the 1970s, the painter Jock McFadyen (an Anne Rees-Mogg protégé) contributed a clutch of films, including the Lacey-like *How to Fall Asleep* (1976), and his wicked re-enactment of the Joyce McKinney Mormon-abduction case *The Case Continues* (1980) based on *The Times*

**122** *How to have a Bath*, Bruce Lacey and Jill Bruce, 1971.

court transcripts, with Helen Chadwick superb as Joyce pursuing her reluctant man. Contributors in the 1990s have included Matt Hulse, Roz Mortimer, Roddy Buchannan and, in their rare and surprisingly light-hearted film excursions, Jake and Dinos Chapman. And in Georgina Starr's object-strewn installations – *Hypnodreamstuff* (1996), *Tuberama* (1998) etc., – one fully expects Bruce Lacey (surely her spiritual father) to make his appearance.[52]

Andrew Kötting (b.1959), active since the late 1980s, has been identified as a committed absurdist, but the surface chaos and anarchy of his films conceal the instincts of a perceptive documentary-maker. Like Larcher, he sees film-making as an extension of his life, his encounters and the activities of his extended family, though where Larcher, the traveller, pursues and documents new experiences, Kötting is the natural outsider who seeks out other misfits and eccentrics, and gives them voice. An early work *Klipperty Klopp* (1984), described by Kötting as 'A post punk piece of pagan sensibility, complete with bestiality, buggery and boundless energy', seems like a fragment, repeated aimlessly but compellingly *ad infinitum*, while *Hub-bub in the Boababs* (1989) contained the first indication of Kötting's extraordinarily acute ear for accents and the vernacular, as the film-maker 'wanders aimlessly' in a forest, besieged by voices 'bombarding him with their folkloric wisdom'. *Acumen* (1990) and *Hoi Polloi* (1990/91, two versions) introduce the first of many invented characters burdened with the clutter of life, 'buried under large piles of their own memorabilia, [and] the weight of their self-importance'.[53] He gained a wider audience and success with his first feature film *Gallivant* (1996), which sent his grandmother Gladys and his own disabled child on a tour of Britain's coastal resorts, recording their encounters with other appropriately marginal characters in a film that was less joyfully anarchic than its predecessors.

**123** *Hoi Polloi*, Andrew Kötting, 1990/91.

## PSYCHEDELIC

Attempts to translate the visual experience of 1960s drug consumption into film resulted in few works of note. In all ways an exception was Mark Boyle's record of a lightshow *Beyond Image* (1969) with music by Soft Machine, of a kind he memorably produced at the UFO club in the mid-1960s. The film was originally shown in a 360-degree projected environment at the ICA, to launch their exhibition *Journey to the Surface of the Earth*,[54] but probably few UFO 'trippers' recognised its relationship to other Boyle Family's projections and performances that included *Son et Lumière Bodily Fluids and Functions*, and *Son et Lumière for Insects, Reptiles and Winter Creatures* (both 1966). Other contemporary documents include the composer Michael Nyman's *Love Love Love* (1964), Anne Rees-Mogg's film of bubbles *Nothing is Something* (1966), Anthony Stern's aggressively pixillated (stop-frame) and solarised *San Francisco* (1968) set to Pink Floyd's 'Interstellar Overdrive', Peter Turner's *Head Rag Hop* (1970) and Arthur John's *Solarflares Burn for You* (1973) with music by Soft Machine's Robert Wyatt. Gordon Payne's film of varying-paced strobe effects that caused 'blink-rate confusion' *Tantra 1* (c.1968), was a product of Latimer's Light-Sound workshop at Hornsey. Other films shown in the 1960s may not have survived; they include the gallery owner Robert Fraser's *Tantra*

**124** *Beyond Image*, Mark Boyle, 1969.

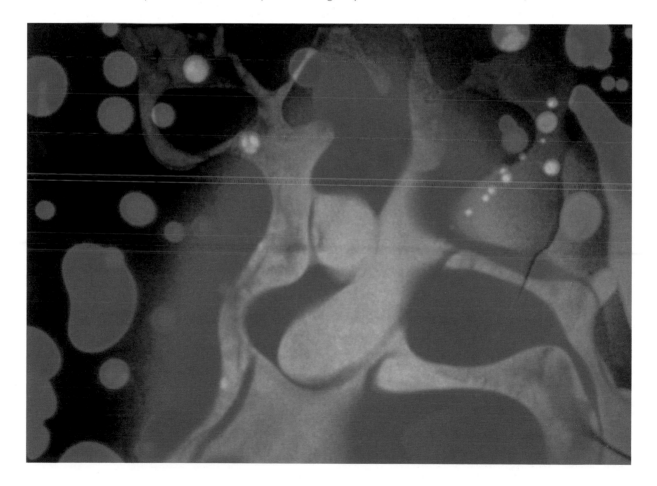

**125 (above)** *Solarflares Burn for You*, Arthur John, 1973.

**126 (above right)** *Head Rag Hop*, Peter Turner 1970.

**127** *83B*, William Turnbull and Allan Forbes, 1951.

(1968) (presumably made on his trip to India?), and Barbara Rubin's record of her time in London with Allen Ginsberg, *Allen for Allen, London, is Peter* (1966).

## SCULPTORS' FILMS

Several artists and film-makers perceived an affinity between sculpture and film during British sculpture's productive 1950s and 1960s. *83B* (1951) was one of two films made by sculptor William Turnbull (b.1922) with film-maker Allan Forbes. It records the shadows cast by Turnbull's sculptures on his studio's walls and ceiling in response to a moving light-source, made even more kinetic by camera movements and fast-paced editing, in counterpoint with percussive, abstracted sounds. Remarkably, the film and its sound were designed to be performed backwards as well as forwards. Dudley Shaw Ashton's *Figures in a Landscape* (1953) funded jointly by the Arts Council and the BFI's Experimental Film Fund and made with Barbara Hepworth's participation, drew analogies between a sculptural group by Hepworth and its out-

**128** Dudley Shaw Ashton
and Barbara Hepworth
during the making of *Figures
in a Landscape*, 1953. (BFI
Stills Collection)

door site, and established how choreography of the film camera could direct and control the
viewer's spatial experience of sculpture. Shaw Ashton himself acknowledged the influence of
the choreographic films of Maya Deren, with whom he corresponded later in the 1950s.[55] Other
sculptors used the camera to record the many stages in the creation of a work, perhaps
encouraged by seeing the evolution of paintings recorded in François Campaux's *Matisse*
(1946) or Henri-Georges Clouzot's *Le Mystere Picasso* (1956), which pioneered the idea and
were widely seen and admired. More recent but at the time less well-known examples
included Robert Smithson's *Spiral Jetty* (USA 1970), Rebecca Horn's *Einhorn* (1970) and
Gordon Matta-Clark's records of sculptural/environmental interventions, *Open House* (1972),
*Splitting* (1974) etc. The English contributions included William Pye's *From Scrap to Sculpture*
(1971), Barry Flanagan's *The Works* (c.1970) and Liliane Lijn's *What is the Sound of One
Hand Clapping* (1973). Pye's later *Reflections* (1972) re-interpreted an existing work, successfully dematerialising its solid mass, using a special camera-mount designed by the sculptor

**129** Peter Dockley shooting *Cast*, 1971, and (right) a contemporary publicity card.

to enable disorientating rotations, creating a film of surfaces – water, landscape and the sculpture's polished chromium.

Graham Stevens was one of several artists in the 1960s to work with inflatables – giant air-filled polythene tubes, squares and cylinders that floated on air or water or bounced across the ground – that exemplified a new 'immaterial' approach to art-making. His films *Atmosfields* (1971) and *Desert Cloud* (1975) record his fascination with the interaction of air and thin membranes, and document the public's response to this mutating and inevitably fugitive sculptural form. *Spaced* (1969–70) recorded a performance around a sculptural installation and performance by Peter Dockley at the Roundhouse with music by Soft Machine. Ephemeral effects and the process of change also were the subject of Peter Dockley's *Cast* (1971), and a series of films made by the American Bill Lundberg including *Corner Fire*, *Two Studies*, *Fire Constructions* (all 1973) and *Noumenon* (1974). In *Cast*, Dockley arranged a number of life-size wax figures around a table decked with bread and wine, as if a moment in time had been frozen. The film scrutinises this tableau in detail as the figures begin to melt in response to an unseen heat-source, and eventually collapse, in a grotesque metaphor of human vulnerability. The interaction of beams of light with fire, smoke and steam were documented by Lundberg (b.1942) who used these elements to define and sometimes animate confined architectural spaces; changes in aperture and focus adding to the sense of near-scientific exploration. These works were exhibited in the context of the Arts Council's *Art Film Tour*, but had limited subsequent exposure, and none of these sculptors persisted with film.

The exception was David Hall. *Vertical* (1970) marks the moment when Hall (b.1937) realised that the moving image, rather than wood and steel, would be his medium. His sculpture in the mid-1960s had explored perspective and the perception of space through constructions and interventions, such as a 'drawing' made on the floor of the ICA gallery using a floor-sanding machine, for the show *Sculpture Out of the Sixties* (1970). Hall saw film and photography as creating 'a new kind of reality … causing perceptual assumptions to be made that are as established as those used to perceive the real world. It is the manipu-

lation of these perceptual notions that forms the basis of *Vertical*'.[56] Hall photographs a series of man-made structures in the landscape, using the camera's position and orientation to determine the viewer's reading of perspective; setting up perceptual notions, then, by moving the camera, disclosing the illusion. His own interest very rapidly moved on to the making of works which consider the nature of television and its position in most people's lives, which became his central preoccupation, leaving others, notably Tony Hill and some of the artists associated with structural film, to continue to explore the interplay of camera and perspective.

## ABSTRACTION

The pursuit of a language of abstract form was another preoccupation carried over into film from painting, though it arrived in this new context at the end of the 1920s, long after the first abstract Vorticist paintings of 1913–14, and the first exhibitions of abstract art from Europe c.1911.[57] One of the reasons for film's slow start was, as always, lack of individual access to an already industry-controlled technology, though the delay was equally pronounced in photography where technology was available; for example Alvin Langdon Coburn's Vortographs only appeared in 1917.

**131** *Abstract Kinetic Painting with Sound*, Duncan Grant, 1914 (Tate Gallery).

The one surviving abstract moving-image work made before the First World War was the *Abstract Kinetic Painting with Sound* (1914) by Duncan Grant (1885–1978), a scroll-painting which explores the changing relationship of a group of geometric shapes through seventeen permutations, to be seen moving from left to right through a little proscenium arch, moved by a motor and accompanied by the music of J. S. Bach. Its flat geometric imagery reflects the short-lived contemporary interest in abstraction shared by Grant's Bloomsbury circle of artists and writers.[58] The work appears not to have been publicly exhibited, and Grant may have been discouraged from further experiments in this area by D. H. Lawrence's thinly disguised mocking portrait of both him and the scroll in *Lady Chatterley's Lover*.[59]

**132 (below right)** *Light Rhythms*, Francis Bruguière and Oswell Blakeston, 1930.

**133 (below and opposite top)** Experimental patterns created by nutmeg grater, Oswell Blakeston, c. 1931.

By the late 1920s, the climate had changed – not least through the efforts of the Film Society – though abstract films were still few in number, and have since been further depleted by accident and loss. The earliest surviving wholly abstract film, *Light Rhythms* (1930), first shown at the Film Society, was made by the partnership of American-born photographer Francis Bruguière (1879–1945) and painter/writer Oswell Blakeston (Henry Joseph Hasslacher 1907–85). Its imagery combines the dramatically lit, cut-and-folded paper shapes familiar from Bruguière's photographic works of 1925 onwards, and the rayogram (cameraless exposure) experiments of

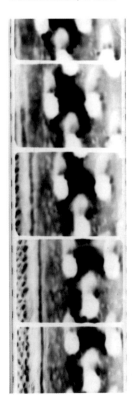

Blakeston, a few of which appeared in *Close Up*. In six sequences, a sharply moving light-source causes dramatic movement of surface-shadows on Bruguiere's cut-and-folded paper abstract compositions, and a scheme of superimpositions adds complexity to the image, further enlivened by a percussive piano score by Jack Ellitt. Whether Bruguière and Blakeston knew of Laszlo Moholy-Nagy's *Ein Lichtspiel schwarz-weiss-grau* (*Lightplay, black-white-grey*) made in Germany the same year, before embarking on their film, or he of theirs, is unrecorded. Both take a sculptural form (in Moholy's case his kinetic *Light Prop or Modulator* sculpture of 1922–30), and embroider the image through dissolves and multiple superimpositions to create a rhythmic, kinetic image. Moholy's film wasn't shown at the Film Society till November 1932, but its existence was widely known. Other film experiments by Blakeston and Bruguière exist only as isolated frames, and no other complete works appear to have survived.[60]

Moholy-Nagy (Hungary 1895–USA 1946) visited the Film Society at the end of 1933 to show his *A.B.C. in Sound* (Germany 1933), an alphabet of sounds derived from visual motifs, and his film-diary *Architectural Congress* (1933) which records the progress through the Mediterranean of delegates to the Congrès International d'Architecture Moderne in Athens aboard the *Patris II*,[61] and while in London sold some leftover footage from *Lightplay* to the GPO for inclusion as an emblem of 'modernity' in *The Coming of the Dial* (Stuart Legg, 1933). He returned to London to study colour film technology at Kodak in 1934 and took up residence in 1935, finding employment mostly as a photographer and designer, his abstract film work being limited to some sculptural light-pattern special effects for Alexander Korda's production *Things to Come* (1936). His interest in film and modernism took a different form in the documentary *The New Architecture at the London Zoo* (1936), which promotes the progressive work by the Tecton group for the Zoological Society's sites in Dudley and London, and the stylish but rather more prosaic commission *The Life of the Lobster* (1936). He left for America in 1937 to set up the short-lived New Bauhaus.

One of the regular contributors to *Film Art*, Robert Fairthorne (1904–2000) is associated with a recently rediscovered abstract film *Equation X+X=0* (1936). In later life Fairthorne wrote on mathematics and information theory and was a recognised pioneer in the field, and it is possible that *X+X=0* was a 'found' film, adopted by Fairthorne to illustrate his assertion (made in *Film Art* the same year), that 'if abstract films are really abstract films … they [should] deal exclusively with those abstract relations that can be expressed in terms of shape and motion';[62] in other words they should be free of the subjective or emotional content claimed for the abstract films of artists such as Oskar Fischinger, Walther Ruttmann and Viking Eggeling. The work was certainly animated by

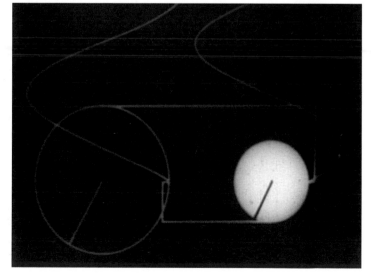

**134 (below)** *Equation X+X=0*, Robert Fairthorne and Brian Salt, 1936.

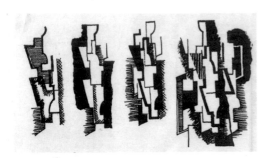

**135** *Developing Forms*,
John Piper, 1936.

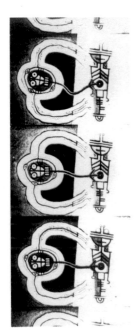

**136** Len Lye: *Tusalava*, 1929.

Brian Salt, about whom all that is known is that he had designed other mathematical diagrams as an aid to teachers and students. The extraordinarily smooth movement of Salt's suitably *non-expressive* geometric figures gives them an uncanny resemblance to the early computer animation of half a century later.[63] Also in *Film Art*, and equally abstract, was a sequence of drawings *Developing Forms* by John Piper which accompanied S. John Woods' discussion of abstraction (that so annoyed Man Ray); Piper possibly having heard of Duncan Grant's scroll, or more probably being aware of Hans Richter's description of the scroll-painting origins of his *Rhythmus* series, shown at the Film Society in 1927.[64]

With the arrival in London of Len Lye (NZ 1901–USA 1980) in 1926, the pace of film activity suddenly quickened. Lye was the most prolific maker of abstract and experimental films in Britain of the inter-war period, and, because most of his works were either commissioned or sponsored, the majority of them have survived. Lye had studied art at the Canterbury College of Art (NZ), and came to London as a painter and sculptor, with an interest in animation and a determination to engage with the European avant-garde. He exhibited batik-paintings with the Seven and Five Society and at the 1936 International Surrealist Exhibition, and became part of the circle of Robert Graves and Laura Riding, designing book-jackets for them, and in turn having some of his writings published by their Seizin Press.[65] En route to London he had visited the Pacific islands and Australia where he filled notebooks with drawings of Aboriginal imagery that inspired the Miro-like imagery in his paintings, and his first film *Tusalava* (1929), its title a Samoan word meaning 'in the end, everything is just the same'. Drawn in bold, abstracted black and white, *Tusalava* showed primeval organic forms – part bacterial, part human, part animal – growing from a field of dots, metamorphosing, engaging in life/death struggles, and withering back into oblivion. For Lye, *Tusalava* initiated a dialogue between imagery drawn from the unconscious, and visual expressions of happiness, 'not hedonism, but happiness of a lasting kind, like art'[66] that would characterise all his work – both painting and kinetic sculpture. Shown at the Film Society, *Tusalava* was praised by Roger Fry who recognised its purpose and wrote to Lye, 'I thought you had seen the essential thing, as no-one had hitherto – I mean you really thought not of forms in themselves but of them as movements-in-time'.[67] Fry might not have seen the work of Eggeling and others at that time, but must have been aware of the extent to which animation was already dominated by cute characters.

Lye himself was frustrated by the time-consuming frame-by-frame animation method, and found a more direct way of making images on film by painting and drawing directly onto the film strip, a technique that has since become commonplace, but was then entirely novel. The new phenomenon of full-colour movie-film seems to have been one inspiration; the squiggles and hand-written instructions that accumulate on the filmstrip during editing perhaps another. In 1936 he published a long essay on the possibilities of accompanying spoken texts with abstract colour imagery, based on a 'recent … test [in which] two voices in conversation were accompanied by colours and patterns moving on the screen … [suggesting] an emotional feeling existing between the … unseen speakers'.[68] Taking this experiment further, through a mutual friend Lye persuaded John Gielgud to record the opening verses of *The Tempest,* and created a collage of hand-painted film and found-footage imagery to go with them. Now lost, *Full Fathom Five* (1935) survives only in a description by Robert Herring in his journal *Life and Letters Today*:

> It is not true to say this it is an illustration to Shakespeare – unless you are willing to concede that a figure '5' floating across the screen is illustrative of the opening line. Nor is it true to describe it as an evocation of similar visual images. Probably I don't know at all what it is, but it seemed to me a pouring out of image and association which leaves a feeling of magic, an under-lit, underwater quality, which the verse has. But in a manner quite different. It is rather like the speech being made; there is mind-movement in the shapes, mind-pictures in the occasional flashes, inserts, of actual photography'.[69]

These experiments interested John Grierson, and Lye was commissioned by the GPO to make *A Colour Box* (1935), advertising the parcel post, in which brilliantly coloured lines, triangles and other abstract shapes dance on the screen, this time loosely synchronised to jazz – *La Belle Creole* by Don Baretto and his Cuban Orchestra. From then on, all Lye's films would be set to music, mostly jazz, making his visual composition an exercise in counterpoint, rather than the pure graphic invention of *Tusalava*. He selected music from his vast personal collection of 78-rpm records; his collaborator Jack Ellitt would edit the recording (sometimes shortening it or combining it with others) then transcribe the essential dynamics into graphic marks that ran along the edge of the filmstrip, and Lye would paint, draw and stencil, responding to these markings. This method reversed the relationship between image and sound of *Tusalava,* where Ellitt had written his score to follow images already animated by Lye.

Widely distributed, *A Colour Box* was not just the first abstract film that many people had seen in the cinema, but one of the first in full colour. The painter Paul Nash was among those struck by Lye's boldness.

> Len Lye conceives of colour film as a direct vehicle for colour sensation. … [Lye] believes, as I believe that he holds in his hands a real power for legitimate popular entertainment. A new form of enjoyment quite independent of literary reference; the simple, direct visual-aural contact of colour and sound through eye and ear. Colour sensation'.[70]

Lye's 'colour sensations' were immediately popular, and gained him commissions from Churchman's Cigarettes *Kaleidoscope* (1935), Imperial Airways *Colour Flight* (1938), and the Ministry of Information – the wartime *Musical Poster* (1940), each a variation on the original in terms of music used, colour palette, type of brush-mark and/or stencil used. During the same period, Lye was also consistently experimenting with other forms of image-making. In a film made jointly with Humphrey Jennings for Shell, *The Birth of the Robot* (1935–6), he worked with model-sets and puppets, his scope for inventiveness being limited to unusual camera-movements, expressive coloured lighting and a bizarre story-line, the

**137** Len Lye: *A Colour Box*, 1935.

**138** Len Lye: (above) *Rainbow Dance*, 1936; (above right) *Trade Tattoo*, 1937

whole being animated a-typically to classical music, a much-abbreviated version of Holst's *The Planets*. Lye approached film technology with fascination but was utterly unorthodox in its use, though he generally managed to gain the respect of the 'experts' and technicians he worked with. He recognised, for example, that the new Gasparcolor and Technicolor systems were related to artists' silk-screen printing techniques,[71] and that using them he could radically alter and intensify colour in the film image. With the help of Technicolor technicians, he made *Rainbow Dance* (1936) for the GPO into an essay in non-natural colour, with moving actors rendered monotone and flat like the stencilled shapes that surround them; everything changing colour following the artist's design, elements of one sequence dissolving into another. For *Trade Tattoo* (aka *In Time With Industry* 1937) he took shots drawn from documentaries being edited by his contemporaries at the GPO, *Night Mail, Drifters,* and *Song of Ceylon*, and turned their imagery into flat, still-readable areas of colour, then assembled them into a film-collage on the theme of international trade. Once again he structured the film to a Cuban jazz score, this time from the Lecuona Band, and accelerated the film's pace with jump-cuts in the action, and interwoven textures of hand-drawn lines, stencilled dots and superimposed words, to 'keep in time' with the music (one of the film's graphic slogans). With *A Colour Box, Rainbow Dance*, and *Trade Tattoo* he achieved a degree of control of pictorial shape, colour and movement rare in film.

Lye's first entirely live-action film *N or NW* (1937), though hampered by awkward actors and a silly story about mail that goes astray because given the wrong postcode (upsetting a romance), becomes a winning demonstration of how to invent your way out of narrative trouble. Lye had already filled the story with inventive camera-angles and visual effects (one shot is taken *through* a table-top), but his skill lay in his restlessly cutting together of fragments of what were obviously poor 'takes', so once again the action (and now speech) proceeds in sideways jumps, keeping in time with the tempo provided by Fats Waller and others.

Lye's wartime live-action films contain isolated sequences of creative camerawork and editing,[72] but generally his scope for invention was limited, and he experienced the same frustrations on moving to New York in 1944 to work for the *March of Time*. In the post-war period and still in the USA, his film-making remained tragically limited by absence of enlightened commissioners or public funding, though he managed to make three acclaimed works, *Color Cry* (1952), *Free Radicals* (1957–63) and *Particles in Space* (c.1966). But most of his creative energy during his American period was channelled into his extraordinary kinetic sculpture[73].

Norman McLaren (1914–87) had already experimented with hand-painted films while a student at the Glasgow School of Art, unaware of Lye's pioneer work in the field, but his first significant films *Seven Till Five* (1933) and *Camera Makes Woopee* (1935) were both live-action studies – the first on a day in the life of the school, the second about its annual Christmas ball – made for the School's Art Film

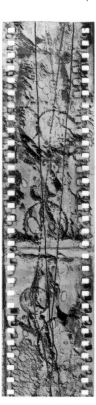

Group. His anti-capital/anti-war film *Hell UnLtd* (1936), made with his fellow sculpture student Helen Biggar, which mixes live-action and model animation, gained him an invitation from John Grierson to work at the GPO Film Unit, where he made several live action films before returning to the paint-on-film technique with the figurative *Love on the Wing* (1938), promoting the 1930s novelty of airmail. An image that it contained of scissors momentarily

**139** Norman McLaren: *Seven Till Five*, 1933; experimental hand-painted strips c. 1940s; (overleaf) strips from *Synchromy*, 1971.

turning into a penis was considered 'too Freudian' by the British film censor, and the film was suppressed, but McLaren had found his style, and the majority of his films from this period onwards were hand-painted, and contained figurative elements stick-men, birds, stars, baroque flourishes etc. Only rarely could he resist the temptation to charm. A pacifist, he moved to the USA at the outbreak of war and was commissioned by Hilla Rebay to make two short 'non-objective'[74] works *Dots* and *Loops* (1940) for the Guggenheim collection. In these he took the synthetic sound experiments of Moholy and others further, accompanying the on-screen acrobatic hand-drawn shapes with abstract sounds generated by marks drawn onto the area of the filmstrip reserved for the soundtrack, and so producing what were probably the first widely seen films to use this technique. While in New York he worked with Mary Ellen Bute who was already

exploring the possibility of using oscilloscopes to make abstract pattern-based films,[75] and he would borrow her method to make two 3-D films of dots and lines that move in deep space *Around is Around* and *Now is the Time* (1951) for the Festival of Britain, set to very 1950s orchestral scores by Louis Applebaum. From New York he moved to Canada, again at John Grierson's invitation, to take up what proved a lifetime's residency at the new National Film Board of Canada. Of his numerous films there, some of the strongest were hand-painted, like Lye's, in loose synchronisation to particular pieces of popular music. His last in New York, the mostly abstract *Boogie Doodle* (1940), was his response to boogie woogie; *Fiddle-de-dee* (1947) to a Canadian Gatineau Valley old-time fiddler's version of *Listen to the Mockingbird*, *Begone Dull Care* (1949) to jazz composed specially by Oscar Peterson.

McLaren's trio of films *Lines Horizontal* (1960), *Lines Vertical* (1962) and *Mosaic* (1965) were experiments made with a frequent collaborator Evelyn Lambert, initially setting out to see whether 'it would be possible to make a film with a single line moving in turn slowly then rapidly'.[76] Lambert engraved the lines directly into the filmstrip using a 19-inch (48cm) ruler, dividing the film into ruler-length segments that marked changes in the number of lines and the pace of their movement across the screen. With *Lines Horizontal* McLaren simply flipped the picture through 90 degrees, using an optical printer. 'I was convinced that the result would be completely different, for gravity no longer exists … you no longer know what animates them'.[77] *Mosaic* was made by superimposing this film upon its predecessor, but revealing only the points where the lines intersect, this time accompanying the image with a hand-drawn soundtrack. McLaren claimed that 'one of the principal advantages of abstract films is that you can stimulate and provoke the spectator's emotions with a fascinating gamut of movements – rapid, calm, precipitous, majestic',[78] but even in this series, his fondness for anthropomorphism is hard to hide; the soundtracks reinforce the suspicion that the lines should be read as behaving as humans might. His final abstract work *Synchromy* (1971) was again the development of an almost mechanistic experiment, designed to show how complex music could be synthesised using patterns of stripes that would simultaneously generate sound and provide imagery for the screen, to explain the structure of sound to an audience. A set of stripes drawn on a card represented a single note; sections from several cards shown side by side produced chords; photographing them onto successive frames produced music. What began as an exercise became a colourful sound/image boogie woogie, a 'chromatic synchronisation' that was complex, novel, even fascinating, but musically hardly the equal of a composition by Oscar Peterson. Later, Lis Rhodes and others would pursue this graphic form of sound/image cinema, but in more radical directions.

One of the most original of all abstract image-sound explorations was *The Eye and the Ear* (1945) made during the last years of the war by the Polish refugees Franciszka (1907–88) and Stefan (1910–88) Themerson. In the 1930s in Poland the Themersons had experimented with filmed shadow-play and moving 'rayograms' in films such as *Europa* (1930), an interpretation of the futurist-style political poem by Anatol Stern. They first explored sound-image relationships in *Short Circuit* (1935), a commissioned film promoting the safe use of electricity made collaboratively with the composer Witold Lutoslawski, in which they attempted

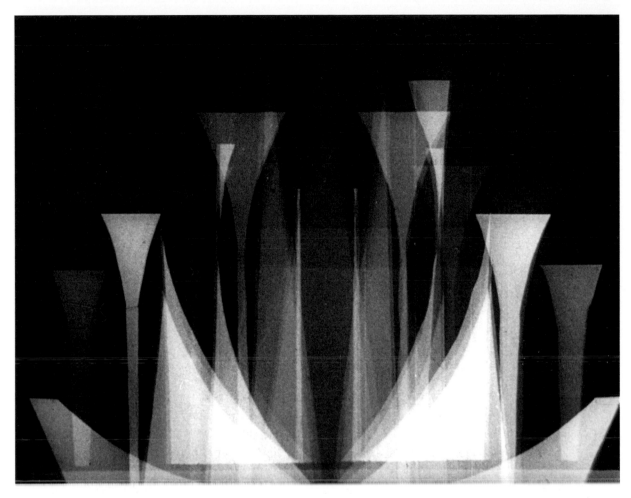

a frame-by-frame transposition of his sound textures into images in one section, and he composed a note-by-note response to their rayogrammed imagery in another.[79] *The Eye and the Ear* took these ideas further, creating analogies between the music of Karol Szymanowski, and patterns of movement made by passing light through lenses and animated and rayogrammed imagery. Their approach to abstraction was more a pursuit of expressiveness than a dogmatic rejection of representation. In his remarkable book on film *The Urge to Create Visions,* Stefan wrote 'I do not think one can make a distinction between content and form when actually making a film. I can well imagine making an abstract film out of realistic rushes, and making a narrative film out of abstract elements … the point is not whether we should stand here or there, the point is that we should move at last into a different sphere.'[80] Though lucky in having the Film Unit of the Polish Ministry of Information in Exile as a sponsor for both this film and their call-to-arms *Calling Mr Smith* (1944, discussed later), neither film found distribution, and the artists retired from film-making after the war, Franciszka continuing to paint and illustrate books, and Stefan writing and running his artists' books publishing venture, the Gaberbocchus Press[81].

**140** *The Eye and the Ear,* Stefan and Franciszka Themerson, 1945.

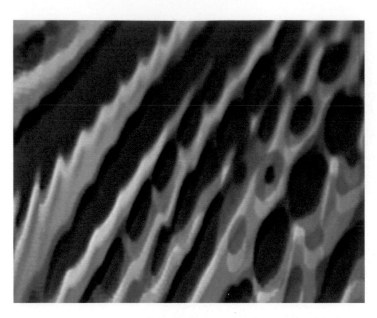

**141** *Horizon*, Lutz Becker, 1966.

Stuart Wynn Jones was one of several members of the Grasshopper Group of film-makers in the late 1950s and early 1960s who made hand-painted abstract films with musical soundtracks, more often following McLaren than Lye. More ambitiously in the late 1970s, the composer and music scholar David Kershaw taught himself animation in order to pursue the kind of abstract image-sound compositions explored in the 1920s by Walther Ruttmann with composer Max Butting (*Opus I-IV*, 1923–24), his own contribution being *Opus One* (1979). But animated abstract films, and films that straddled the abstract/figurative boundary, remained rare until the work of the American animator Robert Breer (active from the late 1950s) became widely known in Britain. Breer's films encouraged the emergence of a new generation of artists including Stuart Hilton, John Parry, John Tappenden and Kayla Parker.

The arrival of new media, colour video and the computer also reinvigorated the abstract tradition. The 'fault' of video-feedback prompted a number of artists to consider the television screen's potential for abstraction (and the famous titles sequence for the BBC's low-budget sci-fi series *Dr Who*). The artist and scholar of Futurism and Soviet Revolutionary-period art Lutz Becker (b.1941 Germany) made a series of tightly controlled abstract works *Experiment 5, Cosmos, Aleph*, and *Horizon* (all 1966) while working experimentally with BBC electronics engineer Ben Palmer. Becker hoped 'we might find some kind of equivalent to electronic music. We explored ways in which visual effects could be created through utilizing a feedback circle between … TV cameras and monitors'.[82] Made when TV was still limited to black and white, and video recording a near impossibility, his imagery was shot from the TV screen onto film, and had colour added later in an optical film printer. *Horizon*, which has an original score by Joy Hall, was transmitted by the BBC in 1969. Five years later, Peter Donebauer (b.1947) had the advantage of having an early colour TV system to experiment with. *Entering* (1974) was one of a series of works he made during a residency at the Royal College of Art, using the colour TV studio donated by ATV. Commissioned by Mark Kidel for BBC2's art programme *Second House*, its mandala-like imagery and synthetic sound were performed 'live' by Donebauer and composer Simon Desorgher, and recorded in real time. Later Donebauer and engineer Richard Monkhouse developed the Videokalos synthesiser, as an image-sound performance instrument that allowed them to work closely with musicians in 'live' largely improvised performances. *Entering* was transmitted by the BBC in 1974. The composer Brian Eno (b.1948) saw colour television more as an instrument for producing coloured light, like the colour-organs of the 18th and 19th centuries, and between 1979 and 1986 made a series

of what he called video 'paintings' (properly sculptures), in which TV sets buried in canvas structures glowed with coloured light in response to his ambient music.[83]

Mineo Aayamaguchi (b.1953 Japan) was one of the few video artists of the 1980s generation to recognise the power of abstract imagery used across a battery of screens in his sculptural multi-monitor video installations. Often his imagery was abstracted from live action, with colour heightened by fragmentation and electronic intensification and movement reflected across screens in linked and mirroring action. The nine screens of *Beyond Colour* (1986) – a cross of five screens enclosed in a square of four – were further mirrored in a grid of polished metal sheets laid on the floor; each of the 25 screens of *Kaleidoscope* (1998) had a metal sheet beneath it – linking the screens together in a field of changing colour. Above all, his is an art of choreography across the multiple image.

**143** *Beyond Colour*,
Mineo Aayamaguchi, 1986.

Colour television as a medium for 'chromatic synchronisation' was almost immediately followed by the domestic computer. Le Grice, Stan Hayward and Denys Irving were all members of the Computer Art Society founded by John Lansdown in 1968, which encouraged the exploration of what was then described as cybernetic art in the fields of painting (computer-controlled drawings), construction, music and film. Stan Hayward (b.1930) was an estab-

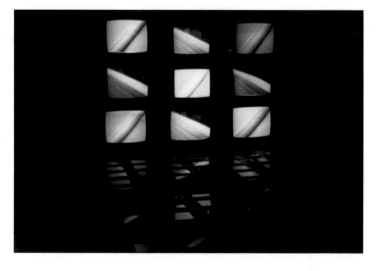

lished scriptwriter who had worked for the BBC radio comics *The Goons* and the animators Richard Williams and George Dunning. His interest in the potential of computer animation led to a partnership with Imperial College in 1971, but his only abstract work was *Square* (1972), a short silent work exploring the harmonics of the square, which was made in collaboration with the young art student George Borzyskowski (b.1948). Hayward provided the design and computer programme, and as with Becker's *Horizon,* in the absence of colour monitors, the film's image was created as three monochrome sequences, then printed through colour filters and superimposed to create full colour.

Denys Irving (1944–76) made two black and white silent computer-drawn films *Now* and *69* (both 1969[84]) of dots moving in mathematically permutated patterns, close in spirit to the work of the American pioneers John and James Whitney. Expanding concentric ellipses appear in Le Grice's multi-screen *Threshold* (1972), the product of six months' experimentation at the Atomic Energy Authority at Harwell. In the early 1970s, Le Grice became an enthusiastic apologist for computer-aided film, organising British screenings of the Whitney brothers' works, and writing extensively on the subject.[85] His own most sustained interventions came later and not in the area of computer-drawn imagery, but in computer-controlled editing, where he designed programmes that would make the essential creative decisions. Examples included *Digital Still Life* and two sections of the Channel 4/Arts Council supported *Sketches for a Sensual Philosophy* (both 1988) where these programmes determined both the sequence of images and their colour transformations. In the image-sound work *Arbitrary Logic* (1988) which was performed live, the computer 'arbitrated' in the battle between a number of different inputs; a repertory of pre-recorded image-sequences and keyboard inputs from Le Grice and musician Keith Rowe (of AMM), their interactivity altering both sound and imagery, colour and tempo.

Darrell Viner (1946–2001) began using computers in the 1970s as a means to explore transformation in drawings and animation, before including them to animate his sculptural work. The silent *Inside/Outside* (1996) follows the logical development of a futurist angular composition, from a flat surface bearing a few simple lines into a complex construction described in deep space. In his kinetic sculpture and interactive environments computers controlled motors which allowed elements to move seemingly under their own momentum, or through interaction with the audience or performers. With access to the super-computers of IBM's research laboratories, William Latham (b.1961) pursued self-generating and replicating biomorphic forms of 'artificial life', in works such as *Evolution of Form* (1989) and *Biogenesis: Artificial Life in Computer Space* (1993). Terrifying in their detail (though rather plastic looking), they prefigured the soulless world of computer games of a decade later. Angus Fairhurst (b.1966) responded more humorously to computers' capacity for replication and repetition *ad absurdum*. His short loop films such as *Concept for a Spectacular (Penis)* and *(Teeth)* (both 1995), *Things That Don't Work (green), (red), (yellow)* and *(blue)* (all 1998) *et. al.* ironically reflected on the obsessive self-absorption of all animation (and most animators) and nerdishness of working with computers. With greater detachment, Tim Head (b.1946) created the silent video-projected installation *Treacherous Light* (2002), setting the computer the chal-

lenge of randomly changing the colour and intensity of each pixel of the image, creating fields of movement that would have been barely perceptible on a TV monitor, but became visible when projected, creating the ultimate pointilliste abstraction.

**144** *Treacherous Light*, Tim Head, 2002

The ubiquity of domestic computers and the arrival of the internet in the 1990s resulted in a new wave of music-related abstract kinetic compositions. Notable figures and groups include Stakker (Mark McClean) who led the way with *Eurotechno* (1989) and *Stakker Westworld* (1995 for Aphex Twin), the Bureau of Inverse Technology and Semiconductor, with commissioning and publishing in the field being stimulated by companies such as WARP records and the festivals Love Bytes in Sheffield, and One Dot Zero at the ICA. Of this generation, Riccardo Iacono (b.1969) uniquely spans the technological divide between digital world and the hand-craft of the Lye hand-painting tradition. He developed his sensibility as a filmmaker while at the Glasgow School of Art, where he produced dense hand-painted films, some, such as *SKZCP* (1997), appearing to be almost in low-relief, before studying digital video at Duncan of Jordanstone College of Art, Dundee. In his later films such as *Cold Tape* (2000), short bursts of rapidly changing digitally generated shapes, in the artist's words 'an interplay of opposites', although entirely synthetic in origin, closely reflect the painterly abstractions of his earlier work.

**145** *Joie de Vivre*,
Anthony Gross and
Hector Hoppin, 1933

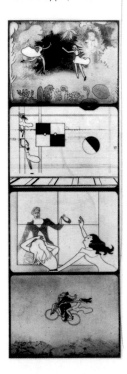

## FIGURATIVE ANIMATION

British paintings of the 1920s and 1930s give little hint of the seriousness with which the artist members of the Film Society took the *Mickey Mouse* and *Felix the Cat* cartoons of the time. Paul Nash for example described Disney as 'one of the few geniuses of the cinema'.

> The early Disney cartoons, which I believe to be authentic Disney, are truly sensitive drawings charged with a rather pale bright colour, reminiscent of certain drawings by William Blake – the Milton series for instance. … Each *[Silly] Symphony* brought new gifts from this fertile source; not merely new flights of nonsense, but accompaniments of design which, apart from their descriptive power, were gems of pictorial fancy.[86]

Yet after Len Lye's brilliant salvo of sponsored experiments in the 30s, animation in Britain (as elsewhere) struggled to persuade either the commercial paying public, or the art-world, to take it seriously. Too often, its artwork was derivative of the look of painting or illustration of decades earlier, or just plain badly drawn, its narrative ideas unsubtle and simplistic, and the choreography of its movement predictable and repetitive. Animation inexorably became the child-orientated and market-driven fast-food that computers now generate with little human intervention. In awe of Disney, as were animators the world over, British animators sought salvation in industrialisation, with established characters around whom a series could be built, assembly-line production methods and dreams of market domination. In reality, British animation's strengths have been associated with individuals with vision, and a cottage-industry production context. In the 1980s and 1990s the commissioning policies of Channel 4 Television and later BBC2 briefly made this a viable option.

Among the exceptions to this gloomy picture was Anthony Gross (1905–84), best known as a printmaker and painter, but also one of the most innovative figurative artist-animators in Europe in the pre-war years. At the Academie Julian in Paris he met Hector Hoppin, who shared his enthusiasm for early Disney, and became his technical partner on most of his film projects. Gross's animation style reflects the distinctive graphic line of his etchings, but add a sophisticated choreography of lines moving in space. *Joie de vivre* (1933) developed its escapist theme from his earlier suite of etchings *Sortie d'usine* (1931) and was followed by *Fox Hunt* (1937), his first work in colour. His film-making was supported by the producer Alexander Korda, until the Second World War intervened and a copyright dispute sunk his ambitious feature-length but incomplete adaptation of Jules Verne's *Around the World in 80 Days* (1936). With sections in the style of Dufy, Indian miniatures, and Alexander Remmington, this anticipated by twenty years the pastiches of 'modernist' painters of the UPA cartoons, and it was finally released as a fragment *The Indian Fantasy* by the BFI in the late 1950s. A distinguished war artist, Gross returned to painting and printmaking, teaching the latter at the Slade until 1971.

The German-born animator Lotte Reiniger (1899–1981) made her first film for Grierson and the GPO *The Toscher* in 1936, and moved to Britain permanently in 1938 to escape the Nazis. In Germany her technique of animated cut-out silhouettes had enjoyed commercial success in the 1920s, and her studio's prodigious output had included the world's first feature-length cartoon *The Adventures of Prince Achmed* (1926), on which Walther Ruttmann and Berthold Bartosch were assistants. In England she continued to make silhouette works for the GPO, the BBC and others, until the end of the 1960s. Technically astonishing, always elegant and charming, they seem to inhabit the 18th century more than the 20th. An exception is a work she apparently made with her husband and producer Carl Koch shortly after arriving in London, in response to the gathering political crisis in Europe; a work which if completed is now lost, but described to their friend the composer Edward Williams who wrote scores for some of her films.[87]

**146** *HPO (Heavenly Post Office)*, Lotte Reiniger, 1938.

It was 'an animated map of the growth and decay of empires, defined in terms of the outlines of territorial conquest. ... A succession of the territorial outlines of the early Egyptian empires, the Mesopotamian (Sumer, Akkad, Ur, Babylon), the Minoan, Chinese, Indian ... Persian; the Macedonian empire of Alexander the Great, they all grew, then decayed and collapsed – but at an accelerating pace. On it went – this continuous, overlapping, bubbling up and dissolving of expanding and collapsing shapes all over the Earth's surface ... Finally, moving at high speed through the shapes describing the changing territorial dominance of the European nations over the last three or four hundred years ... Lotte and Carl ... arrived at their own 'present day' (and the end of their project) in the summer of 1939, just at the point when the outlines of the British Empire – 'on which the sun never sets' – had inflated to almost bursting point ... And abruptly the film stopped. One inference was apparently absolutely and powerfully plain – the British Empire was, *must* be, on the point of Imperial collapse. They were not allowed to show the film publicly.[88]

**147** *The Magic Canvas*, John Halas, 1948.

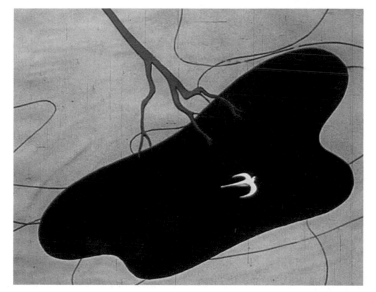

The abstracted figures in John Halas's short film ballet *The Magic Canvas* (1948) showed his admiration for the contemporary sculpture of Henry Moore and Barbara Hepworth, and this film, with the series *Painter and Poet*, exemplified his aspiration to make popular but serious animation for adults. Born in Budapest, Halas (1912–95) came to England in 1936 to work

**148** *A Short Vision*,
Peter and Joan Foldes, 1956.

for the puppet-animator George Pal, but established the Halas & Batchelor studio in 1940 with Joy Batchelor (1914–91), which proved the most viable of all British attempts to emulate the Hollywood factory model, supported by a stream of commissions from government departments via the COI. Their best-known work was *Animal Farm* (1954), Britain's first completed feature-length animation, and a contribution to Cold War propaganda. After an abandoned live-action/animation version of *Pilgrim's Progress,* their subsequent cinema shorts and TV ads were rarely as ambitious. Adaptations of Gerald Hoffnung's much-loved *Punch* cartoons such as *The Palm Court Orchestra* (1964) and their humorous prediction of universal gridlock *Automania 2000* (1963) won awards, but their output became increasingly restricted in visual and emotional range.

A protégé of Halas also born in Budapest, Peter Foldes (1924–77) studied at the Courtauld Institute and the Slade School of Art, London, and received funding from the BFI for two very painterly films, almost literally animated expressionist paintings – *Animated Genesis* (1952), a dark history of the Earth from its birth to mankind's invention of the atomic bomb, and *A Short Vision* (1956), another savage Cold War parable ending in catastrophe, its bleak imagery reflecting the 1950s preoccupation with nuclear annihilation. Although the films were widely shown and well received, Foldes returned to painting, and moved to Paris in 1956. When he returned to film in the mid-1960s, he gained an international reputation as one of the first artists to make figurative computer-drawn animation, working in France and Canada. The BFI also funded what appears to have been the only film made by Peter King, *The Thirteen Cantos of Hell* (1955), a long, silent, black and white version of Dante, peopled by elongated Vorticist-like figures.

The only animators to pick up the Lye/McLaren mantle in the 1950s were both associated with the amateur film-making Grasshopper Group. John Daborn the group's founder made the pixillated (live-action shot frame by frame) *Two's Company* (1953), *Battle of Wangapore* (1955) and *Bride and Groom* (1956), while his colleague Stuart Wynn Jones made the hand-painted alphabet *Short Spell* (1963) and the abstract *Raving Waving, Billowing Bellowing* (1964?) before joining Halas and Batchelor. He returned to individual production with *Organic Canonic Icon* (1981).

Other animators including the Canadians George Dunning and Dick Williams eschewed public funding and took their chances within the commercial industry, which was expanding with the growth of cinema advertising, and particularly of television commercials after the launch of ITV in 1957, hoping to subsidise their more personal work that way. Williams (b.1933) came to Britain in 1954 having studied painting for six years, and used commercial earnings to finance *The Little Island* (1958), a stylish parable about blind pursuit of Goodness, Truth and Beauty set to music by Tristram Carey. After *A Lecture on Man* and the high-camp *Love Me, Love Me, Love Me* (both 1962, and both to texts by Christopher Logue), he became increasingly determined to emulate the detailed animation technique of Disney, and repeatedly financially overstretched himself in this cause, making the titles for Tony Richardson's *The Charge of The Light Brigade* (1968), *A Christmas Carol* (1971) and his long-protracted feature film *The Thief and the Cobbler (aka Nazrudin 1995)*, becoming a producer at Pixar in his

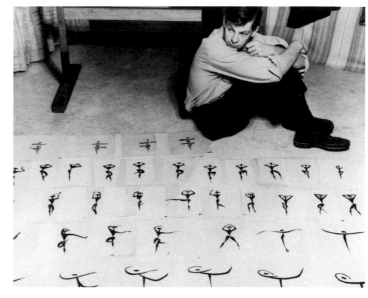

**149** Dick Williams with artwork from *The Little Island*, 1958 (BFI Stills Collection).

later life. George Dunning (1920–79) managed more successfully to make personal works that gained cinema release, such as the simple animated brush-stroke-based *The Apple* and *The Flying Man* (both 1962), and his pencil-line response to an Andrew Marvell poem *Damon the Mower* (1972), which is both a love-letter to the obsessive activity of hand-drawn animation, and a disturbing visual dialogue between male angst and violence. On a larger scale, as in the ambitious Beatles' feature film *Yellow Submarine* (1968), his original ideas about screen-movement were sometimes submerged beneath the psychedelic designs of his collaborator, the graphic designer Heinz Edelman.

The story of figurative animation in the 1970s and onwards is one of a slowly expanding field of small suppliers pursuing the magic balance between an interesting plot and a fresh graphic style, in which the dividing line between 'personal style' and 'experiment' is often blurred. In the 1970s it was still just conceivable to believe that an animated short might be booked to show in front of a feature film, and from that period date the first films of Alison de

**150 (below left)** *Café Bar*, Alison de Vere, 1968 (BFI Stills Collection).

**151 (below)** *Possession*, Phil Mulloy, 1991.

Vere (b.1927 Pakistan), *Café Bar* (1968), *Mr Pascal* (1973), Jeff Dunbar *Ubu* (1978) and Paul Vester (b.1941) *Football Freaks* (1971). By the 1980s cinema exhibition had all but gone, and television, and the happy accident of Channel 4 with a commissioning editor for animation, had come to the rescue. Personal animation flowered during the next fifteen years and engaged hundreds of young artists, and the expanding field, its stylistic movements and various groupings, and the ups and downs of broadcasting policy, deserve a study of their own. Much of the animation in this period become identified with expressions of identity, gender and ethnicity, and stories, where they exist, were psychologically truthful rather than funny; 'problem' films were the norm; in other words animation contributed to the broad themes of the 1980s and 1990s (and individual instances will be discussed in the final chapter).

## NOTES

1. Bursary application to the Arts Council 1977.

2. 'Buried Alive', *Coil,* no. 4, 1997.

3. More directly pre-cinematic were his series of mutoscopes *Crimes of Futility n8, a Set of Meaningless Gestures* (2004), and *Clockwork Cinema,* a motorised thaumatrope (1997).

4. *Follies of an Amateur Photographer* (1996), *Laundramatic* (1998) *et al.*

5. More effectively, he has converted whole rooms into pin-hole cameras, producing a life-size mirror-images of the adjacent space, as in *Introspective* (ICA London 1993) and *Negative Perspective* (Centre for Contemporary Art, Warsaw 1995).

6. Introduction to the programme note for the series of four programmes shown 3–21 March, by the Tate Education department. The twenty-two films included work made between 1970 and 1974 by Raban, Welsby, Croft, David Pearce, Jane Clark and Mike Duckworth.

7. 'William Raban', *A Survey of the Avant-Garde in Britain*, vol. 3 (Gallery House, 1972).

8. *London Filmmakers Co-op Catalogue* 1993.

9. John Du Cane, 'William Raban', *Time Out*, 14 July 1972.

10. 'Interview with Chris Welsby' – Michael O'Pray and William Raban, *Undercut*, no. 7/8, 1983.

11. 'About a third of the composition is taken up by sky. Many people pass through this picture space both on and off the pathway. One frame is to be taken each time a person ... passes into the picture and again when they pass out. Filming is to commence before first light and end after dark'. Artist's notes, 1973.

12. 'Interview with Chris Welsby', op. cit.

13. 'Interview with Chris Welsby', op. cit.

14. Artist's statement 1980, *Chris Welsby: Films Photographs Writings* (London: Arts Council, 1980).

15. Often confused with 2B Butlers Wharf.

16. Artist's statement in a proposal to the Arts Council, 1988.

17. 'I wanted to suggest that the parallel between thought and image in nature was mirrored in the language of the moving electronic image', CMA website.

18. *Issues 1* [leaflet accompanying a Jubilee Gardens design proposal], Florian Beigel, 2001.

19. Louis Lumière described one such family portrait, *Partie d'ecartè [The Card Players]* (1895): 'The partners are: my father Antoine Lumière, who lights a cigar. Opposite him, his friend the conjurer Trewey who is dealing the cards. Trewey was ... the organiser in London of showings of our cinematograph, and is to be

seen in several of the films, *Assiettes tournantes [Spinning Plates]* for instance. The third player, who is pouring some beer, is my father in law, the brewer Winckler of Lyon. The servant, finally, was a man attached to the house. He was born at Confaron – a pure blooded southern Frenchman, full of gaiety and wit, who kept us amused …' 'Lumière the last interview' Georges Sadoul, *Sight and Sound*, vol. 17, no. 66, Summer 1948.

20. Tamara Krikorian, '*On the Mountain* and *Landmakar, Undercut,* no. 7/8, 1983.

21. Margaret Tait, interview for Channel 4 profile.

22. The theme of several publications/exhibitions at the time; *The Destruction of the Country House* 1974; *Change and Decay,* 1977.

23. Anna Thew, 'Anne Rees-Mogg', *A Directory of British Film and Video Artists* (Luton: Arts Council of England/John Libby Press, 1996).

24. *A Directory of British Film and Video Artists* (Arts Council/University of Luton Press, 1996).

25. Barbara Hepworth, Basil Wright, Frederick Ashton, Rudolph Nureyev, Gilbert and George *et. al.*

26. The *Heads* are, as a contemporary programme notes: Charlie Watts, Bill West, Jane, John Blake, Linda Thorson, Marsha Hunt, Steve Dwoskin, Theolonius Monk, Peter Townshend, David Hockney, Marianne Faithfull, Carol Garney-Lawson, David Gale, Richard Hamilton, Dieter Meier, Rufus Collins, Leslie Smith, Anita Pallenberg, Claes Oldenburg, Francis Bacon, Adrian Munsey, Carolee Schneemann, Andrew Garney-Lawson, Jim Dine, Vivian, Prenai, Winston, Gregory Markopoulos, Rosie, Patrick Proctor, Francis Vaughan. A work even more closely modelled on Warhol, *Portrait* (1970), is among many films he has withdrawn.

27. The portraits include Le Grice, Larcher, Tom Chomont, Barbara Schwartz, Lynne Tillmann.

28. A programme note identifies the couples as 'Blinky Palermo and Christina, Sigmar Polke and Karin, Joseph Beuys and Usu, Alfred Schmela and his wife, George Brecht and Takako, Daniel Spoerri and Hette Hunerman, Gerhard Richter and Eva, Robert Filliou and Marianne, Karl Ruhburg and his wife'. Lutz Mommartz is also clearly identifiable.

29. 'Lumière the last interview', op. cit.

30. By coincidence, Jarman's Super 8 camera was given to him by Marc Balet, an American architecture student in Warhol's circle, later the editor of the magazine *Andy Warhol's Interview*.

31. 'Gillian Wearing in Conversation with Carl Freeman' (catalogue) *Gillian Wearing*, Serpentine Gallery, London 2000.

32. *Sam Taylor-Wood*, Hayward Gallery 2002.

33. *Independent Magazine,* 10 December 1999.

34. Artist's statement, LFMC catalogue 1976.

35. A diagram of its climactic mathematically-structured editing was reconstructed by the Viennese artist Peter Weibel for the exhibitions *Film als/as Film* at the Koln Kunstverein and Hayward Gallery, 1978/79.

36. 'As a third of the films was titles and another third was composed of shots from various travel films, there was not a lot of footage for me to shoot, and as these scenes were mostly of myself in disguises in my back garden – which according to the angle of shooting or the arrangement of the background represented anything from the sea to the Sahara – the production expenses were about the lowest on record'. Adrian Brunel, *Nice Work – Thirty Years in British Films* (London: Forbes Robertson Ltd, 1949).

37. The Scholartis Press, 1932. His dates are probably 1902–c.1993. Is he the same C. D. Pegge who wrote 'Caligari: Its Innovations in Editing', *Film Quarterly,* no. 11, 1956/1957.

38. *Surrealism, Permanent Revelation* (London: Studio Vista, 1970); *The Age of Gold, Surrealist Cinema* (New York: Creation Books, 2003).

39. *Paths of Desire: films by Robert Stuart Short* (programme note) 1979.

40. He withdrew to academia in the USA.

41. Promotional card. *Lost Images* was transmitted by BBC2's *The Late* Show, *Rumour of True Things* by Channel 4.

42. John Russell, *Pop Art Redefined* (London: Thames & Hudson, 1969). Russell adds further definitions later in the chapter: 'It was a struggle fought by people for science and against the humanities, for cybernetics against the revival of italic handwriting, for Elvis against pre-electric recordings of Battistini, for American Army Surplus fatigues against waistcoats and watchchains, for the analytical study of General Motors advertising against an hour in the print-room at Colnaghi's. Pop did not count 'ephemeral' as an insult. It was for the present, and even more for the future: it was not for the past, and saw nothing to regret in the changes which had come about in England since 1945'.

43. Claude Lichtenstein and Thomas Schregenberger (eds), *As Found, The Discovery of the Ordinary* (Baden, Switzerland: Lars Muller Publ., 2001).

44. A third film *Mr Machine* (1971) was made by Keith Griffiths from Paolozzi's imagery.

45. Intriguingly, Scott suggests the 'difficult' two-screen format, as well as being appropriate to Oldenburg's ideas about the site for his work, was a way of 'getting my own back on the Arts Council' for the success of *Richard Hamilton*. (Interview with Clive Hodgson, *Film*, July 1973). Scott's collaborations with artists also included *Love's Presentation* (1966) with David Hockney (financed by Alan Power) and *Antoni Tapies* (1974) made with Roland Penrose and the artist.

46. Interviewed in Jack Sargeant, *Cinema Contra Cinema* (Fringecore: 1998).

47. *Jeff Keen Films* (Arts Council & Channel 4, 1985).

48. Artist's statement 1972.

49. Anthony Scott, *Extract from the Longest Most Meaningless Lecture on the Longest Most Meaningless Movie in the World*, 1969. Leaflet in the BAFV Study Collection.

50. James Broughton, *Coming Unbuttoned – A Memoir* (San Francisco: City Lights Books, 1993).

51. Interview with Mathew Noel-Tod 2001.

52. Or 1980s performance artist Silvia Ziranek: *Rubberglovarama* etc.

53. All quotes from LUX distribution catalogue.

54. Jeff Nuttall detected a 'keynote of violence' in the subculture. 'To stand in a pop club in any of the world's larger cities these days is to experience a sensation rather like that of being suspended over a vat of boiling oil. The battery of curdling colours projected round the room, the brutal stroboscopes, the aggressive gobbling of the lead guitars, the belligerent animal wails of the singers, the threat and howling hunger always present in the lyrics – "Why can't we reach the sun" – "I want the world and I want it now" – the throbbing danger of the abused amplifiers, the stunned trance of the crowd and the total bleak despair of the registered junkies always hovering around the door like predatory crows, all contribute to a ritual that can be nothing if not profoundly disruptive of most things that life has been about up till now'. *Bomb Culture*, 1968.

55. Shaw Ashton tried to persuade Deren to undertake a lecture tour of Britain in the mid-1950s. He and his wife were committed modernists; their house 'Landfall' (1938–39) in Poole, Dorset, was designed by Oliver Hill to look like a great white ship with its portholes.

56. Artist's statement on the Arts Council's promotional card, 1970.

57. Wassily Kandinsky showed abstract painting at the AAA from 1911.

58. Notably Vanessa Bell and her sister Virginia Woolf. Grant's work was recorded on film in 1974 by Christopher Mason for the Tate, under the artist's supervision.

59. Lawrence apparently visited Grant's studio in January 1915, where he saw the work, and conveyed his opinion in a letter to a mutual friend.

60. According to James Enyeart's *Bruguière* (New York: Knopf, 1977), he made posters for both Shell and the GPO using similar cut-paper abstractions.

61. 'The film was made under typically amateur conditions, with a hand camera devoid of tripod, with a very limited quantity of film-stock, bought at different times and therefore of differing qualities, and with no prepared scenario or pre-determined order of shots, but was taken when and where occasion offered. The final editing was directed towards displaying the actual work of the congress and national and personal characteristics of the individual delegates. It is by such means, working within a limited compass, Professor Moholy-Nagy believes, that the amateur can make his contribution to the art of film'. Film Society programme note, 10 December 1933.

62. *Film Art*, no. 9, 1936.

63. The similarity of the animated sequence in Moholy's *The New Architecture* suggests the possibility that it, too, was designed by Salt. As a composition of abstract motion, it parallels Ralph Steiner's *Mechanical Principles* (USA 1933).

64. *Film Art*, vol III no.7, 1936.

65. *No Trouble* (London: Seizin Press, 1930).

66. Interview, quoted in Roger Horrocks, *Len Lye a Biography* (Aukland, NZ: Auckland University Press, 2001).

67. Letter, 3 December 1929 in the Lye Archive, New Zealand. Quoted in Horrocks, *Len Lye a Biography*.

68. Len Lye, 'Voice and Colour', *Life and Letters Today*, April 1936.

69. 'Tonga; Trade Tattoo, Full Fathom Five by Len Lye', *Life and Letters Today*, vol. 17 no. 9, Autumn 1937. Ian Hugo's film, *Bells of Atlantis* (USA 1952), with its underwater theme, colour design by Lye and text by Anaïs Nin, contains an echo of this lost work.

70. 'The Colour Film', in Charles Davy (ed.), *Footnotes to the Film* (New York: Oxford University Press, 1938).

71. Early Technicolor was a lithographic process.

72. They included *When the Pie Was Opened* (1941), *Newspaper Train* (1942), *Kill or be Killed* (1942).

73. See the definitive *Len Lye a Biography*.

74. Peggy Guggenheim's preferred terminology.

75. Resulting in *Polkagraph* (1947) and *Mood Contrasts* (1956).

76. Interview, *Norman McLaren,* Scottish Arts Council 1977.

77. Ibid.

78. Ibid.

79. Paul Pawlikowski, 'Art Smugglers', *City Limits* 20 May 1983. *Europa* and *Short Circuit* were both lost in the war, though another film from this period *Apteka* (*Pharmacy* 1930) has recently been reconstructed by Bruce Checefsky from surviving images.

80. *The Urge to Create Visions* [1937–83]: 'When Moholy Nagy saw our film *Europa* in 1936 in London, he also said the film was sophisticated. I was too young then to tell him that he was wrong. That film was primitive. And he couldn't see this because *he* was too sophisticated. For what can be more primitive

than the juxtaposition in time of the picture of a loaf of bread, and a close up of a woman's hips, and a view of her face? Or, a solitary blade of grass squeezed up between two paving stones, its roots struggling with their hardness, breaking them, and the blade growing visibly into a tree that falls down on the roof of the houses?'.

81. From 1948: its output included the first translation of Jarry's *Ubu Roi* in 1951, illustrated by Franciszka.

82. Note to the author 2003. Becker's documentaries include *Art in Revolution* (1971), *Double Headed Eagle* (1972), *Lion of Judah* (1981) and *Vita Fururista* (1987).

83. Such as *Works Constructed with Sound and Light* at the Riverside Studios, Spring 1986. Had he seen David Hall's light-emitting *The Situation Envisaged* (1979).?

84. They *may* have been made in the USA, while he was studying at Columbia University.

85. 'Computer Film as Art' in John Halas (ed.), *Computer Animation* (London: Focal Press, 1974); 'Computer Films', *Time Out* article on the Whitney brothers American Embassy season, 31 December 1970.

86. 'The Colour Film', in Davy (ed.), *Footnotes to the Film*.

87. And for shorts and documentary makers as diverse as Richard Massingham and David Attenborough (*Life on Earth*).

88. Edward Williams, *Lotte Reiniger and Carl Koch – A Geopolitical Animation Project,* 1998 (unpublished).

# 2.2 Narrative: Fiction, Documentary, Polemic

Studies in Thought' **:** 1920s Amateurs **:** Grierson's Avant-Garde **:** War : Post-War Revival **:**
Free Cinema **:** Ambitious Narrative **:** Work **:** The Production of Meaning **:** Image and Voice

## 'STUDIES IN THOUGHT'

If slow to explore abstraction, silent cinema directors of necessity were interested in the
camera's ability to tell stories through images alone, as part of the inevitable first steps in the
development of narrative film-making. Directors looked for images to represent human emotions that could augment, and even replace, shots of the face, and visual metaphor became
one of the building blocks of film-language. Following the introduction of sound after 1928,
it was artists who most systematically pursued this line of pictorial exploration, many continuing
to treat film as if it was a silent medium. Artists eschewed popular cinema's elaborate plots,
sequential structures and well-rounded characters, to focus on cinema's ability to represent
the complexities of perception, thought and emotion through a flow of images. Their narratives reflected the current interest in psychoanalysis and many of the characteristics of the
modernist novels of Joyce and Woolf – fragmentation, absence of strict chronology, emotive
use of location and the subjective 'voice'. That said, visual metaphor also remained a power-

**152** HD in *Wing Beat*,
Kenneth Macpherson, 1927.

ful component within art cinema and even in the tightly plotted
dramas of mainstream directors as diverse as Powell, Hitchcock and
Scorsese; so the difference between the artist's approach to narrative, and that of the most daring of mainstream directors, is often
a matter of intensity only; poetry as against prose. But similarities resonate across the decades between art cinema and the
avant-garde; between the works of Dovzenko, Tarkovsky, Roeg
and Antonioni, and those of Kenneth Macpherson, Steve McQueen,
Chris Newby, and Jane and Louise Wilson. They all give form to
psychological drama through wordless images.

   Not surprisingly, among the first artists to seriously explore narrative were the *Close Up* contributors Kenneth Macpherson, Bryher
and HD. Financed by Bryher's private fortune, Pool Films' first

**153** *Borderline*,
Kenneth Macpherson, 1930:
(above) Eslanda Robeson,
(above right) HD, and (below)
on the cover of HD's booklet,
Paul Robeson (courtesy of
Peter Gidal).

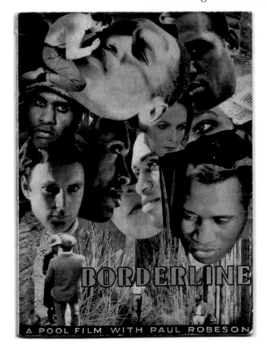

attempted film *Wing Beat* (1927) is attributed to Macpherson (1903–71), and was openly indebted to Pabst, and particularly to his silent film account of psychoanalysis *Secrets of the Soul* (Germany 1925). Successive ads in *Close Up* described *Wing Beat* as 'a study in thought … a free verse poem', and it is a film of glances, gestures, and evocative landscape shots. 'Thought' in this context amounts to evocations of the conflicting feelings of its protagonists – two men seen largely in interior shots (Macpherson himself and Bryher's young brother John Ellerman Jr.) – the younger in turn fascinating and irritating the older – and a woman seen apart in interiors and on a snow-bound hillside (HD). The film survives only as a fragment, and was possibly never completed.[1] *Foothills* (1928), shot by Macpherson but possibly scripted by HD (1886–1960), follows a woman's journey into the country (HD again), and the *longeurs* of the life she endures there. Though never screened at the Film Society, Macpherson and Bryher showed *Foothills* to Pabst while visiting Berlin in 1928, who apparently praised their achievement. *Monkey's Moon* (1929) by Macpherson alone no longer survives, but was, HD tells us, a 'less ambitious film, a document of commercial length of his two pet Douracouli monkeys'.

Macpherson wrote, directed and was cameraman on Pool Films' sole feature-length work, the silent *Borderline* (1930). Set in 'a small borderline town anywhere in Europe' *Borderline* evokes the complex set of relationships linking a group of intellectuals – gay and straight, black and white – that are brought to crisis by the presence of a charismatic outsider (Paul Robeson), the former partner of one of the group. (The sexual tensions and confusions closely reflecting those of the film-makers; both Macpherson and Bryher were bisexual, HD a lover of Bryher's.) HD, who acted in the film (using the pseudonym Helga Doorn), published a long promotional essay in which she describes it as a 'modern attempt to synchronise thought and action, the inner turmoil and the outer', through a chain of images that have individual value and simultaneously contribute to an accumulating set of meanings.

Mr Kenneth Macpherson is himself, you might say, borderline among the young cinema directors. He is not at all allied with the ultramodern abstract school of rhomboid and curve and
cross-beam of tooth pick or coal shovel. I do not mean that Mr Macpherson is out of sympathy
with any form of realistic cinema abstraction, I simply quote him, remember him saying in
casual conversation, 'Why should one trouble to photograph a match stick when a birch tree is
so interesting?' Mr Macpherson finds a white birch tree as interesting, as abstract, as some
people find a toothbrush. [...] But when Mr Macpherson plays upon abstraction, it is in reference to some other abstraction. [...] A little oilcan, for instance (concise modernistic
abstraction) relates to a giant Negro shoulder. Oil and heat are related to a dark brow, that
great head that bends forward, very earth giant. While light and air, indicated in an in-blown
curtain, link onto the Victorian abstraction of a stuffed dead seagull, and thence, by swift
flashes of inevitable sequence, to a weathered woman-face [her own]. That face beats through
the film like the very swift progress of those wings, doomed it is evident, and already extin-
guished in this 'borderline' existence.[2]

Like other films (and novels) that forgo character development and association as means
of engaging an audience, *Borderline* is often hard to follow, and appearing as a silent film in
the first years of sound added to its difficulties. It was hardly seen and, disappointed, the
Pool Films team ceased production, and soon after stopped publishing *Close Up*. Macpherson
left Bryher in 1933 and moved to New York in the early 1940s where, in one last engagement
with film, he co-produced Hans Richter's film *Dreams That Money Can Buy* (1944), before retir-
ing to Italy in 1947, and to life as a writer.[3]

None of the other narrative films associated with *Close Up* and *Film Art* match the ambition and seriousness of the Pool Films' contribution. *Beyond This Open Road* (1934), made by
*Film Art's* editor B. Vivian Braun [dates unknown], reflects the leisure pursuits of London
middle-class youth in the 1930s, fitness, sporty clothing, cycling and rambling beyond the new
suburbs; and, implicitly added to these pastimes, film-making. After the tensions and subjectivities of *Borderline,* it appears shocking in its health-and-efficiency normality, all sunshine,
happy boys and girls, and wholesome outdoor pursuits.[4] Other avant-garde narratives of the

**154** *Beyond This Open
Road*, B. Vivian Braun, 1934.

period are self-conscious exercises in style. *C.O.D. A Mellow
Drama* (1929) was made by a group of technicians led by Desmond
Dickinson at the Stoll Studios, Cricklewood 'during the bleak interval awaiting the installation of sound equipment'.[5] Its story of
gangland skulduggery is told entirely in close-ups of legs and feet
set among dramatic shadows, possibly borrowing this central idea
from *Hands and Feet*, 'a conventional comedy related in an ingeni-
ous manner' (Louis Nalpas, France 1925) shown at the Film Society
in March 1928. Such comic-book visual stylisations of narrative
would become the stock in trade of feature-film titles-sequences
from the 1960s onwards, and music videos in the 1980s. Blakeston's
*I Do Like to be Beside the Seaside* (1928), which has not survived,

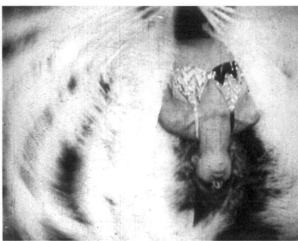

**155** Londoners at work and play: *Everyday*, Hans Richter and others, 1929/67.

was apparently a parody of established 'artistic' film-making styles (one of many such); while *Empire Buyers are Empire Builders* (1930, perhaps not completed), also lost, contained rayogrammed abstractions derived from nutmeg graters and other domestic implements. Another film that started as an exercise was *Everyday* (1929/67), made from material shot at the filmworkshop run for the Film Society in 1929 by Hans Richter (1888–1976), in which Len Lye, Basil Wright and visiting artist Sergei Eisenstein took part.[6] The workshop accompanied the first showing in England of Eisenstein's *Battleship Potemkin* (1925) and a series of lectures in which Eisenstein discussed his theory of 'overtonal montage'. But as edited by Richter nearly forty years later, the workshop footage has been shaped into a familiar avant-garde form – 'a day in the life of a city worker' that repeats *ad nauseam* – its montage including a still-photo cameo of Eisenstein as a London 'bobby', and city-life footage borrowed from *Man with a Movie Camera* and other films in the Society's collection. Disconcertingly, Richter in the 1960s added a soundtrack dominated by an American radio stock-market report, at odds with the 1920s London imagery.[7]

The same theme – the daily drudge of an office worker – was explored with more charm if less self-conscious innovation in Richard Massingham's *And So to Work* (1935), where among the expressionistic shots, a very English comedy of embarrassment is extracted from the unlucky hero's struggles to survive the morning rituals of a suburban boarding house. Massingham (1898–1953) self-financed his early films, and made them while he was still working as a senior medical officer at the London Fever Hospital. His *Tell Me if it Hurts* (1933–35), wickedly designed to increase fear of dentists, exploited this intimate knowledge. From these experiments he developed a successful second career as maker of public information and advertising films, scripting, directing and playing the central character in many of them, and employing domestic locations, family and friends wherever possible. He made numerous information films as part of the war effort, such as the classic *Five Inch Bather* (1942) encouraging water saving, and even a few in the 1950s. As his own eccentric but compelling moon-faced persona became more central, their style became simpler and more conventional and sometimes their length exceeds their invention, but at his best, Massingham's willingness to base his comic ideas on images, rather than dialogue, was that of a natural cineaste. In an obituary tribute, Basil Wright compared his early films to those of Jean Vigo (though Laurel and Hardy equally come to mind):

> like Vigo, Massingham came to film without literary or dramatic preconceptions. For him the logic of the screen image was real and vital. That is why his first films … are, and always will be, so important. For in these, as in *Zéro de conduite*, the logic of the image exists outside the convention (and it *is* a convention) of normal screen continuity. Camera angles and screen movements follow each other according to this logic of the film image, and thereby not only is the comedy enhanced for us, but also a visually flowing pattern of considerable significance emerges.[8]

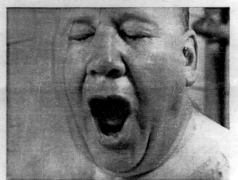

## 1920S AMATEURS

There were artists among the small group of amateurs rich enough to be able to play with film in the pre-war period. Less self-consciously than Brunel, they too were able to affectionately mock the pretensions of the mainstream, and with only a private audience in mind, enjoyed a freedom to openly introduce ideas, such as homosexuality, still taboo in film, but already appearing in contemporary literature.[9] Shot by aspiring director Terence Greenidge, but the brain-child of Evelyn Waugh, *The Scarlet Woman* (1924) involves a plot by the Pope to convert Britain to Catholicism by having an actress (played by Elsa Lanchester) seduce the young Prince of Wales. Waugh himself played two parts, the duffer 'Lord Borrowington' and the Dean of Balliol College, Oxford; the latter himself besotted with the Prince of Wales, and characterised by a startlingly prophetic Andy Warhol wig. Interestingly, five years after scripting the film, Waugh converted to Catholicism, giving the film's attack extra resonance as an Oedipal pre-figuration.

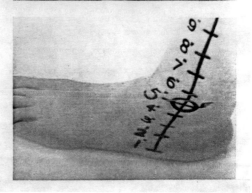

**156** *Five Inch Bather*, Richard Massingham, 1942.

The idea of making a film was probably suggested to the painter Dora Carrington (1893–1932) by her lover Beakus (Bernard) Penrose (1903–88), a sailor/adventurer and younger brother of Roland Penrose, artist and founder of the ICA. Together with friends they made *Dr Turner's Mental Home* and *Topical Budget, Ham Spray September 1929* during a single weekend in 1929. *Topical Budget* was a spoof contribution to the contemporary current affairs film magazine of the same name, and sends up the comings and goings at the house Ham Spray that Carrington shared with the writer Lytton Strachey. The more ambitious *Dr Turner's Mental Home*, with its story of an evil doctor turning his patients into animals, and

**157** *Dr Turner's Mental Home*, Dora Carrington and Beakus Penrose, 1929.

their revenge following the death of one of their number, may have been inspired by H. G. Wells's novel *The Island of Dr Moreau* (1896), which became a popular horror-film subject.[10] Carrington made the costumes and props, Penrose operated the camera, and the film had its first and perhaps only contemporary showing at Virginia and Leonard Woolf's home in Gordon Square, London.[11]

Ostensibly 'industry' films, *Cut it Out: A Day in the Life of a Censor* (1925), *Bluebottles* and *Day-Dreams* (both 1928) were quasi-amateur shorts directed by Ivor Montagu (1904–84), the latter two from storylines provided by H. G. Wells and featuring the young Elsa Lanchester, here paired with her husband Charles Laughton, both rising theatre stars but still new to cinema. A speculative venture by Montagu and Frank Wells (H. G.'s son), their spirit was more Mack Sennett than serious investigation of the boundaries of film or fiction, and they were cheaply shot on available studio sets, but according to Montagu achieved some success. Tongue firmly in cheek, he introduced them to the Film Society as 'comedies of London life written by Mr H. G. Wells [which] display an uncanny insight into the remotest workings of the human heart and mind'.[12]

## GRIERSON'S AVANT-GARDE

'It was something altogether new to be looking at ordinary things as if they were extraordinary'.[13] John Grierson's personal understanding of film's power to reveal previously unseen truths about the world – as had painting and photography before it – was based on making one film as a director, *Drifters* (1929).[14] Grierson (1898–1972) showed *Drifters* at the Film Society,[15] on the same bill as Eisenstein's *Battleship Potemkin* (USSR 1925), which was receiving its British premiere. Grierson had previously written the English inter-titles for Eisenstein's film, and had absorbed its lesson, but limited his own use of montage to the heightening of realism through expressive editing, particularly in the storms scenes (as Hollywood might), forgoing Eisenstein's pursuit of 'third meanings'. For Grierson, 'the task of reality ... [was] not one of reproduction, but of interpretation'.[16] and a film-maker's creativity should serve that end. *Drifters* describes the labour and daily perils of fishermen at sea.

> The men do their own acting, and the sea does its – and if the result does not bear out the *107th Psalm*, it is my fault. Men at their labour are the salt of the earth; the sea is a bigger actor than [Emil] Jannings or [Fyodor] Nitikin or any of them; and if you can tell me a story more plainly dramatic than the gathering of the ships for the herring season, the going out, the shooting at evening, the long drift in the night, the hauling of the nets by infinite agony of

**158** *Drifters*, John Grierson, 1929 (BFI Stills Collection).

shoulder muscle in the teeth of a storm, the drive home against a head sea, and (for finale) the frenzy of the market in which the said agonies are sold at ten shillings a thousand, and iced, salted and barrelled for an unwitting world – if you can tell me a story with a better crescendo of energies, images, atmospherics and all that make up the sum and substance of cinema … I shall make it my next film forthwith.[17]

If *Drifters* fundamentally accepts the social status quo,[18] (where *Potemkin* calls for solidarity with the Revolution), it still importantly demonstrated that the depiction of working-class labour was potentially as rich a subject for the moving image as it already was for literature and the other visual arts.

Grierson's concept of 'realism' built on the example provided by Robert Flaherty's *Nanook of the North* and *Moana*, where prolonged observation led to understanding and interpretation. Flaherty (1884–1951) was notoriously reluctant to commit himself to scripts or detailed storylines, believing, to the frustration of sponsors and collaborators alike, that only through filming and observing the scene would the true subject eventually reveal itself. It was a method that required an unlimited supply of raw film. Grierson observed that 'for Flaherty, it wasn't what he saw or thought he saw that was important, but what the camera over and above, revealed to him. Whence the infinite and infinitely patient experiments with movement; whence … his pioneering work … in the extension of the camera's technical capacities'.[19] Grierson invited Flaherty to England to join his EMB team as an instructor, and set him to work on documenting 'craftsmanship' in Britain's factories, resulting in footage that would become *Industrial Britain* (1931) and a number of other short films. Though

**159** *Man of Aran*,
Robert Flaherty, 1934
(BFI Stills Collection).

Grierson now became the frustrated producer failing to keep the consumption of film stock within his tiny budget (eventually having to take Flaherty off the job), the experience of working alongside the master was invaluable to his British disciples. Edgar Anstey wrote that 'the way in which he would move his camera to anticipate rather than follow the movements of a potter or glass-blower came to be regarded by his documentary colleagues as text-book examples of how to use the camera as something better than a recording machine',[20] and Basil Wright was inspired by his ability 'to look at a landscape and capture all the key elements of that landscape, then translate that into the film image', and learned from him 'the importance of knowing how to "look" through the camera'.[21] From 1931, Michael Balcon and Gaumont-British financed Flaherty's feature project *Man of Aran* (1934), a return to *Nanook*'s theme of man's struggle with nature, this time through a study of a family barely scratching a living from land and sea on the Aran Islands. The film was as anachronistic as *Nanook* and *Moana* were in its description of a way of life of the recent past, not the present (notoriously Flaherty had to persuade his cast of island crofters to hunt a shark as their forefathers had, to provide his film with drama); its 'truth' narrative rather than documentary. Graham Greene was among those who criticised Flaherty's film for its romanticism and departure from the documentary path:

> Photography by itself cannot make poetic cinema. By itself it can only make arty cinema. *Man of Aran* is a glaring example of this. How affected and wearisome were those figures against the skyline, how meaningless that magnificent photography of storm after storm. *Man of Aran* did not even attempt to describe truthfully a way of life'.[22]

Its pursuit of the exotic in a remote place also disappointed Alberto Cavalcanti ('Paris … is just as interesting as Timbuktu or Peking'), though he more tellingly criticised it for its unimaginative use of sound, that was 'little more than a form of musical accompaniment'.[23]

Cavalcanti (1897–1982) had joined the GPO Unit (as the EMB had become) in 1934 specifically to work with its new sound equipment. Astonishingly, all the EMB/GPO films till this moment had been shot silent, with sound and commentary added by the distributor, with or without the Unit's involvement. Cavalcanti's arrival coincided with Basil Wright's return from Sri Lanka with the footage he had shot for *Song of Ceylon* (1934) and with the arrival at the Unit of Humphrey Jennings, and it marked the beginning of a period of sustained experiment. Grierson was keen to capitalise on Cavalcanti's experience of working with sound in France on a series of successful light comedies, and together they conceived *Pett and Pott* (1934), on the use of the phone, in which sound was recorded first, and pictures added later, as an extreme test of the demands of sound composition. Wright (1907–87) and Stuart Legg were

nominally the directors, with Jennings (1907–50) exercising his painterly talents designing the sets. The confidence gained can be seen in the ambitious sound compositions of both Wright's solo *Song of Ceylon* and *Coal Face* (1935) made by Cavalcanti, Harry Watt, William Coldstream, Wright and others. *Coal Face* – essentially another portrait of workers in a heavy industry – takes the unusual form of a collage-film, assembled from bits of Flaherty's *Industrial Britain* and other previously shot material, with extra sequences filmed by Wright and others to fill gaps, and with music, poetry and declamatory statements added to the mix. (Collage was a form Wright had experimented with in his amateur work *Conquest* (1930), which

was entirely constructed from found footage.) Through Wright, W. H. Auden joined the Unit and contributed a madrigal sung by women's voices to accompany the miners' return to the surface at the end of a shift, and at Grierson's invitation a twenty-two-year-old Benjamin Britten provided modernist piano and percussion music; this was the first time that Britten and Auden had worked together. The resulting film is odd if sometimes exhilarating; an oratorio that is in part a promotion for the industry, in part a reminder of harsh working conditions. A men's chorus chants a list of job-titles and industry statistics, and the shocking figure of four deaths and 450 injured in the mines each day[24] is included

without comment; any impulse to criticise the status quo is kept well in check. Wright described it as 'a little test-tube film' in which they tried out 'different uses of the soundtrack in relation to the picture'.[25]

In *Film Art*, Wright and B. Vivian Braun had written a joint manifesto – a transcribed conversation – in which they contemplate the role of abstraction and counterpoint in film-sound:

> *VB:* … music confines itself, very rightly, to noises produced by a limited number of special instruments. [In film] you are at liberty to orchestrate any sound in the world. *W:* Once orchestrated they will become as abstract as music. Orchestrated abstract sound is the true accompaniment to film.[26]

Bolder in form than *Coal Face*, and more fully realised, Wright's own *Song of Ceylon* set images of the Singhalese way of life and belief-system against a rich soundtrack of music and effects assembled by composer Walter Leigh, in which natural sounds were often deliberately un-synchronised with their ostensible source, and – as its only commentary – an account of the island and its peoples given by a European who lived there in the 1640s (cleverly voiced by a contemporary with a Singhalese accent and intonation). The film was intended to promote tea from a source within the Empire, but Wright understood that the culture he was recording would soon be eroded, not least by the trade he was promoting, and his film underlines its fragility. He later described his experience of making the film as 'a religious epiphany', and admitted that he had never again matched its poetry.

*Night Mail* (1936), on the nightly exchange of post between Glasgow and London, more obviously benefited from the experience of *Coal Face*, following the same collaborative method, with most of the same contributors involved, led by Harry Watt and from a script by Wright, with Auden initially acting as assistant director to learn the trade. Surprisingly, the famous sequence that sets Auden's doggerel against the train's progress as it 'crosses the Border' was an afterthought. Grierson saw the assembled film and commented that there was no reference in it to the people who would be getting the mail, and Auden and Britten composed the coda, which Wright edited.

A different but equally innovative response to sound was reflected in *Housing Problems* (1935) directed for the Gas Council by Arthur Elton, Edgar Anstey and Ruby Grierson (one of John's two film-making sisters). This work on slum clearance is often cited as the most politically radical of the Grierson era documentaries on the strength of its makers' decision to film the slum-dwellers in their houses, and to let them speak directly to the cinema audience; a common-place technique in the age of portable 16mm and video equipment, but unprecedented in the 1930s with its imposing cameras and cumbersome sound systems.[27] In static interior shots, the women and men face the camera and speak about damp, vermin and ill health, then are shown happily re-housed in gas-serviced homes. According to fellow documentary maker Paul Rotha, Ruby Grierson was the person who made this intrusive technique work in human terms.

**162** *Housing Problems*,
Arthur Elton, Edgar Anstey
and Ruby Grierson, 1935
(BFI Stills Collection).

'Ruby Grierson's ability to win people's confidence gave a spontaneity and honesty to the 'interviews' that contrasted sharply with the previous, romantic method of handling people'. Grierson himself recalled how Ruby had accused him of looking at the world as if he were in a goldfish bowl, and declared that she was going to break it. She told the slum-dwellers: 'The camera is yours. The microphone is yours. Now tell the bastards exactly what it is like to live in slums'.[28]

Coldstream (1908–87), the credited editor of *Coal Face*,[29] was diffident about his involvement with film, and his contributions as a director have no distinctive style. *The King's Stamp* (1935), on stamp design, has sections in colour, which is rare in GPO films outside animation, and *The Fairy of the Phone* (1936) is a musical on the new telephone exchanges revealing a sense of humour. Auden (Coldstream's lodger during the GPO period) didn't stay long either, briefly returning to teaching before supporting himself by writing, and Jennings, with several works credited to his name[30] but still no clear identity as a film-maker, left in late 1934 to work with Lye on a film at Shell and on other projects that included the *International Surrealist Exhibition* (1936) at the New Burlington Galleries. When Grierson, Wright, Elton and John Taylor also departed to set up Film Centre, Cavalcanti – now in change – brought forward the animators associated with the Unit – Lye, Reiniger and McLaren – to keep production flowing. Jennings returned in 1938 fired up by his involvement in Mass Observation to work on a project about British leisure pursuits, one of two films on British workers proposed that year by the GPO – the other being about factory-work, *British Made* (1939). *Spare Time* (1939), as the leisure film became, was slated to be made in sections farmed out to different

**163** *Spare Time*, Humphrey Jennings, 1939 (BFI Stills Collection).

directors including Richard Massingham (another talent imported by Cavalcanti) and McLaren, as *Mony a Pickle* (1937) had been, but it became Jennings's first individual work. Shot in Lancashire and South Wales around the steel and cotton mills and coal mines, it shows working men and women 'between work and sleep [in] the time we call our own', 'a time when we have a chance to do what we like, a chance to be ourselves'. Apart from these brief scene-setting words spoken by Laurie Lee, the film is without commentary, and seamlessly weaves together its sequences of people in the pub, mending bicycles, tending racing pigeons, watching football, in the dancehall etc., with clever use of overlapping natural sound and music recorded on location. The concept of unmediated recording of people 'doing their thing' is pure Mass Observation, but the poetic montage of images united by a theme would become the signature method of Jennings, here working on his own, but in later films collaborating with his editor and sometimes co-director Stewart McAllister.[31] Writing in the 1980s, the art historian David Mellor noted the value Jennings attached to the visual culture he was recording:

> Prior to the conscious elaboration of Pop Art by the Independent Group at the ICA in the mid 50s *Spare Time* offered perhaps the strongest concentration of pop iconography in any work by a British artist – comic books, pop songs, football-pool advertisements [etc.] … The crucial novelty of the film was the way it revolved about the exploration of the signifiers of pop culture … while in other respects it looks forward even to the intertextual pictorial projects of R. B. Kitaj.[32]

Dai Vaughan, McAllister's biographer, sees both the subject and scope of *Spare Time* as a line of development interrupted by the war, and not picked up again until Free Cinema. (*Spare Time* became part of the British contribution to the New York *World's Fair* of 1939.)

## WAR

The most individual of Jennings's fifteen wartime films built on the strengths of *Spare Time* – his ability to link ideas visually, based on sometimes unexpected but always arresting images. His wartime diaries record his alertness to potential shots: '... coming across Leicester Square just after the sirens are two French soldiers, talking. The three-quarter moonface, very bright, with a few streaks of cloud. A group of white faces outside Lyons looking up watching a great balloon sailing into the sky'.[33] Eerie shots of barrage balloons would appear in *London Can Take It* (1940) and *Fires Were Started* (1943). In *Words for Battle* (1941), one of the first films made with McAllister, the dominant montage is of spoken poetic texts, Jennings deliberately linking Churchill's bleak 'We shall never surrender ...' speech to rousing words from Milton, Blake, Browning, Kipling and Lincoln (identified only in the final credits), and so connecting images of the present struggle and destruction with the enduring humanist values of an Anglophone literary tradition, highlighting what was at stake. In *Listen to Britain* (1942), a portrait of resolve on the domestic front, and *Diary for Timothy* (1946), a snapshot of the exhausted nation as the end of the war approached, which dares to look forward to the post-war era, the primary montage is again visual. *Listen to Britain* is a further example of Jennings's lateral thinking, for its final form combined footage shot for two wholly different film projects,

**164** Humphrey Jennings:
*Listen to Britain*, 1942
(BFI Stills Collection).

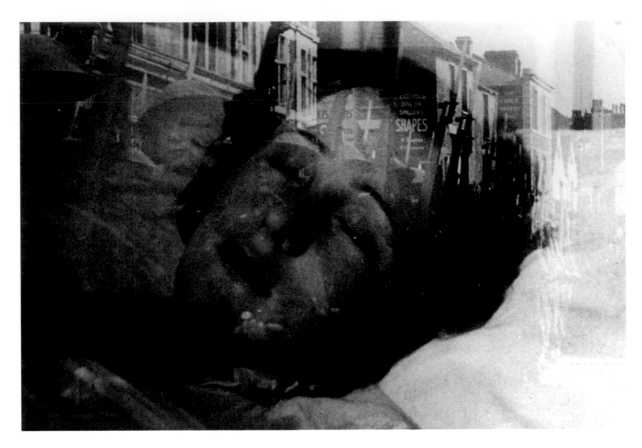

**165** Humphrey Jennings:
*Diary for Timothy*, 1946
(BFI Stills Collection).

a military music film and a sequel to *London Can Take It*, and out-takes from many other sources: 'trees and fields from *Spring Offensive*, coal miners from *Spare Time*, radio valves from *Speaking from America*, the steelworkers and Whitworth bomber factory from *The Heart of Britain*, a Wellington [bomber] from *Target for Tonight*, cutaways for Flanagan and Allen from *Welfare of the Workers* and various transitional shots from here there and everywhere'.[34] *Diary for Timothy* consists of visual notes on the winter of 1944–45 set to words by E. M. Forster, ostensibly recorded for a baby born on the fifth anniversary of the outbreak of the war, to explain the events that have shaped the world he will grow into. Patrick Keiller (to whom Jennings represents an artistic father) describes its effect:

> There are images of rain and fog: of mine-clearing; and of people – queuing for coal, shelter-ing from doodlebugs. The end of the war is expected but continuously postponed. The 1945 election is still in the future. The sense of anticipation is breathtaking. *Diary for Timothy* reflects on what was wrong with Britain before the war, and asks what life will be like afterwards. It is one of the few documents of the period that now feels like science fiction.[35]

Jennings's two story-based films *Fires Were Started* (1943) and *The Silent Village* (1943) showed his increasing boldness and confidence in dealing with 'real' people – the non-actors drafted in to play leading roles. *Fires Were Started* follows the fate of a new recruit to a fire engine crew during one day in the Blitz in 1940, and is memorable for its sequence-construction which builds mood by increments, the surreal imagery of nocturnal London lit by fire, and its depiction of understated heroism and camaraderie among the crew. *The Silent Village* exposed the Nazi reprisals exacted upon the entire population of the village of Lidice in Czechoslovakia in 1943, and Jennings took the unusual decision to involve a Welsh mining community in its re-enactment; a working method that echoes Flaherty but had few other parallels until the community-based projects of Amber Films and others in the 1980s. The villagers of Cwmgiedd and Ystradgynlais in the Brecon Beacons played all the parts and lent their homes to the film, and elected a committee to meet twice a week to discuss the script, view the material already shot, and comment on progress.

Other contributions to the war-effort included Len Lye's *Musical Poster* (1940), an abstract hand-painted film embroidering the slogan 'Careless Talk Costs Lives' that is the equal of his earlier works in this form, and Charles Ridley's *Germany Calling* (1941), wittily edited from forwards-and-backwards printed footage of Nazi soldiers goose-stepping to *The Lambeth Walk* (a tune and title also used by Lye for a hand-painted film, which has caused some attribution confusions). Anthony Gross proposed an equally whimsical animated line-drawn film about air defence, *The Ballad of Barrage Balloons* (1940). His anthropomorphic tale of two female balloons thwarting an invasion reached the story-board stage, but was turned down in favour of a more sober live-action explanation of the balloons' function by Harry Watt, *Squadron 992* (1940), and Gross's War Artist work remained confined to painting and drawing. *The Five Inch Bather* (1942) by Massingham was typical of his many wartime public information films. He responded to the task of promoting water conservation by creating the

**166** Storyboard drawing by Anthony Gross for the unrealized *The Ballad of Barrage Balloons*, 1940.

**167** *Calling Mr Smith*,
Stefan and Franciszka
Themerson, 1944.

simplest of images; he sits in his bath playing with a plastic duck, ladling water over himself
singing 'What to do with the Drunken Sailor?' with a water-level gauge usefully tattooed on
his ankle. Most of his films traded on his oversized, childlike persona, usually depicted as at
odds with, or lost in, the surrounding adult world. In *What a Life* (1948), he and his frequent
sidekick Russell Waters are overwhelmed by post-war depression, and plan suicide from a boat
in the Thames estuary. They jump overboard – but land in just two feet of water, and laughter banishes their gloom.

One of the most original and darkest of the wartime films was Franciszka and Stefan
Themerson's *Calling Mr Smith* (1944). As refugees in London, the Themersons gained their commission from the Film Unit of the Polish Ministry of Information in Exile, and composed an
appeal to the British everyman 'Mr Smith' to join the anti-fascist struggle, and to halt the
Nazis' destruction of Europe's culture, for 'freedom and culture are inseparable'. Images
representing literature, music and architecture are interspersed with drawings, graphics and
shocking footage of atrocities and destruction, all shot through prisms and colour filters in
a remarkable visual collage. Tragically, the British film censor objected to a news image of
a man hanging from the gallows, and like their contemporary work *The Eye and the Ear* the
film was only rarely shown. In making a film that pointed to Hitler's betrayal of the beliefs
of Goethe and Heine, they had – by chance – realised one of Jennings's frustrated film
proposals.

## POST-WAR REVIVAL

The documentaries commissioned for the Festival of Britain included Paul Dickson's sensitive but conventional *David*, a portrait of a Welsh mining community, Wright's *Waters of
Time,* and Jennings's *Family Portrait* (all 1950–51). Wright's film is a river-symphony in the tradition of the city-symphonies of the 1920s, and was sponsored by the Port of London
Authority. It portrays the docks in their last period of full activity before their post-war decline,
and with hindsight seems like an elegy. It, too, reflects the sound-image lessons of *Coal*

**168** *Waters of Time*,
Basil Wright, 1950–1

*Face*, not least in a remarkable sequence where the visual track of dock-workers arriving at dawn by every conceivable mode of transport is edited in counterpoint to a voice chanting a list of their equally innumerable job-titles. Wright considered it his best film after *Song of Ceylon*. Jennings's essay-film *Family Portrait* rather loyally attempts to summarise British national characteristics as they would be represented in the scheme of the Festival's exhibitions, following the pattern of his earlier montage-studies of British society. Lindsay Anderson accused the film of 'lack of passion', and damned it for perpetuating the 'sentimental fiction' of family-life and 'taking refuge in [symbols of] the past'.[36] Jennings may have been uneasy with the idea of a national celebration outside the war context, and frustrated by the limited opportunities in the given theme for exploring social territory unfamiliar to him, the strength of *Spare Time* and *Fires Were Started*. Tragically, he died in 1950 in an accident in Greece while researching a new film, aged just 43, before he had the opportunity to explore new subjects in a new era.

Following *Waters of Time*, Basil Wright made many well-crafted documentaries in the 1950s, but never again worked on the scale of his Festival of Britain film, or achieved the poetry of *The Song of Ceylon*. Such complex essay films would all but disappear till the advent of multi-channel public service television in the 1970s and 1980s. Other documentary film-makers who survived into the post-war era included Massingham and Jacques Brunius (1906–67). Most of Massingham's post-war work is serviceable but rarely inspiring;

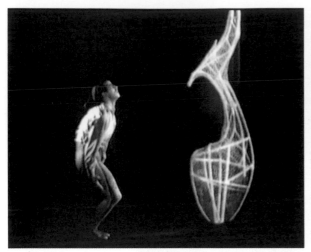

**169** *Between Two Worlds, A Cine Ballet*, Sam Kaner, Guy L Cote and Derrick Knight, 1952.

*Moving House* (1949), *The Cure* (1950*)*, *He Won't Bite You* and *Introducing the New Worker* (both 1951) being indicative titles. *Brief City* (1951–52), directed by Brunius and produced by Massingham, was commissioned by *The Observer* newspaper as a reflection on the achievement of the Festival of Britain – its site a city in microcosm, 'brief' because torn down with indecent haste by the new Conservative government. David Robinson describes the classic surreal trope and 'total surprise' of its opening shots, 'a dream-prospect of wind-whirled litter wrapping itself round the bleak ghost of the former pleasure-ground'.[37] Brunius, who came to England at the invitation of Cavalcanti, was as much a writer as film-maker, and based his long and polemic essay 'Experimental Film in France' for Roger Manvell's *Experiments in the Film* (1949) on his experience as a film-maker and actor and sometimes collaborator with Rene Clair, Jean Renoir, Luis Buñuel, Jacques Prévert and others.[38] The critic Ado Kyrou described him as 'the only surrealist writer who has systematically occupied himself with cinematographic theory'[39], and there are echoes of this critical acuteness in his articles for the BBC's *The Listener*, and the BFI's *Sight and Sound*. He directed one gently subversive film for the Children's Film Foundation *To the Rescue* (1952), and together with Massingham made the *The Blakes Slept Here* (1953 – abbreviated as *Family Album*) which was the last film either made.

In the early 1950s, just as Oxford University was becoming associated with the assertive young film critics gathering around *Sequence*, a different group of artists and film-makers was also running the Oxford Film Group, and embarked on an ambitious dance-film project. *Between Two Worlds, A Cine Ballet* (1952) was the conception of Sam Kaner, an American painter whose ideas were developed by Derrick Knight (later a celebrated documentary maker) and Guy L. Cote, the film's nominal director. With Kaner's themed sequences – one 'monochrome', another 'jazz' – and scheme of abstract sculptural sets, ambitious superimpositions and strong colour, it was surely inspired by the contemporary success of Michael Powell's *The Red Shoes* (1948), and Vincente Minnelli's *An American in Paris* (1951), but was a remarkable achievement for a first, low-budget film. Its principal dancer was Tutte Lemkow, later known as a character actor in countless British and American films.

## FREE CINEMA

Free Cinema was hardly a revolution in film-making ideas; more a wake-up call to a generation who could no longer expect to fulfil their short-film/documentary ambitions in the context of the GPO/Crown Film Unit, and who were left high and dry by the false start of the Festival of Britain commissions. Karel Reisz and Tony Richardson's *Momma Don't Allow* (1955) and the young Swiss film-makers Alain Tanner and Claude Goretta's *Nice Time* (1957) are studies of working-class leisure as *Spare Time* had been, but now specifically about the new phenomenon of youth culture. The sole new ingredient in *Momma Don't Allow* is its highlighting of the class divide where Jennings would have stressed social cohesion. Reisz and Richardson sided with the Teddy Boys and working-class jivers in the featured North London club, rather than the posh-frocked middle-class couples who arrive for a night of 'slumming'. The early section of the film which follows three workers home from work, their preparations to go out, and the similar preparations of the club's attraction Chris Barber's Jazz Band (workers too), is clearly staged, in the manner of Jennings. *Nice Time* is less contrived. Tanner and Goretta's impression of a night's activity in the area around Piccadilly Circus was shot over several weeks, using available light and telephoto-lenses, with wild sound, no commentary, and no central characters. Its implicit voyeurism was indeed modern, and comparable to the

**170** *Nice Time*, Alain Tanner and Claude Goretta, 1957 (BFI Stills Collection).

**171** *Enginemen*, Michael Grigsby, 1958 (BFI Stills Collection).

contemporary observational city-mood films of the photographer (and fellow Swiss) Rudy Burchardt (*The Climate of New York* 1949; *Under Brooklyn Bridge* 1953), Joseph Cornell (*What Mozart Saw on Mulberry Street* USA 1956) or Larry Jordan (*Visions of the City* USA 1957). Lindsay Anderson's portrait of Covent Garden Market *Every Day Except Christmas* (1957) is another worthy continuation of the pre-war tradition, from its subject – workers in their place of work – down to its post-dubbed dialogue, and its sponsorship by the Ford Motor Company (where its producer Reisz worked).[40] Anderson's commentary-less essay on the cheap 'n' cheerful attractions of Margate's amusement park *O Dreamland* (1958) is bolder in its reliance on ironic image-sound juxtapositions alone, though vulnerable to the often-made charge that it reflects an attitude of middle-class superiority. From Unit Five Seven, Michael Grigsby quite openly built on Jennings's legacy in his elegy for steam engines and the men who worked them in *Enginemen* (1958), and his conscious re-working of *Spare Time*'s theme, *Tomorrow's Saturday* (1962). Some of the strongest contributions to Free Cinema were significantly made by outsiders looking in on British society; *Nice Time*,

Mazzetti's fiction film *Together*, Robert Vas's *Refuge England* and *The Vanishing Street* (see below), and arguably by film-makers unknown to Anderson and his critical gang, but more convincingly indicative of a re-awakening – Bruce Lacey, Margaret Tait and an amateur recorder of children's street games who gained the Experimental Film Fund's support, Leslie Daiken (*One Potato, Two Potato* 1957).

## AMBITIOUS NARRATIVE

In the post-war period, ambitious narrative ideas begin to re-appear in marginal places, though unusually Wendy Toye's short *The Stranger Left No Card* (1952), a clever variant on the revenge theme, had a commercial producer. Toye (b.1917) was a dancer and theatre director, and her film was acted as if silent and set to music with the camera as a conspiratorial witness. It was apparently shot to the beat of a metronome, to help stylise the action and allow cutting on the beat.[41] She made a number of more conventional features in the 1950s before returning to stage direction.

Adopted by Lindsay Anderson as a work of Free Cinema Lorenza Mazzetti's *Together* (1955) can equally well be viewed as an exile's contribution to Italian Neo Realism. Mazzetti (b.1928) was a contemporary of Michael Andrews at the Slade School of Art where they both studied painting, and while still a student she made a short film drama based on Kafka's *Metamorphosis*

**172** Michael Andrews and Edouardo Paolozzi in *Together*, Lorenza Mazzetti, 1955 (BFI Stills Collection).

**173** *Herostratus*, Don Levy,
1967 (BFI Stills Collection).

(1953), before embarking on her mini-feature *Together* with Experimental Film Fund support and Anderson as producer. Her story of outsiders at large in an indifferent and even hostile environment leading to tragedy apparently reflected Mazzetti's own traumatic wartime childhood. Its central characters – two deaf-mutes – are played by Andrews and Edouardo Paolozzi, and the film gains from the simplicity of their non-actor performances and from the atmospheric use of the near-empty cityscapes of London's post-war East End, photographed by Walter Lassally. Mazzetti returned to Italy and founded a puppet theatre but made no more films. *Refuge England* (1959) by the Hungarian born Robert Vas (1931–78) again photographed by Lassally, is another depiction of urban alienation – more literally so – that follows a war-camp refugee's first day in London spent searching for his lodgings, having been directed to the wrong 'Love Lane', and viewing with incomprehension John-Bull businessman, shop mannequins, Scots in kilts and empty commuter trams; the experience echoing Vas's own. His sensitive documentary *The Vanishing Street* (1962) records the traditional Jewish street-life of Kessel Street, Whitechapel, in images and sounds, as it awaits destruction by high-rise 'urban improvements', displaying his affectionate, humanist eye for detail.

The literary modernist film tradition re-emerges in some of the many short, purposefully scrambled-stretched-looped narratives supported by the BFI's Experimental Film Fund/Production Board in the 1960s; 'studies in thought', but often no more than a single thought, and only rarely developed into more complex configurations. Examples include David Gladwell's *An Untitled Film* (1964), a moment of nature red in tooth and claw that traumatises a watching child; Ridley Scott's *Boy and Bicycle* (1965), a child playing truant in Hartlepool with his stream-of-consciousness voice-over; and Dunstan Pereira's *Viola* (1967), an image of paranoid delusion shot in stills and dissolves. A rare feature film, Don Levy's *Herostratus* (1967) was also the most daring film of this group, though its critical reception oddly echoes that of the Pool Films' experience with *Borderline*. Levy centres his film on its central character Max's decision to sell his intended suicide to an advertising company. Max's/Herostratus's emotional turmoil is presented alternately in sequences of improvised dialogue shot in fluid, lengthy takes, and shorter tightly-cut sections of contextual imagery, the latter interspersed with recurring leitmotifs – a woman in black leather; some Francis Bacon-like optically-distorted figures. Levy includes these shots ' because they strike the right chord emotionally at a particular time. [They] have a multitude of associations which can vary at different points in the film'[42] Like HD, he describes the film as 'speaking on the direct subconscious level', its structure as 'an emotional one'. And, again like Macpherson and co., he was bitterly disappointed by the critics' mix of indifference and hostility to his work of six years duration.

The first ambitious narrative films and documentaries by black film-makers appeared in this decade. Lloyd Reckord's *Ten Bob in Winter* (1963) was an assured character study of a man living on the breadline in West London, nursing his pride in adverse circumstances, and like South African exile Lionel Ngakane's *Jemima and Johnny* (1966) can be seen as a late contribution to Free Cinema, or a contemporary response to the Nouvelle Vague. The latter won Ngakane an award at the 1966 Venice Film Festival. In the mid-1960s, Horace Ové (b.1939) shot but never completed *Man Out* 'a surreal film about a West Indian novelist who has a

**174** *Ten Bob in Winter*,
Lloyd Reckord, 1963
(BFI Stills Collection).

mental breakdown',[43] before his breakthrough with two remarkable documentaries, an interview portrait of the American writer James Baldwin, *Baldwin's Nigger* (1969), and his prescient
study of the emerging music-form *Reggae* (1970).

Also in the late 1960s, the modernist novelists B. S. Johnson and W. S. Burroughs found
opportunities to become directly involved in film-making. Johnson (1933–73), who consciously pursued in his novels the direct lineage of Joyce and Laurence Sterne, wrote several
screenplays and directed at least two films himself. *You're Human Like the Rest of Them*
(1967), funded by the Experimental Film Fund, was an opportunity for Johnson to experiment with congruent word and editing patterns. The dialogue is delivered in (well-disguised)
decasyllabic verse, the editing paralleling its rhythm, with (as planned – but not fully executed)
the camera angle changing at the end of every line, occasionally with each syllable, according to a tight scheme, flash frames 'referencing' various individual words. His reasoning was
in part based on nostalgia for the richness of Elizabethan stage language; in part a desire to
explore parallel treatment of visual track and text.

I think every poet regrets that no-one uses verse in the theatre any longer ... And I wanted to experiment, to see if I could make verse work ... The images and the language reinforce one another – they work together – they're welded together in a way which isn't possible if you just have a speech given from one angle.[44]

**175** *You're Human Like the Rest of Them*, B. S. Johnson, 1967 (BFI Stills Collection).

*Paradigm* (1969), a dark comment on the writer's condition funded by a Belgian producer, consisted of just six shots, filmed in red and white that observe 'the writer', initially naked as a baby, finally old and grey, speaking to camera. He speaks in an entirely invented language but has ever less to say, becoming silent in the final shot. Johnson planned other works with Beresford, including the promisingly called *Up Yours Too, Guillaume Apollinaire!* (1968), but they remained unrealised.[45]

Not funded by the BFI, but partly shot in the BFI Boardroom and with a small part played by the BFI's long-serving officer John Gillett, *Towers Open Fire* (1963) by Burroughs (1914–97) and Anthony Balch (1937–80) is a kind of avant-garde art home-movie; certainly an experi-

**176** *Towers Open Fire,*
W. S. Burroughs and
Anthony Balch, 1963.
(BFI Stills Collection).

ment, and one in which the surrealist method of random juxtaposition was a guiding principle. An assault on linear narrative and good taste, the film brings together readings by Burroughs, apparently unrelated film sequences, and the linking image of Brion Gysin's prototype *Dreamachine* – inducer of hallucinations and mental stimulation. Balch was a commercial film distributor and cinema owner, who handled an eclectic mix of art cinema and sexploitation films, and he was able to launch *Towers Open Fire* at London's Paris Pullman cinema in 1964, paired with a re-release of Tod Browning's 1930s *film maudit Freaks*. *The Cut-Ups* (1966), as its title suggests, more rigorously followed Burroughs's literary compositional method of chopping up and re-ordering text according to a pre-existing system, in this case based on one-foot lengths of film. Other joint films were made simply as private experiments, such as *Bill & Tony* (1972), filmed close-ups of the writer and film-maker made to be projected back onto the face – the filmed face of one projected onto the living face of the other, forming un-aging masks, and potentially merged personae.[46]

David Larcher's two-and-a-half-hour-long *Mare's Tail* (1969) was the first work of scale and ambition by a filmmaker associated with the Filmmakers Co-op, and its appearance was harbinger of a period of sustained interest by artists in long-form films. Larcher (b.1942) had studied archaeology and anthropology at Cambridge before attending a post-graduate year in Film at the RCA, and by the mid-1960s was a professional photographer. *KO* (1965) made while at the RCA was an accomplished student work, marked by its photography and frequent use of the then fashionable fish-eye lens. *Mare's Tail* and the films that followed couldn't have been more different, except in their often-remarkable photography. Described by Larcher as 'primitive, picaresque cinema', *Mare's Tail* is autobiographical, introspective film-making on the heroic scale of Brakhage's *The Art of Vision* (1965) shown in London by Sitney in 1968. Imagery filmed on impulse – a web-tangled fly buzzing on a tabletop – set against brilliantly staged effects – light apparently pouring from a pregnant figure in a bath – is taken

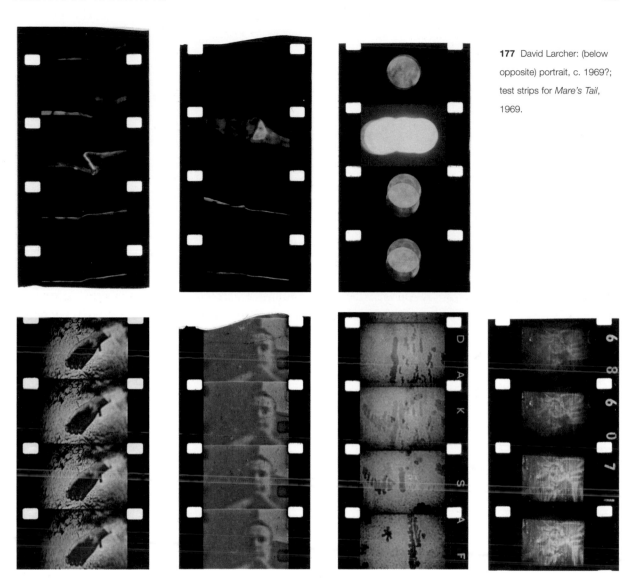

177 David Larcher: (below opposite) portrait, c. 1969?; test strips for *Mare's Tail*, 1969.

as raw material for visual analysis and the construction of metaphors for consciousness and perception. Working before the Co-op's workshops were up and running, Larcher added expressivity to his footage by working directly on the image with heat and chemicals (as had Brakhage and Schneemann), superimposing footage (sometimes in camera), and re-filming sequences from the screen. He described the process as 'starting in the beginning *at the* beginning ... organic ... prima materia ... impressionable massa confusa ... out of which some original naming and ordering processes spring ...',[47] a method familiar enough to painters but unknown till this point among British film-makers. *Monkey's Birthday* (1975), six hours long, follows the artist and his family in their pantechnicon-van home as it travels across Europe into Asia, encountering and recording remarkable landscapes and peoples, and experiencing the romantic artists' life of poverty and visionary experience. Here his

**178** David Larcher,
*VideØvoid*, 1993–5.

assembled images are embroidered by optical printing to achieve a layering of time and image of extraordinary intensity. (He was also the first film-maker to make colour positive prints using the Co-op's contact printer.) The accompanying music and recorded sounds include sections during which Larcher speculates philosophically about the image, quoting Gurdjieff, in what would become a familiar feature of his later work. These works complete, Larcher was silent for a decade, but re-emerged with *E ETC* (1986), 'E' representing Elizabeth, the name of both his partner and his sister; another meditation on relationships and scenes from daily life in Scotland and France, but with more emphasis than before on speculation about the condition of 'the image', and with even greater powers of invention in its manipulation and development of the visual track. This work also represented the mid-point in Larcher's evolution from a film-maker obsessed with celluloid to a video-artist uniquely in control of the electronic image. The work is full of visual references to the material of celluloid, its stains, light-leaks and scratches, but it is entirely through video that the image is spun, flipped, composited and squeezed, and its colours and tonalities reversed. In the 1980s Larcher became artist in residence at first CICV (Centre International de Creation Video) at Montbelliard in France, then later at ZKM (Zentrum fur Kunst und Media) in Karlsruhe in Germany, where he had access to the most advanced digital post-production facilities. Funded by partnerships between these laboratories and Channel 4, the BFI and the Arts Council, he made a series of works *Granny's Is* 1989, two versions of *VideØvoid* (1993–5) and *Ich Tank* (1998), with the same mix of autobiographical material, philosophical speculation and dazzling visual invention. The mix now included imagery generated from the electronic signal itself (with patterning derived from its faults), which Larcher wove into elaborate abstractions, which then sometimes tore themselves apart to reveal the live-action imagery being carried by the signal. The critic Sean Cubitt admiringly commented on Larcher's ability to turn 'the dead-end of the aesthetics of medium-specificity [into] a Zen encounter with the void at the heart of the work, and by inference, the medium of electronic imaging itself.'[48]

Both *Mare's Tail* and *Monkey's Birthday* were funded by the art collector Alan Power. Stephen Dwoskin, the only other artist to break into long form in the early 1970s, had to self-fund or go abroad for support for his *DynAmo* (1972), *Tod und Teufel* (1973) and *Behindert* (1974); not till the mid-1970s did the BFI sufficiently recover from the trauma of its overspends on *Herostratus* to venture support for his *Central Bazaar* (1976), after which the floodgates opened.

The mid-1960s saw the emergence of the first 'independent' film-making professionals, 16mm lone operators, of whom the two most notable were products of Thorold Dickinson's film course at the Slade, Peter Whitehead and Don Levy. Their careers, widely discussed at the time, contributed to the perception that it was desirable – and indeed viable – to set your own agenda as a film-maker, whether artist or 'auteur'. Whitehead came to personify the *nouvelle vague* concept of *le caméra stylo* (camera-pen); camera-on-shoulder, he was present at most significant arts happenings, rock concerts and political events of the period. In his kinetic short films made for the emerging group The Rolling Stones (such as *Lady Jane* in *Charlie Is My Darling* 1964) he has been credited with inventing the music-video form; while his self-financed record of the night the poets took over the Albert Hall, *Wholly Communion* (1965), became the model for a new form of engaged arts documentary. He went on to make feature documentaries such as *The Fall* (1968) in which he tried to involve himself directly with the US student protest movement at Columbia University from behind the camera, and a semi-autobiographical feature

**179**  Peter Whitehead:
*Wholly Communion*, 1965.

**180** Peter Whiteread shooting *The Fall*, 1969.

*Daddy* (1974) made with sculptor Niki St Phalle, before suddenly dropping out and developing a second career as a falconer to Arab princes.[49] While at the Slade, Don Levy made the meticulously crafted sponsored shorts *Time Is* (1964) and *Crafts of Fez* (1966) for the Nuffield Unit for the History of Ideas (which had loaned its equipment to the school), which in turn supplied images to his *Five Short Films* or *Five Film Poems* (1967), tiny, perfectly-crafted essays in style that counterpoint the spoken word with images, made concurrently with *Herostratus*, discussed above.

The Tattooists – Dick Fontaine, Mike Myers and others – represented another new model in the late 1960s; hip young film-makers who made enough money from selling their skills to television and advertising to support an independent film-making habit. Fontaine and Myers, who moved in the circle of the photographer David Bailey and model Jean Shrimpton, made films that were variously witty, self-indulgent, provocative and serious, and stylishly gave them numerical titles such as *Tattooist # 5 Talk Film,* in which Myers abuses the audience direct to camera, *Tattooist # 8,* a cinéma-vérité study of Norman Mailer's campaign to become Mayor of New York, and *Tattooist # 10, Messages from the Lost Planet,* in Jan Dawson's description 'a dizzying, dazzling montage of single-frame shots of advertisements, street signs, urban American architecture, carefully cut to a first-rate pop score and powerfully conveying the impression of a disintegrating civilisation'[50] (all c.1967–70). This ideal of a dual economy in which commercial work supported more individual 'cultural' projects was pursued by many (if achieved by few) in the 1980s and 1990s.

**181** The Tattooists

## WORK

Responses to the rising sense of political crisis in the early 1970s provided an area of overlap and exchange between film-makers and gallery artists. Two themes were prominent; opposition to the Heath government's anti-union legislation and rising unemployment, and at the same time, the growing awareness of the unions' failure to advance the rights of women in the workplace. Surprisingly, the opening moves were made not by documentary film-makers, but by gallery artists. Conrad Atkinson (b.1940) made his symbolic (and rather enigmatic) performance to camera *Industrial Relations Bill* (1971) as a response to the government's Bill of 1970 (the Act of 1971), which restricted trade union rights, and led to strikes by dock-workers and miners.[51] Atkinson showed his film in the random-survey-of-the-avant-garde context of *Art Spectrum*, but on other occasions he used documentary material as an element in solo exhibitions about specific industrial disputes, including one at a factory in his home town of Cleator Moor, represented in text, still-images and video in *Strike at Brannans* (ICA 1972). This followed *Garbage Strike* at the Sigi Krauss Gallery 1970, and led to *Work, Wages and Prices* at the ICA in 1974.

Film and video remained peripheral to Atkinson's work, but the New Zealand artist Darcy Lange (b.1945), who was active in Britain between 1970 and 1978, devoted himself uniquely to filmed representations of British working life and the British class system. His studies began while he was a sculpture student at the RCA with clay portraits of *Irish Road Workers in Oxford Street* (1971) but were followed by film, video and photographic studies (shot simultaneously) of people from contrasting social classes, at work, in education and in their domestic environments. His titles illustrate the scope of his undertaking: *Breaker Metal Works, Balsall Heath, Birmingham* and *Mr and Mrs Mates & Family, Pimlico* (both 1972), *Craigdarroch Hill Sheep Run, Scotland* (1973), the multi-part series *A Documentation of Bradford Working Life* (1974) that looked at steel smelting and rolling, woollen mills, piston-ring production and a mail order factory, commissioned by the Bradford City Art Gallery and Museum, and the *Studies in Comprehensive and Grammar Schools* (1977) shot in Birmingham. Without

**182** *Industrial Relations Bill*, Conrad Atkinson, 1971.

**183** *Osborn Steelworks*
from *A Documentation of*
*Bradford Working Life*, Darcy
Lange, 1974 (Bradford
Industrial Museum).

commentary, he saw these as 'performance analysis; they searched the monotony of the work, they questioned the workload and the suffering due to the work',[52] but as recorded, they are remarkable for their neutrality and empathy. The takes are extremely long, the editing minimal and the subjects acknowledge and respond to the camera's presence. Now they seem extraordinary social documents of abandoned industries and archaic social attitudes. Lange's studies were exhibited at the Jack Wendler Gallery (1973), the ICA (1975) and in Bradford, the last only after Lange's return to New Zealand. There he started a new series *Artists at Work* in 1998.

The individual rights of women and their contemporary working conditions were the subject of *Women and Work: A document on the Division of Labour in Industry 1973–75*, made by Mary Kelly with Kay Hunt and Margaret Harrison, and exhibited at the South London Gallery in 1975. This took the form of charts, questionnaires, photographs and video documentation – essentially Lange-like unmediated scenes of women on the factory floor – that together drew attention to gender inequalities in the workplace. Kelly also participated in the Berwick Street Film Collective's *Nightcleaners* (1975), a film that began as a campaigning documentary about a long-running battle for better working conditions for women cleaning offices at night, and the failure of their union to support them. At the end of four years, it emerged as almost a meditation on work and the endurance of the individual human spirit, as a result of its repeated searching of the women's faces in extreme close-up, re-filmed and slowed down to the point of near-stasis, accompanied by their overheard conversations, and contrasted with fly-on-the-wall shots of fruitless political meetings. The Collective was formed in 1970, with members Richard Mordaunt, Marc Karlin, James Scott and Humphrey Trevelyan, with the aim of producing 'films that take politics as their subject both in terms of film-making and film content' that entail 'an examination of the processes of perception which in turn requires a re-examination of film-language'.[53] *Nightcleaners* and its follow-up *36–77* (1978) were their most extreme

statements, intended for but ill-suited to the campaign trail; hard to watch in cinema or gallery, yet extraordinary artistic statements. Clare Johnston reviewing *Nightcleaners* in *Spare Rib* described it as 'a material object in which meanings are produced, not by the filmmaker alone, but by the filmmaker and the viewer together',[54] an acknowledgement of its 'difficulty' but also an indication of how far the critical language of structural film had penetrated the wider independent cinema.

**184** *Nightcleaners*, The Berwick Street Film Collective, 1975.

Other contemporary responses to 'work' included Haselden's *MFV 'Maureen'*, discussed later, and works by the Four Corners group that included Joanna Davis and Mary Pat Leece's *On Allotments* (1976) about a threatened community of gardeners, and Davis's *Often During the Day* (1979) a structural near-poem on the sociology of housework that quotes from Ann Oakley's contemporary study of the subject.[55] Wollen and Mulvey's *Riddles of the Sphinx* (discussed below), again with Kelly's participation, was one of the most substantial contributions to the debate. Mike Dunford's *One Million Unemployed in Winter 1971* (1971) was one of the few works from the Co-op group to acknowledge the contemporary politics of work directly, though Gidal might rightfully claim that *all* his work implicitly addressed the subject, and Le Grice provided his own elegant summary in the form of his *Time and Motion Study* (1976), a record of the artist doing the after-dinner washing-up.[56]

**185** *Riddles of the Sphinx*, Laura Mulvey and Peter Wollen, 1977 (BFI Stills Collection).

## THE PRODUCTION OF MEANING

With rare exceptions, Bruce Beresford's vision of how the Experimental Film Fund might assist future feature directors had focused on the production of 'calling-card' short films; a decade later, Peter Sainsbury saw the BFI Production Board (as it now was) best serving 'the new social function of cinema' by producing feature-length films in-house.[57]

Catalysts to many who followed, Laura Mulvey (b.1941) and Peter Wollen (b.1938) began their film-making partnership simultaneously with their most sustained intervention into cinema studies as theorists, one activity growing out of and feeding the other.[58] Sharing Sainsbury's vision, they addressed the mainstream from the position of practitioners attempting the fusion of the 'two avant-gardes' as advocated by Wollen in his *Studio International* article of 1975, and with the benefit of their insights into psychoanalytic theories of spectatorship. Their succession of fiction and documentary works explored contemporary social and political issues within highly formal film structures or frameworks, the latter their means of resisting the 'monolithic accumulation of traditional film conventions' (Mulvey's phrase). Their first feature *Penthesilea* (1974) is in five very different parts; a fixed camera record of a mime performance of Kleist's play of the same title about the Queen of the Amazons; a monologue about the play by a prowling Peter Wollen, witnessed by a independently prowling camera; a slide show of ancient representations of Amazons; an aside on the Suffragette discourse; and a final section recapitulating the four sections already presented, seen simultaneously on four video screens. *Riddles of the Sphinx* (1977) similarly brackets a series of tableaux describing 'easily recognisable situations from a [working] mother's life', set in 'kitchen, canteen, shopping, playground', with a direct address to camera by Mulvey, a narrative by Mary Kelly, and enigmatic, optically printed footage of the Sphinx in Gaza, 'representing a repressed instance of the female unconscious', the camera viewing the tableaux in thirteen completely circular panning-movements. Echoing contemporary statements of intention by Gidal and Le Grice, Wollen explained 'Our aim is the production of meaning rather than transparency of meaning. The key words are montage, camera strategy and heterogeneity'. Mulvey continued (highlighting a divergence from the Co-op group):

> We wanted a definite camera strategy, but the 360 degree pans aren't just a formal device, It's important that they interact with the content too. They fit in with the claustrophobia and caught-ness that the woman's story is about. Circumscribed circles. As well as that, they make it perfectly clear where the camera is in relation to the spectator and to the screen. There's a kind of tension between the [spectator's] lack of knowledge of what is going to slip onto the screen next, and their knowledge that the shot is not going to veer away or cut till it's returned to its original recognisable point of departure. Each shot ends of its own accord; nothing to do with the idiosyncratic volition of the filmmakers' mind or eye.[59]

The idea that the viewers' experience of a film should be one of 'the production of meaning' – there's work to be done while viewing – was a dominant preoccupation of the 1970s avant-garde, and is also present in Wollen and Mulvey's subsequent features *Crystal Gazing*

(1981) and *The Bad Sister* (1983), though the 'idiosyncratic volition of the filmmakers' mind and eye' (aesthetic decision making?) reasserts itself in direct proportion to their decrease in structural formality. These narratives have, at times, the feeling of high-level seminars on film language and social politics – a collection of brilliantly expressed ideas with the films' central characters as exemplary illustrations – but their truth and appropriateness to their time derives from their common theme of the contradictory position of an active woman in contemporary society. And iconic images of powerful women from their films – the trapeze artist whose performance punctuates *Riddles* and the woman singer/saxophonist (Lora Logic) from *Crystal Gazing* – resonated in subsequent feminist artists' film-making.[60] Wollen and Mulvey's non-fiction work includes the docu-drama *AMY!* (1980) on the aviator Amy Johnson, and a study of the artists *Frida Kahlo and Tina Modotti* (1982) for the Arts Council. The importance to other artists of Mulvey's writing and of this body of film-making is discussed further below.

James Scott (b.1941), son of painter William Scott, and himself a Slade-trained painter, conceived his first completed feature *Adult Fun* (1972) as a Godardian fragmented tale of 'small-time thuggery' while also working on *Nightcleaners*. Though happy with its mix of 'fantasy' and 'the real', he concluded that the film had failed to achieve 'a dramatic whole' and saw his next step being 'to try to unify these contradictory elements without losing the arbitrary way things happen. In theatre, Brecht managed to do it ... but I've never seen it done in a film. No film for me for me has the quality of Brecht, or what Joyce did with the novel'.[61] Given this aspiration, the subject and treatment of Scott's next film was surprising, but it resulted in the most radical narrative experiment of this highly experimental period. The origin of *Coilin and Platonida* (1976) was in an observation by Walter Benjamin about the folk-tales recorded by the Russian writer/poet Nicholai Leskov, of how 'the spoken word is enriched from generation to generation by the experience of the story-teller of the time'. Scott linked this to the history of early photography, and the ways that photographs and film 'can penetrate beneath the surface' to reveal the iconic or symbolic image. This led him re-tell a Leskov story of an unmarried Russian peasant who brings up her son as a girl in a convent, then hopes they can find peace living together with an unhappily married cousin. Scott set his version in 20th century Connemara (an area 'uncontaminated by capitalism'), and shot it on Super 8, which he blew up to 16mm to make it grainy, sometimes including two or more scenes on screen, side by side.

> Technically I would have preferred to return to the beginnings of photography instead of making use of the technically highly developed commercial methods of today. However, to develop an individual film emulsion would have been time consuming. ... I believe that a perfect picture gives a too perfect, almost unapproachable impression, and leaves too little room for the process of discovery which is so central to the oral tradition of story-telling.[62]

Originally shown silent, with elaborate inter-titles setting the scene and carrying the dialogue, the film met such indifference and even hostility that Scott reissued it two years later

with a soundtrack of piano music, but it remains a neglected, little-known work. His film on his father's formative years *Every Picture Tells a Story* (1984) is more conventional in form, and Scott has subsequently returned to painting.

The origins of Ken McMullen's *Resistance* (1976), which spans the borders between fiction and documentary, are equally unusual. McMullen (b.1948 – another Slade School graduate) worked on the film's development with doctor/psychiatrist Arnold Lincoln and historian Rod Kelward, and took transcripts of therapy sessions with traumatised former French Resistance members as his starting point. Collaborators on the project also included professional actors and the performance artists Stuart Brisley, Marc Chaimowicz and Anna Kolpy, who were read transcripts and given parts to play, and later encouraged by Lincoln (on screen) to 're'-enact 'their' individual memories of rivalry, betrayal and guilt for actions done or undone. The staging of this psychodrama is interspersed with archival footage and photographs, posing questions of authenticity (which representation is more true?), and moves to deeper levels as the participants' unconscious motivations begin to surface. Formally, the film mixes directly shot sequences with re-filmed video and the archive footage, adding to its multi-layered textures. McMullen has continued to make collaborative documentaries and records of performance art, and ambitious features such as *Ghost Dance* (1983) and *1871* (1990).

Like Scott, Malcolm Le Grice came to making feature-length works as a well-established film-maker, already with a clear agenda (his work is mostly discussed in the next chapter). A transitional work between his short films and the long-form was *After Manet, After Giorgione, le Dèjeuner sur l'Herbe or Fête Champêtre* (1975), an hour-long deconstruction of the process of filming a picnic, shown on four adjacent screens, that (unlike Manet) gives all the picnic participants, Le Grice himself, and his film-maker friends Raban, Nicolson and Eatherley, an active role – each is responsible for the camerawork of one screen following Le Grice's varied directions – thus exploring 'the conceptual relationship of the camera to the scene in spatial terms'.[63] The film also elegantly catalogues cinema's palette, with sequences in positive and negative, black and white and colour, silence and sound, static and moving camera.[64] *Blackbird*

**186 (opposite)** *Coilin and Platonida*, James Scott, 1976

**187** Malcolm Le Grice, *After Manet, After Giorgione, Le Dèjeuner sur l'Herbe or Fête Champêtre*, 1975.

*Descending – Tense Alignment* (1977) plays its game of 'temporal deconstruction' on one screen and within a domestic setting (Le Grice's home), limiting its action to a series of domestic tasks, hanging out washing, pruning a tree in the garden, making coffee, typing a script, answering the phone; all observed in extremely long takes (echoing those in the simultaneously shot *Riddles*).[65] His deconstruction paradoxically involves a construction of screen time and space of a Chinese-box complexity; time advances in a two-steps forward one-step back routine, the camera moving position at each halt to follow the different participants, while (as in *After Manet*) progressing through a repertory of camera-strategies. It also becomes clear, as the film moves towards its crescendo of superimpositions, that the script being written is that of the film itself. The writer-typist was played by Lis Rhodes (standing in for Le Grice), and the long sequences of voice-over in which she reads the script's detailed outline of the action in a neutral voice anticipate her own now celebrated use of this technique, first found in her own more abstract work of deconstruction *Light Reading* (1978, see below).

Le Grice's *Emily – Third Party Speculation* (1978) was built round his own performance to camera, and presented many of his familiar concerns in verbal form, with even more limited visual action (table-polishing is a recurring motif) becoming word-bound and claustrophobic. *Finnegan's Chin – Temporal Economy* (1981) is more expansive with a more complex scheme of action, and returns to the device of having a surrogate for the artist, this time his film-maker neighbour Jack Murray. The 'narrative event' explored is the routine of getting up and shaving, eating an egg, leaving the house; its repetitive shape echoing the children's round 'There was an old man called Michael Finnegan/He grew whiskers on his chin-igan ...' (with its obvious link to Joyce, patron saint of deconstruction). Like the song, the shot-sequences permutate, here according to a complex mathematical system, again to question and un-pick time and viewpoint, action and re-action, 'naturalism' and fantasy. Despite *Finnegan's* comparative critical success.[66] Le Grice withdrew from feature-length films for nearly a decade, returning only when digital cameras and computer-controlled editing allowed a more hands-on form of working. *Sketches for a Sensual Philosophy* (1988) announced a more positive acceptance of subjectivity, and at the same time Le Grice's return to an interest in ideas thrown up by interaction with the computer. He described the work as 'nine short video "songs" conceived like a musical album, some [made] in collaboration with other artists or musicians, three exploring computer generated image and sound. Each begins from its own artistic proposition drawn from sensual responses to sound or picture'.[67] Here the 'picture' sometimes derives from home-movie footage, but often becomes highly abstracted, and some sequences are wholly computer-generated abstract sound-image constructions. *Chronos Fragmented* (1995) shares this 'song–sequence' structure, but more extensively and openly uses informally shot footage to reference his life and experience. Sequences draw on the artist's travels in China, Mediterranean culture, images recalling his father who had recently died, and showing a film-maker friend in the fragmenting former Yugoslavia; the editing prompted, but not wholly determined, by suggestions made by programmes he had written for his computer.

Other feature films funded by the BFI in the late 1970s which more self-conciously attempted to intervene in the mainstream with a political engagement equivalent to that of Godard and Straub/Huillet, often using re-enactment as a means of illuminating a historical subject, included *Justine* by Stuart Mackinnon, Clive Myer and Nigel Perkins (aka the Film Work Group 1976), Ed Bennett's *The Life Story of Baal* (1978) based on Brecht's play, Phil Mulloy's *In the Forest* (1978), Anna Ambrose's *Phoelix* (1979), Sue Clayton and Jonathan Curling's *The Song of The Shirt* (1979), Richard Woolley's *Brothers and Sisters* (1980) and Anthea Kennedy and Nick Burton's *At the Fountainhead* (1980). Most of these were heavily didactic and many embraced Brechtian 'alienation' techniques, often characterised by flat acting, flatter delivery and immobile staging, and only rarely exhibited the fluid, cinematic camera-style of the valorised early Godard (or Fassbinder) or the economic editing of Straub/Huillet. They were dubbed by sceptics at the time 'post-Straubian Costume Dramas' and contributed to the developing sense in the early 1980s that British independent feature 'experiments' were a doomed investment, thus making life hard for those with feature ambitions that followed, including Derek Jarman, Peter Greenaway and Sally Potter.

The star to which the Production Board next hitched itself at the end of the 1970s was Peter Greenaway (b.1942). Trained as a painter, Greenaway spent a decade at the Central Office of Information editing documentaries and learning film craft, emerging in 1976 with a group of tightly constructed self-funded short films to his name. His early works show many characteristics of structural cinema, though made outside the fraternity, but with *Vertical Features Remake* (1978) and his first (very) long film *The Falls* (1980) literary ideas and a fondness for cataloguing and lists began to dominate – his highly structured image-flow

**189** Promotional card for
*The Falls*, Peter Greenaway,
1980.

becoming increasingly subservient to a voice-over that plays its own elaborate narrative games, while in a detached way re-contexting the image. His BFI-funded feature *The Draughtsman's Contract* (1982) was the first to have a conventional story-line – a chilly Restoration romp – and gained him critical success and a following, and led to further feature projects *A Zed and Two Noughts* (1985), *The Belly of an Architect* (1987), *The Cook, The Thief, His Wife, Her Lover* (1989), *The Baby of Macon* (1993) and others, with equally dystopian narratives, and containing brilliantly staged scenes that alternately dazzled and shocked, seemingly their prime purpose. He found a happier balance between verbal narrative and image in some of his video works, such as his digitally-illuminated manuscript version of 'The Divine Comedy' *A TV Dante (Cantos I-VII)* (1989) made with painter Tom Phillips using the latest video paint-box technology, and the beautifully crafted documentaries *Four American Composers* (1983), both made for Channel 4. In these, richer texts and the demands of collaboration kept his more baroque tendencies in check. His essay on the naturalist *Darwin* (1992) was an interesting experiment in high-definition TV that appeared to be executed in a single shot, tracking into and out from its elaborately staged tableau vivant. The collage possibilities of digital editing also gave added layers of visual interest to later features such as *Prospero's Books* (1991) and *The Pillow Book* (1996). Another conduit for his encyclopaedia-mania has been exhibition-making, including his installation *In the Dark*, shown as part of *Spellbound: Art and Film* at the Hayward Gallery (1996), that deconstructed the whole process of preparing a feature film – from culling ideas from newspapers to the casting of actors (the latter coldly displayed, live, in glass cases).

Sally Potter's (b.1949) feminist classic short *Thriller* (1979, discussed in the final chapter) convinced the Production Board to support her first feature film *The Gold Diggers* (1983), 'a musical describing a female quest' in which the unlikely partnership between an economically oppressed black woman and a glamorous but equally exploited film-star she befriends leads the star (Julie Christie) to an understanding of her own oppression. The film asks questions 'about the illusion of female powerlessness; about the *actual* search for gold and the *inner* search for gold; about imagery in the subconscious and its relationship to the power of cinema […], seeing the history of cinema itself as our collective memory of how we see ourselves, and of how we – as women – are seen'.[68] Beautifully photographed by Babette Mangolte, the film's long-held shots and narrative repetitions reflected Potter's early association with the Filmmakers Co-op and the theories of Mulvey and Le Grice, and contributed to its box-office failure. The short dance-based narrative *The London Story* (1986) and two documentary series followed, and their greater success led finally to her more conventionally realised *Orlando* (1992) based on Virginia Woolf's novel, with Tilda Swinton as the gender-changing lead and, less happily, Billy

**190** *The Gold Diggers*,
Sally Potter, 1983

Zane as her lover, but a clever supporting cast of British eccentrics including Heathcote Williams and Quentin Crisp (the latter as Queen Elizabeth). With *The Tango Lesson* (1997), a fictional but very personal work in which she herself played the lead, she was able to draw on her own life-long entanglement with dance, and achieved a critical and popular success.

Also funded by the BFI were a number of one-off projects, some containing reflections of distinguished contemporary cineastes from abroad. Raban and Halford's *Black & Silver* (1981) a deconstruction of Oscar Wilde's story of a dwarf at the Court of the Spanish Infanta, and simultaneously of Wilde's source *Las Meninas* by Velasquez, recalls Yvonne Rainer's film/dance mix in films such as *Lives of Performers* (1972).[69] More importantly, it signalled Raban's determination to work on a larger scale, and also the sustained interest in dance and performance as narrative forms of his then collaborator and partner Marilyn Halford. Chris Petit's *Radio On* (1979) emulated the existential road-movies of Wim Wenders (to the extent of being produced by Wenders, and using Wenders' signature-cameraman of the time Martin Schäfer), but achieved an odd lyricism in its stylish combination of casual mystery and music by Kraftwerk, David Bowie and Eddie Cochran. Similarly, Robina Rose's *Nightshift* (1981), funded by the Arts Council and with cameraman Jon Jost, was a string of episodes involving eccentric hotel-guests; a politer version of Warhol's *Chelsea Girls* (1965–6) that incidentally recorded portraits of the contemporary film/art-world.

## IMAGE AND VOICE

At the close of the 1980s, David Finch (b.1956) wrote an article for the Film Co-op's magazine *Undercut* in which he tried to pin down the essence of 'poetry' in film, and its relationship to narrative, which he defined as being different from (but often confused with) 'drama'; arguing that 'drama [the driving force in popular film] is the replacement of narration, the method of epic poetry, by presentation'.[70] His was the first call in *Undercut* for a film-making philosophy to replace that of structural (or structural/materialist) film, and it expressed his own frustration with the 'anti-narrative' project. 'My work is narrative, not anti-narrative. It's an attempt at a critical kind of poetry: the resolution of narrative into an elliptical form that both excludes and invites identification. ... I do not accept that narrative is "illusionist".'[71] Its publication, which would have been impossible in a Co-op magazine a decade earlier, indicated the extent to which interest in narrative had regained momentum. Finch's own narratives included re-tellings of classic tales such as Edgar Allan Poe's *The Fall of the House of Usher* (1981), a film in ten tableaux, with voice-overs giving different versions of the story, before developing into a looser mix of documentary and fiction in *1983* (1983) and others, anticipating the work younger artists such as Oliver Payne and Nick Relph of two decades later. Finch's poetic autobiographical works have already been described. Another story-teller who began to make an impact in the early 1980s was Ian Bourn (b.1953), who converted the familiar monologue-to-camera of early video into a wholly fictional form with none of the video-specific allusions of his predecessors. Beginning with *Wedding Speech* (1978), ostensibly a tape recorded by an absent best-man, he created a series of fictional selves, witty and sometimes sad portraits of East End characters: the obsessive model-plane maker in *B29 (Three Nights In)* (1979); two half-vacant minds – a video-game addict (the artist) and his sunbathing partner (Helen Chadwick) in *The End of The World* (1982); a failed punter trying to sell on his gambling 'method' in *Sick as a Dog* (1989), this last simultaneously an affectionate portrait of the declining London sport of greyhound racing, and a parody of instructional videos. His humour and deadpan delivery led to his involvement as a writer-performer in films by John Smith and Paul Bush.[72]

**191** *The End of The World*, Ian Bourn, 1982.

**192** *London*, Patrick Keiller,
1994 (BFI Stills Collection).

Others chose to explore narrative largely without actors, through the relationship of images, spoken texts and sound alone. The unseen narrator formed an essential building block of feminist film and video in the 1980s, for example in the work of Lis Rhodes, Mona Hatoum or Nina Danino; it also shaped the fictions of Patrick Keiller (b.1950), Cordelia Swann (b.1953) and Gad Hollander (b.1948) and was central to the quasi-documentary projects of Steve Hawley (b.1952) and John Smith (b.1952). It was also the preferred medium of gallery artists Jaki Irvine (b.1966) and (implicitly) Tacita Dean (b.1965 ) who are discussed in the final chapter. Of these, the unlikely trailblazer was Keiller. In the slide-tape works he made while still at the RCA, *The Tourists' Return* and *The View Behind Wormwood Scrubs Prison*[73] (both 1980) he established the balance between independence and relatedness of sound and image that would characterise the work of these artists over the next two decades. In these works, words neither directly follow nor describe the images, but qualify their meaning. Keiller wrote at the time (in cod eighteenth-century prose, following his hero Laurence Sterne):

> These entertainments have their origins in real life, in moments when place, time, mood and weather coincide in a prospect that is somehow *true*. In making public such revelations, I have found that, instead of trying to reconstruct them, it is better to invent new ones. These are combinations of photographs or film with spoken narratives derived from them. … There are often no people in the pictures as this leaves more room for the narrator's creations.[74]

Keiller's own compositional method was highly unorthodox. His films were shot and edited before he wrote their scripts, often beginning with a photo-essay laid out in linear form on a paper scroll as a prompt to his narrative invention. As in his slide-tapes, their imagery was of static, classically framed landscapes and cityscapes, with no more than incidental movement within the frame. His narrator's voice-over describes journeys; across Europe in *The End* (1986), from England to Scotland in *Valtos* (1988), crossing and re-crossing London in the feature-length *London* (1994), making observations along the road. This highly literary and discursive form allowed Keiller, a trained architect, to comment on social and cultural history, to 'read' and interpret the human interventions in the changing scene, while almost incidentally hinting at the events and circumstances that have shaped the narrator's life – his cultured down and out in *The End*; 'Robinson', a man returning from years abroad in *London*. The viewer of a Keiller film can identify with the lead character, but only with his mind (his protagonists are invariably male); there is no physical form to bond with.

Gad Hollander starts from the other end with existing narratives, drawing freely from ancient Greek myths to shape his own speculations on the theme of being alive and an artist in contemporary London. *Mnemosyne* (1985), *Euripides' Movie* (1987) and *Diary of a Sane Man* (1990) variously describe the author's predicament as he searches for money and inspiration. The storyline of *Euripides' Movie* is characteristic:

> On the advice of Sophocles, a failed playwright adopts the name Euripides. Several thousand years later Eisenstein suggests he makes a film of his play Medea. Euripides takes up the idea and submits a proposal to the Arts Council (of an unnamed country!). Unfortunately, the proposal is rejected. Depressed, but undeterred, he decides to go ahead with the film anyway, soliciting the receptionist at the Arts Council for the part of Medea.[75]

Shot mostly on Super 8 (the third film was part-funded by Channel 4 and included 35mm filming in Tuscany), they make a virtue of their poverty, depending on voice-over 'diary', improvisation (as ancient narrators would), roping in celebrated friends,[76] and filling in narrative gaps with the film-maker's direct address to camera. Hollander's is a cinema of indulged digressions. Cordelia Swann's first mature work *The Citadel* (1992) followed Finch and Hollander in borrowing its structure from an ancient tale – Dido and the fall of Carthage – to shape a portrait of London under Thatcher, decked out for the Falklands War 'victory' celebrations. Her more typical later works *Out West* (1992), *Desert Rose* (1996) and *Back East* (2000) are essays in fictional autobiography, dark incidents from an unnamed female protagonist's childhood in the 1950s described in voice-over monologue, and set against spectacular long-held shots of 1990s American landscapes and cityscapes.

Steve Hawley sets words and images more pointedly against each other, so each questions the status and veracity of the other. His early works, mostly shot on video, included the nicely subversive *We Have Fun Drawing Conclusions* (1982), based on the then-standard *Janet and John* children's books, that undermined their unrealistically optimistic and stereotype-reinforcing images and texts with a subtly rewritten story in voice-over. He used a semi-documentary

form for *Language Lessons* (1994) made with Tony Steyger, which sought out speakers of the invented languages Iso, Esperanto, Volapuk, Logopandecteision, Lips Kth, the musical language Solresol and others, encountering colourful individuals en route, and cumulatively unseating the authority of the mongrel-construction 'English' of its own commentary. In *Human and Natural History* (1996), he wittily accompanied images of an emotional triangle involving a man, a woman and a tape recorder, with a perfectly matching soundtrack from television documentary about the mating rituals of tropical fish. He demonstrates that language is a construct, not to be trusted, but a possible source of pleasure. John Smith is equally alert to the hidden potential in language's instability. Smith adopted the quasi-documentary form with which he is now associated only after some years of structural film-making, through observation of the urban landscape, an insistence on the clarity of the film's structure and even structural film's trope of rapid repetitions are consistent features of his mature work. *The Girl Chewing Gum* (1976) established his characteristic questioning of the narrative voice, and his fondness for creating and then exposing an illusion. An unseen speaker appears to be uncannily directing not just the camera's movements, but the choreography of pedestrians and vehicles at a busy street corner, before the film's one cut and change of location reveals the speaker to be in a distant field, reading from a transcript of the previously filmed action. (Or is this, too, an illusion?).

**193** *Out West*, Cordelia Swann, 1992.

**194** *The Black Tower*,
John Smith, 1987.

A number of the films I've made have very much to do with taking the viewer to the edge of psychological immersion, but then pulling out again, so one is more aware of the construction of the film. The fact that the films reveal their artifice is important to all of them. That's an ideology that comes from the Co-op. Although I use narrative, the work is still anti-illusionist.[77]

*The Black Tower* (1987) similarly subverts the viewer's trust in the image. While the unseen protagonist voices increasing paranoia triggered by the sudden appearance of an ominous building and its apparently growing number of clones, the image both confirms the phenomenon (the tower *is* omnipresent), and hints at the power of photographic framing and viewpoint that could explain the phenomenon. The unseen narrator in *Slow Glass* (1991) is a glazier, and his stories, asides and descriptions of glass-making illuminate his subject, while the image tells its own social history of glass and its role in lower-middle-class life, using an array of visual puns and asides.

Thanks in part to television patronage, the documentary essay-film that bears the film-maker's strong individual voice enjoyed a period of renewal in the 1990s. Wright's *Waters of Time* and Harvey Harrison's *City of Ships* (1939) were a direct inspiration to William Raban as he prepared *Thames Film* (1986), his essay on the changing face of London's river over three centuries. This film, with *From 60°North* (1991), marked Raban's return to an interest in landscape, but unlike his analytical films of the early 1970s and his structural/spatial studies of the mid-1970s, his vision now embraced history and politics. *Thames Film* follows a voyage downriver from Tower Bridge and out into the Estuary to the point where river ends and sea begins, and then retraces its route back to the heart of the City; its shape echoing equally the pattern of the tides, the journal of Thomas Pennant who made the same journey in 1787, and the symmetry of structural film. Raban interweaves his colour footage with black and white shots taken of the same locations by Wright and Harrison, and of the engravings in Pennant's journal to produce not a lament for the past but a reflection upon the apparently unstoppable forces of commerce, politics and nature that together drive change. Raban's voice-over narrations on both *Thames Film* and *From 60°North* (on the fate of the Spanish Armada ships as they tried to circumnavigate the British Isles) are their most conventional aspect. With his later and more politically-charged Isle of Dogs trilogy *Sundial* (1992), *A13* (1994) and *Island Race* (1996) he trusted his images to work without commentary, accompanying them only with richly worked soundtracks of intensified 'natural' sound. These were

195 *A13*, William Raban,
1994.

his response to the rapidly changing physical and social landscape of East London where he lives; to the brash new office towers and motorways of Thatcher's enterprise culture that displaced old industries and old communities, but have created their own collage of unexpected images; pockets of the old surviving in the shadow of the new, street markets, immigrant families, a gangland funeral, the London Marathon race, an urban farm, British National Party (fascist) candidates buoyant in local elections. Another, more predictable television essayist was Iain Sinclair (working with writer/critic Chris Petit), their joint works including *The Falconer* (1998), a subversive portrait of film-maker Peter Whitehead, and *London Orbital* (2002), a response to the new landscapes bordering London's outer-ring motorway, the M25; obsessive works littered with asides and sharp observations.

A looser essay-form – the willing hold-all, or the snail-trail of the urban *flâneur* – has appealed to a younger generation of film-makers, notably to Oliver Payne and Nick Relph. Their *Driftwood* (1999) and *Gentlemen* (2003) take a distant cue from the musings of Keiller's Robinson as he wandered across London. Their own travels result in a seemingly haphazard assemblage of sounds and images; an assertive voice-over text on the failures of city planning, snippets of history, a colourful spoken account of a third-party's encounter with the police, accompanied by chunks of suburban documentation, rough home-movie footage of skateboarders, graffiti, poster-hoardings, passing buses, long takes of bands playing; images of a troubled but energetic city.

## NOTES

1. In her monograph on *Borderline,* HD appears to suggest that Macpherson suppressed it.

2. *Borderline* (London: Mercury Press, 1930).

3. His colourful life in New York, where he shared a duplex with Peggy Guggenheim, is described in Guggenheim's autobiography *Out of This Century, Confessions of an Art Addict* (New York: Anchor Books, 1980).

4. Of three other films Braun may have made, all that apparently survives is an image from *Exhilaration* (1933, with Irene Nicholson) reproduced in *Film Art*, no. 1, 1933.

5. Film Society programme note, 5 May 1929.

6. Richter's abstract films were shown at the Society on three occasions in the 1920s. He left Nazi Germany in 1933, emigrating to the USA in 1940.

7. Given that the film was being edited in the USA in 1966–67, these 'ad nauseam' repetitions may be a joke by Richter at the expense of the new stars of American structural film.

8. 'Foreword', *Richard Massingham,* (London: Shenval Press, 1955). In the same obituary tribute, Henri Langlois calls Massingham 'the greatest technician and greatest poet of British cinema'.

9. Ian Christie suggests these 'elaborate "home-movies" ... might be considered Britain's true avant-garde (as indeed many revered French avant-garde films were sponsored by wealthy patrons)'. Programme note: *Avant-Garde Film of the 20s*, NFT, 21 January 2004.

10. Wells's story was not filmed under its original title till 1933, but the American film *A Blind Bargain* (1922) was a free adaptation, and was possibly shown in England.

11. 'Saxon Sydney-Turner played the doctor; Rachel MacCarthy played the heroine, "a simple girl called Daisy" who got drowned in the bath by the greenhouse, and everyone else played the lunatics with Frances [Partridge] excelling as "a human quadruped lunatic wearing riding boots on her arms". Carrington's enthusiasm for the project was infectious, but none went so far as joining her at 7 o'clock on Sunday morning and the following Monday making dummies and masks and finding properties for the cast. When the film was shown the following Thursday at 41 Gordon Square it was a big success; Bunny [David Garnett] recalled that Saxon wore an expression of such malice as he peered around the door at the luckless Daisy; the film had a "macabre quality" he had never witnessed before.' Jane Hill, *The Art of Dora Carrington* (London: Herbert Press, 1994).

12. 31 January 1932.

13. John Grierson, 'I Remember I Remember' (1970), ibid.

14. He was also particularly proud of his contribution to *Granton Trawler* (1934).

15. 10 November 1929 – with Epstein's *The Fall of the House of Usher* and Disney's *The Barn Dance*.

16. 'Untitled Lecture on Documentary', 1927–32, Ian Aitken (ed.), *The Documentary Film Movement – An Anthology* (Edinburgh: Edinburgh University Press, 1998).

17. 'Drifters', *The Documentary Film Movement – An Anthology*.

18. Ray Durgnat described Grierson's whole project as 'bourgeois-jingoistic' and the films 'just beautiful enough to set my students, rightly, writhing with rage at their serene establishmentarianism'. 'Brain Drains, Drifters, Avant-Gardes & Kitchen Sinks', *Cinema*, no. 3, 1969.

19. 'Flaherty as an Innovator', John Grierson, *Sight and Sound*, July 1951.

20. *Experiments in the Film* (London: Grey Walls Press, 1949).

21. 'Basil Wright Interview with Ian Aitken' (1987) *The Documentary Film Movement – An Anthology*.

22. *Footnotes to the Film*, 1937, quoted in *Sight and Sound*, July 1951.

23. 'The British Contribution' (1952), reprinted in *The Documentary Film Movement – An Anthology*.

24. Out of a workforce of 750,000.

25. Wright interviewed by Elizabeth Sussex in *The Rise and Fall of British Documentary* (Berkeley: University of California Press, 1976)

26. 'Manifesto (1) Dialogue on Sound', *Film Art*, vol. 1 no. 3, 1934.

27. It interestingly anticipates George Orwell's *The Road to Wigan Pier* by two years.

28. Sussex, *The Rise and Fall of British Documentary*.

29. Coldstream's name is on the credits, but Cavalcanti was the more likely editor.

30. These included *Post Haste, Locomotives, The Story of the Wheel,* all released in 1934.

31. 1914–62; trained as a painter at Glasgow School of Art, in the same cohort as McLaren.

32. 'A Sketch for an Historical Portrait of Humphrey Jennings', in Mary-Lou Jennings (ed.), *Humphrey Jennings: Filmmaker, Painter, Poet,* (London: BFI, 1982).

33. October 1940 Quoted in *Humphrey Jennings: Filmmaker, Painter, Poet.*

34. Dia Vaughan, p. 88.

35. 'Patrick Keiller on *Diary for Timothy'*, *The Guardian*, 10 November 1997.

36. Anderson's postscript to his famous 1954 *Sight & Sound* article on Jennings, 'Only Connect', reprinted in *Humphrey Jennings, Filmmaker, Painter, Poet.*

37. Obituary notice, ibid.

38. Grey Wall Press, 1949. (If only he'd been asked to write the British section, which Manvell gave instead to Anstey, who was resistant to the concept of artistic experiment.) Brunius's witty and pioneering film on 'outsider art', *Violons d'Ingres* (1939 aka *Hobbies Across the Sea*) was shown in the French pavilion at the New York World's Fair, and his collection of pre-cinema optical toys formed the founding core of the Pollock's Toy Museum in London.

39. Obituary notice in *Sight and Sound*, 1967.

40. Durgnat, who has little time for Free Cinema, sees *Every Day* … as 'a subaltern's view of Covent Garden porters, "rough diamonds, you know, but jolly good fellows"'. Raymond Durgnat, *A Mirror for England* (London: Faber & Faber, 1970).

Drawing by Jacques Brunius, undated.

41. As was Macpherson's *Borderline*, HD suggests in her pamphlet.

42. Bruce Beresford, 'Don Levy – A *Cinema* Interview', *Cinema*, no. 2, March 1969. *Herostratus*'s alternating sequences echo those of Shirley Clarke's *The Cool World* (USA 1963), as its use of improvised dialogue reflects her *The Connection* (USA 1961), films Levy publicly admired.

43. Inge Blackman, BFI Online 2004. The BFI rejected Ové's bid for funding for this film, but partially made amends by supporting his *Pressure* (1975).

44. Interview with Bruce Beresford and Eric Rhodes (unpublished), Production Board files, BFI Library. My thanks to Christophe Dupin for leading me to this.

45. The television documentaries *Fat Man on the Beach* (Harlech TV 1973) and *The Unfortunates* (1968) in which he appears are also very much his own creation. See Jonathan Coe's biography *Like a Fiery Elephant: The Story of BS Johnson* (Cambridge: Picador, 2004).

46. See Peter Wollen's definitive study of Burroughs's film work, 'Guerrilla Conditions [the original title of *Towers Open Fire*] The Cinema of William Seward Burroughs', *Pix*, no. 3, 2001, BFI.

47. *Filmmakers On Tour* catalogue 1980.

48. Sean Cubitt, 'David Larcher', *A Directory of British Film & Video Artists* (Luton: Arts Council/University of Luton Press, 1996).

49. His eccentric life-story is the subject of *The Falconer* (1998) by Chris Petit and Iain Sinclair.

50. 'More British Sounds', *Sight and Sound*, Summer 1970.

51. B S Johnson's *Unfair* (1970), made for friends in the ACTT union, more directly addressed the Bill's proposal that judges alone would decide 'what's fair' in an industrial dispute.

52. Artist's notes on the Bradford studies.

53. Statement in a funding application by the Collective to GLAA, 1974. Both Kelly and Trevelyan contributed to the earlier and more conventional documentary *Women of the Rhondda* (1972/73) made by Esther Ronay, Margaret Dickinson and others, which explored the position of women in traditional mining communities, and memories of the 1926 miners' strike.

54. *Spare Rib* no. 40, October 1975.

55. Ann Oakley, *The Sociology of Housework* (New York: Pantheon Books/Random House, 1974).

56. Mike Stubbs and other artists also contributed to the campaigning *Miners Tapes* at this time.

57. Bill Douglas's BFI-produced trilogy *My Childhood* (1972), *My Ain Folk* (1973), and *My Way Home* (1977) – a moving but filmically conservative autobiography – interestingly links these periods.

58. For example, Laura Mulvey, 'Visual Pleasure in Narrative Cinema', *Screen*, 1975; Peter Wollen, *Signs and Meaning in the Cinema* (London: BFI, 1969).

59. Don Ranvaud, 'Laura Mulvey, Peter Wollen, An Interview', *Framework*, no. 9, 1979.

60. For example in Jeanette Iljon's *The Conjurer's Assistant* (1979), Tina Keane's *Circus Troupe* (1990) and *Neon Diver* (1991); Jayne Parker's *Cold Jazz* (1993).

61. Clive Hodgson, 'From Artists to Cleaners', *Film*, July 1973.

62. All quotes from ZDF Programme note, reprinted as LFMC note 31 March 1976.

63. LFMC Catalogue 1976. Mike Figgis adopted a similar four-screen format to explore multiple viewpoints in a more conventional narrative context in *Timecode* (2000). Figgis may have seen Le Grice's earlier work when performing with Nuttall and The People Show at the Robert Street Arts Lab.

64. Unlike the other long films discussed here, *After Manet, Blackbird Descending* and *Emily* were funded by the Arts Council; *Finnegan* by the Production Board.

65. Hitchcock's 'one-shot' *Rope* was re-released in the UK around this time, but J. L. Godard's *One Plus One* (1968), shot in London, had already re-awakened interest in the ten-minute take.

66. Chris Auty in *City Limits* (23 October 1981) enjoyed its wit: 'It's not often that you laugh out loud alone in a preview theatre. Not often that a joke from Joyce meets a man shaving in the deep night or a mime artist playing chamber music on a handsaw … [etc; concluding] only one word for it: magic.' Gidal's was the voice of dissent. describing it in *Undercut* no. 5 (1982) as 'the last gasp of a dying patriarchy'; in which 'The soundtrack and every single shot without exception has an image, a word, a phrase, a series of acts, a symbol, a metaphor for male erection', finally despairing 'How could this have happened to Le Grice?'.

67. LFMC catalogue.

68. Sally Potter, 'British Independents – *The Gold Diggers*', *Framework* no. 24, 1984.

69. Rainer was in London at the time making *Working Title: Journeys from Berlin / 1971* (1980) which was co-funded by the BFI.

70. 'A Third Something: Montage, Film and Poetry', *Undercut* no. 18, 1989.

71. *Film Makers On Tour 1984–85*, Arts Council of Great Britain.

72. Penny Webb and Tim Bruce were other pioneers of narrative in the LFMC context.

73. Shown at the Tate 23 August to 19 September 1982.

74. Programme note for Tate screenings 23 August to 19 September 1982.

75. Lux catalogue description of *Euripides' Movie*.

76. Yonti Solomon plays Bach's *Goldberg Variations* in *Diary*.

77. Brian Frye, 'Mr Smith' [interview], *Film West* [Ireland], Winter 2001.

# 2.3 Expanded Cinema and Video Art

Film as Film **:** Conceptual Art and Early Installations **:** Video Art and Television **:** Expanded Cinema **:** Other Structures **:** Gidal's Legacy **:** Later Installations

## FILM AS FILM

Structural film in Britain in its most distinctive form was pioneered by Malcolm Le Grice, and its later theorised formulation, the structural/materialist film, was the brainchild of Peter Gidal, whose personal artistic philosophy it represented. A. L. Rees defined it concisely:

> Structural film proposed that the shaping of film's material – light, time and process – could create a new form of aesthetic pleasure, free of symbolism or narrative. It typically combined predetermination (for example, camera position, number of frames or exposures, repetition) with chance (the unpredictable events that occur at the moment of shooting).[1]

Structural *materialist* film differs only in the extent of its emphasis on 'freedom from narrative' and the consistency of its resistance to representation. In his defining essay Gidal wrote: 'The Structural/materialist film must minimize the content of its overpowering, imagistically seductive sense, in an attempt to get through this miasmic area of "experience" and proceed with film as film';[2] (the syntax may be eccentric, but the message clear).

Le Grice's conception of what an artist might do with film was already fully formed at the time of his first substantial public show at the Drury Lane Arts Lab in November 1968. It derived directly from his experience as a painter teaching at Saint Martins, and from his involvement with improvised music and jazz,[3] and developed, crucially, before he had any exposure to the emerging American avant-garde. He didn't attend Knokke 1967/68, nor any of the New American Cinema programmes brought to England in April that year by P. Adams Sitney, though he did see Michael Snow's screening of

**(Opposite)** *Hand Grenade*, Gill Eatherley, 1971.

**196 (below)** Poster by Le Grice and Biddy Peppin, 1968; the images are from *Castle One*, 1966.

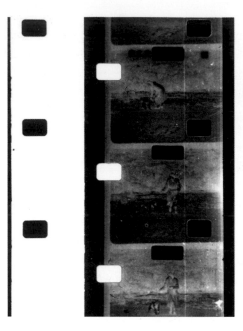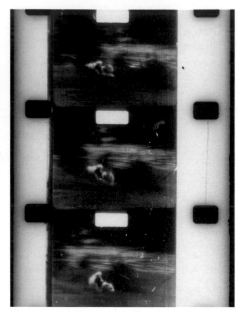

*Wavelength* at the Arts Lab in September, just before his own show. With its prescient title *Location? Duration? Films Films Paintings Plus,* his show included films and large canvases with free-floating abstract motifs, some textured, some apparently stencilled, others with lines drawn in colour straight from the tube, reflecting the approach to painting established by Harold Cohen at the Slade where Le Grice had recently studied. His programme of films[4] *Castle One (The Light Bulb Film)* (1966), *Castle Two, Little Dog For Roger, Blind White Duration, Talla, Yes No Maybe Maybe Not* (all 1967) was unlike any that had been seen in Britain, and introduced all the characteristics that would later be associated with the English development of structural film; use of found footage, mathematical or random structures, re-filming from the screen as a means of re-framing and re-interpreting the image, startling *repoussoirs* (the real light-bulb that flashed at random intervals during *Castle One* 'returning the audience to their actual situation') and twin-screen projection. The films' imagery was equally unusual. *Castle One* was assembled from found documentary footage of the industrial and political world (Employment Minister Barbara Castle addressing a conference, a woman handling a laboratory pipette, the Harrier jump-jet taking off); the sound 'a scramble of the various commentaries, music and dialogue which gradually become identified with their respective images during the [twenty minute] course of the film'. (An emphasis on duration, as he had warned, would become a characteristic of his work.) *Little Dog* took as its starting place imagery from 9.5mm home-movie footage shot by the artist's father, re-filmed from the screen and woven into repeating cycles of action, to heighten the viewer's awareness of film-time and the film-image. In these early films, found footage provided Le Grice with a way of referencing mainstream cinema and television and its links to the industrial/political machine, while his treatment of it asked the viewer to observe how cinema traditionally operates to disempower the viewer. But increasingly his primary material becomes film he shot himself, often scenes of his own domestic and working life.

Gidal (b.1946) arrived on the scene less immediately sure of his subjects. *George Segal Sculptor* (1967) was an act of documentary homage made while still in America that he later suppressed; as he suppressed *Lovelight* (1968–69) 'a painter's exploration of the love-object (subject)',[5] a nude with two light-bulbs. Similarly personally engaged were *Still Andy* (1968), a portrait of Warhol in his studio 'Factory', shot in stills; *Subject/Object/Portrait* (1970), a study of his partner Sally Harding in which the camera's role is as eroticised as in any Dwoskin film; and *Heads* (1969), the essay in Warhol-like portraiture of cultural heroes discussed earlier; these only hinted at things to come. His most familiar subject – his own domestic space – first appeared in *Room – Double Take* (1967). a portrait of his student bed-sit in London, more transparently so than in later studies, but already with the restless, searching camerawork that would become distinctly his, and the whole film is repeated in its entirety, introducing another familiar trope.[6] His growing unease with photographic reproduction/representation was given almost humorous form in the near-empty frame of *Clouds* (1969), his first fully recognisable work. *Clouds*, in black and white, depicts just sky with an occasional plane nudging the edge of the screen, keeping the viewer guessing just *what* – if anything – is moving; camera, clouds, plane? Gidal wrote later 'The anti-illusionistic project engaged by *Clouds* is that of dialectic materialism. There is virtually nothing ON screen, in the sense of IN screen'. Then he disarmingly defends its repetitions: 'Obsessive repetition as materialist practice, not psychoanalytic indulgence',[7] (a swipe possibly at Stuart Brisley's *Arbeit Macht Frei* (1973) or perhaps at *Nightcleaners*; films in which repetition carried an emotional charge). The *Theory and Definition of Structural/Materialist Film* continues:

**198** *Clouds*, Peter Gidal, 1969.

Devices such as loops or seeming loops, as well as a whole series of technical possibilities, can, carefully constructed to operate in the correct manner, serve to veer [steer?] the point of contact with the film *past* internal content. The content thus serves as a function upon which, time and time again, a filmmaker *works* to bring forth the filmic event' [italics mine].

*8mm Film Notes on 16mm* (1971) and *Upside Down Feature* (1972) began to define different aspects of Gidal's mature style; extreme duration (forty and seventy-six minutes long respectively); interrogation of pre-existing imagery (the artist's own), its further re-presentation obscuring subject matter that is already obscure; repetitions that are not always immediately identifiable, but with an obsessive attention to image-quality which allows viewers *some* aesthetic reward for their perseverance. Though a fierce champion of the Co-op, after the mid-1970s Gidal rarely used its workshop facilities, instead becoming one of the commercial film labs' most exacting customers, respected by them for his knowledge of film-stocks, printing-lights etc. *Upside Down Feature* atypically featured quantities of fast-scrolling text (too fast to read, even if it hadn't been the dense writing of Beckett on Proust on the subject

**199** *Room Film 1973*, Peter Gidal, 1973.

of Time). Here Gidal revealed both his credentials as a conceptualist and his life-long devotion to Beckett, on whose work he has frequently written. Briefly in the mid-1970s, Gidal exhibited with some of his conceptual peers, the four Johns: Stezaker, Latham, Hilliard and Blake.[8]

Mature Gidal appears with *Room Film 1973* (1973), a reworking of the theme of *Room – Double Take*, first shown at the 1973 Festival, and immediately singled out for praise by Mekas, Michael Snow and others. In his *Studio International* report, Le Grice perceptively wrote 'there is no describable content, but one watches with fascination the representation of the objective world through the agency of light and its absence ... Gidal ... poses the problem of the dialectic of representation, *through* representation'.[9] *Film Print* (1974), first shown in *Codes and Structures* at the RCA 1975:

> deals with a particular space through a series of photographs each representing a specific site. The film deals with levels of reproduction. The repetitious camera movements over successive photographs are intended to function as [a] distancing device relatable to mechanical repetitions such as film loops. The 'subject' of the film is the material operation, or, rather, it is a film in its own right and an explication of the mechanisms and techniques inherent in its making. It is not a documentary of those mechanisms and techniques.[10]

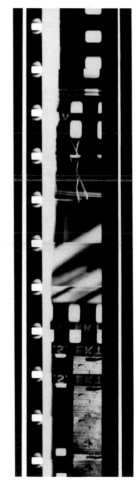

**200** *Shapes*, Annabel Nicolson, 1970.

From now on, each new Gidal film obsessively revisited this 'problematic', with, in the lengthening gaps between their appearances, the publication of polemical essays of increasing complexity, many pointing to the failure of 'progressive' film theorists to confront it.

At the end of the 1960s, Le Grice's students at Saint Martins and Goldsmiths were already being productive, but their work at this time shows little of his direct influence. Fred Drummond's *Photo Film* (1967) was an animation of Muybridge's studies of locomotion; Roger Ackling's *Boot Film* (1967) a gentle still-life; Mike Dunford's portrait *Angie* (1968), and *Weeds* (1969) a structured study of wasteland with Sally Potter striding through it.[11] In his relationship with students and peers, Le Grice was an enabler. With the setting up of the Filmmakers Co-op workshop at the Robert Street Arts Lab (RAT) in late 1969, others began to have access to the kind of equipment that Le Grice had originally constructed for his own use, and work with the 'material of film' suddenly became widespread. Films made during the first months of the workshop's operation in 1969 that featured loop-printing and optical printing, colouring of the film image through filters, etc., included Roger Hammond's *High Stepping*, Drummond's *Maja Replicate*, and Le Grice's own *Spot the Microdot*. By the time the equipment had been re-installed in the Co-op's next base 'The Dairy' in Prince of Wales Crescent in mid-1971, Crosswaite and Dunford were also making re-filmed and re-printed works, and the core group had been joined by Annabel Nicolson (b.1946), Gill Eatherley (b.1950), Mike Leggett (b.1945), who had been making personal films since 1965 (some jointly with Ian Breakwell and while supporting himself with work for television) and John Du Cane (b.1949), a Cambridge-educated aspiring journalist.

The publication of P. Adams Sitney's essay 'Structural Film' in the American avant-garde

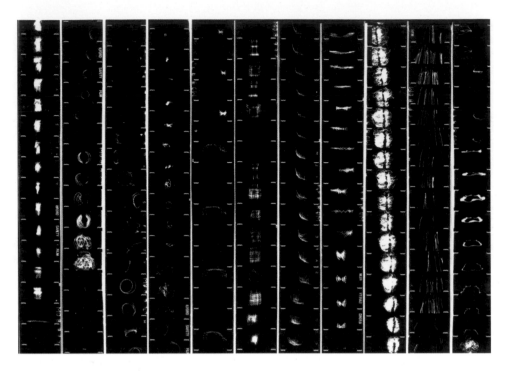

journal *Film Culture* in 1969,[12] followed by the appearance at the NFT Festival in 1970 of many of the American film-makers he discussed (notably Michael Snow and Paul Sharits), gave this fledgling English movement a label, 'structural film-makers', though it was one that many resisted. For some artists emerging at the time, like Nicolson and Eatherley, the excitement of the Co-op workshop was that it offered a way of handling film as directly and physically as they had previously handled paint. Nicolson joined the Co-op in 1969 having studied painting at Hornsey and Edinburgh before Saint Martins. Her *Shapes* (1970) is an abstract vision of colours and rhythms derived from elements in her studio, filmed, projected, and re-filmed from the screen, sometimes further slowed down and superimposed in the printer. In it, she welcomed 'the incidental tactile qualities of film', such as dust particles, which extensive re-working of the image sometimes produced. Her *Slides* (1971) and *Frames* (1972) are forms of collage, based on introducing tiny fragments of filmed image into the printer and sometimes longer sections that contain filmed movement; their subjects being 'looking' and the boundaries between movement and stasis.

For *Hand Grenade* (1971), Eatherley developed a technique of 'drawing' images in the camera, frame by frame, using a moving light-source as a 'pencil' and a long time exposure of each frame to accumulate a tangle of lines, that in projection created a kinetic, rhythmic performance based on a chair motif. 'Malcolm helped me with [the] stills – the chairs traced with light – then … we started on 16mm. We shot only 100 feet on black and white in pitch dark, and then took it to the Co-op and spent ages printing it all out on the printer there', where the superimpositions, slippage and brilliant colours were introduced.[13] Raban and Welsby became involved the Co-op in 1971 but brought with them their own interest in

landscape, time-lapse photography and elaborate shooting-systems described earlier, further stretching the concept of structural film, and broadening its practice.

**202** John Du Cane: (above) *Zoomlapse*, 1975; (below) *Sign*, 1974.

The film-makers closest to Gidal at this point were Hammond, Dunford and Du Cane. Du Cane arrived with no art-school or film background, but instantly became the Co-op's most prolific film-maker, pouring out works which systematically interrogated perception and the film recording process, through different camera and film-printing strategies. His note on *Relative Duration* (1973) reads: 'Shots from a small courtyard space [increase] from single-frame rate to about half a minute [720 frames] in a straightforward progression; the whole section is then repeated upside down, back to front and with a change in colour balance. The shots are broken up into sections indicating change of zoom, focus and light intensity'.[14] If this tends towards dry experiment, *Zoomlapse* (1975), which on paper sounds equally mechanistic, presented an engaging if ethereal visual experience. Du Cane combined the action of the zoom lens, which repeatedly brings-close a distant view of a warehouse then throws it back again, with a time-exposure on each film frame, so both perceived time and screen-depth are compressed, resulting in overlapping veils of time and space. 'I wanted the viewer to be pretty conscious that what they're seeing is *not* something that exists on celluloid; that there's a way it's manufactured in the viewing process.'[15] Hammond (1947?–2005) was always more spontaneous; his films' frequent lack of such etiquette as front and end titles adding to the impression that he had – on impulse – just picked up the camera and jotted down the work. He was as close at this time to David Larcher – for whom that was a legitimate way of gathering material – as he was to Gidal. Under Gidal's influence

he moved from making formulaic re-printed films such as *Knee High* (1970) to more loosely structured assemblages of obscurely shot footage – sometimes re-filmed, sometimes shown in negative, sometimes under-exposed, often enigmatically beautiful, such as *Window Box* (1972), a nocturnal study of windows in negative, greeted as 'a small masterpiece', by Gidal.[16] Dunford (b.1946) responded to the political and conceptual challenge posed by Gidal, each new film becoming 'a kind of hypothesis, or a questioning statement'.[17] The series *Synch Sound, Lens Tissue, Deep Space* (1972–73) are like test demonstrations, though *Tautology* (1973) with its single, repeating ironic assertion (this is a) 'tautology' is more simply conceptual – and illustrates how closely structural film and conceptual art were related. *Still Life with Pear* (1974), Dunford's richest film of this period, forgoes all the standard 'structural' camera and printing procedures, and counterpoints the classically composed and lit still-life image with an apparently simultaneous voice off-set of instructions to the 'production crew', who, it soon becomes apparent, are operating to quite another system; as effective a subversion of 'representation' as any. The film won a prize at Knokke in 1974/75 though Dunford later rejected it along with all his early work for 'preventing [the] questioning of the political nature of bourgeois perception, treating it as given and hiding the reality of the class struggle … I no longer make such films',[18] and his retirement from film-making lasted for more than a decade, but he began making video work again in the early 1990s.

## CONCEPTUAL ART AND EARLY INSTALLATIONS

During the early 1970s, other artists, less involved or not involved at all with the Filmmakers Co-op, were also exploring different ways of exhibiting film. David Dye (b.1945) and Anthony McCall (b.1946) took film into the gallery in a particularly sculptural form. For John Latham (b.1921), John Hilliard (b.1945) and David Tremlett (b.1945), film was primarily a documenting medium, an extension of the function of a still camera, or a means of recording statements and proposing ideas to be seen alongside related works in other media displayed in the gallery. Film in its most cinematic form became a serious preoccupation for a few conceptual artists, such as Yoko Ono (b.1933), David Lamelas (b.1944), Tony Morgan (b.1938) and John Blake (b.1945), albeit for a short period of time, while John Stezaker (b.1949) saw the *idea* for a film – the concept committed to the page – as enough in itself, with no need to progress further.[19] At the same time, David Hall, Ian Breakwell and others were pioneering video as a gallery medium.

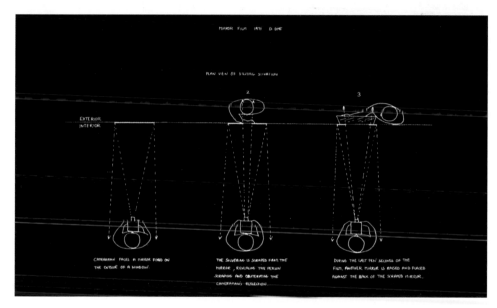

204 David Dye: drawings for installations – (below) *Unsigning II*, 1972, and (left) *Mirror Film*, 1971.

David Dye, like Eatherley and Hill a graduate of the sculpture department at Saint Martins, avoided close contact with the Filmmakers Co-op, but shared much of the Le Grice/Raban/Nicolson interest in the phenomenon of projection and its relationship to production. *Film onto Film* (1970) for example projected the image of a moving filmstrip *onto* itself; onto a section of the moving film-loop that he arranged to pass in front of the screen, before it returned to the projector, and round again. Similarly, *Projection/Introjection* (1971) projected the image of a projector back onto itself, through mirrors. Loops of film (this time running in reverse) were central to *Unsigning for 8 Projectors* (1972) shown in *The New Art* at the Hayward Gallery that year, an 'anti-ego trip' in which the artist's

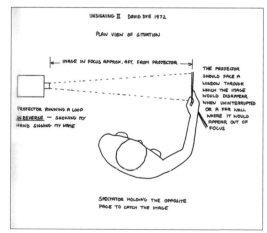

hand in close-up is seen un-writing the letters of his name. The same action being repeated out of synch on eight projectors projecting onto a single dangling and sometimes spinning screen further fragmented the image, and animated the adjacent walls as light spilt onto them. This was possibly the first continuous film installation seen by a large public in Britain, and was made possible by the artist's decision to use loops and cheap and reliable Super 8 film. Though this too was expanded cinema, he contrasted his mode of operation with that of his contemporaries:

> I use [film] in a very direct way … I don't get hung up with all the paraphernalia that can so easily make you slick, and you start making films which cost a lot of money and bring in the whole film world. I feel I've approached film sidelong. I've tried to get back to square one with film, as if I'd never seen a film before'.[20]

McCall's early films were souvenirs of serial-action performance-works, such as *Landscape for White Squares* (1972), which documented performers walking with squares of canvas, and *Landscape of Fire* of the same year, which illustrated the essential cyclical pattern of a thirteen-hour performance of lighting/extinguishing a grid of fires. Permutations and serial ideas would remain a strong element in his work.[21] His *Line Describing a Cone* (1973) was a radical departure: a film which fully addressed the relationship between the spectator, the work and the nature of film as a medium, and which elegantly summarised many of the concerns of the Filmaktion artists and the Co-op group, though at that stage he had no formal relationship with them.[22] It was also a film of great simplicity. Over half an hour, a white dot on a black screen

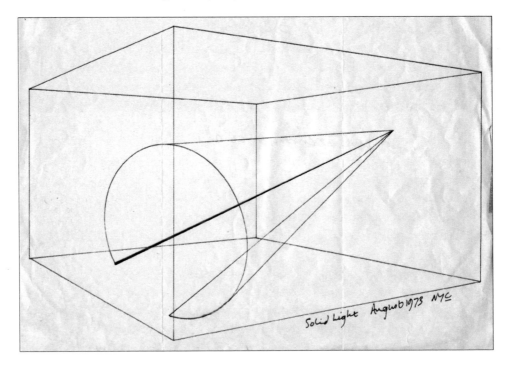

**205** Anthony McCall, *Line Describing a Cone*, (left) conceptual drawing, 1973; and (opposite top) installation view at Artists' Space, New York, 1974 (photo: Peter Moore).

was animated to move through 360 degrees, slowly becoming a circle. Projected into a smoke-filled room, a hollow cone of 'solid light' was formed, with its apex in the projector lens. McCall wrote:

> *Line Describing a Cone* deals with one of the irreducible, necessary conditions of film: projected light. It deals with this phenomenon directly, independently of any other consideration. It is the first film to exist in real, three-dimensional space. This film exists only in the present: the moment of projection. It refers to nothing beyond this real time. It contains no illusion. It is a primary experience, not secondary: i.e., the space is real, not referential: the time is real, not referential'.[23]

Other variants soon followed. *Partial Cone* (1974) introduced a flicker, with the drawing on intermittent frames; *Long Film for Four Projectors* (1974), first shown at the London Filmmakers Co-op, then at *Documenta* 6 in 1977, sets its four projectors close to the room's longer walls, so their moving light-beams create interpenetrating planes of intermittent light which sweep the entire space, creating a changing three-dimensional sculpture through which the spectators negotiate their passage.

Latham began film-making as a means of recording the evolution of his burnt and painted book-assemblages, as in *Unedited Material from 'Star'* (aka *Film Star* 1960), but his practice developed to embrace films such as *Speak* (1962–65) a rapid-fire animation of circles and dots, and *Erth* (aka *Britannica* 1971), a page-by-page condensation of the encyclopaedia, both occasionally screened in the context of his exhibitions and installations. The *Star* footage was also apparently shown in the context of a paper-tearing performance (figures covered in paper busily shredding each other), while *Speak* was projected as an element in *Juliet and Romeo,* a performance within an inflatable environment created with his frequent collaborator Jeffrey Shaw (with whom he had founded the Event-Structure Research Group) at the Knokke 1967–68 Competition. An 'event-structure' was Latham's measure of all things scientific and artistic, and much of his art-making was concerned with interrogating concepts of time and information. His enigmatic statement accompanying the showing of *Britannica* at the *Prospect 71 – Projection* exhibition in Dusseldorf (1971) read 'TIME IS UNREAL as a real idea'. John Hilliard's film-making directly extended his photographic works which exhibited many of the symptoms of structuralism; systematic exploration of space, reflexive games with the camera (the camera recording its own image through a sequence of aperture changes), etc. To make *From and To* (1971), he provided detailed instructions to his two camera operators; one was to stand in the middle of a circle and rotate slowly, filming outwards, the other to film inwards from points on the perimeter of the circle, recording the first. The resulting two films were projected, and each cameraman gave a verbal account of their actions, the work consisting of these instructions and the divergent records of the same event. The work's only showing was at *Prospect 71 – Projection*, until it was re-discovered and reassembled in 2003.[24]

Typical of many artists, Tremlett made a small group of films within a short period of time in the early 1970s, showed them once alongside photo-pieces at *Prospect 71*, then passed on to other things. *Untitled (Piano)* (1970) juxtaposes the static lines of a large grid-like drawing with a continuous recording of a piano tuner at work. The drawing was made specifically for the

**206** *From and To,*
John Hilliard, 1971.

film, and its repetitive structure relates to looped sound tapes the artist had been making. The sound, which was recorded and added after filming the drawing, gives the work its sense of purpose. To Tremlett, 'the film represented a way of thinking; as an object it was less important'.[25] For Stezaker, to *think* of an idea for a film work was enough in itself. The first of his series of *Time Deletions*, whose only tangible form is notes printed in the catalogue to *Codes and Structures* at the RCA in January 1975, indicate his awareness of the work of his Co-op contemporaries:

*1A*. Film as Footage. Walking the length of a room filming ahead, at such a speed as will result in footage of film equalling the length of the room, i.e. walking at 24 frames a second. The resulting footage of film is shown without a projector unrolled along the original path of the walk, with a suitable means of making it visible to the naked eye – lighting below. A second copy of the film is shown on a loop projector (thus occupying effectively half the room). The procedure is made more evident by walking towards a large mirror at the end of the room in the original walk.

The series is progressive: *1B* begins 'The Film from *1A* when installed alongside the original path of the walk is itself filmed …' etc.

This relationship of the moving image to the still was similarly explored in *Cumulative Script* (1971) by Lamelas, which followed Dunford and Hammond as they larked about on Primrose Hill near the Filmmakers Co-op, and was exhibited as a series of sets of contact strips (a visual synopsis of the film) alongside its projected self, in *A Survey of the Avant-Garde in Britain* and at the Nigel Greenwood Gallery in 1972. Similarly Darcy Lange showed

**207** Detail of the photo-sequence from *Cumulative Script*, David Lamelas, 1971 (reproduced in *Art Magazine*, France, Summer, 1973)

Cumulative script. 16 mm couleur. 15 minutes. 1971 (galerie Wide White Space. Anvers)

15

films, photos and videos shot simultaneously of the same subject in the same space, as related but independent records (discussed earlier). Even closer to Stezaker's concept was John Blake's intended layout of *Arrest* (1970) – a ten-minute single take of his head in profile moving in and out of shot – where the projected film was to be accompanied by a print-out of the filmstrip graphically revealing its patterns of movement. The ensemble was tried out in a space lent by the Situations Gallery, and reprised with a smaller strip at the Victoria and Albert Museum, but

Blake was only able to show the film alone at *A Survey of the Avant-Garde in Britain* at Gallery House. *Arrest* was shot by Gidal, and Blake, echoing Gidal, accompanied its making with the publication of a dense, theoretical text. Other Blake films were occasionally shown (and were equally at home) in the Co-op cinema. His *Bridges* (1974 aka *Bridge Film*), for example, contained the radical Gidallian decision to film the remarkable architecture of two Thomas Telford bridges *totally* out of focus, though in rich, velvet-like black and white. *Untitled (Juggler)* (1972) showed a very Co-op-like interest in screen-space, created in this

**208** *Arrest*, John Blake, 1970, (right) frame from the film – self-portrait; (below) installation shot revealing the movement of the subject in successive frames.

case by projecting two images – the juggler on one, the flying balls on the other – on top of each other, simultaneously creating and unmasking an illusion.

While conceptual artists and the Co-op group were separately beginning to define the ways in which the moving image could operate in the gallery, the intellectual common cause between these groups, personified by the friendship of Gidal and Blake, was also working to dissolve tidy definitions of what belonged in gallery and what belonged in the cinema. The eroded boundary between white cube and black box that has characterised the moving image since the late 1990s has its roots here in the mid-1970s. After 1975 Gidal no longer participated in gallery shows, recognising that the address of his works was uniquely to cinema, but he became increasingly the exception, not the rule.[26]

Tony Morgan made nearly fifty film and videos between 1968 and 1976 and exhibited them widely, participating in *Documenta 4* (1970), *Information* (MOMA NY, 1970) and *Prospect 71* in Dusseldorf, the city that became his home for a number of years, and where he created his own exhibition space *Produkt Cinema (im Keller)*. Some of his films recorded performances or events (*Haircut*, 1975); others were nicely paradoxical sculptural installations such as *Wall Slap* (filmed hand slaps wall) and *Black Corner* (a black corner projected into a black corner), both shown at the Lisson Gallery in 1972; many involved collaboration with other artists such as Robert Filliou, Rebecca Horn, George Brecht, Lutz Mommartz and Bob Law. Morgan returned to painting in the late 1980s, occasionally making films and tapes from then on. Lamelas's works included single-idea films such as *Milk and Glass* (1973) – a series of close-ups of a glass being filled from an unseen source, sometimes overflowing – serving as metaphors for the construction of meaning in film. 'I wanted to find symbols for "container" and "contents" – to represent how the camera frames what is shown on screen … The eight sequences end with … the glass being shattered and the milk splattering all over the table, which implies that there is no way to contain information'. But increasingly his films became more ambitious, finding ways of contrasting physical and environmental structures with their social counterparts, often mixing formal and documentary strategies. *A Study of the Relationships Between Inner and Outer Space* (1969), shot in the Camden Arts Centre and around the Whitechapel Art Gallery, juxtaposes shots of the Arts Centre's galleries and staff, with vox-pops filmed on the street as the Americans were making their first moon landing (relating inner to outer space). He exhibited at *Prospect 71*, and at the Nigel Greenwood and Jack Wendler Galleries in London from 1972, before moving to California in 1974 where he made the short road-movie that mutates into a series of interviews *The Desert People* (1974).

Yoko Ono had already contributed a number of films to Fluxus events in New York before travelling to London in 1966 to take part with her performance *Cutting Piece* in the Destruction in Art Symposium. Remaining in London, her first works including her celebrated feature *No.4* (1966), the 'bottoms' film, and *No.5* (aka *Smile* 1968), John Lennon's face shot at 333 frames a second, [27] both longer remakes of earlier Fluxus works. With her new partner Lennon (1940–80), and with access to professional resources, she embarked on even more ambitious films, mostly jointly credited, including *Rape* (1969) in which an unsuspecting female tourist is pursued mercilessly by a camera crew (Ono's response to her own sudden celebrity?) and

**209** *Apotheosis*, Yoko Ono and John Lennon, 1970: (above) image from the film and (above right) cover of the press pack that accompanied its launch at the ICA.

*Erection* (1971), a time-lapse record of a dull South Kensington hotel being built (a Lennon pun?). *Two Virgins* (1968) consists of self-portraits that drift out of focus and superimpose in a game of merged identities, reminiscent of those played by Balch and Burroughs, while *Bed In* (1969) documents a happening/media event, but *Apotheosis* (1970) with its simple structure – one idea, one action – is more consistent with Ono's larger body of work. The camera rises from the ground in the Market Square in Lavenham, Suffolk, passes John and Yoko (whose black cloaks conceal the film's first cut), and continues to ascend, passing though thick clouds (causing a long section of 'blank' screen and concealing another cut), and sailing on above them till the film runs out. The idea of filming an apotheosis, a 'release from earthly life', was apparently Lennon's.

## VIDEO ART AND TELEVISION

Video first crept into the gallery space at the end of the 1960s in the form of live events; the Portapak wasn't capable of continuous playback, and the novelty was the 'live' image of closed-circuit TV (CCTV). Le Grice and Dunford created a two-week long *Drama in a Wide Media Environment* (1968) for the Drury Lane Arts Lab, and Susan Hiller created a three-hour interactive video for ten participants called *Pray (Prayer)* (1969) for the Serpentine. (Self-evidently, little remains of either.) Ian Breakwell (1943–2005) used closed-circuit video to relay images of men shifting piles of earth with shovels inside the Angela Flowers Gallery to the gallery's ground-floor window in 1971, while NASA's Apollo 14 astronauts were digging on the moon, his wobbly black and white images wittily mirroring the more hard-won scenes currently displayed in TV shop windows across the land. (In an odd later echo, Kerry Trengove would relay his more strenuous excavation of the Acme Gallery's floor to its street-front window in *An Eight Day Passage* (1976), essentially a video in the service of performance – and on this occasion, literally the artist's only means of communicating with the outside world, but with no conscious address to television.) Breakwell's event *Birthday* celebrated the Gallery's first year of operation, and was also recorded on film by Leggett as *One* (1971), and it led to a jointly issued diatribe against domestic TV, *Moving Wallpaper in the TV Lounge*, one of the first of many by artists:

> Study and observe the piece of equipment known as a television receiver in its most common environment; the living room, the lounge, the drawing room, whatever you may call it. … Functioning perfectly, is it not just simply a 21″ picture window? Another standard lamp in the corner? A constantly changing pattern of new wallpaper? … Between 20 and 30 million people watch television each night: the engaging guest who's staying permanently, who's impossible to ignore and won't tolerate being turned off. For so many people to entertain such an insufferable guest is intolerable'.[28]

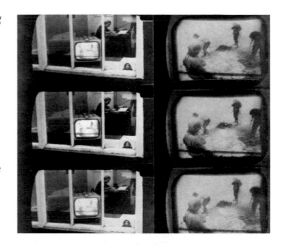

Leggett and Breakwell had collaborated earlier on *Sheet* (1970), another 'event-process' film which documented actions performed with a nine-foot square of material in a number of locations. Leggett wrote 'Ian had discovered the moving-pavements at Montparnasse Bienvenue Metro Station, and thought they needed filming with something in frame. So he did various things with the sheet while I filmed it'. Breakwell's nineteen proposals for sheet-actions included '(1) Drape sheet over a bush; (2) Pull sheet through letterbox; (3) Drop sheet from top floor window;'etc.[29] and the film records their execution in a number of domestic and exotic locations (though they made up other actions as they went along). *Nine Jokes* (1971), made by Breakwell alone, was a series of one-line performance jokes that parody the excessive seriousness of some contemporary conceptual art.[30] More typical of his later work was *Repertory* (1973), a long continuous tracking-shot around the outside of a closed theatre, accompanied by a voice-over in which he imagines (and makes the viewer imagine) a

**210** *One*, Ian Breakwell and Mike Leggett, 1971 (from *The Video Show* catalogue, 1975).

**211** *Repertory*, Ian Breakwell, 1973

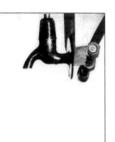

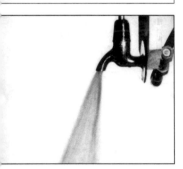

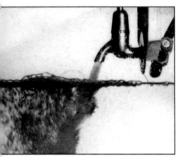

programme of gently surreal stage-tableaux and presentations. During the 1970s and 1980s he would publish a series of *Diaries* in book and video form, observing the absurd juxtapositions of daily life, recording dreams and memories, the latter reaching a wide public when transmitted by Channel 4 in 1984.

Television itself became a venue and medium for artists' works with David Hall's *Television Interventions* (aka *Seven TV Pieces*) transmitted by Scottish Television in 1971. Inspired by Schum's un-introduced German broadcasts of *Land Art* and *Identifications* (1969) that had included works by Long, Flanagan, Gilbert and George, Keith Arnatt, and Hamish Fulton, but unlike them addressing his works to television itself, Hall created a number of visual surprises – durational events and paradoxes involving the proscenium of the TV set, designed to be inserted unannounced into the evening's schedule, to 'redirect attention back to the box as object':

> Often I attempted to interface reality and image, apparatus and illusion – the spatio/temporal ambiguities of the medium. In one a water-tap appears in the top corner of the blank screen. The tap is turned on and the cathode ray tube 'fills with water'. The tap is removed. The water is drained out, this time with the water obliquely inclined to the expected horizontal. The screen is blank again – normal service is resumed, and the illusion restored.[31]

Television – both 'the 21" picture window' and 'the engaging guest' – was his constant subject and victim over the next twenty years. *60 TV Sets* (1972) shown as part of *A Survey of the Avant-Garde in Britain* and its remake as *101 TV Sets* (1975) for the Serpentine *Video Show* (both made with Tony Sinden) were assaults via overkill; the motley collection of old domestic sets (some only half alive) tuned to create a visual and aural cacophony, surrounding the viewer in serried rows. *This is a Video Monitor* (1974), remade for the BBC as *This is a Television Receiver* (1976), combined this shock tactic with an early assertion of *video as video*, what Hall called 'a wholly videological experience'. In both, a speaker reads a text about the material construction of the television sound/image illusion (recalling Le Grice and Nicolson), which is repeated several times, each repeat being re-videoed so image and sound become increasingly degraded and distorted, to the point of abstraction, with in the second version the clever conceit of having Richard Baker – the BBC's then most popular newsreader/face of authority – as the speaker. *Vidicon Inscriptions* (1974–75) played with a fault unique to early video cameras – the way in which the shape of any tonal highlight in a scene would briefly 'burn' itself into the vidicon tube, and so transfer a ghost image or streak of light to the transmitted image; more video materiality. *TV Fighter (Cam Era Plane)* (1977), like the *This is* duo, was a classic piece of deconstruction through repetition, in this instance of 'hot' wartime archive footage, and with variations in the camera-movement within each repeat. Hall's endorsement of many of the tropes of structural film led to their widespread transfer to video, and their replication with greater and lesser degrees of interest in video materiality, in the work of his younger LVA colleagues, not least in the early work of Chris Meigh Andrews, *The Distracted Driver* (1980), Peter Savage, and later into the 1980s with Mike Stubbs, Steve Littmann, Jez Welsh and others, again reflecting the pattern of film.

**212** David Hall: (above) sequence from *Television Interventions* (aka *Seven TV Pieces*), 1971; (opposite top) *Progressive Recession*, 1975; (opposite) *The Situation Envisaged*, (various versions) 1978-88.

Hall's *Progressive Recession* (1975), exhibited at the Serpentine *Video Show*, was a return to his earlier activity as a sculptor working with spatial paradoxes, but also reflected the growing awareness by British artists of contemporary conceptual video from the USA. Both this work and Roger Barnard's *Corridor* (1974, installed at the Tate's *Video Show* in 1976) confront the spectator with a disorientating representation of their own live image via CCTV cameras set within a sculptural construction, echoing Bruce Nauman's installation *Going Round the Corner* (USA 1970). Equally, the late-1960s/early-1970s body-action films of Nauman, Richard Serra and Dennis Oppenheim had their counterparts in Denis Masi's *Lipsmear* (1971) (lips smearing the camera lens), Clive Richardson's simple exercise-like *Video Studies* (1972), Bruce McLean's and Silvia Ziranek's *Crease Crisis* (1970) and some of Tony Morgan's collaborations.

In the late 1970s and through the 1980s, Hall developed a series of large-scale sculptural assemblages with the common title *The Situation Envisaged* (1978–88) that returned to the theme of television's overload of information. In these, the TV monitors were tuned to ever-more stations and stacked in solid wall-like arrangements, now with their backs turned to the viewer, so only their cumulative coloured glow was visible, with, behind them, one forward-facing screen that could be glimpsed in fragments through the wall's gaps; an imposing metaphor for the box's many frustrations.

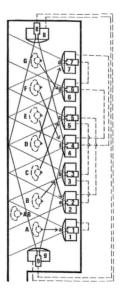

PROGRESSIVE RECESSION 1974
Installation plan drawing © David Hall

**213** *Monitor 1*,
Steven Partridge, 1975.

Among the most elegant early video pieces to explore the medium's unique visual language were Steven Partridge's *Monitor 1* (1975). Partridge (b.1953) set his camera to record a close-up of the monitor to which it was linked, so the monitor displayed its own image, and another within that, *ad infinitum*. A hand appeared and slowly rotated the monitor through 90 degrees, causing a vortex of movement within its image; a slight delay in the signal from camera to monitor exaggerating the time/space distortion. Many artists capitalised on the limitations of early reel-to-reel recorders by constructing uninterrupted performances to camera. Stuart Marshall (1949–93), David Critchley, (b.1953) and Keith Frake (b.1955) conceived clever variations on this theme while highlighting video as video. Marshall's *Go Through the Motions* (1974) consisted of a continuous close-up of the artist's mouth miming to a sound tape loop. At first it appears to be a live performance, but as the mouth suddenly freezes and the sound continues, the illusion ruptures, and 'from then on, a play is set up between speech and mime, live sound and commentary, which involves the patterned semantic deconstruction of the speech loop' (artist's statement). The three-reel *Trialogue* (1977) by Critchley elaborates the theme; in reel one he delivered an oddly fragmented statement directly to camera; in reel two he filled in some of the gaps while a monitor beside him replayed the first recording; and in the third, with the monitor now replaying reel two, he completes the message, uniting three layers of time. Frake's *An Interaction of Meaning* (1977)

**214** *Trialogue*,
David Critchley, 1977.

offered a close-up view of a blackboard on which letters are being written and rubbed-out/altered according to a hidden system, the writer periodically halting to allow an unseen speaker to try to pronounce the letters in their current form. The work continues till the speaker admits defeat and the tape runs out. All three pieces can be seen as 'structural games', paralleling contemporary developments in film. Critchley's *Pieces I Never Did* (1979), another conceptual dig at conceptualism, also involved his description to camera of a series of potential conceptual works, his delivery being periodically interrupted by one such work in which he shouts 'Shut up' to the camera (and himself) at maximum volume, until his voice gives out.

**215** *Television Interview*,
Kevin Atherton, 1986.

Hall's critique of broadcast TV was picked up by several artists, notably, but more ambigu-
ously (and humorously), by the sculptor/performer/video artist Kevin Atherton (b.1950). In
*Home is Where the Art Is* (1976) he describes in voice-over the domestic space in which his
TV resides and in which the work is being shot, while the camera focuses on him drawing its
layout on his naked chest. Once these various descriptions have been completed, he holds up
a mirror so the reflected real space replaces the drawing, then zooms out to reveal the entire
scene. In the 1980s he introduced a TV set as a stand-up comic in performances at the ICA,
and for the Ikon Gallery in Birmingham created *Video Times* (1984) in which the single image
of the artist watching TV was deconstructed in a printed magazine, itself an elaborate pastiche
of a popular TV-guide. In his most celebrated piece, *Television Interview* (1986) made for
*The British Art Show,* he quizzed the cast of the soap opera *Coronation Street* on the nature
of television, he on one monitor, they on another, their 'replies' to his questions cleverly
edited from transmitted programmes.

One response to the task of occupying gallery space was simply to replicate the video
image across many screens (as in a TV shop window). The novelty soon tired, but not before
some effective use of the device was made. Marshall's *Orientation Studies* (1976), shown in
the Tate *Video Show* and in a second version at the Paris Biennale in 1977, copied the same
signal to eight (later ten) screens set in a row but, through superimpositions, camera movement
and editing, built the momentary illusion that the images were joined, then allowed them
to fragment again. Similarly in Sinden's solo work *Behold Vertical Devices* (various versions
1974–76), where the monitors are placed on their sides and on a slope, a running figure

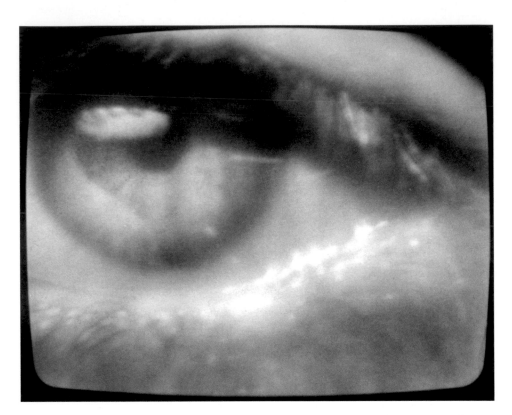

seemed to progress along their length. *Disintegrating Forms* (1976) by Tamara Krikorian (b.1944) shown at the Tate's *Video Show,* imaginatively installed its linked monitors in two descending series of four, placed high on plinths in a darkened gallery, so her repeated imagery of clouds appeared suspended in an undefined space, an allusion to their natural home and to the apparent source of TV imagery as signals in the skies.

In other works, Krikorian took the video installation into less formal directions, introducing wider cultural references and more reflective ways of discussing the video image, often involving self-portraiture as one of the elements. *Vanitas* (1977) was inspired by the painting *An Allegory of Justice and Vanity* attributed to Nicolas Tournier in the Ashmolean Museum, Oxford, her version including her own image, a still life and a TV set relaying the news, seen through a mirror, to form an allegory of the ephemeral nature of television. Of the origins of *In the Mind's Eye* (1977) she wrote:

> I thought about ways of approaching formalism through some sort of restricted narrative, and I
> used Rimbaud's poem *In Winter* [describing a railway journey] as the structure of the work, while
> retaining obvious self-referral devices ... concerned with the perception of video/TV *per se*'.[32]

We hear her read the poem in French, then see first the changing view from a train window; then its re-played image on a TV monitor; then (remarkably) its image reflected in her eye. In *Unassembled Information* (1977) the screen is dominated by the back of her head, past which can be glimpsed fragments of her face in the small mirror she is holding, while a radio is playing. Thus she negated the elaborately constructed image of the TV presenter; with the radio a reminder of importance of the spectator's imagination, so rarely addressed by television. Within the early LVA group, Krikorian pioneered the inclusion of more personal subjects. Hardly discussed in contemporary reviews of the Serpentine *Video Show* were the tapes by feminist artists from Europe and America: Linda Benglis, Hermione Freed, Frederike Pezold, Ulrike Rosenbach and others. Their ideas only really took root in Britain in the 1980s with the work of Zoe Redman, Katherine Meynell, Cate Elwes and Mona Hatoum, but Krikorian provided an early link and, through her teaching in Maidstone and Newcastle, support for many emerging talents.

Performance-related tapes provided another safe haven for subjectivity and 'the personal' in this formalist period. Several of Marc Camille Chaimowicz's (b.1947) tapes were made initially as part of live events, though he subsequently allowed them to stand on their own. In live versions of *Doubts … A Sketch for Video Camera and Audience* (1977), the artist sat facing away from the audience, swinging a pendulum, his image simultaneously relayed to a monitor on the stage. He would exit, leaving a pre-recorded tape to show scenes from his domestic life – writing, looking out of the window, having tea with another figure, sleeping naked on a bed – formally framed, shown at length, and transparently staged, with a melancholy Lou Reed song adding its own atmosphere. The tape version ends as it begins with a shot of the empty stage and the monitor, that now shows the sleeping figure; a reminder that this intimate image was, too, just that – an image. Tina Keane's *Playpen* (1979) and *Media Snake* (1985) were other early intimations of the new welcome to subjectivity, and are discussed later.

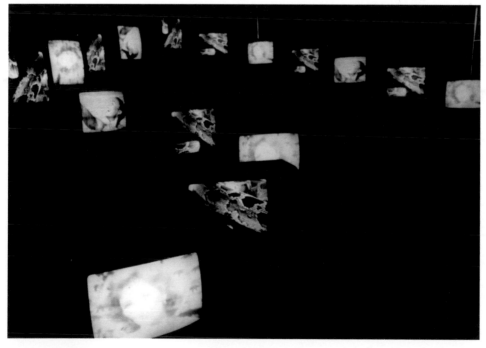

**217** *Media Snake*, Tina Keane, 1985.

## EXPANDED CINEMA

Le Grice's influence was at its greatest in the context of the development of expanded cinema in the early 1970s, and in particular through a series of events in 1972–73 to which he gave the name Filmaktion.[33] Twin-screen films had been part of Le Grice's repertoire from the beginning, and with *Horror Film* (1971) he had added a live element to the mix, performing, naked, a Leonardo-like man-as-measure-of-the-screen, casting his shadow to its four corners. To Le Grice, expanded cinema represented:

> the establishment of the third region of time/space experience [the actual time/space of the film's presentation] as *primary* … where the material factors of the screening situation, the celluloid, the light, the screen and the duration of [the viewer's] attention is clearly established as the first instance.[34]

**218** Poster design by David Crosswaite for Filmaktion at the Walker Art Gallery, Liverpool, 1973. Its imagery shows the Film Co-op workshops at The Diary, and portraits of many Co-op artists and activists.

He saw his own *White Field Duration* (1972) and Raban's *2.45* (1973) as exemplary in their challenge to 'the significance of cine-photography/recording as a retrospective process.' (cinema's preoccupation with reproducing things staged in the past). In different ways, both works dramatised the viewer's experience of the present film-projection event, heightening awareness of the elements that contributed to it. *White Field Duration* was a composition across two screens of tiny bursts of image and long but irregular image-less intervals; *2.45* a performance that uniquely combined shooting and screening in a simultaneous event, designed to be repeated on successive nights to add a visual layering of time.[35] In his works made for Filmaktion, Raban temporarily put aside his landscape/systems interests (they would re-appear only months later, transformed), and produced some of the most elegant demonstrations of Le Grice's principles. His *Take Measure* (1973) brilliantly dramatised the physicality of the projector's beam of light, turning its length – from projector lens to screen – into the 'measure' of the projected filmstrip thus determining its duration, and in *Diagonal* (1973), in which he built a kinetic multi-screen performance from re-filmed images of projected light. Nicolson, too, was captivated by projected light.

> Thinking back to earlier work with film, it occurred to me that I liked projectors as instruments to be played. The cone of light that we see as a beam expands in size as it diminishes in brightness. This beam is visible but often overlooked because attention is directed only to the screen, where the cone of light collides with a surface. This area of light is rich in particles of light making up an image.
>
> Light allows information to travel. Projection is essentially transient. The image travels through space but can be arrested at any point on its path.[36]

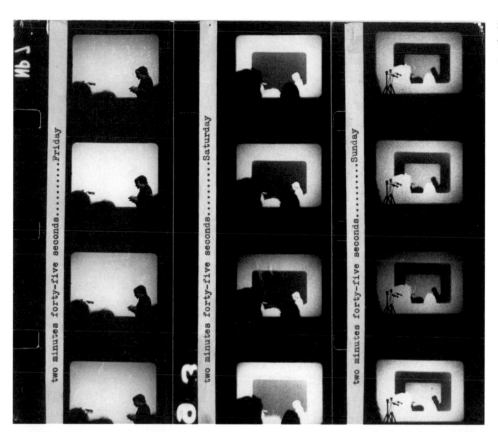

**219** Photo-synopsis by William Raban of his *2.45*, 1973.

**220** Multi-projection by Filmaktion at Gallery House, London, 1973. (l. to r.) Le Grice, Crosswaite (?), Eatherley and Raban.

**221 (right)** *Take Measure*,
William Raban, 1973.

**222 (below)** Performing
with film: *Reel Time*,
Annabel Nicolson, 1973.

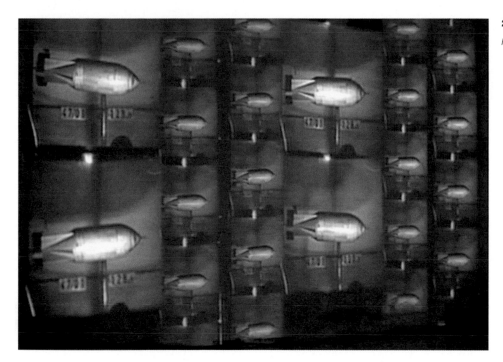

**223** Film installation: *Sicher Heits*, Gill Eatherley, 1973.

Other key works in Filmaktion's changing programme included Nicolson's *Reel Time* (1973), in which the artist sat at a sewing-machine and stitched directly into a filmstrip containing her image sewing, which passed in a loop to the projector, then back into the sewing machine, circulating between them until it fell to bits. This clever combination of production and exhibition (also self-portrait and demonstration of film's material frailty) was a witty variant on Le Grice's *Pre Production* piece for four performers and two slide projectors (1973), in which texts about principles of cinematography were solemnly read; Nicolson had readers alternately quote the 'how to thread the machine' sections of Singer's sewing machine manual and a Bell & Howell projector manual (the readers halting as the projector periodically choked on sewn film, plunging them into darkness), allowing spectators to note their remarkable mechanical similarities, and their bizarrely contrasting gender associations.[37] Eatherley's *Light Occupations – Aperture Sweep* (1973) questioned the status of the reproduced image equally playfully, and involved her sweeping her own shadow off the screen, with sound coming from the amplified head of the brush.[38] Crosswaite, Drummond, Dunford and Sally Potter also showed works that used two or more screens in this context.[39] Some contributions were less concerned with drawing attention to 'the third region of time', and simply evidenced the growing contemporary interest in multi-screen presentation. A Potter film of this period was *Play* (1971), a two-screen film in which three pairs of twins playing in the street are recorded from an upper window by two cameras simultaneously, creating an engaging piece of choreography of action on, across, and 'off' the screens. Eatherley's four-screen *Chair Film* (1971), in which a fluorescent-painted 'real' chair interacts with its animated screen equivalents, was developed into a performance from an earlier *Hand-Grenade*-like study, but her *Sicher Heits* (1973) – a loop of found footage of a

224 Performing with
projectors: *Gross Fog*,
Malcolm Le Grice, 1973.

bomb dangling from a rope, overlapped by slides of the same image in its filmstrip form – was new in that it was conceived as a installation that could run unattended for as long as was needed. Film loops installations had been seen on occasion elsewhere and previously, but were new in the Filmmakers Co-op context. Le Grice contributed his own spectacular loop works including *Gross Fog* (1973) based on long sequences of richly coloured 'fogged' film with flashes of found imagery (drawn from *Matrix* of the same year); a work sometimes 'performed' by the artist by moving the running projectors to change the screen-image juxtapositions and combinations, but often left static and allowed to run unaccompanied.

The Festival of Expanded Cinema at the ICA gallery in 1976 celebrated this extra-cinema activity at its peak, yet the expanded cinema events at the Film London festival only three

225 *Angles of Incidence*,
William Raban, 1973.
(right and opposite)
In twin-screen projection;
schematic drawing of the
parameters of the camera-
movements employed in its
making; and film strip.

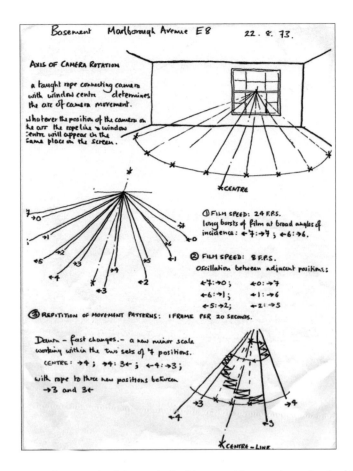

years later marked the end of widespread interest by artists in this activity. Videos shown on monitors were now in the ascendant, and future interest would focus on installations per se. And as Le Grice's agenda was passed over by others (and as he himself began to pursue it in single-screen long-form films), the film-loop, re-filming and multi-screen projection became (simply) popular ways of freeing film from its narrative straitjacket, and allowing exploration of other formal issues. 'Structural film' became synonymous with formal film, as the title of the 1979 exhibition *Film as Film – Formal Experiment in Film* tacitly acknowledged. These other concerns were already apparent among the Filmaktion performances. Eatherley's *Light Occupations* series included single-screen works such as *Lens and Mirror Film* (1973), which responded to the brilliance of a sun-lit beach, while also drawing attention to the function of the lens recording the scene. Raban's *Angles of Incidence* (1973) was 'the starting point of a continuous investigation into ways of presenting Cubist space in terms of the flat surface of the film screen. The film image is a view through a window, the window-frame providing a constant spatial reference point, as the view beyond is modified by a series of major and minor variations in camera viewpoint'.[40] Neither particularly draws attention to 'the third region of time', both pursue *film as film*, the shared concern of many if not all the film-makers associated with the Co-op.

## OTHER STRUCTURES

In the 1970s at the Filmmakers Co-op, the film printer became a creative tool sometimes to the exclusion of the camera, reconnecting with the tradition of Lye and Man Ray. The resulting focus on the filmstrip and its image-carrying surface is particularly associated with a group of Guy Sherwin's students at North East London Polytechnic, who were introduced to the Co-op's printing machines as part of their course. By imposing his own meticulous standards, Sherwin himself extracted prints from the Co-op's machines of an unprecedented quality and degree of control, even when (as often) they involved complex superimpositions and repeat printing. His *Newsprint* and *Cycles 1* (1972-77) and Lis Rhodes's *Dresden Dynamo* (1974), all made without a camera, are graphic works with an image-quality akin to screen-printing (and the inspiration for Steve Farrer's *Silk Screen Films* (1974), which were literally that – images screen-printed onto 16mm film). For *Dresden Dynamo* Rhodes fixed Letraset and Letratone onto clear film, then ran it through the film-printer in different combinations, finally adding colour through filters and extending the image into the area reserved for audio recording, so simultaneously generating synthetic sound. In her most dramatic film of this form *Light Music* (1975), Rhodes spread her imagery of black and white lines of varying widths across two screens, again simultaneously generating sound and playing it from two sources, creating an overwhelming but orchestrated aural-visual assault. In some presentations she projected from opposite ends of the viewing space, and following Anthony McCall's example (see below) filled the void with smoke, so making tangible the pulsing light-beams. Another example of this graphic cinema, Sherwin's *At The Academy* (1974) took the standardised length of film which provides a visual countdown to assist projectionists with timing and focus – the 'academy leader' – and systematically looped and repeat-printed it to develop layers of superimposition

**226** Lis Rhodes: (below) *Dresden Dynamo*, 1974; (below right) *Light Music*, 1975.

that on-screen appear as numbers in spectral bas-relief, their cyclical development playing games with the audience's expectations. Farrer's *Ten Drawings* (1976) exists in two forms, a series of 'drawings' to be exhibited on a wall in which lines were drawn onto strips of clear film arranged in large rectangles, and these same strips projected in succession, the projector transforming the pattern of lines into movements and sounds on the screen. To Farrer it fulfilled the desire to 'deal with a film with one stroke; to say, well – slash – I've dealt with beginning, middle and end in one go'.[41] Sherwin's *Railings* and *Musical Stairs* (both 1977) are further elegant examples of films in which the image, flipped into the soundtrack area, generates the sound.

Structural film could be shaped by mathematics, which offered a formal beauty or, equally, the pattern of a game, which offered a particular form of engagement to the viewer. Particularly elegant examples of the latter were the games-based works of Halford, *Hands Knees and Boompsa Daisy* (1973) where she performs (live) the children's hand-game with her projected negative filmed self, and *Footsteps* (1974) where she takes the game Grandmother's Footsteps as a means of dramatising the usually hidden relationship between film camera and its subject.[42] Chris Garratt (later well known as one of the *Guardian*'s *Biff* cartoonists – a partnership with Co-op distribution worker Mick Kidd) used structural film's device of repeat-printing/looping footage as a way of generating humorous *musique concrete* out of found images and sound – in films such as *Romantic Italy* (1975), *Versailles* (1976) and *Filmmusic* (1977). Jo Millett and Rob Gawthrop's *The Miller and the Sweep* (1984) wittily re-made a British film comedy of 1898,[43] in which the protagonists fight each other with soot and flour, adding their own structural games of

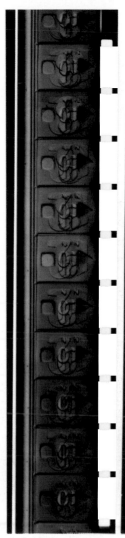

**227** Strips from *At The Academy*, Guy Sherwin, 1974.

reverse-motion, superimpositions, and pos-neg alternations, to the black-to-white / white-to-black tonal transformations of the original. In time, the most dedicated structural/formal film-maker would prove to be Peter Greenaway, whose early work *Intervals* (1969) cut up and mathematically permutated a long sequence showing pedestrians walking on a Venetian canal-side pavement, with an alphabetically re-arranged voice-over, prefiguring the structural games that characterise many of his later features (discussed earlier). The most celebrated of such game-structured films is *Zorn's Lemma* (USA 1970) by Hollis Frampton, an artist admired by Greenaway and Gidal alike. John Smith's *Associations* (1975) takes its punning word-per-image game (Ass, Sew, Sea, Asians etc.) from Frampton, though even this atypical early work already reveals Smith's particular eye for the particularities of the London urban scene.

Some artists used formal structures as a means of exploring space (as in the landscape films discussed earlier). David Hall's *Phased Time* (1974) employed an intricate mathematical system of progressive repetitions, superimpositions and 'matting' (partial obscuring of the image during a take, allowing 'filling in' later) to construct a complex spatial reading of a bourgeois interior space. Robert Fearns's *Rocking and Rolling* (1978) plays Tony Hill-like games with the viewer, engaging the camera in a repeated head-over-heels journey across the bleak, dark space that was the Co-op's Gloucester Avenue cinema. David Parsons (b.1943), an influential teacher at NELP and later Saint Martins, combined spatial exploration with an exhaustive cataloguing of all the camera's possibilities, 'its lenses, the film transportation mechanism, the shift of the turret, hand-holding or tripod mounting'.[44] Gidal admired Parsons's 'extreme' use of 'film and the apparatus and machinery as its subject matter', noting that in *Picture Planes* (1979), 'the subject matter and the content *is* the filters, the camera, [the act of] putting a lens onto a camera which is running without one, and having an image take place, then disappear, then change colour when a colour filter is put up in front; switching to negative and doing the same operation in negative reverse'.[45] Parsons himself saw his process as painterly; a fusing together 'of the everyday familiarity of being in a work-space, with a distanced appraisal of its dimensions and function', and compared it to Matisse's pictorial use of his studio, 'where one becomes aware of the constant looking and re-looking at the same space, through spatial decisions on the picture plane'.[46] Stuart Pound was almost as prolific as John Du Cane and equally devoted to the Co-op's film-printer. His *Slow Down* (1971) included in *Perspectives on British Avant-Garde Film* at the Hayward Gallery, with its acceleration of permutating found and filmed images, was as tightly mathematically ordered as Du Cane's work at its most extreme, but with its own distinctive sensuality that derived from Pound's polished combination of images in the optical printing process. *Clocktime* (1972) sets spontaneously filmed portraits of Eatherley, Nicolson and Le Grice against a blizzard of details superimposed in flat colours, Pound's intention being 'to make films which fight against the kind of "cinematic reality" which we usually find so engaging in narrative cinema … and to assert themselves as physical strips of film'.[47] His *Codex* (1979) – images of nocturnal London with film-frames animated by multiple-printing, set to music by Philip Glass – won a prize at Toulon/Hyeres in 1979, and transported the writer Marguerite Duras, one of the judges, to another world:

> The film is without past, with no becoming. The film beats with a metronomic regularity. It is just that, regularity and presence … One can also say that we have here a pure cinema of intelligence and that the nature of this intelligence is one based on the simultaneity of image and sound. Simply that; an intelligence of that, but one that is intoxicating.[48]

## GIDAL'S LEGACY

Gidal stopped working at the Co-op in 1973, but taught continuously at the Royal College of Art from 1971 to 1983, and continued to be a major force, as example, mentor and polemicist. Ten years after, the task of introducing a programme of British work to audiences at the Collective for Living Cinema in New York in March 1983 (where Simon Field was acting as programmer) allowed him to take stock of the scene. Included were works by Leggett, Lucy

Panteli (b.1954) and Nicky Hamlyn (b.1954) who were among those now seriously engaged with the structural/materialist project.[49] Also shown was Leggett's *Friday Fried* (1981) which took its point of departure from postcard imagery with permutating 'plausible' sounds, and played with image-sound synchronisation, a subject Leggett, as an industry-trained film-editor, was well placed to deconstruct and contest. (In a different context it might be seen as another 'game' film.) It was also possibly a critical response to Le Grice's current engagement with narrative in *Blackbird Descending* et al., which had disturbed many of his colleagues. Gidal, having first rebuked New York's avant-gardists for their attempts to 'commodify and patriarchialize aesthetic production-processes, and in one way or another titillate the viewer's senses, again to constantly reproduce voyeurism', pointed to his colleague's resistance of these traps. He praised Leggett's use of repetition and his image's 'constant reconstruction towards – and simultaneously against – narrativisation'. He admired the interruption of the post-card sequences by 'durational sequences of frying eggs (an image which in England conjures up a domestic lower-middle-class "scene"' making it 'endless, tedious and humorific'.[50] He praised Panteli's *Across the Field of Vision* (1982) for:

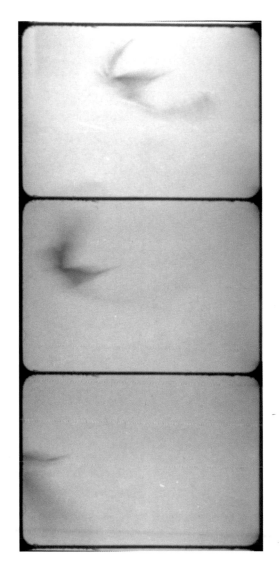

> inculcating in the viewer the need (and yet only occasionally the
> desire) to look at *and through* the frame, unstoppably; [so] attempting
> to annihilate the dramatic interest of the ostensible subject matter –
> birds flying and gliding at different speeds, seen from different
> camera positions and against differing 'backgrounds' of tonality –
> white to grey to dark blue. In this attempt, carefully composed
> durations (as opposed to perspectively orientated montage) operate.

(Panteli's film was surely inspired by Nancy Graves's *Aves, Magnificent Frigate Bird, Great Flamingo* (USA 1973), another celebration of birds, seemingly free of gravity, effortlessly stretching and redefining screen-space). The sound in Hamlyn's *Not to See Again* (1980), Gidal described as working:

**228** *Across the Field of Vision*, Lucy Panteli, 1982.

> in as complex and at the same time understated a manner as the image, where the need to
> listen whilst deciphering, and attempting to decipher sound (often against the 'meaning' that
> the simultaneous image is 'giving'), forces work by the viewer that disallows consumption
> and satisfaction. ... Thus, for example, the *moment* of sound, a fragment (of a sentence) is
> clearly understood, and then 'lost', (similar to the way a radio is tuned).

 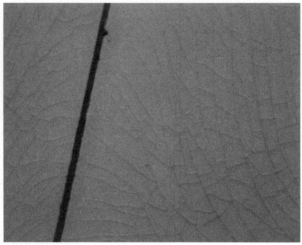

**229** *Guesswork*,
Nicky Hamlyn, 1979.

Of these artists Hamlyn has been the most consistent in supporting Gidal's project. His own summary of *Not to See Again* echoes Gidal, but introduces his own clarity of purpose (he would become one of the best writers on artists' film of his generation):

> A film of misrecognitions, simulacra etc. The film is anti-montage, a series of discrete shots that nevertheless gel at one or two points to produce simple meanings … Like *Guesswork* [1979] the film hovers on the line between abstraction and representation, hopefully problematising both'.[51]

His later works are increasingly distinctive and, while withholding description, offer more clues as to location, admitting personal involvement, even to the point of being openly auto-biographical. Of *Telly* (1995), he wrote:

> I have become interested in the role of the body in negotiating space, because of how it contrasts with the implicit detachment of the monocular perspectival gaze, that is the camera's view. *Telly* is concerned with the spurious visual phenomena generated by the TV box itself, and by the light it both emits and reflects'.[52]

**230 (opposite)** *Cézanne's Eye*, Michael Maziere, 1988

Michael Maziere (b.1957 France) was equally prolific as a film-maker, and initially equally committed to the Gidallian position, though through the 1990s, and as he moved into video, his attitude to subject matter and the issue of the 'representation' of things moved far from its place of origin. His *Untitled* (1980), made while he was still at the RCA, was a construction of super-impositions, camera-movements and sound-dislocations that questioned the representation of space in film in the authentic Gidal manner. 'The film can be read as an existential journey through interior spaces or as a phenomenological inquiry into the relationship between what is seen and the act of seeing'. But in the late 1980s – encouraged perhaps by Le Grice's *Academic Still Life, Cézanne* (1976), or inspired by trips to his parental home of Aix en Provence – he

embarked on a series of Cézanne studies which allowed him to combine Gidallian rapid camera-movements, streaks and blurs, with his own musical rhythms and frozen frames, and, in the later studies, actual music; re-introducing emotion and subjectivity. *The Bathers Series – Les Baigneurs* (1986) and *Swimmer* (1987), filmed on the Mediterranean, were followed by *Cézanne's Eye 1* and *2* (1988–91), which revisited some of the master's subjects; the quarries and dam at Bibemus and the slopes of Mont Saint-Victoire. Gidal's philosophy was also important to artists who responded to his challenge less overtly. Will Milne (b.1952) made several studies of interiors and bodies such as *Fattendre* (1978) and *Same* (1980) which, though static and deeply introspective, still reflected Gidal's withholding of representation and identification. The work of Lis Rhodes, Jean Matthee and Nina Danino (discussed later) similarly developed his arguments about the (non)representation of the image of women, in new and different ways.

## LATER INSTALLATIONS

While the interest in performed cinema diminished in the latter part of the 1970s, large-scale film installations became an occasional but increasingly important part of the landscape, thanks to the development of artist-run organisations such as Acme and 2B Butler's Wharf (discussed earlier). The artists who came to prominence as makers of film installations at this time included Chris Welsby and Raban (also discussed earlier), and Sinden, Jane Rigby (b.1954), and Ron Haselden (b.1944).

Tony Sinden uniquely worked equally in film and video during the late 1970s, and was prolific in both. *Cinema of Projection* (1975), shown at the ICA Gallery and reprieved at the Arnolfini, was his first film installation, and comprised ten projectors with long loops made from footage from his contemporary film *Wipers and Whippersnappers* – a film of rhythm and re-film-

**231** *Another Aspect, Another Time – The Exhibition*, Tony Sinden, Hayward Gallery, 1979.

ing based on Lumière's *L'Arroseur arrosé* (an 1895 joke about a garden hose), his version containing the imaginative *repoussoire* of windscreen wipers apparently sweeping the camera lens. Where other film-makers had been happy to improvise the set-up of their installations (so long as the sight-lines were good, the projectors matched, the sound worked), Sinden insisted that lay-out of projectors, plinths and loops, together with the architectural space they were in, the surrounding lighting, were all part of the work. To this end, he would sometimes add slide projections to mirror props he had included, or to introduce his own ghostly presence in life-size silhouette. He described this relationship of on-screen to off-screen space in relation to *Another Aspect Another Time – The Exhibition* shown in the Hayward Annual in 1979:

> For instance, I might walk onto the screen carrying a chair or bouncing a ball, you glance
> away from the screen and notice the same chair placed in front of the screen, and the ball rest-
> ing on the floor at the other end of the gallery; an event that creates a sense of illusion
> extending itself to the physical space – in which you are standing. Alternatively, you might
> decide to sit down on the chair and look away from the screen, across the room, and notice
> that your position is reflected back to your angle of view, in a sense back into the illusion, as a
> displacement of the physical self.[53]

It was not surprising that he became a founding member of Housewatch in the 1980s, a group dedicated to animating large architectural spaces with moving images,[54] though he continues to make solo work.

Haselden's installation *MFV 'Maureen' Fishing Out of Eyemouth* (1975), shown at the New 57 Gallery in Edinburgh and the Acme Gallery in London, was in part a documentary

**232** *MFV 'Maureen' Fishing Out of Eyemouth*: Ron Haselden with projectors, Edinburgh, 1975.

project evoking North Sea fishing in the tradition of *Drifters,* but equally a record of the artist's
evolving response to the material he had shot. Six shots of the activity at sea were projected
simultaneously as loops of different lengths in a row, forming a changing collage of details
through which a composite reconstruction of the boat emerges, with a videotape interview with
some of the fisherman playing on a monitor nearby. During the progress of the exhibition,
Haselden re-shot some of the footage as it was projected, reframing and re-timing it, so by the
end of a week, the exhibited loops had changed and developed. Still images and frame-
blow-ups from earlier stages of the installation added a history of its development.[55] *Lady
Dog* shown at the ICA Festival of Expanded Cinema in January and its sibling *Sticks for the Dog*
at the Acme Gallery in November 1976 teased out the different experiences of 'framing' and
'time' in still and moving images, juxtaposing a small projected image of the artist's dog
jumping for a stick, with print-outs from the same footage positioned on the wall following the
line of the original camera movement, translating represented screen-space into real-space,
and (in the later multi-screen version) mapping the lines of represented movement in three
dimensions.

Rigby was almost as prolific an installation-maker as Sinden at this time, but worked only with film, her work being characterised by the formal symmetry of structural film, and a concern for the immediate psychological impact of her image-compositions. The four different-length loops that formed *Graffiti* (1975), projected as a quartered square, displayed texts about the nature of film, made alternately credible and contradictory by their permutation. A fifth projector added a layer of visual graffiti, building to a climax. In *Figures in a Landscape* (1978), shown at Film London, she used matte boxes in her camera to generate two adjacent but successively filmed images on each frame, each sweeping up landscape imagery in a long pan, but in mirrored actions. Projected as three slightly overlapping loops – the landscapes sometimes linking up, sometimes not – the 'figures' were introduced by the spectator's own shadows as they penetrated the installation. In later works such as *Ambient Vision* (1979) shown at the Acme, and the related *Counter Poise* (1980) shown in *About Time* at the ICA, the figures were filmed dancers, their engaging and expressive choreography contrasting with her own highly formal and schematic camera-movements. In another early 1980s project (which sadly remained a one-off), the artist Charles Garrad initiated a new installation form with *Cinema* (1983), a detailed film-set *scene of the crime* built in the Serpentine Gallery, which allowing the spectator only limited, camera-like perspectives on the view. This architectural concept lay dormant till Peter Greenaway's large-scale cinematic installations of the mid- and late 1990s, such as *In the Dark* (Hayward Gallery, 1996), described earlier.

## NOTES

1. A.L. Rees, *A History of Experimental Film and Video* (London: BFI, 1999).

2. 'Theory and definition of the Structural/Materialist Film', in Peter Gidal (ed.), *Structural Film Anthology*, (London: BFI, 1976).

3. 'Through my contact with guitarist Keith Rowe, I did a few performances of sound and light devices with AMM, then including Cornelius Cardew, at 26 Kingley Street Gallery.' 'Flashbacks', *Filmwaves*, no. 14, 2001.

4. Shown 1, 2 and 10 November 1968. He had shown *Castle One* for a week at the Arts Lab in October 1967, but introduced it as the work of 'Mihima Haus [Mickey Mouse] and Doe Nagduk'.

5. *London Filmmakers Co-op Catalogue*, 1969.

6. He blames the author for suggesting this: 'A week or two later I took *Room...* to the open screening at David Curtis's Arts Lab film night ... As there were two copies on one reel, and I had no equipment, I asked David what to do to get them separated, and he said "Why not leave them together", which I thought a wonderful idea'. 'Flashbacks – Peter Gidal', *Filmwaves*, no. 7, 1999.

7. Peter Gidal, *Arte Inglese Oggi* (Milano: British Council/Electra Editrice, 1976).

8. *Codes and Structures*, RCA, January 1975; *Structure and Function in Time* (organised by Rosetta Brooks), Sunderland Arts Centre, February 1975.

9. *Studio International*, October 1973.

10. Peter Gidal, *Arte Inglese Oggi*, op. cit.

11. Not a Le Grice student, but close to this group, David Crosswaite made *Pigeon Film* and *Puddle* (both 1969), sensitive studies that reveal an emerging accomplished photographer.

12. Elaborated in P. Adams Sitney, *Visionary Film* (New York: Oxford University Press, 1974).

13. Gill Eatherley to the author 2002 for Illuminations TV.

14. London Filmmakers Co-op Catalogue, 1976.

15. Interviewed by Mark Webber for *Shoot Shoot Shoot*, 2002.

16. NFT programme note, *English Independent Cinema: 2* (1972).

17. Programme note, 2nd International Avant-garde Festival 1973.

18. Statement in *Arte Inglese Oggi* (Milano: British Council/Electra Editrice, 1976).

19. This approach originated with the New York Fluxus group, with examples by Ono and others.

20. 'David Dye', interviewed by Anne Seymour, *The New Art*, Hayward Gallery, 1972.

21. '[In 1974] I created a set of photographs based on the four characters in Manet's painting *Le Dejuner sur l'herbe* which represented every possible state of dress and undress (the models for this included myself and Carolee [Schneemann]. Malcolm Le Grice saw this piece in New York … and later called to tell me that it had got him thinking, and that (if I didn't object) he was going to do a *dejuner sur l'herbe* piece of his own [*After Manet*].' McCall, email to author, 25 August 2001.

22. He had exhibited with Raban, Du Cane and others in *A Survey of the Avant-Garde in Britain*. *Line Describing* was conceived on the boat as he emigrated to New York with Schneemann.

23. Artist's statement to Fifth International Experimental Film Competition (Knokke Le Zoute), 1974.

24. For *A Century of Artists' Film in Britain* at Tate Britain, April 2003–March 2004.

25. Conversation with the author 2003.

26. Even Gidal had signed up with the commercial distributor PAP and the gallery Gimpel Fils in 1973, but these initiatives foundered. More surprisingly Raban too sided with the black box: 'I prefer to show films involving the live space of the audience in conventional viewing theatres. Both *2.45* and *Take Measure* depend on the formal context of the cinema for their full effect'. *Festival of Expanded Cinema* catalogue 1976.

27. The original was *Disappearing Music for Face* by Chieko Shiomi, where the smile filmed was Yoko's (see *Fluxus Anthology*, 1966).

28. A4 flier accompanying a workshop by Leggett and Breakwell at Plymouth College of Art, 19 April–16 June 1971.

29. Flier accompanying its premiere at the Robert Street Arts Lab.

30. Sending up conceptual art was a popular pastime even among conceptualists. Keith Arnatt's *Self Burial* (1969), a series of nine still images in which he disappears into the ground, included in Schum's TV Gallery show *Identifications* 'was originally made as a comment upon the notion of "the disappearance of the art object". It seemed a logical corollary that the artist should also disappear'. Keith Arnatt 1979.

31. LVA first catalogue, 1978.

32. LVA first catalogue, 1978.

33. First staged at Gallery House in March 1973 as 'film action and installations', then as Filmaktion at the Walker Art Gallery in June, Arts Council Gallery Edinburgh in July and at the 2nd International Avant-Garde Festival in September. There were isolated performances thereafter.

34. Paper delivered at LFMC, 10 February 1976.

35. He would create an interesting variant on this theme in the installation *Pink Trousers* at the Acme Gallery in 1977.

36. 'To the Projector', part of a reciprocal lesson; Nicolson to Paul Burwell, c. 1976.

37. '... few commentators have considered [*Reel Time*'s] proto-feminist aspect: bringing together the domestic sphere of sewing and the public space of performance. The Singer sewing machine (invented some 45 years before the Lumières' Cinematograph) is both a familiar household object and a potent symbol of women's hidden labour in the home and in sweatshops; by contrast the film projector, traditionally hidden above and behind cinema spectators in a closed off box and operated by male projectionists, symbolises a vast male-dominated entertainment industry.' Felicity Sparrow, *Annabel Nicolson*, Lux Online.

38. 'Light meaning lightweight or menial occupations, like sweeping; or light meaning light from the sky, or light from the projector, artificial light.' Gill Eatherley in *Relating*, a tape/prose piece by Annabel Nicolson 1979.

39. Hammond and Dunford also exhibited together as *Theatre Optique*.

40. William Raban, *LFMC Catalogue,* 1993.

41. 'Steve Farrer', *A Perspective on English Avant-Garde Film*, 1978.

42. '*Footsteps* is in the manner of a game re-enacted. The game in making was between the camera and actor, the actor and cameraman, and one hundred feet of film.' Marilyn Halford, 1977.

43. Made by George Albert Smith/James Williamson of the Brighton School.

44. 'Flashback – Picture Planes', *Filmwaves*, no. 2, 1997.

45. 'Organising the Avant-Garde – A Conversation with Peter Gidal', Jonathan Rosenbaum, *Film the Front Line* (Denver, CO: Arden Press, 1983).

46. Application to the Arts Council, February 1981.

47. Stuart Pound, letter to Deke Dusinberre (undated), c.1976 in BAFVSC.

48. 'Les Yeux Vert – Le Cinema Different' *Cahiers du Cinema*, June 1980 (translated M. Maziere).

49. Also shown were works by Guy Sherwin, Margaret Tait, Lis Rhodes and Deborah Lowensburg.

50. Scripted speech for *British Avant Garde Film* Collective for Living Cinema, New York, 15/16 April 1983.

51. LUX online distribution catalogue.

52. LUX online distribution catalogue.

53. Interviewed by William Furlong, *Hayward Annual*, Hayward Gallery, 1979.

54. Such as *Cinematic Architecture for Pedestrians* (1985), *Little Big Horn* (1993).

55. Also displayed was his detailed written diary of his time on the trawler, concluding with a list of the 23 species of sea creature caught; 'Haddock, Codling, Cod, Lemon Soul, Plaice, Monkfish,' etc.

# 2.4 Politics and Identity

Sexual Liberation? : Feminism : New Romantics : Identity : The Body : Social Space

## SEXUAL LIBERATION?

Besides the sexual freedom introduced by 'the pill', the 1960s in Britain are associated with the ending of censorship in literature and theatre, and the rise of a political and social counter-culture that found expression in the events of May 1968 and the 'underground'. In his response to the period *Bomb Culture*, Jeff Nuttall suggests that 'movies and magazines were called Underground because they were so totally divorced from the established communicating chan-nels, and because they were intensely concerned with [turning society's] … obsession with sex and religion into a weapon against the spiritual bankruptcy which begat the bomb'.[1] As a part of its anti-establishment libertarian agenda, the British underground press – *IT, OZ, Ink, Friends* – noisily opposed censorship and demanded honesty in representations of sex and discussion of sexuality (though it was generally happy to perpetuate the exploitation of women in its own choice of images), and championed new British writers who explored these themes. Yet the iconic underground 'sex' films screened in London in the 1960s were all American – Anger's *Scorpio Rising* (USA 1963) with its fetishisation of the male body, Andy Warhol's *Couch* (USA 1964), *Chelsea Girls* (USA 1966) *et al.* with their various couplings, Tom Chomont's homo-erotic psychedelia *Phases of the Moon* (USA 1968) and *Love Objects* (USA 1971). Nuttall – whose sometimes erotic drawings graced many of the early editions of *IT* – recalled a conversation on the subject in a Bayswater café in 1964: 'Tony [Balch] and Bill [Burroughs] were talking about films. They were unimpressed by Jack Smith's *Flaming Creatures* [USA 1963] – Tony had seen a Brakhage birth film [*Window Water Baby Moving*, USA 1959] at Knokke, was enthusiastic. He had passed out watching it'[2] (one measure of a film's integrity). The only contemporary artists working in Britain to similarly challenge the sexual evasions and euphemisms of mainstream cinema were also American – Carolee Schneemann, Sandy Daley and Stephen Dwoskin.

Schneemann (b.1939), who worked in London from the late 1960s into the early 1970s, brought with her the recently completed *Fuses* (USA 1964–67), a celebration of lovemaking ingeniously filmed by herself and her lover James Tenney, the camera both passing between

(Opposite) *Arbeit Macht Frei (Work Makes Free),* Stuart Brisley, 1973.

partners and being operated by them remotely; the resulting filmstrip and its images later cut, collaged and painted on to heighten its expressive context. Schneemann, who was a close friend of Brakhage, said later:

> [*Fuses* was made] in conversation with *Window Water Baby Moving*. I had mixed feelings
> about the power of the male partner; the artist subsuming the primal creation of giving birth as
> a bridge between male constructions of sexuality as either medical or pornographic.
> Brakhage's incredible authenticity and bravery was to take this risk, to focus on what was
> actual and real, actually looking at the body's reality and leaving the protection of a con-
> structed mythology ... You must understand that in the early 60s, the terminology, the analysis
> of traditional bias was totally embedded. [In *Fuses*] I really wanted to see what 'the fuck' is,
> and locate that in terms of a lived sense of equality. What would it look like?.[3]

The idea of an honest and 'equal' documentation of the changing dynamics within a relationship also informed *Reel Time* (1972), a diary begun in London jointly with Anthony McCall, but left incomplete at the time.[4] Schneemann's primary medium was performance and the other films she worked on in London, including *Plumb Line* (1972) and *Up To and Including Her Limits* (various versions before 1974; one section taped by Hoppy) were both performance based, and she exercised a strong influence on the development of contemporary experimental live art in London, not least at IRAT/the New Arts Lab, where she sometimes worked in the theatre-space with John Lifton.[5]

Daley and Dwoskin (b.1939) both took Warhol – rather than Brakhage – as their reference point. In her one London-period film *Robert Having His Nipple Pierced* (made for the International Underground Film Festival of 1970) Daley followed the method of Warhol's early sound films, recording in long unbroken takes the rambling and inconsequential but

**234** Carolee Schneemann: (right) contemporary announcement of work on *Reel Time*, which became *Kitch's Last Meal*, 1973–5; (opposite top) drawing for the installation/ performance *Up To and Including Her Limits*, c. 1974.

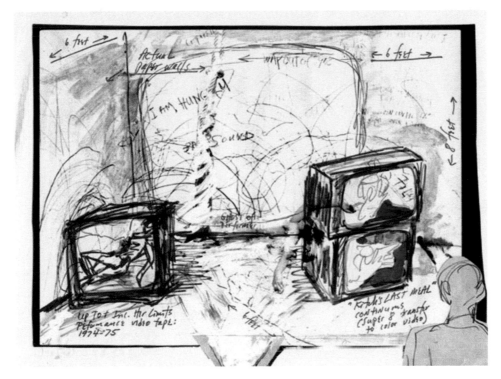

intensely 'real' chatter that accompanies a semi-public sexual encounter, in this case the interplay of Robert Mapplethorpe and his lover, as Mapplethorpe undergoes a procedure he hopes will enhance his love-life.

Dwoskin drew from silent-period Warhol, Warhol the obsessive observer whose camera-stare sucks a performance out of its transfixed victim. *Moment* (1968), Dwoskin's most explicit but still oblique early film, observes a woman smoking and masturbating in solitude, and like all his work says as much about the maker and the current viewer, as about its ostensible subject. Dwoskin had worked professionally as a designer in New York[6] before coming to London in 1964, where he initially worked as a designer before securing lecturing posts at the London College of Printing and the Royal College of Art, and the relationship of the observed with the camera-eye/I would be his most consistent subject in the following decades. Paul Willemen noted how *Moment*'s power derived from Dwoskin's refusal of conventional camera and editing techniques:

> The fixity [of the camera-view], although paralleling the spectator's position, nevertheless marks itself off as 'different' from our view because it refuses the complex system of cuts, movements, 'invisible' transitions etc. which classic cinema developed to capture our 'subjectivity' and absorb it into the filmic text. In this way, the distinction between the camera and the viewer is emphasized. Moreover, the sadistic components inherent in the pleasurable exercise of the 'controlling' gaze are returned to the viewer, as it is he/she who must construct the 'scenario' by combining a reading of the image with an imagined (but suggested) series of happenings off-screen.[7]

**235** *Times For*, Steve
Dwoskin, 1971; Photo
synopsis written by J G
Ballard for *Running Man*
magazine while the film was
in progress – Schneemann
was one of the performers.

*Trixi* (1969), another erotic encounter between camera and a single woman, is accompanied by a sound-loop by Gavin Bryars that obsessively repeats its subject/victim's name, the sound's modulated monotony contrasting with 'Trixi's' changing responses to Dwoskin's camera, 'from initial shyness, fear and withdrawal through teasing and posturing to naked surrender and final exhaustion'.[8] *Dyn Amo* (1972), based on a stage play by Chris Wilkinson, places this voyeuristic game in the narrative context of a strip-club, where a succession of girls 'perform' on a satin-covered bed. Here Dwoskin's subject more overtly includes the relationship of 'self' to performance and role-playing, and (implicitly) willingness to adopt a role that conforms to others' exploitative interests. In the 1970s, the dynamic in Dwoskin's films shifts from his camera's direct erotic relationship with its (his) subject to a more distant observation of the relationships that develop between actors – invariably extracted from daily life and placed without scripted lines in some featureless limbo, trapped like lab-specimens by his camera. In *Times For* (1971) he and his subjects are confined for twenty-four hours in a bathroom, and experience the inevitable succession of emotions – self-consciousness, irritation, bravado, and tentative attempts at emotional exchanges, always aware of – and responding to – the camera's controlling gaze, (Dwoskin here more gainfully exploring a territory revisited forty years later by television's 'reality' show *Big Brother*). In the 1980s and after, Dwoskin's camera oscillates between the roles of participant and neutral observer; his subjects now including documentaries and autobiographical works that boldly address his identity as a sexual, disabled man. In the first of these, *Behindert (Hindered)* (Germany 1974), he followed the evolution of a relationship through semi-documentary sequences that touch on the daily frustrations of living in a non-adapted world (the well-intentioned but unimaginative attempt by a waiter to help him get seated in a restaurant), intimate scenes in which his girlfriend tries on his leg-irons and crutches, and sequences staged in a theatre that illustrate a dozen ways in which a woman can 'fell' a man on crutches – with erotic intention; even a 'ballet' staged between the prostrate film-maker and two dancers.

Dwoskin's example inspired many disabled artists in the 1980s and 1990s;[9] yet in the 1960s and 1970s it is remarkable how *little* the works of these American pioneers impacted on the development of the British film-making scene, despite their relatively wide circulation at the time. Schneemann herself identified one reason. In a sound tape that accompanied her Super 8 film *Kitch's Last Meal* (1973–75) she recites:

I met a happy man
a structuralist filmmaker
– but don't call me that – it's something else I do –
he said we are fond of you
you are charming
but don't ask us to look at your films
we cannot
there are certain films we cannot look at:
the personal clutter
the persistence of feelings
the hand-touch sensibility
the diaristic indulgence
the painterly mess
the dense gestalt
the primitive techniques
(I don't take the advice of men, they only talk to themselves).[10]

Some contemporary structuralists working at the Filmmakers Co-op *were* tempted by 'hot' imagery; in the period 1969–71 Fred Drummond, Mike Leggett and Roger Hammond all made films based on erotic footage, but abstracted the action through repetition and reprinting of the image to the point where it became unrecognisable, ultimately denying its sexual charge. All David Larcher's films reflect upon the intensity and messiness of human relationships to a greater or lesser extent, and while nakedness is common, they only rarely include openly sexual imagery.[11] By the mid-1970s Gidal's stern injunctions against representation, and particularly any depiction of women, had taken hold among the Co-op group, and Dwoskin, the only one of the 1960s Americans to take root in Britain, had become a loner in his pursuits. From outside the structuralist group, the contemporary *How to Have a Bath* (1971) by Lacey and Bruce is innocent and asexual, despite its detailed nakedness. Ian Breakwell – ever the rebel – allowed sexual reveries to enter his filmed monologues such as *The Journey* (1975) but stuck to words, withholding all but mental images, and not until the women's movement – and particularly the work of Mary Kelly and Helen Chadwick – and later the double tragedy of Clause 28 (Thatcher's notorious criminalisation of any 'promotion' of homosexuality) and AIDS would representations of the body and the issues of gender and sexuality

gain centre stage in British artists' film-making. Then, the context was often that of affirmations of sexual difference and studies of forbidden Eros, or explorations of sexuality in the mother/child relationship; celebrations of heterosexual love remain rare – presumably because associated too closely with the dominant mainstream.[12] Paradoxically, and Dwoskin apart, the most thoughtful explorations of sexual and gender relations in Britain in the 1960s were contained in feature films – *Blow-Up* (Michelangelo Antonioni 1966), Levy's *Herostratus* and *Performance* (Nicolas Roeg/Donald Cammell 1968).

Schneemann also commented on the lack of critical response to her films in Britain, citing an example which – if a little unfair in its reading of the chronology of events – at least interestingly serves to highlight the time-delay between the arrival of feminist film theory (marked by the *Women and Cinema* event at the Edinburgh Film Festival in 1972),[13] and the beginnings of film-*making* by native feminist artists, issued in by Mulvey's own *Penthesilea* (1974).

> *Fuses* was being shown in London, 1968, 1969, through the early 70s when I lived there – as Mulvey began writing her film essays. Mulvey talked to me about the rupture *Fuses* made in pornography – how important *Fuses* was as an erotic vision. It was going to change the whole argument and discussion of filmic representation of sexuality, and … then she couldn't touch it! Mulvey has never mentioned my films. But perhaps it was a touchstone behind critical theory for Mulvey. We were there at the same time, at the same moment, in parallel.[14]

Schneemann is overlooking the fact that the focus of Mulvey's seminal essay 'Visual Pleasure and Narrative Cinema'[15] was exactly that – the function of mainstream cinema (a focus implicitly shared by *Penthesilea*) – and her article *does* look forward to an 'alternative cinema … which is radical in both a political and aesthetic sense, and challenges the assumptions of the mainstream film'; a development to which both she and Schneemann crucially contributed.

Schneemann's integration of performance with film-making did provide a model for a number of British artists over the following decades. Stuart Brisley – one of the first – had his own direct connections with the Happenings and performance art outside Britain, following four student years spent in the USA and further time on a DAAD scholarship in Berlin, and his encounter with the Vienna Action artists – Otto Muehl, Hermann Nitsch, Gunter Brus and film-maker Kurt Kren – at the *Destruction in Art Symposium* in 1966. His performance *And for Today … Nothing* (1972) staged at the *Survey of the Avant-Garde in Britain* at Gallery House, which involved him remaining in a bath full of watery offal for seven days, provides the core imagery of his claustrophobically filmed *Arbeit Macht Frei* (*Work Makes Free* 1973), which takes its title from the shocking motto written over the gates of Auschwitz, suggesting that the artist's essential labour concerns the endurance of the human spirit. Schneemann's metaphorical use of body-performance finds echoes in many of the feminist works of the late 1970s and 1980s discussed below, but Brisley's legacy is clearest in tapes made in the 1990s based on extreme performances such as Andre Stitt's *Second Skin* (1996) and Franco B's *When I Grow Up I Want to Be Beautiful* (1993) and *Dead Mother* (1995).

**236** (above and opposite) *Arbeit Macht Frei (Work Makes Free)*, Stuart Brisley, 1973.

 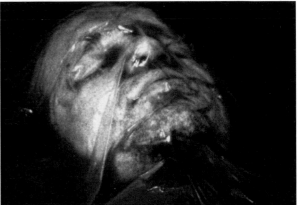

The 'liberation through transgression' theme common (if in very different ways) to Schneemann's and Muehl's performances was light-heartedly echoed in Tony Morgan's film *Beefsteak (Resurrection)* (1968), made with the French artist Daniel Spoerri – which details the transformation of a living cow into cooked meat, and onwards into shit and back to earth, but shows the process entirely in reverse motion. He claims it was the product of a heated discussion between the artists 'about the English aesthetic of cleanliness, and the French aesthetic of shit'.[16] With Kren's *16/67: September 20* (aka *The Eating Drinking Shitting and Pissing Film,* Austria 1967) it is one of the few films to confront these material connections.

There is an irony in the fact that even as Gidal's influence and the formalist pursuit of film as film / video as video reached its height in the late 1970s, the work of feminist film and video artists was already re-validating the subjective and asserting 'the personal as the political' – and thereby helping to establish an agenda that would dominate the next two decades.

## FEMINISM

In a lecture specifically about film and the avant-garde delivered just two years after the publication of 'Visual Pleasure and Narrative Cinema', Mulvey sees the challenge to women artists as being to 'discover a means of expression that [breaks] with an art that has depended, for its existence, on an exclusively masculine conception of creativity', and asks:

> What would women's cultural practice be like? What would art and literature within an ideology that did not oppress women be like? … On the one hand, there is a desire to explore the suppressed meaning of femininity, to assert a women's language as a slap in the face for patriarchy, a polemic and pleasure of self-discovery combined. On the other hand, there is a drive to forge an aesthetic that attacks language and representation, not as something naturally linked with the male, but rather as something that soaks up dominant ideology, as a sponge soaks up water.[17]

The shift from feminist theory to artistic practice occurred simultaneously across several fronts in the mid-1970s – in independent documentaries and feature films, in the gallery, and

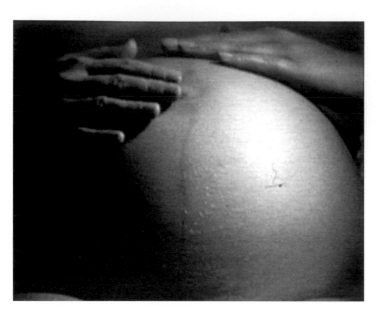

**237** *Ante-Partum Loop*,
Mary Kelly, 1973.

among the Co-op group (the last of these contributing to the schism that occurred in 1979). As Mulvey was formulating her own film ideas with Wollen, their friend and sometime collaborator Mary Kelly (b.1941) was already using film as an element in her own exhibitions – recording documentary footage of factory work for *Women and Work* (1975, discussed earlier) and a meditative fixed-frame close-up of the subtle surface-movements on her own pregnant belly (*Ante-Partum Loop* 1973), as a preface to her evolving *Post-Partum Document* (1973–79). In this latter project she documented the first years of the mother–son relationship through a display of recorded 'evidence' (almost as in an instance of Mass Observation), but within a framework of psychoanalytic theory, and with the gallery as the intended display-space. She noted a mother's daily work, new responses and exchanges with her child such as the arrival of first words, food ingested and rejected, and even (notoriously) offered an analysis of faecal traces on soiled nappy liners – in the process creating one of the most discussed art-actions of the period. Including motherhood and the tasks of parenting within an artwork offered one means of exploring 'the suppressed meaning of femininity' and 'asserting a women's language'.

The influence of Kelly's documentary studies is apparent in *Bred and Born* (Mary Pat Leece and Joanna Davis 1983) which looked at the relationships between different generations of women in London's East End and the documentary-making process itself, as the film evolved over a period of years. But it is more subtly at work in the artist-mother/daughter theme that underpins Tina Keane's *Shadow Woman* performance (1977) and videos *Playpen* and *Clapping Songs* (both 1979), and *Hopscotch* (1985) and Carola Klein's *Mirror Phase* (1978) and *Children's Games: Studies in Documentary* (1981) that draw on Lacanian theory. And even in Kate Meynell's study of her daughter *Hannah's Song* (1986), and Cate Elwes's *With Child* and *There is a Myth* (both 1984), *Play* and *Gunfighters* (both 1986) and *Grown Up* (1990 – with her son substituting of necessity).[18] Guy Sherwin's *Messages* (1984), based on his daughter's drawings and observations of the world, reflects many of the same concerns and psychological insights. Even later, Gillian Wearing contributed to the genre with her *Sacha and Mum* (1996) – the daughter now a grown-up and the relationship viewed at second-hand, but remaining as fraught as ever. Jayne Parker (b.1957) memorably reversed the dynamics in *Almost Out* (1984) where she – grown-up but naked as an infant – confronts her mother, also naked, with the eternal questions about being, power, and desire; its tone more poetic than psychoanalytic. 'My mother is a symbol of power, authority, control I feel that she is inside me. She is very heavy. I want to push her out, gently, because I care for her and don't want to hurt her'.[19] There are echoes of Kelly's interest in women's daily work in Bobby Baker's ironic cooking performances (some designed for video) such as *The Kitchen Show* (1991) and *Spitting Mad* (1993), though by now the focus of the critique was more on the unreal depiction of women's domestic work in magazines and daytime television, than on factory enslavement.

Elwes (b.1952) was a member of the Women Artists' Collective and co-organised the influential *About Time* exhibitions at the ICA and Arnolfini in 1980 which was accompanied at the ICA by a film and video programme *Women's Own,* organised by Sparrow, Deborah Lowensberg and Chris Rodley. Sparrow also contributed to the nationwide celebration of women's work *Women Live* (1982), programming films and videos to be shown at the NFT, London Filmmakers Co-op and elsewhere.

**238** *There is a Myth*, Cate Elwes, 1984.

The project of recording and documenting the 'feminine' was also applied by women to their own bodies. The tape-slide works *Water Into Wine* (1980) and *Sea Dreams* (1981) by Judith Higginbottom (b.1955) were based on responses systematically gathered from 27 women to questions about the link between menstrual cycles and creativity.

> For 13 lunar months … I recorded details of lengths of cycles, how they corresponded to the lunar cycles, and information concerning patterns of dreaming, creativity, elation and depression … The images which make up the piece come from my own and other women's experiences of menstrual time, and from menstrual dreams … The soundtrack consists of extracts from the reports which the women wrote for me.[20]

The hand-painted animated film *Cage of Flame* (1992) by Kayla Parker, and Maya Chowdry's *Monsoon* (1993) are other works that drew their structure and imagery from menstrual cycles and their relation to the natural order.

Helen Chadwick (1953–96) and Roberta M. Graham (b.1954) explored femininity and self-image more metaphorically, initiating a form of body-representation new in British film, if familiar from the work of 1930s painters and sculptors such as Dora Carrington, Barbara Hepworth and Ithell Colquhoun, and the American film-maker Maya Deren. The photo-montaged imagery of body-parts, x-ray plates and images of raw flesh in Graham's light-box installation *Life Sentence/Death Insight* and her tape-slide on plastic surgery *Short Cuts to Sharp Looks* (both c.1980) evoke an awareness of the mortality of all flesh, in which the artist's body becomes, in the words of film-maker Penny Webb, 'the site of a struggle for expression of shared unconscious fears'.[21] Chadwick's performance-related videos such as

 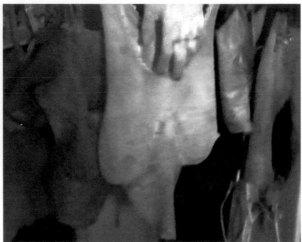

**239** *Domestic Sanitation: (2) Latex Glamour Rodeo*, Helen Chadwick, 1976.

*L Skin (Three Experiments With Video)* and Super 8 films *Domestic Sanitation: (1) Bargain Bedroom Bonanza; (2) Latex Glamour Rodeo* (all c.1976) take a more subversive route, mocking the glamour industry and women's engagement with it, while at the same time showing women enjoying making and putting on prosthetic skin and fantasy costumes.[22] The humour in Chadwick's work, which embraced performance, photography, installation and sculpture, challenged the intense seriousness of much political art of the period, and antici- pates the more playful but no less subversive approach adopted by many women artists in the 1990s, such as Sarah Lucas (*My Sausage and Me* 1990), Clio Barnard (*Dirt and Science* 1990), Sarah Miles (*Damsel Jam* 1992), Lucy Gunning (*Horse Impressionists* 1997) and others.

**240** *Descent of the Seductress*, Jean Matthee, 1987.

More typical of the 'serious', theory-driven 1980s, Marion Urch (b.1957) used the technique of chroma-key – which allows the electronic replacement of one part of an image by another based on colour – to question the ideals of 'female beauty' created by women's magazines in her tape *The Fascinating Art of the Ritual Feast* (1979). As a woman applies make-up to change

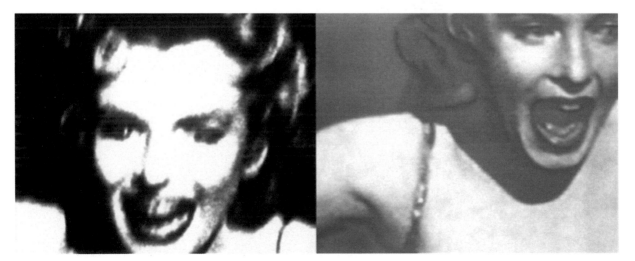

her appearance to more closely resemble the 'ideal', 'the camera closes in, and [by means of chroma-key] the ideological and commercial images that determine her goal are literally jig-sawed over her image. She becomes a single element among a conglomerate of media images, and then finally is entirely effaced'.[23] Jean Matthee (b.1954) drew on her own experience of Lacanian psychoanalysis to explore the iconic female images of Hollywood melodrama – particularly those of Marilyn Monroe and Dorothy Malone – in her films *Neon Queen* (1986) and *Descent of the Seductress* (1987). Taking fragments of scenes, she used freeze-frames and structural film's endless repetition of loops to isolate and deliberately fetishise the image, providing through excess her own answer to Gidal's challenge of representing the female form without 'participating in its exploitation'. Nina Danino (b.1955) provocatively added the Catholic religion to the brew in *Stabat Mater* (1990), in her own words:

> a purposeful, 'perverse', re-reading of the eternal feminine of Chapter 16 of Joyce's *Ulysses* …
> a short *oracion*, opened and closed by two songs – it is the voice of my mother singing – two
> *saetas*, laments sung during Holy Week to the *Mater Dolorosa*. The frenetic hand held images
> define the movement of the body, the slipping cadences of the song enunciate the upper body
> and throat, the breathlessness of the unpunctuated speech evokes the eroticism of the body –
> a maternal, homoerotic body. It attempts to locate a lost territory, unrecouperable mother – site
> of plenitude and loss.[24]

She developed these themes in *Now I Am Yours* (two versions 1993), bringing together other representations of the ecstatic – the singing of Diamanda Galas and images of Bernini's sculpture *Ecstasy of Saint Teresa* in Rome – gathered by her camera in erotically charged sweeping movements. Susan Hiller's installations from the end of the 1990s *Wild Talents* (1998)

**241** *Wild Talents*,
Susan Hiller, 1998.

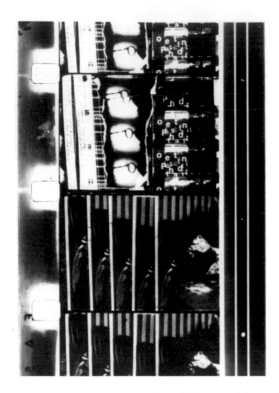

**242** Lis Rhodes: (above)
*Light Reading*, 1978;
(opposite top) *Orifso*, 1998.

and *Psi Girls* (1999) also drew from representations of exceptionally empowered women – but from popular cinema, and representations constructed by men, and of women exercising the dangerous supernatural power of telekinesis, clipped from films as diverse as Andrei Tarkovsky's *Stalker* (USSR 1979) and Danny DeVito's *Matilda* (USA 1996). As she played on male fears, she also offered a reminder of the root-links between creativity and the irrational. Paranormal experience was also explored by Graham Gussin in *Remote Viewer* (2002).

Though the works of Mulvey and Wollen and Sally Potter were more widely discussed at the time than any other contemporary feminist films (being lighted upon by American academics), the film-maker who arguably exercised the strongest influence on film-making by women in Britain in the 1970s was Lis Rhodes. Her first gendered work *Light Reading* (1978)[25] gives the spoken and written word a central role – after a decade in which silent and mute images had dominated. It was being completed as the Film Co-op held its *Feminism, Fiction and the Avant-Garde*[26] conference, organised by Dusinberre, led by the Californian editors of *Camera Obscura,* and accompanied by a week-long programme of voice-led works by Chantal Akerman, Marguerite Duras and Babette Mangolte. The American high theory – welcomed in some quarters – was poorly received by local makers,[27] but from *Light Reading* and other works shown flowed a wave of film-making in which the woman's voice plays a central role. In Rhodes's films, the speaker is never seen; speech is fragmented and repeated, and accompanied by rapid camera-movements, reprinted shots (many of them photographic collages, animated under a rostrum) and an insistent soundtrack. The characteristics of structural film are all present, but take on a new expressive meaning. After lending her image and voice as 'the film-maker' to Le Grice's *Blackbird Descending, Light Reading* offers a different take on the same subject. Where Le Grice felt able coolly to deconstruct his scene of film-making from a dozen viewpoints, each carefully plotted and interlocking with its neighbours, Rhodes's film presented the jumble of impulses that accompany the creative act, in an overlapping and cascading sequence. Although using her own voice – which would become more recognisable with each succeeding film – she resisted identification as 'author' (perhaps warned by her experience with *Blackbird*). Instead, as she states on the soundtrack, 'she watched herself being looked at / she looked at herself being watched / but she couldn't perceive herself as the subject of the sentence'. After a series of short atypically sloganising pieces *Hang on a Minute* (1985) made with Joanna Davis for Channel 4, she returned to her ongoing cycle of voice-centred works with *A Cold Draft* (1988), *Deadline* (1992), *Just About Now* (1993), *Running Light* (1996), *Orifso* (1998), and others, each building on the interplay of a poetic text and a set of fragmented images; each renegotiating the boundaries of representation and abstraction. Sarah Turner's *Sheller Shares Her Secret* and Alia Syed's *Delilah* (both 1994) are among the many works that show her influence.

The voice plays a central role in Sally Potter's ironically titled *Thriller* (1979), a re-reading of the position of Mimi the seamstress, the victim of Puccini's opera *La Bohème,* in which Potter strips the story of all drama and gives centre-stage to Mimi, who offers her own flatly-delivered anti-romantic account of her victim-hood, and asks why can't she be the hero? Potter set this in a montage of sound from the opera, the shrieking attack-music from *Psycho* and occasional unexpected highly choreographed movements, contrasting the mundane realities of Mimi's position with the requirement for melodrama in high art. The same question formed the core of her later feature films (discussed earlier). Tina Keane (b.1948) often drew on women's traditions of story-telling, work-songs and playground rhymes in her works. *Shadow of a Journey* (1980) on the Scottish clearances includes keening (melancholy wordless wails) and verbal accounts of traumatic events passed down through generations of women; *Hey Mack* (1982), her response to the oversize 'masculine' trucks on New York's streets, is accompanied by scatological songs by the women's performance group Disband; the installation *Demolition Escape* (1983) wryly includes the sexist children's clapping song 'My Girl's a Co-or-ker'; her political instal-

lation *In Our Hands, Greenham* (1984), made in support of the women picketing the American military presence at Greenham Common, includes women's protest songs, etc. Susan Hiller's first video installation *Belshazzar's Feast/The Writing on Your Wall* (1984) is even clearer in its evocation of aural traditions and their relation to the imagination, its image simply a burning fire, the traditional site of story-telling, its sound whispered accounts from newspapers of phantom images seen late at night on 'empty' TV screens, a child's voice (her son) trying to describe Rembrandt's painting of Belshazzar, and her own incanting/ wailing voice.

**243** *Shadow of a Journey,* Tina Keane, 1980.

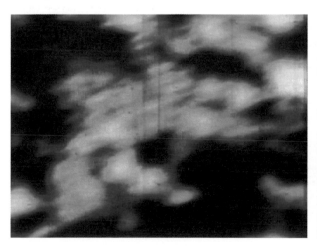

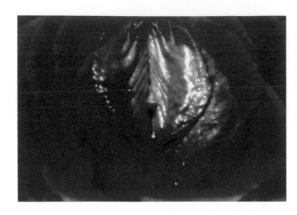

**244** *The Story of I*, Jo Ann
Kaplan, 1997.

In contrast to *Almost Out,* most of Jayne Parker's work has
avoided the spoken word, instead depending upon performed
actions and telling props – fire, water, eels, oysters, and even
(apparently) her own intestines – in Deren-like photoplays.
Often, as in *K* (1989) and *The Pool* (1991), Parker herself is the
central performer, her closely observed performances building
through repetition and montage into metaphors for states of
mind or being. Equally eloquently, Sandra Lahire (1950–2001)
animated an expression of her own struggle with anorexia in
*Arrows* (1984), and constructed analogies between her wast-
ing body and the devastated lives and ravaged landscapes of
a community in Ontario scarred by uranium mining in the series of films *Plutonium Blond*
(1987), *Uranium Hex* (1988) and *Serpent River* (1989).

The boldest images of the sexual female body – and the first to equal Schneemann's in
their raw explicitness – were made by the American-born artist Jo Ann Kaplan, painter, film editor
and occasional film-maker. In her *The Story of I* (1997), she responds to George Bataille's surrealist erotic novel, transferring its focus from male to female – so the (imagined) experiences
of a teenage man acquire the voice and the 'eye/I' of a mature woman. Yet the most intimate
images of the 1990s – those in which the camera-lens was most fully invited to assault the
artist's own body – were contained in Mona Hatoum's *Corps Étranger* (1994) filmed with an
endoscope that penetrated her body, the image being projected on the floor of a claustrophobic circular cell in which the viewer must stand, heightening the sense of invasion.

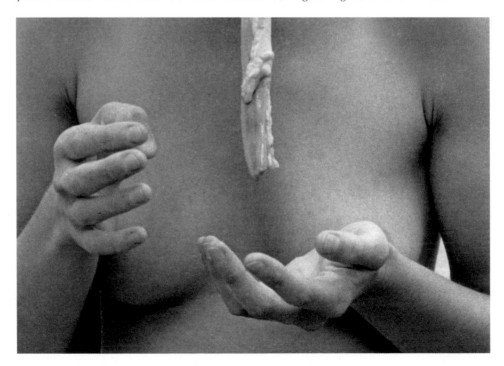

**245** *'K'*, Jayne Parker,
1989.

In the 1980s and 1990s, the feminist project was widely pursued in the field of animation, notably by Vera Neubauer, *Animation for Live Action* (1978), *The Lady of the Lake* (1995); Marjut Rimminen, *I'm Not a Feminist But..* (1985), *The Stain* (1991); Ruth Lingford, *What She Wants* (1994); Candy Guard and many others.[28]

## NEW ROMANTICS

Like Dwoskin and Greenaway (but few others), Derek Jarman (1942–94) was able to make enough features to be able to experiment with the form on the basis of experience, in his case managing to make large budget works and no-budget works with equal freedom as circumstances dictated. Unlike most of his contemporaries, he came to film with no mission to be avant-garde, no interest in Marxist politics or progressive film theory, and held the unfashionable belief that his work was directly connected to – and an extension of – the classical traditions of English music and literature and painting. He was radical in his belief that his work should reflect his identity as an openly gay man in a still intolerant country, (in this he would draw from Warhol, rather than his admired Benjamin Britten), and in his embrace of the anarchic, anti-establishment creativity of Punk. These qualities gave his work its political edge. Jarman came to film almost by accident. His training in theatre design at the Slade led to work on film sets for Ken Russell's *The Devils* (1971), and he was simultaneously encouraged to take up Super 8 film-making by his Bankside Studios neighbour, the artist Andrew Logan, using a camera donated by a friend. From then on, he kept a Super 8 diary recording daily life in his studio, the people he met, lovers, holidays and excursions.[29] His first feature *Sebastiane* (1976)[30] took an imagined life of the martyred saint as the basis for a fantasy on the

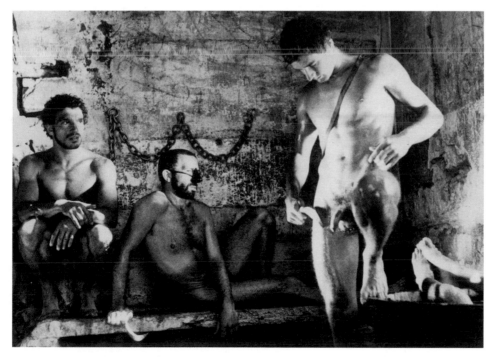

**246** *Sebastiane*,
Derek Jarman, 1976.

**247** *The Last of England,*
Derek Jarman, 1987.

theme of frustrated desire and its consequences in an all-male remote Roman garrison. In film terms it was conventional, and its subject, the nudity of the actors and its schoolboy-Latin dialogue contributed to its atmosphere of a public-school prank, but it broke ground as an original and unapologetic treatment of a gay subject. With his next features *The Tempest* (after Shakespeare) and *Jubilee* (an acerbic portrait of a spiritually exhausted England at a time of royal celebrations) made simultaneously in 1977–78, Jarman established his most successful method of composing long films, assembling them from disparate bits gathered around a theme – acted sequences, songs and sections of home-movie re-filmed from the screen, which were held together by inter-titles, poetry, and his eclectic choice of accompanying music. Often this collage process would begin in book-form where Jarman would draw image-ideas, assemble photographs of people and objects, gather quotations and write notes on locations and dialogue in his elegant italic hand. These books would form his real scripts. *Imagining October* (1984), *The Last of England* (1987) and *The Garden* (1990) were all made this way and, with *Jubilee*, were his most personal and most original works.

The mix in *The Last of England* is typical. Home-movie footage of the child Jarman shot by his airforce father intercut with scenes of his own domestic life; shots of London's urban decay, and scenes from 'an imagined movie' filmed in the wastes of dockland featuring terrorist gunmen, cowed immigrants (reflecting the contemporary troubles in Northern Ireland, but oddly prescient of scenes in Iraq and economic/political migrants in twenty-first-century Europe) and outbursts of anarchic dancing. Interspersed with these were his history-plays about iconic but problematic gay figures *Caravaggio* (1986), *Edward II* (1991) and *Wittgenstein* (1993), which were more dependent upon scripted dialogue and their performers' delivery for their success. Jarman's solution was to add theatre-trained actors to his cast of friends and non-professionals, with predictably uneven results, the former often dominating the action and constraining his directorial freedom. An exception was Tilda Swinton, who understood and could work with the camera's natural egalitarianism (which can allow non-actors to shine), becoming his muse and the anchor-figure in some of his more personal works. In *The Angelic Conversation* (1985) and *War Requiem* (1989) he constructed what were essentially visual tracks to accompany existing texts and music (Shakespeare's *Sonnets* in the first, Britten and Wilfred Owen in the second).

To Jarman Super 8 represented a freedom from engagement with film as film, and he remained loyal to it throughout his life. 'The great thing about Super 8 is that you can switch it onto automatic and get beyond all those technicalities. I was working in Super 8 because I was technically incompetent.' Both *The Angelic Conversation* and *The Last of England* were shot on Super 8 and blown up to 35mm for release. Showing his home-movies, he gave his spontaneously shot images a degree of formality and abstraction by a radical trick of projection.

> Shooting and [then] projecting at three frames per second means that [to the spectator] it syn-chronised with the heartbeat. Every time a frame goes through you are forced to refocus slightly, which makes you really look at it. Of course, there are good economic reasons, because you can make twenty minutes of film from nothing! You can make amazingly long films with no money'.[31]

His very public endorsement of this do-it-yourself cinema was highly influential among a generation of young artists who had no desire to print and process their own films, and pitied the grant-dependency of their college tutors and seniors, and it also provided an unexpected but welcome boost to some grey-haired narrow-gauge enthusiasts – such as the gallerist Victor Musgrave[32] and writer Gray Watson, of the contemporary London Super 8 Group.

Jarman's absence of film-schooling contrasts with the experience of his protégées Cerith Wyn-Evans (b.1958) and John Maybury (b.1958) who were imbued with classic underground texts as they engaged with film – not the 'structural' films made by their art-school tutors at NELP, Saint Martins and the RCA, but the earlier films of Warhol, Kenneth Anger and Jean Cocteau, icons of taste and style to young gay film-makers. Encouraged by Jarman to work with Super 8, and sup-porting each other's development, they made films of lush colour and music and languorous pace, celebrating the (male) body (contra-Gidal), decor, and visual excess. As in Jarman's home-movies, portraiture is a central theme in many of their works – images of contemporaries and lovers, loosely interwoven with symbolic imagery. Wyn Evans was the more cerebral, the mix in his films including philosophical quotations in voice-over and sometimes pages of text shown on screen. He later described his first film *Still Life with Phrenology Head* (1980), made while he was still a student at the RCA, as 'a kind of sculpture. … I was interested in the idea that you could take things that had various trajectories, histories, meanings and associations and make a collage-like assemblage that would generate different micro-discourses'.[33] He was intensely active for just

 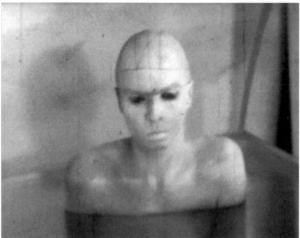

**248** Cerith Wyn-Evans:
(above) *Still Life with
Phrenology Head*, 1980;
(right) *Degrees of Blindness*,
1988.

four years making exotically titled films such as *The Attitude Assumed 2 – Beauty is Only Screen Deep* and *Have You Seen Orphée Recently?* (both 1981*)* and then came to an abrupt stop after his BFI-funded video experiment *Degrees of Blindness* (1988). In the 1990s he made occasional conceptual sculptures, and even rarer video installations.

Maybury, who worked with Jarman on *Jubilee, War Requiem* and *The Last of England,* seemed to inherit Jarman's more engaged and passionate involvement with the image, adding his own commitment to London's gay subculture. Michael O'Pray, the first critic to champion Jarman and his school, summarised Maybury's subjects as 'cultural narcissism, sex, drugs [in] a dark claustrophobic world … constructed out of borrowings from Surrealism and aes-

thetic devices hijacked from structural filmmaking'.[34] Maybury's
early films were peopled by angelically beautiful young men,
joined later by cultural icons from the art world (performance
artist Leigh Bowery, dancer Michael Clark) and assorted drag
queens and gay porn stars – contemporary equivalents to Cocteau's
entourage in the 1940s and 1950s. His debt to structural cinema
extended to a fondness for endlessly held shots in the early Super
8 works (1978–83), and frequent sequence-repetitions in his later
video works, here functioning as a superficial gloss of cool detachment imposed on dangerous, personal imagery. His primary
composition method, like Jarman's, was collage. In his Super 8
works such as *Sunbathing for Idols* (1978), *A Fall of Angles*
(1981 for three screens) and *Court of Miracles* (1982), editing was
limited, and his capacity to elaborate the image was restricted to
in-camera superimpositions and re-filming from the projected
image. In the later video works, made either on the back of music-
video commissions,[35] or with Arts Council and Channel 4 funding,
he had access to digital editing technology, and exploited it to
the full, collaging one image into another, re-timing actions and
replaying imagery, placing his characters in virtual worlds. His
long films in this vein such as *Remembrance of Things Fast* (1993)

and *Read Only Memory* (1996) are unruly shouts of pain and anger around the theme of desire
in the age of HIV/AIDS – dazzling in their imagery and moving in their testimony, but bleak
and bludgeoning in their impact. Interspersed with these he made the more conventionally
structured dramas *Man to Man* (1992 for the BBC) from Manfred Karge's one woman play,
and his well-received fictionalised life of Francis Bacon, *Love is The Devil* (1998), which
reached a wider audience.

**249** *Remembrance of
Things Fast*, John Maybury,
1993.

Other artists who mined this rich vein, in many cases encouraged by Jarman, included
Michael Kostiff, Holly Warburton, Daniel Landin, Richard Heslop, Steve Chivers, Sophie
Muller and John Scarlett Davis. Some showed together in *Salons*
programmed for the ICA and Filmmakers Co-op during 1984 by
Cordelia Swann, who at the time was one of their number; others
were gathered together by Mike O'Pray under the banner
*Synchronisation of the Senses,* again at the ICA in 1985, where his
subtitle 'The New Romantics' stuck, despite their protests.

Equally a romantic, but of a very different temperament, Chris
Newby (b.withheld) might have been more at home in among the
silent film-makers of the 1920s than in the post-Gidal 1980s, when
he first emerged. As with Macpherson, his work suggests sexual
feelings through visual metaphor. *Hoy* (1984), made while he was
still at the RCA, was the first of a series of short films which were

**250** *Stromboli,*
Chris Newby, 1997.

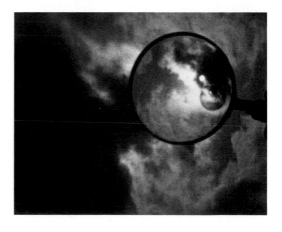

lyrical portraits of particular places – the islands of Hoy and Stromboli, the ports of Whitby in Yorkshire and Amsterdam – while at the same exploring another subject, the human body, its mortality and its desires through the erotic charge contained in their images. This theme was explicit in the Whitby portrait *The Old Man and the Sea* (1990), where a bedridden old man tugs at a line connecting him to the sea and to memories of youth, but it remained implied to greater effect in the later *Stromboli* (1997) and *Amsterdam* (1999, unprinted).[36]

## IDENTITY

In earlier video works by Hatoum (b.1952 Lebanon) the subject is more often the experience of exile-hood, the pain of separation and the sense of not fully belonging to the culture in which you find yourself. In different forms, individual responses to 'not belonging' or displacement became one of the dominant themes of the 1980s and 1990s. Hatoum's *Measures of Distance* (1988) centres on letters written to the artist in London by her mother in Beirut (in yet another exploration of this relationship), which appear as Arabic text on-screen but are read in English by the artist in voice-over. Interrupting these letters are taped conversations in Arabic between mother and daughter: 'Although the main thing that comes across is a very close and emotional relationship between mother and daughter, it also speaks of exile, displacement, disorientation and a tremendous sense of loss as a result of the separation caused by war.'[37] Marion Urch has shown through the main body of her work how this sense of displacement can still be powerful a generation on, and how nostalgia for even an oppressive culture can be entrapping. Her tape-slice work *Speak English Cathleen* (1982) reflects the traditional identity of an Irish woman 'who has always existed as the mother of ... the daughter of ... the wife of ... and the crumbling of that identification, as the basis for it recedes more firmly into the past. The denial of the central character's Irish-ness within an English marriage is echoed in the title which refers to the English repression of Gaelic at the turn of the 20th century'.[38] In her two-track ten-monitor installation *Distant Drums* (1989):

**251** *Measures of Distance*, Mona Hatoum, 1988.

A nostalgia for rural Ireland and our parents' feeling of loss and exile become entangled with the stories of Irish suffering and British oppression, told to us as we grew. Yet we have no language, accent or skin colour to make us visible, either to Irish people or to second generation Irish people, and often our parents are the first to point out to us that we are English![39]

**252** *Turas*, Frances Hegarty, 1991–4.

Fran Hegarty's *Turas* (1991–94) confronts this dilemma and the wounds of Ireland's division by a positive act of reclamation, asking her Irish-speaking mother to help her to:

re learn language
re gain mother tongue
re possess speech
re claim culture
re claim history.[40]

Violent displacement from one's roots is also the theme in her *Voice Over* (1996) where unseen women, recorded at a centre for victims of war in Croatia, speak of their shattered lives.

**253** *The Left Hand Should Know*, Breda Beban and Hervoje Horvatric,1994.

The sequence of tapes *Geography* (1989), *For Tara* (1991), *The Lifeline Letter* (1992) and *The Left Hand Should Know* (1994) made by the artists Breda Beban (b.1952) and Hrvoje Horvatic (1958–97) marked stages on their progress from being internal exiles within their divided homelands in the former Yugoslavia, to statelessness, and eventual exile in London; a journey described through metaphor and stark images of landscape, performed actions and poetic texts. In *Absence She Said* (1994), a coming-to-terms with their new context, fragmented details of domestic interiors are interwoven with shots of impersonal, archetypical land-scapes. Together with written captions, these images evoke the state of mind of the central character who remains nameless and silent, eloquently performed by Beban. Alia Syed (b.1964) has described the fragile way in which images and sounds can trigger glimpses of a past set in another culture. In *Fatima's Letter* (1994), a woman reads a letter to a friend remembering an event that took place in Pakistan, her voice heard off-screen, speaking in Urdu, with a fragmented translation printed over the film's images. Syed's editing makes the viewer people the story with the unknown faces she films in London's underground system, as the letter-writer did. 'Being unhappy in London, you remember other places. When travelling on the East London line or visiting Whitechapel, I would encounter smells that reminded me of India or

Pakistan.'[41] Zarina Bhimji (b.1963) in her installation *Out of the Blue* (made for *Documenta 11*, 2002) addresses the complex subject of Britain's colonial past, through her own family's memories of ejection from Uganda following the dictator Idi Amin's decree in 1972. With a faint recording of Amin's broadcast as its only contemporary reference, Bhimji sets images of deserted homes, a prison and wrecked airport buildings in Uganda against African landscapes of extraordinary beauty, in a poignant evocation of violence, displacement and loss.

Memory, and its function in the connections and separations experienced between family generations, have been explored by many artists. Jez Welsh's *Immemorial* (1989) looked back and forward across three generations; Barbara Meter's *Departure on Arrival* (1996) and *Appearances* (2000) added loss and 'the slipping away' of individual memories which photographs only partially restore; Elwes was able to question her father on his wartime experiences in France for *The Liaison Officer* (1997) where Marshall had to reconstruct the absent figure of his father by interviewing relatives and re-visiting locations for his *Robert Marshall* (1991) but, tellingly, neither is able to assemble 'the whole story'. The American artist Dan Reeves (based in Scotland in the mid-1990s) bravely unburied memories of an abused childhood that had preceded his experiences as a teenage soldier in Vietnam, in his remarkable *Obsessive Becoming* (1995), made for the Arts Council and Channel 4

The 1980s were characterised by songs of protest, essays in self-definition, elegies, and attempts to retrieve overlooked histories. In Isaac Julien's (b.1960) first work with Sankofa, *Territories* (1984), he proclaimed his identity as a gay black artist and, in an insistent, looping voice-over, demanded the writing of 'new histories; new *her*-stories'. The first part of his tape presents a collage of carnival, black diaspora culture in Britain and the 1976 Notting Hill Gate riots, while the second more poetically seeks out a personal space in the midst of this chaos of impressions, centring on his own image – locked in an embrace with another black man. '*Territories*', explained a contemporary press release from Julien's fledgling film-making collective Sankofa, 'refers not only to geographical spaces, but to the occupied and controlled spaces of race, class and sexuality.' It was made in the same year as Lahire's *Arrows*, and in the same creative hot-house, the Saint Martins School of Art. Julien's next works alternately explored black history and gay identity, and often (transgressively?) strayed from cinema and television into the gallery, being re-versioned to suit the new context. The

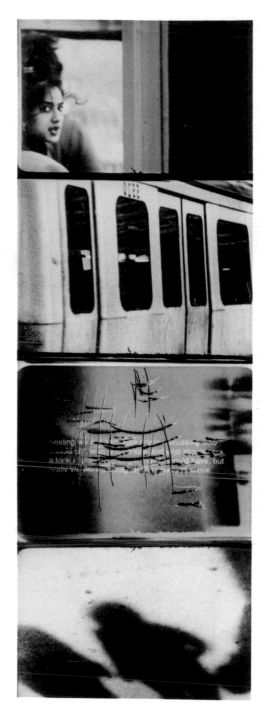

**254** *Fatima's Letter*, Alia Syed, 1994.

**255** Isaac Julien: (above) *Territories*, 1984; (below) *The Long Road to Mazatlán*, 2000 (Victoria Miro Gallery).

feature-length *The Passion of Remembrance* (1986), made collectively by Sankofa, dealt with black female sexuality, and was deliberately controversial:

> we didn't want … to repeat some of the very boring, academicised and … embarrassingly anti-pleasure discussions around the body and around concepts of desire which had become, in the British context at least, frozen by a kind of structuralist bind on everything.[42]

*Frantz Fanon: Black Skin, White Mask* (1996) looked at the psychological interdependence of coloniser and colonised in black history, while *Looking for Langston* (1988), on the poet Langston Hughes, and his narrative feature *Young Soul Rebels* (1991) considered gay male sexuality, while the TV documentary *The Darker Side of Black* (1994) addressed homophobia in black popular music. Disillusioned with feature films, Julien's later work was increasingly made for gallery alone, though it retains his interest in cinematic editing and narrative. *The Attendant* (1992), *The Conservator's Dream* (1999) and *Vagabondia* (2000) were his take on the cultural heritage of the colonial era, gathered, catalogued and displayed in museums by the white colonisers, into which he none the less found room to insert 'pleasure and fantasy'.

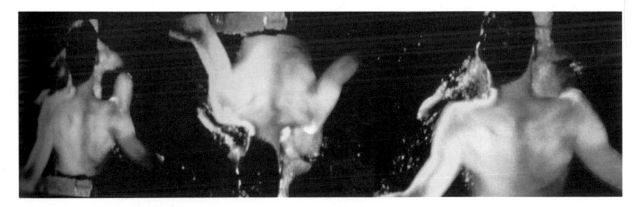

*Three* (1999) and *The Long Road to Mazatlán* (2000) were multi-screen danced-narratives of repressed and awakening desire, shot with big budgets and high production values, and helped secure his nomination for the Tate's Turner Prize, but essentially developing a language of choreographed movement, look and gesture that would have been familiar to the American pioneer Maya Deren.

The Black Audio Film Collective of young artists first made its mark with a slide-tape programme at the Filmmakers Co-op in 1984, *Signs of Empire/Images of Nationality*.[43] Like Keith Piper's contemporary first shows at the Black Arts Gallery in London and his MA degree show

**256** John Akomfrah: (above) *Handsworth Songs*, 1986; (below) *Seven Songs for Malcolm X*, 1993.

of graphics and slide-projections at the Royal College of Art 1986, these were fierce collages of texts, sounds and images drawn from African and West Indian cultural life, set against shots of the oppressors – police aggression on English city streets, the National Front and the forbidding imperial monuments that litter Britain and her former colonies. *Handsworth Songs* (1986) directed by John Akomfrah (b.1957) was the Collective's first major film, and had a more immediately urgent subject, the causes of the uprisings by black communities in Handsworth, Birmingham, in 1985. With its angry yet meditative text woven from first-hand testimonies and re-filmed documentary footage, its title signalled its different mode of address, as Michael O'Pray recognised: 'The song is a cultural form which can dig as deep as any analysis ... The poetry of song ... is a potent weapon, that for centuries has been used powerfully by the colonisers themselves.'[44] Akomfrah went on to make many documentary films for television distinguished by their thoughtfulness and formal design, that unpacked different aspects of black culture – such as *A Touch of the Tar Brush* (1991) on J. B. Priestley's prescient if limited vision of Britain's multi-cultural future, *Seven Songs for Malcolm X* (1993) and *Martin Luther King – Days of Hope* (1997).[45] Also part of Black Audio, Reece Auguiste (b.1958) continued the group's critique of racist Britain with his passionate outcry against the deaths of black men while in police custody *Mysteries of July* (1991), and Martina Attille of Sankofa made the similarly poetic *Dreaming Rivers* (1988).

Keith Piper (b.1960) only slowly moved from still-images and slide-tape installations to video, one of his first moving-image works being a contribution to the *Nelson Mandela 60th Birthday* video (1988) shown at the Wembley Stadium concert protesting against Mandela's continuing imprisonment. His subsequent video installations retain a painter's fondness for bold outlines and flat planes of colour, his technique being close to animation and well-suited to digital manipulation. In the three-part *A Ship Called Jesus* (1991 various venues) he explored the complex, contradictory history of the Christian church in black life, from the moment black slaves embarked in a ship called 'Jesus' (donated to the trade by Queen Elizabeth I in 1564), to their descendants' rejection by white Christians on their arrival in England the 1950s, in what they believed to be their mother country (ruled by another Elizabeth). In *Cargo*

**257** *Cargo Cultures/ Trade Winds*, Keith Piper, 1992.

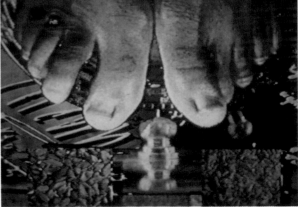

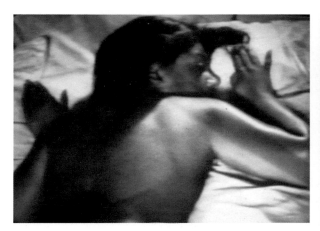
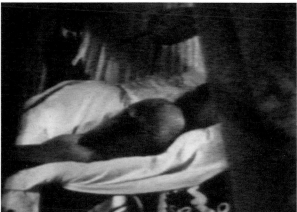

Cultures/Trade Winds (1992) made for Liverpool's Maritime Museum he more directly explored the history of slavery and its legacy, and in his contribution to the Manchester Olympic bid The Nation's Finest (1990) simultaneously challenged contemporary media stereotypes of black sports stars and interrogated black men's own construction of their masculinity. Amanda Holiday similarly imported her painter's feeling for colour into her astute reflection on black gender relationships Umbrage (1989) and her live-action/video-paintbox work Manao Tupapau (1990) made for the Arts Council/BBC2 One Minute Television scheme, a response to Gauguin's painting in which she gave a voice to the artist's long-silent Tahitian model/mistress. Holiday was already representative of a younger generation who used narrative and humour to describe the experience of the new urban black middle-class. She returned to painting, but Pier Wilkie (b.1964) and Alnoor Dewshi (b.1964) both made sharp, witty narratives that explored the different expectations and experiences of their own and their parents' generations, in films such as How Wilkie Discovered England (Wilkie 1992) and Latifah and Himli's Nomadic Uncle (Dewshi 1992). Both went on to work in television.

Gay and lesbian artists also battled to replace negative stereotypes with more positive images, and additionally had to contend with the repressive legislation and press-bigotry of the 1980s that were spreading fear of 'a gay plague', and misinformation about HIV and AIDS. It was no help that gayness had generally been depicted as a 'problem' in film – equally in well-intentioned mainstream melodramas such as Victim (1961, Basil Dearden), and the work of pioneering independents such as Terence Davis in his trilogy Children (1976), Madonna and Child (1980) and Death and Transfiguration (1983), and even Ron Peck's Nighthawks (1978). This down-beat tradition was blown apart by Derek Jarman's assertive, even celebratory approach to depicting gay life, and his example and friendship helped launch the careers of many of the most successful gay artists and film-makers, Wyn Evans, Maybury and Julien among them. Typically, Jarman's response to the threat of Clause 28 included a demonstration of public kissing outside the Bow Street Magistrates' Court, an event documented by Steve Farrer in Kiss 25 Goodbye (1992). Stuart Marshall's was to make a comic, pseudo-teaching-aid interview with performance artist Neil Bartlett, Pedagogue

**258** *Manao Tupapau*, Amanda Holiday, 1990.

**259** *A Journal of the Plague Year*, Stuart Marshall, 1984.

(1988), which gleefully transgressed both good taste and the threatened law. A sense of urgency had entered Stuart Marshall's work when he came out as a gay man in the late 1970s, and he abandoned video formalism and the tiny dedicated audience for single-screen videos (for which he had made *The Love Show – Parts 1–3* 1980), and first made one of the few serious video installation works to address AIDS, the five-screen and text installation *A Journal of the Plague Year* (1984, after Defoe),[46] then focused on television, gaining a series of commissions from Channel 4 to document gay history and politics in *Bright Eyes* (1984), *Desire* (1989), *Comrades in Arms* (1990), *Blue Boys* (1992) and others. Equally militant was Julien's *This is Not an AIDS Advertisment* (1987). Witty responses came from a reinvigorated Peck, whose *What Can I do With a Male Nude?* (1985) mocked the prudishness and censorship of an earlier age, and Richard Kwietniowski's visually-punning gay alphabet *Alfalfa* (1987) and *Flames of Passion* (1989), a gay, slimmed-down version of *Brief Encounter* (David Lean 1946). While most of these artists had trained in art-school or university, others of the new generation emerged (like the Scratch video artists) from community video workshops. *Framed Youth* (1983), a shout of protest from Julian Cole, Connie Giannaris and others, came from the Oval Video project, and set Cole on a course of music video-making for the Pet Shop Boys and other bands, and Giannaris onto a career that led to feature films, but en-route included his poetic *Jean Genet is Dead* (1987) which set a child's voice reading Genet to homoerotic images (again in an act of deliberate transgression), *Trojans* (1989) on Cavafy, and an American ménage-à-trois road movie *North of Vortex* (1991). Like Julien, Pratibha Parmar (b.1955 Kenya) initially made works that addressed race alone – like *Sari Red* (1988), a poem of remembrance for a young Asian woman killed by British racists – then added the more complex issue of gender in *Khush* (1991) – 'ecstatic pleasure' in Urdu – a fusion of dance and documentary footage on the theme of gay and lesbian love in Asian Britain.[47]

At the same time, the issues of gender and race were becoming subsumed within the broader theme of personal identity; the question 'who am I?' now being addressed as often in the first-person-singular as in the third-person-plural. Rhodes, Parker, Julien and Hatoum had been the trail-blazers; others who followed included Sarah Turner (*She Wanted Green Lawns* 1990), Sarah Pucill (*Swollen Stigma* 1998), Vicky Smith (*Fixation* 2001), Syed and Bhimji, and many installation-makers. The slower, more meditative pace of the video installation – rather than the fast montage of shots in films made for cinema or television – suited introspection, and by the middle of the 1990s, the body – its representation, its interrogation and use as metaphor or measure – had assumed a centrality in the moving image that it had traditionally enjoyed in all the other visual arts.

## THE BODY

Of the yBa generation of film-makers, Tracey Emin (b.1963) most directly engaged with this pursuit of personal identity, in her drawings, installations and (rare) Super 8 films. *Why I Never Became a Dancer* (1994, aka *Why I Didn't Become a Dancer*) is an account of the end of her childhood in Margate, and her humiliation by local youths. To camera, in home-movie confessional style, she describes her disaster on the dance-floor, then the moment when she seized control of her life and triumphed over her oppressors. It was a theme she returned to in her feature film *Top Spot* (2004), but now with a teenage cast and a more direct reference to the sexual abuse that she herself had suffered. It was also the amateur-gauge camera's potential as mirror and confessional that appealed to Gillian Wearing, whose early works are self-portraits *in extremis*. Anticipating the identity-revealing games she would later inflict on others, she bravely made a spectacle of herself in *Dancing in Peckham* (1994), dancing wildly in a shopping mall to music on headphones we can't hear, and in *Homage to the Woman With the Bandaged Face Who I Saw Yesterday Down Walworth Road* (1995) walked the length of the street

**260** *Why I Never Became a Dancer* (aka *Why I Didn't Become a Dancer*), Tracey Emin, 1994. (White Cube)

**261** *Deadpan*,
Steve McQueen, 1998
(Thomas Dane).

**262** *Mouth to Mouth (aka*
*Sustain)*, Stephanie Smith
and Ed Stewart, 1995
(Film & Video Umbrella).

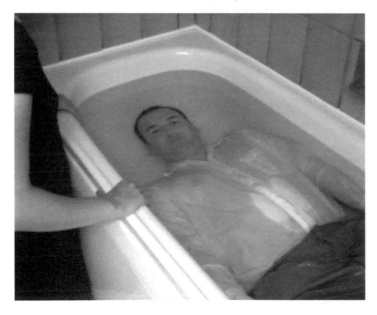

in mummy-like headgear, testing the medium and her own courage. With *Confess All on Video. Don't Worry You Will Be in Disguise. Intrigued? Call Gillian…* (1994) she turned the camera on others and launched her mature career. Steve McQueen (b.1969) also began film-making with performance-based self-revelation. In *Bear* (1993) (a pun) he wrestles naked with another black man; neither is graceful; the editing and camerawork are lively but there is no discernible choreography and the film says little more than a bold 'this is who we are; look at us'. In *Five Easy Pieces* (1993) he begins to construct a self-portrait as Kenneth Macpherson might have – not composed of mirror reflections, but of 'images personal to me [and to] how I define myself and my experiences'. Shots of figures performing with hula-hoops suggest erotic tension and release, and a linking sequence of a tightrope walker is 'the perfect image of a combination of vulnerability and strength'.[48] McQueen makes work exclusively for gallery installation, but more than most embraces cinematic spectacle. In *Deadpan* (1998) he places himself in the famous scene in *Steamboat Bill Jr.* (Buster Keaton 1928) where the end-wall of a wooden house falls on Keaton, who miraculously remains standing, thanks to an artfully placed open window. In McQueen's looped re-staging, this brilliant cinematic trick is transformed into an image of artistic perseverance in the face of danger. With the paired installations *Caribs' Leap* and *Western Deep* (2002), McQueen links another image of endurance – the black miners working in the extreme conditions of the world's deepest goldmine in South Africa – to a moment of ultimate resistance in black history, the suicidal leap of hundreds of the native people of Grenada who, having briefly experienced autonomy, chose death rather than surrender to French soldiers and a return to servitude. Grim, claustrophobic documentary scenes in the mines contrast with McQueen's looped images showing a distant body viewed from far below silhouetted against a heavenly blue sky, eternally flying through the air, suspended somewhere between apotheosis and self-obliteration.

The installations of Stephanie Smith (b.1968) and Ed Stewart (b.1961) explore the boundaries of eroticism and pain through simpler metaphors

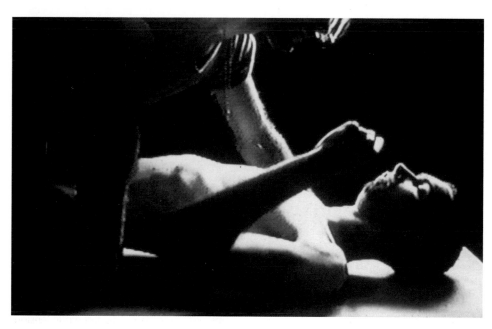

**263** *Amami se Vuoi*,
Michael Curran, 1994.

based on their interaction as performers. In *Intercourse* (1993) the slow-motion repeated action of one mouth spitting – seemingly across the void between two screens – into the mouth of another suggests intimacy and trust; in *Mouth to Mouth* (1995 aka *Sustain*) Smith repeatedly feeds air by mouth to Stewart submerged below the water in a bath, in an anxious-making image of dependency (or a reassuring one of care). Michael Curran (b.1963) took the premise of *Intercourse* one stage further (knowingly or unknowingly) in his *Amami se Vuoi* (1994), where the exchange is between himself and another man, foregrounding the risk involved in the age of AIDS, and providing a dark metaphor for the necessity of risk in all art. Lighter in tone, the videos of John Wood (b.1969 Hong Kong) and Paul Harrison (b.1966) are game-like performances played to camera that involve them in a set of physical actions – dodging balls fired by a tennis-practice machine when tied together in *Three-Legged* (1996); being manipulated by a rope leading off-screen in *Volunteer* (1998) – often presented in series, each piece a variation upon, or development of, an initial idea. Their empty white-box set and use of carefully built props give a sense of theatre that is undercut by the transparency of their illusions; the strongest impression remaining is of infinite inventiveness and – as with Smith and Stewart – the participants' mutual trust.

**264** Episodes from *Device*,
John Wood and
Paul Harrison, 1996.

**265** *Eyelashes*, Jaki Irvine, 1996 (Frith Street Gallery).

Jaki Irvine's *Eyelashes* (1996) appears to tell two stories at the same time. Her images observe a couple talking over a breakfast table, perhaps discussing their relationship, while on the soundtrack a woman's voice describes a man's obsession with another woman's eyelashes, which make him feel uneasy. The viewers' task is to look for conjunctions and attempt a synthesis, and so construct their own story. Irvine's films are almost always shot on Super 8, and have the appearance of being fragments torn from longer stories. As a gallery artist, she can further deconstruct the narrative by showing different sections on separate screens, giving viewers additional assembling to do. In *Another Difficult Sunset* (1996) five screens in different spaces show a man and a woman separately travelling on the underground and (possibly) meeting at the Zoo, where a tiger paces up and down; a newspaper headline read by one en-route hints at a prior tragedy in the tiger's cage. The action on each screen is looped so chronological order is unclear and nothing is overtly stated, so many readings of the tiger's menace, these journeys and their outcomes are possible. Tacita Dean, who also makes films predominantly for the gallery, initially used narrative more directly to shape her works. *The Martyrdom of St Agatha (In Several Parts)* (1994) and *Bag of Air* (1995) set images against a voice-over text, an account of the Sicilian saint's dismemberment and the fate of her relics in the former, an alchemical recipe in the latter. In more recent works such as *Disappearance at Sea* (1996) and *Disappearance at Sea II (Voyage de Guérison)* (1997) the images stand on their own, but in relation to a 'hidden' narrative. Both feature lighthouses, the first seen at dusk as it lights up, the second in daylight, with the camera replacing the source of light, and sweeping the horizon as a metaphor for hope and endurance. In written narratives published separately, Dean relates the first to the story of Donald Crowhurst who cheated during a Golden Globe round-the-world yacht race, but lost his reason in wild speculations about time and jumped overboard before his deception was uncovered; the second to the story of Tristan and Isolde and Tristan's 'voyage de guérison' (voyage of healing). Sometimes her narrative is nearer to the surface. *Sound Mirrors* and *Bubble House* (both 1999) document extraordinary architectural structures, an abandoned rich man's folly in the Cayman Islands and a wartime experimental early warning system on the Kent

coast, each hinting at its own complex history. Indeed, *Fernsehturm* (2001), which consists of a long cinemascope shot taken at twilight from within the revolving restaurant atop East Berlin's television tower, suggests that for Dean the starting point is always an arresting image with a history, about which the viewer is encouraged to speculate.

**266** *Disappearance at Sea*, Tacita Dean, 1997 (Frith Street Gallery).

Installations sometimes trade on the voyeuristic pleasure of reading the body language of others. In Sam Taylor-Wood's four-screen *Killing Time* (1994), her fixed-frame cameras watch four 'ordinary' people filmed separately in mundane domestic surroundings, as they attempt to lip-synch the absurdly out-of-context singing of the four principles in Straus's *Elektra*, pleasuring the spectator with their show of impatience, extreme boredom and rare moments of anticipation. Cerith Wyn Evans's *Kim Wilde Auditions* (1996) places the camera in the position of judge as a succession of auditioning male models run through a repertory of attitudes from coyness to narcissistic display for its benefit. Monika Oeschler sets up games for her subjects to play designed to allow maximum observation of human idiosyncrasies, in installations such as *Necking* (1999), school children passing the apple from neck to neck; in *Johari's Window* (2000) the highs and lows of four women involved in a poker game; and in *The Chase* (2001) male/female competitiveness on the running-track. Many of Lucy Gunning's videos such as *The Horse Impressionists* and *The Singing Lesson* (both 1997) record conscious child-play and unconscious behavioural tics.

**267** *Killing Time*, Sam Taylor Wood, 1994 (White Cube).

**268** *Wait*, Dryden Goodwin, 2000.

Sometimes the language depicted is deliberately ambiguous. The people filmed by Nick Stewart (b.1952) for *Face Up* (2000) were clearly watching some spectacle in the night sky, his tight framing of their faces and slow motion inviting us to interpret their expressions; is this awe, or perhaps fear? In other works he has combined the 'reading' of fleeting human emotions with an exploration of architectural space and landscape. Dryden Goodwin (b.1971) is more coolly analytical. People selected apparently at random and observed in the street are a frequent subject in his films. In the single-screen late-structural film *Hold* (1996), a different person is seen in each frame of film, although sometimes their image is repeated, allowing it to register more strongly when projected at normal speed. In the five-screen *Wait* (2000), faces are held in slow-motion close-up as emotions (of anticipation?) slide across their surface. Though image-manipulation, time is stretched and sometimes reversed, drawing out every glance of the eye and move of the facial muscles, deepening the mystery. A theme in Goodwin's work has been the pursuit of the relationship between the drawn image and its film equivalent in an interrogation of the boundary between movement and stasis. He has made drawings from individual film-frames (*One Thousand Nine Hundred and Ninety Eight* 1998); drawn directly on photographs (*Capture* 2001), and projected linear elements into live-action video (*Closer* three-screen 2002).

Digital technology, with its potential for electronic collage and even interactivity between spectator and the image, allowed for the construction of new forms of body-image, and analogies involving the body and different concepts of space. In *Hermaphrodite Bikini* (1995), Clio Barnard (b.1965 USA) created a garden full of fabulous winged hermaphrodites through digital embroidery, to accompany a young man describing his more prosaic adventures in cross-dressing. More directly alluding to the art of the past, Judith Goddard (b.1956) constructed her three-screen *Garden of Earthly Delights* (1991 after Hieronymus Bosch) from many moving video fragments collaged together, offering a dystopian view of life in 1990s London, and

**269** *Garden of Earthly Delights*, Judith Goddard, 1991.

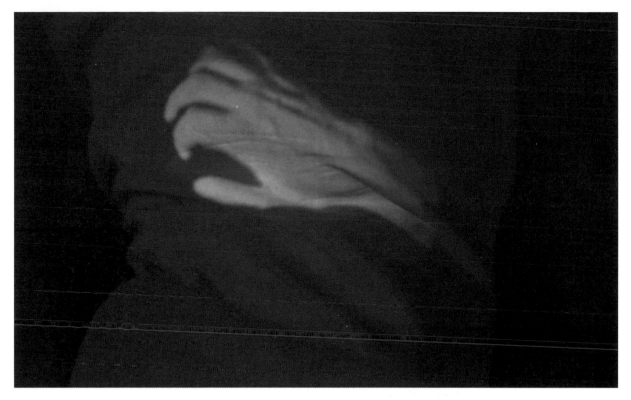

relishing the multiple viewpoints and perspectives inhabited by her central female figure. The **270** *Touched*,
boundaries of the real and the imaginary body were explored in Jane Prophet's interactive Susan Collins, 1996.
DVD *The Internal Organs of a Cyborg* (1998), and similar technology allowed viewers of
Simon Biggs's *Shadows* (1992–93) to interact with life-size projected human figures, and to be
touched up by ghostly disembodied hands in Susan Collins's *Touched* (1996).

## SOCIAL SPACE

Compared to the flood of artists investigating identity (their own and others) during the 1980s
and afterwards, it is surprising how few made works that addressed the most urgent social
themes of the period. Jarman's direct critique of his age was an exception, as were the pointed
collages of Scratch video. Other rare examples have included Jeremy Welsh's *Forest Fires*
(1983–90)[49] and Andrew Stones's *Salmon Song* (1986) that alluded to environmental concerns; the Butler Brothers' sardonic computer-animated 'celebration' of consumer choice
and the triumph of free-market capitalism by *World Peace Thru Free Trade* (1989); and works
that mocked raw militarism such as Rose Finn Kelcey's *Glory* (1983) (based on a performance), Ann Course and Paul Clark's mock-primitive animation *Recruitment Video* (2000), and
*Death Valley Days*, *War Machine* (both 1984) and others by the Scratch video artists. Finn
Kelcey also commented on money's distortion of the art-world's values in her *Bureau de
Change* (1988–92), based on an installation in which she reproduced Van Gogh's *Sunflowers*
using £1,000 worth of coins – the convincing reproduction appearing on-screen via a

**271** *Forest Fires*,
Jeremy Welsh, 1983–90.

surveillance camera. (In a less focused gesture, 'Gimpo' of the K Foundation made *Watch the K Foundation Burning a Million Quid* (1994), in which the former band did just that, in a desultory fashion.) Before Willie Doherty's arrival on the scene, Simon Robertshaw's early work *Shot Dead in Armagh* (1984) and the photographer Paul Graham's *Troubled Land* (1987)

**272** Rose Finn-Kelcey:
(right) *Glory*, 1983; (opposite
top) *Bureau de Change*,
1988–92.

were among the few works to reflect Britain's involvement in a sectarian, post-colonial conflict on its doorstep in any way. Throughout the 1990s, Doherty (b.1959) proved the reliable poet of Northern Ireland's struggles, showing in films and photographs their everyday face – distant checkpoints, blocked roads, military lighting in the nightscape – rather than the sensational images of marches and the aftermath of bombs; his titling a further provocation to thought: *The Only Good One is a Dead One* (1993), *At The End of the Day* (1994), *Control Zone* (1997). The Anglo-American adventure in Iraq and failure to deal with Palestine was reflected John Smith's series of *Hotel Diaries – Frozen War* (2001) and *Museum Piece* (2004), while many of Phil Mulloy's animations from the *Cowboys* series (1991) onwards have reflected on humankind's strange compulsion to create enemies of strangers, and to engage them in battle.

In his later works, Robertshaw (b.1960) has drawn attention to ethical issues in public life, particularly within science and medicine. *Biometrica* (1987) and *From Generation to Generation* (1989) documented the dubious arguments made by the Eugenics Society in the nineteenth-century, their parallels in Nazi Germany and echoes still sounding. A more complex theme running through his work is observation, which embraces both scientific study and surveillance as a means of social control. In *The Observatory* (1993) he drew on ideas from Michel Foucault (who in turn drew from Jeremy Bentham, proposer of the Panopticon),

**273** *Same Old Story*, Willie Doherty, 1997.

and applied them to modern science and modern technologies, while *The Nature of History* (1995), made with scientist Sinclair Stammers and designed to fill an entire gallery of London's Natural History Museum, related methods of scientific observation to history, and used inter-activity with the spectator as a way of dramatising individual decision making within a contained social structure. Another memorable engagement with social medicine was *Rehearsal of Memory* (1994), a CD-ROM by the artist Harwood (Graham Harwood) produced with prisoners in the Ashworth hospital for the criminally insane that gave the participants some form of public voice in the form of a collaged, composite self-image.

A similarly collective work made a decade later, Jeremy Deller's *The Battle of Orgreave* (2002) was shot and edited by Mike Figgis and documents the artist's re-enactment of the final violent confrontation of picketing Yorkshire miners and the police at the end of the Thatcher government's battle with the labour unions; Thatcher notoriously having identified the National Union of Mineworkers as 'the enemy within'. Deller choreographed the event to include participation by many of those originally involved, but Figgis's film reveals the artist's interest to be the catalytic social function of a collective performance, here a belated healing of the divisions between strikers, 'scabs' and police in a formerly tight-knit com-munity. Channel 4 contributed to the project and screened the film, belatedly atoning for the anti-miner reporting of the news media in the 1980s. Deller's *Memory Bucket,* a quirky essay on President George Bush's backwoods home-town, was made without TV money for the 2004 Turner Prize exhibition (and won him the prize), but presents the viewer with the slightly surreal (but increasingly familiar) experience of watching a TV essay-film while seated in the gallery.

The video installations *Class* (1990) and *The Nature of Their Joy* (1994) by Andrew Stones (b.1960) shared Robertshaw's interest in the deconstruction of British social history. The spec-

**274 (opposite)** *The Nature of History*, Simon Robertshaw, 1995.

**275** *Class*, Andrew Stones, 1990.

tacular construction of *Class* – an assemblage of children's desks with illuminated panels, inverted window-cleaners' ladders (ladders of opportunity?), slide-projected diagrams and video projections – speaks of instilled constraints determining social position, and challenges 'a sense of cultural archaism still present in Britain after the dissolution of the Empire. Latin maxims [printed on giant rulers] … are yardsticks whereby the right of residence in a given place may be granted or rejected'.[50] *The Nature of Their Joy* unpicked the archaic image of Britain and her Empire reflected in H. V. Morton's introduction to the illustrated *A Pageant of History* (c.1933), and included fragmented printed images of crowds greeting the declaration of the first World War and the Armistice Day celebrations, isolating individual faces from the crowd and suspending them in liquid in transparent tubes, to be projected via a series of micro-fiche readers, where chance might briefly illuminate them before they dissolved into the medium carrying them. In more recent work Stones's critique is subtler, but no less spec-tacular in its execution. In *Outside Inside* (2004), his camera explores the extraordinary structure and vast scale of the particle accelerator at CERN, the camera's choreography and the artist's manipulation of time and changing spatial relationships within the image and across six screens leading to a sense of both awe and fear of science operating at the extremes of knowledge.

These are very public works, however individual their signature, which suggest that the video installation is beginning to operate on the grand scale of nineteenth-century history paint-ing, allowing current public anxieties and responses to recent events to be aired though spectacle (though not always providing an establishment view as their nineteenth-century forebears would have). Other examples might include Mark Wallinger's *Royal Ascot* (1994) – at first sight the 'same' footage of the Queen's progress in her carriage down the length of the racecourse repeated across four screens; in fact four successive days of BBC transmis-sions – the repetition a measure of Britain's continuing deference to a redundant social system. Equally his installation *Prometheus* (1999), a dark view of the stealing of fire or little death that is creativity, realised in the form of a full-sized room built on its side containing an electric chair, into which the artist's image is projected, singing 'Full fathom five …', slowed down, then jerk-ily rewinding. On the same scale, Graham Ellard and Stephen Johnstone's *Passagen* (1993 after Walter Benjamin) and *Geneva Express* (1997) return full-circle to pre-cinema spectacle. In the former, interactivity summons up aerial views of London, Paris and Berlin on sur-rounding, diorama-like screens, while captions connect Benjamin's thoughts on the nineteenth-century urban landscape and labyrinths, with their parallels in the construction of cyberspace; in the latter, two screens present an enveloping mid-runway view of jumbo-jets taking off at Gatwick, echoing the Lumières' *Train Entering a Station*, but now a chillingly universal image of modern communication networks, human rootlessness and absence of individuality.

The public realm of cinema continues to fascinate many artists. Adam Chodzko often engages volunteers in the interrogation of cinematic ideas, as in his *A Place for The End* (1999) in which citizens of Birmingham were invited to nominate locations for imaginary final shots, which he then realised with them in moving and still images. In the earlier two-

screen installation *Nightvision* (1998) he drew attention to the 'hidden' artists of film-lighting
in a collaboration with the 'sparks' who facilitate lighting for clubs, raves and concerts. 'I
wanted to work with people who normally remain out of visibility, in the semi-darkness of back-
stage space. They are asked to light a wood at night as though it was heaven.'[51] For the series
*Flasher* (1998) he hired feature films from video rental shops and recorded a single fifty-
second shot of a flash-illuminated landscape at their ends, as an unexpected gift and intellectual
challenge to the next viewer. Typical of many artists of his generation, he works in many
media. His *Plan for a Spell* (2002) involved a computer program designed to randomly and endlessly search through contemporary folk websites in pursuit of the magic combination of
image and sound that constitute 'a spell'.

The most assured fabricators of the modern history spectacle are Jane and Louise Wilson.
After the quiet surrealism of their *Crawlspace* (1995 various versions) they began a series of
works that explored major public buildings – investigating their fame or notoriety through
use of their prowling camera, the choreography of movement across mirroring screens, and
occasional disturbing interventions. *Stasi City* (1997) explored the abandoned former East

**276** *A Free and Anonymous
Monument*, Jane and Louise
Wilson, 2003 (Film & Video
Umbrella).

German Secret Police headquarters, its surveillance equipment, old-fashioned telephones, abandoned papers, padded doors and suggestive marks on its peeling walls, and odd glimpses of uniformed figures, and – even more disorientating – moments when figures suddenly exit the frame by levitating. In *Gamma* (1999), the abandoned scene was that of Greenham Common, site of the women's protest twenty years earlier. Here the artists' sympathy with their predecessors was marked by the steely coldness of their filming, made even harsher by low light levels, a blue cast, and the precision of the image's mirroring across the four panels of the installation. *Parliament (A Third House)* (1999) failed to dent the richness and glamour of Pugin's architecture despite including the pipes and tunnels beneath the chambers, but *A Free and Anonymous Monument* (2003), made to fill the Baltic art space in Gateshead, moved on and developed a portrait of England's North East through a collage of spaces projected onto a myriad of screens above and around the viewer – changing, fast-moving fragmentary images of an oil rig, a computer-chip factory, an automated machine-production line, a 1960s multistorey car park, Victor Passmore's abandoned *Apollo Pavilion* at Peterlee New Town, brilliantly encapsulating the unsettling new landscapes, false hopes and visual chaos associated with rapid changes in society.

## NOTES

1. Jeff Nuttall, *Bomb Culture* (London: Paladin Books, 1970), p.165.

2. *Bomb Culture*, p.145.

3. Interview with Carolee Schneemann by Kate Haug', *Wide Angle*, vol. 20 no. 1, 1997.

4. 'The film with Anthony is about how the *perception* of a relationship *changes* the relationship. We made tapes with each other's friends, and when listening to one tape I discovered how much he loved me, I got so upset, so he put on another tape, so we have a tape recording the discovery of another dimension of our feeling. How to handle that in relationship to the visual stuff is really interesting'. 'Interviews With Three Filmmakers', Verina Glaessner, *Time Out*, 17 March 1972.

5. They jointly performed *Thames Crawling* at the 1970 NFT International Underground Film Festival.

6. He designed covers for the first three distribution catalogues for the London Filmmakers Co-op.

7. Quoted in *Shoot Shoot Shoot* broadsheet 2000.

8. Tony Rayns, *LUX Distribution catalogue* (online).

9. Jo Pearson, Sophie Outram *et al*.

10. Transcript in the BAFV Study Collection.

11. As in *Mare's Tail* (1969).

12. Chris Cunningham's overblown *Flex* (2000) is an unhappy exception.

13. Organised by Lynda Myles, Claire Johnston and Laura Mulvey.

14. Kate Haug, *Wide Angle*, vol. 20 no. 1, 1997.

15. 'Visual Pleasure and Narrative Cinema', *Screen*, 1975.

16. Note in *Some Films From Tony Morgan* – self-published, c.1998, in BAFV Study Collection.

17. 'Film, Feminism and the Avant-Garde', Laura Mulvey, *Women Writing and Writing About Women* reprinted in Michael O'Pray (ed.), *A Director of British Film and Video Artists* (Luton: Arts Council/University of Luton Press, 1996).

18. Elwes interestingly rejects other feminists' assumption that the camera's point of view is 'male', proposing instead it can represent 'a mother's timeless watching'.

19. Jayne Parker (1984) quoted in O'Pray (ed.), *A Directory of British Film & Video Artists* (Arts Council/University of Luton Press, 1996).

20. Programme note for a screening at LFMC 1980. Elwes was using menstrual cycles within performance works at the Slade at this time. 'The cycle is a structure within which experience is filtered and regenerated into expressive imagery. It both constrains and illuminates the relationships between the physical, emotional and intellectual life.' Elwes quoted in 'Feminist Perceptions' Alexis Hunter *Artscribe,* Oct 1980.

21. 'Bringing About the Present', *Undercut*, 14/15, 'Special Issue on Women's Work', 1985.

22. Though her own film work was limited to 1976–77, she also appeared as a performer in films by Ian Bourn, Jock McFadyen and others.

23. Start Marshall, *Video Developing Technology and Practice*, Serpentine Gallery, April 1982.

24. LUX Online distribution catalogue.

25. Her earlier abstract work was discussed in 2.1.

26. 6–7 May 1978.

27. For this recollection, I am grateful to Felicity Sparrow.

28. See Jayne Pilling, *Women and Animation – A Compendium,* BFI, 1992.

29. Such as *A Journey to Avebury* (1971) and *Fire Island* (1974).

30. Largely self-funded, it received a small grant from the Arts Council.

31. Derek Jarman, *ICA Video Library Guide*, ICA, 1987. In 1976 he claimed to have made 'about 24 hours of film which cover a rather vast area … from rather faltering beginnings to I suppose some of the most complicated work in the medium'. Adding in an aside 'I find all English filmmaking with the exception of social documentaries and David Larcher, excruciating'. Letter to Ron Haselden, January 1976. Jarman was shortlisted for the Turner Prize in 1986, 'in recognition of the outstanding visual quality of his films', in particular *Sebastiane, Jubilee, The Tempest* and *Caravaggio.*

32. Promoter of Outsider art; poet; husband of photographer Ida Karr, he ran Gallery One (1953–63). A champion of Fluxus, he co-produced Yoko Ono's *No.4 (The Bottoms Film)* (1966).

33. 'Innocence and Experience', *Frieze* No. 71, November/December 2002.

34. 'John Maybury', in O'Pray (ed.), *A Director of British Film and Video Artists*.

35. He has made videos for Neneh Cherry, Sinead O'Connor and Boy George, among many others.

36. Newby has also directed two feature films, *Anchoress* (1993) and *Madagascar Skin* (1995).

37. Artist's statement 1997.

38. Marion Urch programme note for LFMC Screening, July 1982.

39. Marion Urch, flier accompanying its installation at Video Positive 89, Liverpool 1989.

40. Caption in *Turas.*

41. LUX Online catalogue.

42. 'Reel Stories' interview with Erika Muhammad, *Index* no. 6–7, USA 2000.

43. 14 December 1984 Billed as *Expedition – Tape/Slides on Race and Nation by The Black Audio Film Collective.* The group met as students at Portsmouth Polytechnic.

44. *The Elusive Sign* (London: Arts Council/British Council, 1988).

45. Akomfrah also helped design the Arts Council's *Black Arts Video* scheme, which funded documentaries on black arts subjects by new black film-makers, such as Peter Harvey's *Blue Too,* Shafeeq Velani's *Walking Away With the Music* (on WOMAD), Pratiba Parmar's *Memory Pictures* (on Sunil Gupta's photography), Susannah Lopez's *Polishing Black Diamonds* (on Munirah theatre company) and Patricia Diaz's *The Hidden Wisdom,* first screened at the ICA in July 1989.

46. Shown at *Video 84* Canada, *Cross Currents* RCA Gallery, London (both 1984), *Signs of the Times* MOMA Oxford (1990), and subsequent British Council Tour.

47. Her documentary *The Colour of Britain* (1994) looks at the work of British Asian artists – Anish Kapoor, Jatinder Verma, Shobana Jeyasingh, Supta Biswas, Chila Burman and Zarina Bhimji. *Exiles of Love* (1992) by Toby Kalitowski documents the work of gay artists Jarman, Giannaris and Bartlett.

48. Statement in an application to the Arts Council 1993.

49. 'The present version of *Forest Fires* is unambivalently concerned with the ever present threat of ecological disaster. The installation uses two of the media that deliver us images of the ravaged natural environment – video and photography [slides] – and is concerned with the ambiguities of the Media's position. While alerting us to the dangers, it is nonetheless inescapably implicated in the processes of destruction.' Artist's statement, *Signs of the Times*, MOMA Oxford 1990.

50. Artist's statement in O'Pray (ed.), *A Directory of British Film and Video Artists*.

51. *Tate* magazine, Summer 1999.

# Conclusion

One of the prompts to the writing of this book was the absence of any comprehensive history of the support-organisations designed *by* and *for* British moving-image artists. Bits of the story (the GPO phenomenon; the Film Co-op's early days) are relatively well known, but an overview that shows the links and recurring patterns has not been attempted before.

As written here, agencies of the State – the GPO, the BFI, the Arts Council, the British Council and Channel 4 – loom large, which would imply a dependency by British artists upon State support greater than that of their contemporaries abroad. How true this is will remain conjecture until more European nations have written their own stories. Certainly this account implicitly illustrates the reality that State involvement in the arts can be a mixed blessing. It can be slow to act and vulnerable to policy changes – and like any intervention designed to influence a natural ecology, almost invariably stimulates the mediocre alongside the good. (When involved in Arts Council funding, I was often made keenly aware of the limited effectiveness of our decision-making, not least by the ability of some our true originals, such as Jeff Keen and Margaret Tait, to be prolific makers with little or no institutional support). Probably more in common with developments in mainland Europe, a continuing strength of the British scene has been the role of artist-led organisations, exhibition spaces and magazines; pragmatic, do-it-yourself utopianism being the recipe for their success.

An enduring undercurrent in British work was established by the documentary makers of the 1930s with films that set out to provoke changes in society (*Housing Problems*), or simply to *astonish* by showing how things are (*Song of Ceylon*). This broad, humanist tradition links Grierson and Jennings with Tait, The Berwick Film Street Collective, Stones and Robertshaw, Kötting and Wearing. Contrastingly, British artists – with the glorious exception of Len Lye – have only rarely shown a sustained interest in abstraction in film; no-one in the post-war period dedicated a lifetime to making abstract works as did the American artists Paul Sharits and Stan Brakhage. And while British investigation of narrative has been strong and extremely varied, only rarely has it resulted in works as formally radical as those of say, Markopoulos or

even Godard. Similarly, the involvement of British conceptualists in the 1970s (which hope-fully this book will do something to rescue from obscurity) was short-lived beside that of their American peers, though paradoxically, much current gallery-work is very productively re-mining this territory.

Besides the work of the documentary pioneers, the most original and sustained achieve-ment of the British school developed in the productive 1970s out of an intense interest in the politics of representation. This heterogeneous British movement encompassed 'structural materialist' film, early video art, Feminist film and video, even the post-Straubian costume drama, and much else besides. At its best, it was as daring and innovative as any contemporary body of work abroad. Not least, it began the still continuing debate about how cinema might be expanded, conceptually and physically. And from that period emerged the major theme of *identity*, which still dominates artists' image-making in Britain today, in gallery and cinema. Much of the founding work of the 1970s has fallen out of circulation and become invisible. Structural film, one of the cornerstones, became popularly associated with the tortuous theor-etical language developed by a few of its practitioners and was all but forgotten. But the process of reassessment has begun, and re-screened 30 years on, the works themselves, such as the expanded cinema Filmaktion performances of Le Grice, Eatherley, Raban and Nicolson – and even the austere single-screen works of Gidal – reveal their formal originality and their transparent pleasure in the image.[1]

Moving-image artists in the 21st century still face the challenge of getting the work seen, and the debates about the ideal viewing space for the moving image are far from resolved. The art-market remains the only source of any real financial return on work made, but benefits a very few.  On the other hand, digital technology *has* come to the artist's rescue by radically reducing the costs of filming and editing, making it now as easy (or as difficult) to make films, as to make paintings. Artists' websites on the internet offer a more effective means of self-promotion than any distributor's catalogue ever did, and copies made at home on VHS or DVD offer low-cost means of sending moving images to anyone who shows an interest.[2]

Technological developments have also contributed to a rise in scholarly interest. The Arts and Humanities Research Board ('Council' since 2005), which supports University-based research, has funded several projects which combine documentation of the lives of artists with digital preservation of their works and the building of comprehensive websites. Among these are REWIND (Universities of Westminster and Dundee) which is documenting the early analogue years of British video art, CACHE (Birkbeck College, University of London) which mapped the first years of computer-based art; and the British Artists' Film & Video Study Collection at Central Saint Martins (University of the Arts, London), the research-base where I now work. LUX, the child of the LFMC and LEA, gained funding from another National Lottery-funded *quango* the New Opportunities Fund (NOF) to develop its LUX Online web-site, which provides detailed information about a growing number of British artists, and even 'streamed' clips. The LUX, like the BFI, is publishing collections of artists' works on DVD to sell to individuals as well as institutions, marking a significant shift towards the domestic in its core market. So opportunities for individuals to gain knowledge of the field are becom-

**277 (opposite)**

*One Thousand One Nine Hundred and Ninety Six* (detail), Dryden Goodwin, 1996.

ing more widespread. Higher education is now also a key patron of artists, offering research leave and funding to artists, and in importance has come to equal the former role of the Arts Council and BFI.

There are signs that attitudes in museums are beginning to change. The BFI has finally appointed a curator for artists' film and Video within its National Film & Television Archive and the Henry Moore Foundation is happy to recognise the moving-image as 'sculpture'. Tate Modern was designed with a series of small spaces intended for projection within its suites of galleries, and promisingly its opening displays included the continuous projection of *Le Ballet mécanique*, (though the Trustees passed on the opportunity to bring a print of this key work of film modernism into the permanent collection). Tate Britain commissioned the year-long display of British work *A Century of Artists Film in Britain* (2003–4), which incidentally prompted this book. Tate purchases have played their part in confirming the importance of the YBA generation of filmmaking artists, though the museum has yet to show that it recognises the significance of the older generations (these artists' spiritual parents), such as (to name but a few) Dye, Gidal, Larcher, Le Grice, Rhodes and Parker, or even Lye and Jennings. (This book will hopefully suggest a few more candidates). The museum world's fixation with contemporary 'limited edition' works continues. This *will* change. In an age when 'gallery' artists *demand* that museums build them cinema-like screening spaces (McQueen; Julien) and 'cinema artists' (Chris Marker and Chantal Akerman) are busy invading the museum with multi-screen re-edits of their feature films, no curatorial prejudice is safe.

*Nizas, France, June 2006*

## NOTES

1. The performances and installations by artists associated with Filmaktion were one of the revelations of the exhibitions *Live in Your Head* (2000) and *Shoot Shoot Shoot* (2002–4), and were documented for posterity by Illuminations TV.

2. When researching *Experimental Cinema* in 1969, I had no alternative but to pursue 16mm prints wherever I could find them – Paris, New York, LA, San Francisco – and hope that I could remember what I had seen after one projection.

# Index

Page numbers in **bold** denote detailed treatment; those in *italic* refer to illustrations (or captions). *n* = endnote.